WRITING THE GETTYSBURG ADDRESS

Writing

GETTYSB

THE

Gettysburg Address

Martin P. Johnson

University Press of Kansas

© 2013 by the University Press of Kansas

Published by the University Press of Kansas (Lawrence, Kansas
66045), which was organized by the Kansas Board of Regents and is
operated and funded by Emporia State University, Fort Hays State
University, Kansas State University, Pittsburg State University,
the University of Kansas, and Wichita State University

Library of Congress Cataloging-in-Publication Data

Johnson, Martin P.
Writing the Gettysburg Address / Martin P. Johnson
pages cm
Includes bibliographical references and index.
ISBN 978-0-7006-1933-7 (hardback)
1. Lincoln, Abraham, 1809–1865. Gettysburg address. 2. Lincoln,
Abraham, 1809–1865—Political and social views. I. Title.
E475.55.J65 2013
973.7'349—dc23
2013020162

British Library Cataloguing-in-Publication Data is available.

Printed in the United States of America

10 9 8 7 6 5 4 3 2 1

The paper used in this publication meets the minimum requirements
of the American National Standard for Permanence of Paper for
Printed Library Materials Z39.48-1992.

For Kelli

Contents

A photo section appears following page 111.

Acknowledgments

This project began when I, like many before me, became intrigued and puzzled by the mysteries of the Gettysburg Address. It seemed odd that the origins and writing of a speech that had become such an important part of American identity should be surrounded by so many questions. Early on, it became clear that much of the confusion arose from the encrustation of error accumulated over the decades, of stories repeated but never verified, and of supposedly eyewitness accounts by persons who were merely reporting what they thought others had said. Then the task became a matter of seeking the earliest and most reliable evidence and putting the fragmented history of the events together with the silent testimony of the texts. I was astonished at the story I discovered of Lincoln's own understanding of the eventful journey that brought him to create a speech he knew to be remarkable, and I hope that this history of Lincoln's journey to the "new birth of freedom" helps reveal a new depth to America's most admired speech and to its most beloved president.

I am deeply thankful to the many friends and colleagues whose help and advice has been invaluable during this project. Research support was provided by the Department of History, the College of Arts and Sciences, and the Office of the Provost at Miami University. In addition, I would like to thank the legion of archivists and librarians who were unstinting with their time and efforts, among them Mary Jo Kline and Mario Fernandez for their help with the John M. Hay Papers at the John M. Hay Library, Brown University; Katherine Reagan and Lucy Burgess at the Carl A. Kroch Library Rare and Manuscript Collections, Cornell University; Patty Mosher of the Galesburg (Illinois) Public Library; Karen Dupell Drickamer of the Musselman Library, Gettysburg College; John Rhodehamel at the Huntington Library in San Marino, California; Thomas Schwartz of the Illinois State Historical Society, Springfield, Illinois; William Grace at the Kansas State Historical Society, Topeka; Matt Norman for his help with the Clark E. Carr Papers at the Knox College Archives in Galesburg, Illinois; Ilhan Citak for his help with the John R. Bartlett Papers at the Linderman Library, Lehigh University; Cindy VanHorn of the former Lincoln Museum in Fort Wayne, Indiana; Steve Nielson for his help with the Alexander Ramsey Papers, Minnesota State Historical Society; Nicholas Graham for his help with the Edward Everett Papers, Massachusetts State Historical Society; Maida Goodwin for her help with the Hale Family Papers, Smith College, Northampton, Massachusetts; Mary H. Huth for her help with the William H. Seward Papers, University of Rochester Library, Rochester, New York; and Lila Fourhman-Shaull at the York County Heritage Trust, York, Pennsylvania.

WRITING THE GETTYSBURG

ADDRESS

Introduction:
The Mysteries of the
Manuscripts

A brilliant November day. Ten thousand mourners wait. He rises.

> The throng of eager listeners was swayed by his stirring words. Their
> hearts swelled with deeper emotions as the speaker poured out the
> fervor of his own patriotic soul, always in full sympathy with the brave
> defenders of the country, over the nameless graves which consecrated
> that field of blood.
> "The world will little note, nor long remember, what *we say* here;
> but it can never forget what they did here."
> Noble words of a true-hearted patriot! Such honor to the brave does
> not often hallow their sleeping dust. . . . His generous nature clasped
> the lifeless forms of those who saved their country by nobly sacrificing
> themselves; and he would recognize the obligations of the living to the
> martyred dead.[1]

Lincoln at Gettysburg. Few images of the American past run deeper in
the national memory than that of the tall martyr president dedicating the
cemetery for the honored dead of the greatest battle of the Civil War. But in
our postheroic era, depictions like this one, published by William Makepeace Thayer less than a year after the ceremony—even before Lincoln was
reelected—seem irretrievably remote. It may be that the iconic scenes and

1

well-worn passages of this story have been told and retold so many times that the tale has changed from vividly classic to hopelessly archaic, any semblance of vitality lost beneath tradition, homily, and trivia.[2] Controversy and debate have swirled around what exactly Lincoln said, what he wore, what he meant, the response of the crowd, the color of his horse, whether he wrote on the train, and a myriad of other matters. As early as 1906 a beleaguered book reviewer expressed only half-joking surprise that "so minor an incident as the delivery of an address, strictly occasional, by a man who was not a noted orator" should inspire three books in that year alone. Forty years later, James G. Randall, one of the first academic historians to specialize in Lincoln and the war, bemoaned "the unprofitable realm of Lincoln-at-Gettysburg apocrypha."[3]

No area of that realm has been more unprofitable than the quest to know how Lincoln wrote and revised the Gettysburg Address. Some of the first newspaper articles about the Gettysburg dedication ceremony, 150 years ago, noted that Lincoln's words were reported inaccurately, and the 1870s saw the first debate about which of the handwritten copies of the speech he may have held while speaking; to the present these questions have remained unanswered. These mysteries of the manuscripts are important because the search for a secure history of Lincoln's best-known speech is at heart an effort to understand his ideas and purposes at a crucial moment in the war, for there is no more effective way to enter into people's thinking than to look over their shoulder as they compose and revise. It is in the spaces between words, in the differences and choices made between one sentence or phrase and another, that we approach most closely the enigma of creativity and thought. Yet for the Gettysburg Address, confusion and uncertainty about such fundamental issues as which of the five handwritten versions Lincoln wrote first, which manuscript was the one— if any—he read from at the ceremony, and which report of his words is most reliable have prevented comprehensive analysis of Lincoln's vision and a clear sense of the evolution of his thought as he wrote and spoke about the central issues of the great Civil War and the nature of the American experiment.

Many of the mysteries of the manuscripts arise because, although the Gettysburg Address is the most admired work by our most admired president, the dramatic and surprising story of Lincoln's speech has never been fully told.[4] For Lincoln, getting to the speech—as a statement of ideas and as an event—was both an intellectual and a physical journey. Lincoln began to compose his words in Washington with one set of ideas, incorporated in the draft of the speech that he took with him when he left the White House. Yet by the time Lincoln stood on the platform at Gettysburg a day later, he had traveled a long road, one that had become more meaningful with each step. He had journeyed by carriage, train, and horseback, passing in part over familiar terrain that he now saw in a new light. He had experienced for the first time the battlefield of Gettysburg and the little town in the grip of patriotic celebration of loyalty and commemoration. And he had deeply felt the solemn funeral rites for 3,000 heroes and more.

Lincoln's journey to Gettysburg is encoded in the manuscripts and words of his speech and reflected in the texts of his revisions. Through these documents we can trace, at times word by word, the arc of his thought. Lincoln's own words reveal that he experienced writing the Gettysburg Address as an eventful process that was fraught with the possibility of failure but that he knew finally resulted in a success beyond expectation. A year after the Gettysburg ceremony, when Lincoln told his old friend James Speed about how he came to write his speech, he rehearsed a three-act drama of contemplation, composition, and revision that was surrounded by anxiety and permeated by doubt, but he saw that this story of sudden reversals and unlooked-for achievement gave a particular cast to the words that he wrote and spoke. As an accomplished storyteller, Lincoln knew that the narrative he spun that night to his friend explained the nature of the final speech, a journey he experienced as paradoxical, surprising, and, he recognized, triumphant.

Lincoln's own story of how he wrote the Gettysburg Address, and the words of the speech themselves, cannot be fully comprehended without a clear chronology of composition and succession of manuscripts and words. Five versions of the speech in Lincoln's handwriting survive, but the heart of the mystery lies in determining the chronological and editorial relationships of just two of them: the so-called Nicolay text described and published in facsimile by John Nicolay, Lincoln's secretary, in 1894, and the so-called Hay text, found in the papers of Lincoln's assistant secretary John Hay and first published in 1908.[5] Perhaps because it was thought that the history of the speech was already known and was inconclusive as to the order of the texts, efforts to solve the issue have centered on textual approaches such as counting word differences among documents to see which are most closely related. This is a useful approach, but texts can be edited for many purposes, and as it turns out, the nature of Lincoln's editorial changes, drawing first on one document and then on another, precludes resolving chronological or editorial relationships on the basis of counting words only. Establishing the order of these two documents and the other versions of the speech requires in addition fixing for the first time the timing and stages of Lincoln's composition and revision process, often to the very hour, because the evidence of the texts can only be read in context: the history of those days surrounding the ceremony clarifies the mysteries of the manuscripts.

Bringing together the events and the words in a comprehensive narrative for the first time reveals a secure order for Lincoln's manuscripts, an order that is confirmed by the near totality of evidence, both textual and contextual. New sources and old evidence interpreted in a new light at last can provide confidence in a historically verifiable and textually supported chain of composition, performance, and revision that is written in Lincoln's movements and inscribed in his texts. The story that Lincoln told to Speed, read in the context of events and the evidence of the manuscripts, precludes the possibility that the Hay and all other existing texts were written before the speech; that story, again in conjunction with the texts and the events, confirms that the Nicolay document was the delivery manuscript. It alone is the sole surviving textual evidence and documentation of the compositional history that Lincoln told to Speed as a dramatic narrative; it encompasses a whole series of episodes of writing and revision that brought Lincoln from Washington to the stand at Gettysburg, and from an early, discarded conception of his speech to a new and more powerful vision pronounced on the battlefield. The chief witness in that story, through the recollections of Speed and seconded by the history of the texts and the events, is Lincoln himself.

As Lincoln saw, the speech that became the Gettysburg Address was not preordained; it was created, and its eventful history of composition reveals its contours and shape in ways that cannot be seen without the lens of Lincoln's lived experience. On the very morning of his speech, for example, Lincoln toured the battlefield and visited the site where his "gallant and brave friend, Gen Reynolds," had died.[6] On returning to his quarters to review his manuscript, Lincoln initiated an unexpected revision, changing the text he had prepared the night before and bringing a new vision to his speech. He included a wholly new second page incorporating a more assertive sense of dedication into his speech, and he underlined one word and one word only on the first page that he had retained from the draft he had brought from Washington: "The world will little note, nor long remember what we say here; while it can never forget what they did here." On the speakers' platform, Lincoln's deeply felt dedication to the cause and to the sacrifices of soldiers like his friend Reynolds led him to pronounce those words with such feeling that many listeners were moved to tears, difficult as that might be to believe in a postheroic world. This same powerful emotional impulse prompted him to add the words "under God" to his speech—words incorporated today in the Pledge of Allegiance because of this—though they are not found in his earlier drafts.

In that moment was born the authentic legend of Lincoln at Gettysburg; this is how the "few appropriate remarks" Lincoln was asked to give at the ceremony became the Gettysburg Address, history and memory intersecting to make an American myth. It is a myth that happened to be true for many who lived it, and it is a legend that is real for those who experienced it as such and who still believe in its power to transform. At first only some of those who witnessed that day expressed a sense of the emotional power of the scenes that unfolded before them. Over time, and in part because of the assiduous work of partisans and boosters, moralizers and patriots, the small cohort who carried the flame became the legions of a cause, part of the larger Cause Victorious, a myth nurtured in the North and among Unionists that inversely mirrored the secessionist myth of the Lost Cause.[7] The legend grew in schoolrooms, from pulpits, and in the pages of the daily press, and it was continued even a century later from the steps of the Lincoln Memorial by a prophet who still had a dream, but it began in a historical event whose reality resides in the details and trivia of a moment.

The texts tell the tale, but we can only see their history through the sources available to us, refracted by time and distorted by the lens of myth and memory. Recognizing the processes that created the legend of Gettysburg allows us to correct for these layers, taking us down through the accumulated sediments of memory to the bedrock of lived experience and a myth that has shaped American identity. Reconstructing Lincoln's journey to Gettysburg, a journey that as a people we have all made with him, allows us to trace across Lincoln's manuscripts the development of the new and more radical vision of the war's meaning announced by the "new birth of freedom." As individuals, we recognize that memory, with all its inaccuracies and distortions, gives us identity and makes us who we are. As humans in social communities, we find meaning in memory, myth, and legend, allowing us to make sense of lived and shared experience in ways that serve our need to feel connected to others and to larger purposes. In a sense, the Gettysburg Address remade America, but it might also be said that through the processes of reflection, repetition, and revision, America has constantly remade the Gettysburg Address.[8] The Gettysburg myth was built by veterans and partisans, opportunists and ideologues (and sometimes these were all the same), but the legend prospered and thrived because it reflected the ideals of, first, a people at war, and then, a nation defining its character during an era that created a new and somewhat terrifying vision of what a people united could be: "The unprecedented power," as *Harper's Weekly* put it welcoming Lincoln's second inauguration, "of a Government founded upon the popular will."[9]

His entire political life, Lincoln recognized the power of the people's will, and he sought to guide and lead that force toward what he considered its proper ends. For Lincoln, the great danger within Stephen Douglas's "popular sovereignty" was that it threatened to seize authentic democracy and replace it with rule by the will of only a part of the whole. The same ideas and tools that Lincoln developed during the 1850s in his struggle against Douglas and popular sovereignty served also in the struggle against secession, which Lincoln similarly defined as the effort of a part of the people to dictate to the whole.[10] However, by 1863 the massive transformations and new issues brought by the war demanded new responses; emancipation was one such, but it was a first step, not a culmination. A Union restored on the basis of the Emancipation Proclamation would have remained a house divided, part slave, part free. The real break in Lincoln's vision and policies came in mid-to-late 1863 and arose from the accumulated weight of decisions and policies by which the administration felt its way forward. Lincoln saw this clearly and described it quite forthrightly in the Annual Message of December 1863, written precisely during the two weeks bracketing the Gettysburg Address, in which he outlined the path by which he came to what he called a "new review" and a "new reckoning" about the course and destination of the war.

Most crucial in the new reckoning were the radical implications of administration policies regarding recruiting and arming formerly enslaved blacks. Building upon the policy that blacks could be citizens, in July 1863, and in response to Confederate massacres of African American soldiers, the Lincoln administration forthrightly proclaimed, "It is the duty of every government to give protection to its citizens, of whatever class, color, or condition," and then began to impose this view in its economic and Reconstruction policies. In early October 1863 the Lincoln administration, over the strong objection of some border state Unionists, instituted a remarkable and little-known policy of compulsory emancipation of enslaved men, with compensation to their previous owners, in most of the border states and of their enrollment in the army, effectively extending the draft to slaves and providing the essential foundation for the extension of full citizenship.[11] Most crucially for Reconstruction, the Annual Message of 1863 announced for the first time that only states that had abolished slavery would be readmitted to the Union: there would be no reunion with slaveholders. At the same time, Lincoln also pushed behind the scenes for state governments then in formation in the occupied South to enfranchise blacks who had served the Union.[12] This set the stage for his public statement of April 1865 in support of voting rights for some of the freedmen, perhaps the most radical and controversial public statement made by a president to that time. Hearing that speech, John Wilkes Booth resolved to strike.

Taken together, these and other new departures of 1863 and 1864 were already beginning to implement some of the ideas and policies that can be found in the three great postwar amendments to the Constitution that collectively created what some recognize as the Second American Republic: eradication of slavery throughout the nation, as in the Thirteenth Amendment, symbolically signed by Lincoln in 1865; declaration of equal protection of rights under the law regardless of race, as in the Fourteenth Amendment (1868); and extension of voting rights (albeit limited at first) for freedmen, as in the Fifteenth Amendment (1870).[13] In an early and still nascent form, this was the "great task" evoked at Gettysburg, which in 1864 Lincoln several times defined quite precisely, telling an Ohio regiment, for example, "what the country is now engaged in," which was nothing less than assuring the survival of "a free Government where every man has a right to be equal with every other man." Driving the point home, he declared that "every form of human right is endangered if our enemies succeed."[14]

Emancipation had been a middle ground, a military strategy with deliberately limited social and political implications. By 1863 and 1864, however, Lincoln was coming to see that the new nation born of the war would include blacks and whites coexisting in a single society, as affirmed by his silent retreat from advocacy of colonization. That society, in Lincoln's emerging vision, would be founded upon equal rights in civic life and before the law for all. This may seem an inevitable progression, but in part that is because Lincoln helped make it seem inevitable, for these issues divided Americans for the next century. In new forms, they divide us still.

Lincoln in his debates with Douglas and before had already recognized the natural rights that were denied to the enslaved: the right to one's own labor and the right to determine one's own life. This was the conceptual foundation of the emancipation policy, imposed and justified by military necessity. It was only after mid-1863 that he implemented the far more politically volatile and radical extension of civil and political rights, which were not asserted in the emancipation strategy of 1862. These were the issues that divided the nation during Reconstruction, the issues that brought forth the three great amendments, and the issues that eventually broke the Republican Party's commitment to equality of rights, allowing demagogues and Ku Klux Klan terrorists to reverse for a century and more the political and social gains of the war and Reconstruction. The "new birth of freedom" of the Gettysburg Address, then, was not mere poetry—it was also a statement of new and evolving governing principles that added up to a revolutionary transformation. "However it may have been in the past," Lincoln was quoted in news reports as saying within days of his return from Gettysburg, "I think the country now is ready for radical measures."[15]

And here is where a secure sequence of composition and revisions of the Gettysburg Address can illuminate these larger political and conceptual evolutions. Lincoln had trouble with the second half of his speech, with the majestic last sentence that resolved upon a "new birth of freedom," and we can see the difficulties he encountered in the ungrammatical, penciled revisions in his manuscript made on the very morning of the ceremony itself. But this is only apparent if we recognize that this document, the Nicolay document, and no other, was indeed his Battlefield Draft, held while looking out across the freshly mounded graves. The speech Lincoln gave there, on the battlefield, was whole and complete. Lincoln would later reframe certain phrases, but as noted by Lincoln scholar Douglas Wilson, the relatively few changes Lincoln made to his speech culminating in his last handwritten version in March 1864 were "more about texture than meaning."[16]

In the texts of Lincoln's manuscripts and his spoken words can be discerned the development of his evolving vision, revealing the Gettysburg speech to be a crucial milestone, when Lincoln crafted and refined the keynote phrases and central political vocabulary through which he made sense of the new reckoning and defended the new policies of his presidency.

Seeing this requires at last solving the mysteries of the manuscripts. If we do not know which manuscript Lincoln held when he first said the words "a new birth of freedom," we cannot know the difficult and eventful process by which those words came to be written, a process that Lincoln himself recognized. If we cannot place in proper sequence his revisions and handwritten copies of the speech, then we cannot understand the reasons and contexts for his spontaneous declaration, on the speakers' platform, with the mourning crowd before him: "This nation, under God . . . , shall not perish." And without standing in the crowd and witnessing the impact of his powerful invocation of "what they <u>did</u> here," we cannot understand the birth of the authentic legend of Gettysburg, the collective project that eventually brought to bear the energies of an entire nation in defining what has become the Gettysburg Address.

That moment depicted by William Makepeace Thayer, who was among the first to celebrate the scene of "Lincoln at Gettysburg" that comes to stand for the meaning and majesty of the Civil War and of the American experiment, was indeed a vision worthy of note, iconic and powerful. But we must have confidence in our knowledge of Lincoln's words before we can hear what he said. Lincoln's speech has helped make the battlefield and the cemetery at Gettysburg into landmarks of the American imagination, but Lincoln's journey to Gettysburg made both his manuscript and his spoken words. It was by writing the Gettysburg Address that Lincoln arrived at the "new birth of freedom."

"It Will Be an Interesting Ceremony"

Abraham Lincoln was irritated. It was Tuesday, November 17, 1863, the usual day the cabinet met, but his secretary of the treasury, Salmon Chase, had not shown up, nor had he sent an explanation. "I expected to see you here at [the] Cabinet meeting," Lincoln wrote in rebuke, the missing definite article nicely expressing his hasty chagrin, for there was pressing business. Lincoln had finally decided just two or three days before that he would be able to attend the dedication ceremony of the Gettysburg cemetery on November 19 for the honored dead of the Union's greatest victory, but he was also in the midst of writing an Annual Message that would at last present his formal plan for Reconstruction to Congress; a major battle was looming at Chattanooga, Tennessee, to seize the vital rail route to Atlanta; little Tad Lincoln was worrisomely ill; and on top of all the cares of the presidency in wartime, the railroad schedule for going to Gettysburg that had been given to him that morning had not been to his liking and had to be redone. So when Chase had not come to the meeting, Lincoln felt compelled in his note to let him know that he was displeased—"I expected to see you here at Cabinet meeting"—before getting to the matter at hand: "and to say something about going to Gettysburg. There will be a train to take and return us. The time for starting is not yet fixed; but when it shall be, I will notify you."[1]

The uncertainty about the train schedule reflected in Lincoln's imperious note to Chase was of Lincoln's own making, for he had waited until the last possible moment to decide about the Gettysburg trip, creating confusion in the press, at the White House, and in the administration more generally about the travel arrangements. Secretary of War Edwin Stanton had queried the railroads about a travel schedule, probably on Monday the sixteenth, and, acting under the assumption that "economy of time" was essential, they responded with an itinerary that had the presidential party departing Washington, D.C., on Thursday, the day of the ceremony, at 6:00 a.m. and returning that same day by midnight. Stanton had reason to believe that Lincoln particularly wanted to visit the battlefield, and he assured Lincoln that the train would arrive in Gettysburg by noon, "thus giving two hours to view the ground before the dedication ceremonies commence."[2]

Some of the newspaper reports datelined Washington, November 16, that first reported Lincoln's decision to attend the ceremony included this one-day schedule, but on the morning of the seventeenth Lincoln wrote to Stanton, "I do not like this arrangement. I do not wish to so go that by the slightest accident we fail entirely, and, at the best, the whole to be a mere breathless running of the gauntlet."[3] It was not only Chase who was receiving marks of presidential disfavor that day. Probably Lincoln had heard about the difficult rail journey to Gettysburg from his friend Ward Hill Lamon, who was serving as the master of ceremonies at the dedication, for Lamon had returned a few days before from a trip to Gettysburg and the two men had several times conferred about the ceremony.[4] In any case, economy of time for Lincoln was not the highest priority: he wanted to be sure that he arrived in time for what he was to call the "interesting ceremony."

Without a travel schedule, Lincoln could not announce a departure time, or even a date, at the midday cabinet meeting as he had hoped. Because Lincoln wished to bring some or all of his cabinet with him, late into Tuesday afternoon the office of Secretary of State William Seward still did not know whether he, Lincoln, and the others in the official party would be conducting business as usual in Washington on Wednesday or traveling to Gettysburg.[5] At some point on that busy Tuesday, Stanton and Lincoln finally arrived at a schedule more to the president's liking that had Lincoln leaving Washington at noon on the eighteenth, the day before the ceremony, and returning just after the ceremony on the evening of the nineteenth.[6] The *New York Express* and other papers reported that this schedule was designed to get Lincoln to the ceremony "without fail," which is undoubtedly an echo of Lincoln's determination not to "fail entirely" by attempting the trip in one day. The railroads telegraphed their acceptance of this new schedule at 3:50 p.m. on Tuesday, November 17, and the issue was finally settled. Lincoln was going to Gettysburg—the next day.

These chaotic arrangements for an iconic journey perfectly express the mixture of make-do and majesty that defines the history of the Gettysburg Address, and especially its origins in Washington and at Gettysburg. Lincoln himself sensed this peculiarity, most especially in the contrast between the process of writing the speech, as illustrated here by the disorder of the days before leaving, and the achievement he knew his speech to be. Lincoln had a remarkable ability to stand outside an issue and consider it from a perspective besides his own, a trait that is one element in what contemporaries called his "honesty" and that we might call objectivity. An ungainly boy and man, tall, awkward, and odd, he early on developed a sense of his effect on others and an ability to look at questions from several angles, as he knew others were looking at him. He was also a problem solver, and though he did not strike people as mentally quick—except when telling a joke or a story—by the time he became president more people than mere partisans had come to recognize his ability to frame an argument and identify the heart of a question. One problem Lincoln had set for himself was trying to understand the notable contrast between the way he had come to write his speech for the ceremony at Gettysburg and the high praise and esteem the speech had earned.

We can hear Lincoln working out for himself the paradox of his speech during a conversation with an old friend, James Speed, one night after Lincoln's reelection in 1864, just over a year after he had given the speech. Speed's story is mentioned in every history of the speech, but it has not been fully recognized as our best and most complete testimony about what Lincoln was thinking about and hoped to accomplish as he was writing and revising the Gettysburg Address.[7] Speed was not at Washington or Gettysburg at the time of the dedication ceremony, so his recollection of what Lincoln told him that night was not affected by his own memories of the event. Instead, what he tells us Lincoln said about the Gettysburg Address conforms so well to the record of events and seems to reflect Lincoln's outlook and understanding so closely that Lincoln himself seems to be speaking to us, telling us how he experienced and thought about writing the speech. And Lincoln had quite a tale to tell.

Lincoln was generally guarded about current concerns, but at the end of a long day he would sometimes look back at some incident in the past and speak more freely of his thoughts and motives. Talking with James Speed on that night in December 1864 or early 1865, Lincoln was evidently feeling particularly expansive, perhaps because he had known Speed for over three decades. Speed was the brother of Lincoln's best friend from the early Springfield years, but the two had grown to know each other well only during the war, when Speed, from one of the richest families in Kentucky, had helped keep the state from seceding. In December 1864, as Lincoln's second term was about to begin, Speed came to Washington to take up the duties of attorney general, and it was then that Lincoln, "one night in familiar conversation," told Speed about how he wrote his speech at Gettysburg.[8]

Lincoln's reasons for discussing his speech that night become apparent when we consider why Speed felt compelled in 1879 to repeat the story. Speed had started the war as a Democrat, but like many others, he had been radicalized by the fight against secession.[9] After Lincoln's assassination he had remained in Andrew Johnson's cabinet until July 1866, when he resigned in disgust and returned to Kentucky. He attempted to launch a political career—even receiving twenty-two votes for the 1868 Republican vice-presidential nomination—but eventually returned full-time to his successful law practice. In the meantime, the Gettysburg Address had made its way into school readers, handbooks of literature and rhetoric, and political and patriotic texts of all kinds. Speed, again like many others, had come to see the speech as a near-perfect expression of the central conflict of the war, or as he put it in 1887 when summarizing the war: "The question of the ages had come to a test. Can a nation endure dedicated to the proposition that all men are free and equal?"[10] This outlook helps explain why in 1879 Speed was dismayed to read in the newspapers that Ward Lamon had claimed that the greatness of the speech was not initially recognized. Speed vigorously contradicted Lamon and then set about demonstrating that Lincoln himself knew that his speech had been appreciated.

Though Lincoln did not live long enough to see the full resolution of the issues he faced in the war, he did witness the first year and more of the nascent Gettysburg legend. When talking with Speed, Lincoln saw that the speech, and the compliments it inspired, needed to be explained. It was not yet a myth; it was more a persistent memory with a growing reputation, an enduring and widening ripple that was unusual when so many great speeches had caused comment and then faded with the next oration or next issue. During Lincoln's life the speech did not yet have a clearly defined name, and it was not yet a universally known cultural entity that could be invoked with the assurance that everyone would know what was intended. Still, in the intersecting worlds of Republican political leaders and respected intellectual figures, the speech had already earned persistent acclaim and the label "immortal."[11]

By the time he spoke with Speed that night, Lincoln knew, for example, that the respected author John Pendleton Kennedy and the premier American historian of the time, George Bancroft (whom Lincoln had consulted about the history of habeas corpus), had asked him for handwritten versions of the speech for inclusion in a prestigious collection of facsimile copies of illustrious literary and patriotic texts in the handwriting of their authors. The first item in the collection, as Lincoln knew, was to be the "Star Spangled Banner," in the hand of Francis Scott Key, but the second was to be Lincoln's "Address Delivered at the Dedication of the Cemetery at Gettysburg," a name first given the speech by Kennedy in that volume, titled *Autograph Leaves of our Country's Authors*. Due to an error, Lincoln wrote two versions for the collection, the second of which, called the Bliss copy from the family that long owned it, was the last of his five surviving handwritten copies and is today considered the definitive wording of the Gettysburg Address.

When Lincoln was talking with Speed he also probably knew of—and probably dismissed—the praise for the speech found in most of the campaign biographies of 1864, including the milestone myth-making words of William Makepeace Thayer, editor of the *Nation*, quoted in the introduction to this book. Lincoln had provided Thayer with some information for an 1863 biography, and it seems likely that Lincoln owned both the 1863 and 1864 volumes.[12] Undoubtedly, too, Lincoln heard occasionally of the times his Gettysburg speech was quoted in the popular press and in political speeches across 1864—but such marks of attention were not unusual, particularly in an election year.

By March 1865 Lincoln did know of, and certainly did not dismiss, the praise of Elizabeth Granville, Duchess of Argyll, and of Goldwin Smith, Regius Professor of Modern History at Oxford University; both for different reasons held a good deal of cultural authority in a United States that still sometimes felt itself inferior to its well-bred European elders. Charles Sumner, the great radical senator from Massachusetts, brought to Lincoln a letter from the duchess in which she mentioned Smith and added, "I like his Article in McMillan on the Prest and think the speech at the Gettysburg Cemetery must live." The chair of the Senate Foreign Relations Committee, Sumner probably knew that Lincoln would be interested in the prescient comments of the duchess, who Lincoln knew was one of Sumner's usual informants on foreign opinion. And Sumner might even have known that Lincoln had met Professor Smith at the White House the previous fall when, as a rare prominent British supporter of the Union, he had been feted across the North. Lincoln rewarded Sumner's thoughtfulness, for he was so much interested in the letter that he took the time to copy out that part of the letter and file it away with the endorsement "Duchess of Argyll." Less than three months later Sumner would make the Gettysburg Address one of the keynotes of his own speech memorializing the assassinated president as a champion of human rights.[13]

The *Macmillan's Magazine* (London) with Goldwin Smith's praise for the speech was available in the United States when Lincoln copied the quotation, and the article was also reprinted in several U.S. publications before Lincoln's death; he would have been more than human had he not sought out the article and felt some pride upon reading the Regius Professor's comment, "It may be doubted whether any king in Europe would have expressed himself more royally than the peasant's son. And, even as to the form, we cannot help remarking that simplicity of structure and pregnancy of meaning are the true characteristics of the classical style."[14] Remarkably, this story returns upon itself, for on Smith's tour of the Union in 1864, George Bancroft, even then the owner of the first of the copies of Lincoln's speech written for the *Autograph Leaves* volume, had been his host in Newport, Rhode Island, and had given Smith a lot to think about for his planned book, at least according to Smith's almost comically condensed diary: "The Fort and its commandant. A great number of deserters, owing to the Bounty system. The President's address at Gettysburg—very good. The army—good men on the whole brought forward."[15] Whether or not Bancroft showed Smith his copy of the Gettysburg Address written by Lincoln, this discussion of it was surely one reason why Smith reprinted the entirety of the speech in his *Macmillan's* article, sparking the praise of the duchess and eventually leading Lincoln himself to copy the quotation about his own words.

Against the backdrop of these and other marks of the nascent Gettysburg legend in 1864–1865, many of them apparent to Lincoln, Speed affirmed that on that night in conversation Lincoln had said "that he had never received a compliment he prized more highly than that contained in a letter from Edward Everett, written to him a few days after that speech was delivered, and commenting upon it." Speed added, "He produced the letter and allowed me to read it." Lincoln was indeed proud of Everett's letter, which he received on November 20, 1863, the day after the ceremony at Gettysburg, for Lincoln greatly respected Everett, the country's most esteemed public speaker and a former secretary of state, who had given the main oration at the dedication ceremony; several times already Lincoln and Everett had met to discuss the war and foreign policy more particularly.

Everett's compliments to Lincoln reveal deep insight into the exigencies of the ceremony that he and Lincoln had just participated in, as well as keen sympathy for the task of speakers on such occasions, as is understandable coming from one with such long experience in public speaking. "Permit me also," wrote the reigning master of the podium, "to express my great admiration of the thoughts expressed by you, with such eloquent simplicity & appropriateness, at the consecration of the Cemetery. I should be glad, if I could flatter myself that I came as near to the central idea of the occasion, in two hours, as you did in two minutes." This was not only flattery for a president; rather, Everett's choice of these particular points to make the object of his flattery ring as truthful commentary on the requirements of ceremonial speeches. For months, Everett had pondered the "central idea of the occasion," yet the Boston Brahmin saw instantly that Lincoln had hit the point with as much economy of force as a rail-splitter wielding a well-aimed maul.[16]

Lincoln's reply to Everett revealed that he, too, understood the necessities of the occasion and the expectations of the day. "In our respective parts, yesterday," Lincoln graciously responded, "you could not have been excused to make a short address, nor I a long one."[17] Lincoln saw that both he and Everett had roles to play in the ceremony, like actors with their "respective parts." Excused by whom? Excused for transgressing what line of conduct or expectation? By taking his cue from Everett and referring to the difference in the length of the two speeches, Lincoln shows us that he meant at least in part to refer to the expectations of the event organizers, who had dictated the "respective parts" to the two speakers.

Clearly, Lincoln had been thinking about the imperatives of the occasion over the previous days when writing his remarks, and this probably made Everett's compliment even more meaningful to him.

Within hours of receiving Everett's complimentary note, Lincoln mentioned it to Advocate General Joseph Holt, and when his son Robert visited from Harvard sometime later, Lincoln even read it aloud to him.[18] Although stories had circulated since at least 1866 that Everett had complimented Lincoln while on the platform at Gettysburg, Speed's recollection of 1879 is the first mention in print of Everett's letter to Lincoln, providing strong support for his conversation with Lincoln. The letter "was laudatory almost to an extravagant degree; it was as complimentary as it could possibly have been," Speed recalled. "I do not remember his expressions, but I remember well the extremely handsome and flattering tone of the letter."[19]

Everett's letter of November 20 praising Lincoln's speech was evidently the starting point and focus of Lincoln's remarks to Speed as they talked that night in late 1864 or early 1865; it was so important that Lincoln even took the time to find it among his voluminous correspondence and show it to Speed, just as he had shown it to his son Robert perhaps a year before. For Lincoln, an accomplished storyteller with an eye for narrative structure, the plot of the story he told Speed flowed from the letter because as Lincoln told it, Everett's letter, and his own speech that gave rise to it, had an interesting and even surprising backstory. And so, Speed continued, "Mr. Lincoln at this time gave me an account of the preparation and delivery of the speech," revealing that Lincoln had in effect wrapped the story of writing the speech inside the moral or meaning provided by Everett's complimentary letter. Looking backward to see what steps to take on the road ahead was the standard structure of virtually all of Lincoln's most important speeches and writings, and he even applied that historical method in understanding how he came to write a speech that provoked a compliment he prized above all others.

Lincoln a year after the events provided a complete retrospective of how he had thought about and written his remarks from first receiving his invitation to speak at Gettysburg, to writing the speech, to revising it for publication after the ceremony on November 19, 1863. The path of development outlined by Lincoln, supplemented by other witnesses and the texts themselves, can serve as a guide in the following chapters as we move though the stages of the composition story Lincoln told; as a first step, however, it is essential to see the whole story as Lincoln told it, because only the entire story can untangle the mysteries of the manuscripts. Lincoln was the first historian of his remarks, and by following his account as given to James Speed we can follow his own journey to the Gettysburg Address.

Lincoln in his conversation with Speed recalled experiencing an eventful compositional journey: contemplation, which we can date from November 3 or 4 to November 14 or 15, a time when Lincoln was thinking about his role in the event and considering whether he could attend; composition, from about November 14 to November 19, when Lincoln actually wrote his speech; and resolution, when the speech was presented and inspired notable approval. This was a complete compositional narrative in three phases, or perhaps, a drama in three acts: development, crisis, and redemption.

First, contemplation and development. "When requested to deliver an address on the occasion of the dedication of the National Cemetery at Gettysburg," Speed recalled Lincoln telling him, "he was very uncertain whether his duties would not detain him at Washington—but was anxious to go—and desired to be prepared to say some appropriate thing." Speed's use of the word "appropriate" here is striking because that very word is found in the key phrase in the letter of invitation sent to Lincoln by the chief organizer of the Gettysburg cemetery, David Wills, on November 2, 1863, which asked Lincoln for "a few appropriate remarks." Like Everett's complimentary note of November 20, the letter from Wills had not been published at the time Speed was writing and was not mentioned in public accounts. Speed's use of the word "appropriate" in a context so similar to the phrase used in the letter further confirms that he was accurately reporting Lincoln's words, which reflected a certain concern about saying "some appropriate thing."[20] Speed's recollection of what Lincoln told him also precisely matches the chronology of Lincoln's invitation to Gettysburg, which suggests that Lincoln first learned of his invitation to speak in early November.[21]

Lincoln's first response to his invitation was not to immediately and definitely accept. Rather, in classic Lincoln fashion, he temporized. November 19 at Gettysburg occurred at a vital juncture in the war, when the military and political events that made 1863 the pivot point of the war were beginning to reshape the landscape. It was becoming increasingly clear that with perseverance the North could win the war, but it was still very unclear whether, and under what conditions, the Union could be reconstructed, focusing tremendous attention on the upcoming Annual Message and Lincoln's much heralded but still unknown plan for Reconstruction. Overshadowing everything was the impending presidential campaign of 1864, which opened semiofficially with the recent end of the state elections in the fall of 1863—the last votes were being reported in the paper Lincoln read on the train going to Gettysburg. Lincoln fully believed that if he were defeated for reelection in 1864, the Union would be lost, and with it the ideals he held even higher than the Constitution itself; some of this potent mixture of idealism and political interest would inevitably find its way into Lincoln's speech.

During these busy weeks, a few news reports appeared in newspapers expressing the hopes of the ceremony organizers that Lincoln would attend, or even Lincoln's own desire to do so, but Wills himself in an official announcement on November 7 stated only that Lincoln had been invited, not that he had accepted, and as of November 14 Wills was still uncertain about Lincoln's plans.[22] On November 12 and 13 Ward Lamon visited Gettysburg to consult with Wills about the ceremony, and on the fourteenth we find Wills asking Secretary of State Seward to perform the dedicatory service if Lincoln did not come to the ceremony.[23] Wills's wording to Seward probably reflects what Lincoln had told Lamon, that Lincoln would be able to attend "unless prevented by unforeseen circumstances," and Wills clearly thought it best to hedge his bets by arranging Seward as a backup.[24]

This first phase of contemplation and development ended sometime during the weekend of Saturday and Sunday, November 14 and 15, 1863, when Lincoln finally committed himself to going to Gettysburg. The reasons will require discussion, but the record is clear as to timing: up until Saturday the fourteenth, newspaper articles mentioned the attendance of governors and high officials in general, almost always with no indication that Lincoln would attend; as late as the fourteenth, several reporters even thought that Lincoln had decided against going.[25] Then, on Monday, November 16, a barrage of authoritatively phrased newspaper reports went out over the telegraph under a Washington dateline stating that Lincoln would attend the ceremony: "The President has finally determined to attend the inauguration of the Gettysburg cemetery," declared the *Baltimore Daily Gazette,* the phrasing suggesting that David Wills and the cemetery agents in Gettysburg were not the only ones who had been awaiting a presidential decision.[26]

The second act of the compositional drama that Lincoln described to Speed, the actual writing of the speech, almost certainly did not begin in any significant way before Lincoln's final decision during the weekend of November 14 to attend the ceremony. Writing the speech unfolded in two, discontinuous segments. "The day before he left Washington," Lincoln told Speed, "he found time to write about half of a speech." The precision of the date Lincoln indicated is remarkable. Lincoln left Washington on November 18 for the ceremony in Gettysburg on the nineteenth; in Speed's telling, Lincoln was referring specifically to the last day that Lincoln would have been in Washington with time and opportunity to write: not the day before the ceremony itself, but "the day before he left," Tuesday, November 17, the day of his irritated notes to cabinet officers and the scramble to set the rail schedule. We will hear that date again.

Lincoln then described a second segment of writing. "He took what he had written with him to Gettysburg," Speed recalled, "then he was put in an upper room in a house, and he asked to be left alone for a time. He then prepared a speech, but concluded it so shortly before it was to be delivered he had not time to memorize it."[27] Lincoln thought he had gotten a late start on his speech, and because of the discontinuous process of writing in two locations, on top of the unsettled conditions inevitably brought by an overnight visit, he felt pressed by the deadline of the ceremony, as indicated by the fact that he had hoped to memorize the speech and thought it a fault that from lack of time he could not do so. This unease, this feeling of getting through in the nick of time, was similar in some ways to the uncertainty and anxiety of the period of preparation before writing. This same tone continued as Lincoln related to Speed one consequence of the hurried finale of his compositional journey: "After the speech was delivered and taken down by the reporters, he compared what he had actually said to what he had written, and the difference was so slight he allowed what he had said to remain unchanged." The "upper room" so accurately described by Speed, in the home of Lincoln's host at Gettysburg, David Wills, is now a museum marking Lincoln's stay and commemorating the place where the delivery text of the Gettysburg Address was completed.

This eventful story that Lincoln told, from contemplation to composition, was the foundation of the third act: resolution and redemption, when Speed recalled that Lincoln "told me that he had never received a compliment he prized more highly." Speed had begun his recollection of the conversation with this introductory remark, and within the story of the speech as told by Lincoln it forms the end point chronologically and thematically. Here, as at several other points in the story, Lincoln not only told what happened but also gave some indication of how he felt at the time, a sense of the emotions he experienced during a process that moved chronologically from anxious, uncertain, and hurried toward a conclusion of a prized compliment. Indeed, one of the most notable elements of Lincoln's description of how he wrote his speech is this dramatic plot that he imposed upon his composition process.

Already, just over a year after the speech, we can sense the effect of the growing Gettysburg legend on Lincoln himself, because when he spoke with Speed, the address was for him a memorable or interesting event that needed to be explained and understood. Most immediately for Lincoln, Everett's remarkable—and to Lincoln, perhaps even surprising—praise for the speech required explaining, which he did by spinning a story describing how the speech that was begun with the idea of simply saying, as he told Speed, "some appropriate thing" and that was written during such an eventful process inspired a recognition he prized above all others—in other words, how the "few appropriate remarks" requested from him by David Wills became the Gettysburg Address. Lincoln was not just giving Speed information during "familiar conversation"; he was telling a story with an uncertain beginning, dramatic complications, and an ending of surprising achievement beyond expectation.

Lincoln indicated to Speed that he had been "anxious to go" to Gettysburg, but his desire to say "some appropriate thing" arose from the nature of the occasion and the request to dedicate the ground by a "few appropriate remarks," not from anything Lincoln himself felt compelled to say. Lincoln does not depict himself working on his remarks for weeks or burning with specific inspiration or seeking just the right venue to speak words he had to express. Rather, the Gettysburg Address was an occasional speech, created for a particular event and tailored to fit carefully crafted instructions, as outlined in the November 2 letter of invitation from David Wills. The Gettysburg Address did not arise solely from Lincoln at the center of the Civil War in Washington; it has in addition roots in the clay of a Pennsylvania market town and the decisions of obscure men planning to dedicate a cemetery.

The Gettysburg origins of Lincoln's speech can be found on the battlefield itself.[28] After the battle the crisis caused by decomposing bodies and thousands of injured soldiers had quickly overwhelmed the improvised local response. Within days of the battle, the governor of Pennsylvania, Andrew Curtin, visited the town in order to help organize care for the wounded and the dead; it was the first step on his own path toward being associated with the Gettysburg Address. Earlier in the year, Curtin had hesitated about running for reelection because he was uncertain of his chances, but he seems to have recognized very quickly that anger at Robert E. Lee's invasion and a backlash of patriotism created more favorable conditions for his candidacy.[29] Soon a party convention obligingly drafted him to stand for reelection, and he ran in large part on his credentials as "the soldier's friend." From the first, Curtin recognized that he had both humanitarian and political reasons to respond quickly to the crisis at Gettysburg.

When Governor Curtin left Gettysburg in mid-July, he appointed David Wills as his agent for "alleviating the sufferings and ministering to the wants of the wounded and dying," a task that became the foundation of the soldiers' cemetery.[30] A successful thirty-four-year-old lawyer, Wills was also the driving force and central figure in the organization of the dedication ceremony. As it would be for many of those associated with the cemetery and its dedication, the event became a milestone marking his rise to a more prominent role, and in 1874 he would be elevated to the bench and become known as Judge Wills, a figure respected in later decades for bringing Lincoln to Gettysburg. A Republican in a predominantly Democratic town, Wills was aligned with the radical wing of the party in the region— he had studied law in the office of Thaddeus Stevens—and hence his close association with Curtin, whom he had probably come to know during their common work on state educational boards in the 1850s.[31]

Having secured land and arranged numberless details, David Wills in late August reported to Governor Curtin that he anticipated beginning the reinterments in November and that "in the meantime the grounds should be artistically laid out, and consecrated by appropriate ceremonies." This is the first mention of the event that would bring Lincoln to Gettysburg, and from the beginning Wills and the dozen or so officials from several states who worked with him at various times sought to stage a dedication ceremony equal to the importance of the battle and to the heroism of the fallen. The cemetery was designed, and the burials carried out, Wills later affirmed, mindful of the "national character" of the project, and his descriptions of the cemetery used elevated and sacramental language to place the cemetery within the grand struggle of the war for the Union:

It is the ground which formed the apex of our triangular line of battle, and the key to our line of defences. It embraces the highest point on Cemetery Hill, and overlooks the whole battle field. It is the spot which should be specially consecrated to this sacred purpose. It is here that such immense quantities of our artillery were massed, and during Thursday and Friday of the battle, from this most important point on the field, dealt out death and destruction to the Rebel army in every direction of their advance.[32]

Wills in a newspaper interview went so far as to promise that this would be "one of the grandest and most imposing affairs ever beheld in the United States." It was hoped that all the governors of the loyal states would participate, but selecting the proper orator to give the keynote speech and set the tone for the ceremonies was the first and most important concern. "The Honorable Edward Everett, of Massachusetts, was then regarded as the greatest living American orator," recalled Clark E. Carr, a state agent from Illinois working with Wills, "and it was decided to invite him to deliver the oration." And so, six weeks after the battle, the cemetery was well under way, with the ceremony planning also seemingly complete, from the opening music to the final benediction.[33]

But there was a significant omission, at least to posterity, for Abraham Lincoln is nowhere to be found in Wills's papers or correspondence for the first three months of the cemetery project—his letter of invitation of November 2 is the first sign in the official correspondence that Lincoln was to be involved in any way. Indeed, according to Carr, Lincoln was very nearly not invited to speak at the ceremony. Although Carr's recollections over several decades present some inconsistencies, all versions agree that among the state agents and others working with Wills, the question of inviting Lincoln to attend the ceremony was not controversial, but Lincoln's invitation "to speak" was a late decision, and some cemetery agents in 1863 opposed the idea entirely.

"It was said that this would not be an occasion suitable to his accustomed manner of speaking," Carr said in his first extended account, published in the *Chicago Tribune* on February 12, 1900, "that, while in forensic debate or in the discussion of legal or political problems he excelled, he could scarcely be expected to be equal to such a memorial occasion." Carr was even more forthright in a 1913 interview, when he was quoted as saying, "Lincoln hadn't struck the other members as being just the right speaker for the occasion." In 1915 Carr repeated these earlier points in a speech and then flatly stated that some cemetery organizers had argued that "this was to be a great funeral, and that it was entirely outside his [Lincoln's] line of speaking." Overall, Carr's writings and the newspaper articles about him suggest that opposition to Lincoln's speaking arose mainly from fear that this stump speaker from Illinois, relatively unknown in the East, was at best simply not suited for the elevated proceedings being planned, and at worst might bring the tone down to the level of a frontier tavern.[34]

Moreover, the final decision to invite Lincoln was evidently not made by the cemetery agents or even by the undisputed leader of the project, David Wills, for on October 23 he wrote to Governor Curtin in Harrisburg, Pennsylvania, asking for a meeting to discuss the "arrangements" for the ceremony consecrating the grounds. Wills and Curtin had communicated by post and telegraph for months, so this request for a personal meeting probably signals that Wills had particularly delicate or complex matters to discuss with the governor. Then, on October 30, like a dam bursting, invitations poured forth from David Wills in Gettysburg to federal officials and officers in Washington, beginning with Ward Lamon and including, on November 2, Abraham Lincoln.[35]

Curtin's apparent role in approving Lincoln's invitation suggests that a later recollection by a reporter who had spoken with Carr may be significant: the reporter stated that some of the cemetery agents opposed Lincoln's speaking because of "political attitudes," seemingly referring to divisions within the Republican Party. Several of the cemetery agents were closely associated with radical politics, most notably Governor Curtin himself, and Curtin's supporters were even putting him forward for president in 1864. Although that idea fizzled, well into 1864 Curtin still hoped to nominate a more radical candidate than Lincoln, supporting John Charles Frémont in particular.[36]

Carr mentioned in 1900 that those opposed to asking Lincoln to speak did not want a "political speech," seemingly because it would bring down the tone of the event, but later reports inspired by Carr, and the circumstances of the meeting between Wills and Curtin, suggest that some of the cemetery agents also wanted to avoid a speech that expressed Lincoln's particular brand of politics or did not want to give the Lincoln administration an important role in their great patriotic ceremony. These considerations might also explain why the most prominent mention of Lincoln in

David Wills's official report on the cemetery written in early 1864 was tucked among notices of various invitations sent and letters of regret received, noting, "The President of the United States was present, and participated in these solemnities, delivering a brief dedicatory address."[37] Wills did not even print his letter of invitation to Lincoln in his official report, even though such documents were an almost mandatory part of the innumerable nineteenth-century publications presenting speeches, consecrations, and other public events. Wills may well have been among those who opposed asking Lincoln to speak; it seems that at a minimum he recognized that inviting the president and other Lincoln administration officials required consulting Curtin.

Just as Carr described, the November 2 letter of invitation that Wills sent to Lincoln, most probably only after getting Curtin's approval, encodes the compromise among the cemetery agents that cleared the way for Lincoln to speak at Gettysburg:

> These Grounds will be Consecrated and set apart to this sacred purpose, by appropriate Ceremonies, on Thursday, the 19th instant,—
>   Hon. Edward Everett will deliver the Oration.
>   I am authorized by the Governors of the different States to invite You to be present, and participate in these Ceremonies, which will doubtless be very imposing and solemnly impressive.
>   It is the desire that, after the Oration, You, as Chief Executive of the Nation, formally set apart these grounds to their Sacred use by a few appropriate remarks.

First, Wills asked Lincoln "to be present, and participate," a recurring phrase that refers to taking part in the formal procession and other events but does not imply a speaking role, as when Wills similarly stated that "the public generally were invited to be present and participate." Only in the next paragraph did Wills ask Lincoln to "set apart these grounds to their Sacred use" and at that, "by a few appropriate remarks."[38] Wills accompanied his letter of invitation with a personal note inviting Lincoln to stay at his home, which also emphasized Lincoln's presence and did not mention any words he might speak.

These letters of invitation were Lincoln's best evidence of what was expected when he first learned of his invitation. Together, the two notes described the "appropriate Ceremonies" as "very imposing and solemnly impressive." Then, too, Wills's vocabulary of "consecration," of "this last sad rite," of the "Sacred" purpose of the cemetery, and his evocation of widows and orphans and of the soldiers "now in the tented field or nobly meeting the foe" was clearly intended to play upon patriotic and sentimental themes that had become so powerful in the Union during the war. Wills's description of the ceremonies as a civic ritual, an act of political religion, set the framework for Lincoln's own speech. Wills also twice mentioned the participation and patronage of the powerful governors sponsoring the cemetery and twice mentioned the respected name of Edward Everett, suggesting that Lincoln would be in good company should he attend.

Most important, at least eight times in these two letters Wills underscored the request to "have you here personally" or "participate" or "come here," but only once did Wills mention that Lincoln should actually speak by making some "remarks." As Carr put it in 1906, the cemetery organizers "supposed and expected that the President would, in what he said, simply dedicate the ground," which is what Wills asked in his two letters.[39] Those opposed to a speaking role for Lincoln very nearly prevailed: Lincoln was not so much asked to give a speech at Gettysburg as to be present and to participate in a ceremony.

And Lincoln knew it. His letter to Everett the day after the ceremony mentioning the length of the speeches reveals that he knew the limited role expected of him. News reports coming out of the White House or Washington reflected this view: reports up to and including the official announcements of November 16 that Lincoln would go to Gettysburg all mentioned only that Lincoln would attend, or sometimes that he would "participate." None mentioned a speech or any words that Lincoln might say, doubtless a reflection of the way the reporters were given the information by the White House. As far as the cemetery organizers, the press, the larger public, and Lincoln himself were concerned, he was not going to Gettysburg to give a speech.

Why, then, did he go? It was an unprecedented decision for Lincoln. Never before in his presidency had he left Washington with the express purpose of participating in a public event or to give a speech. The first clues to Lincoln's reasons for going to Gettysburg can be found in a conversation he had with Ward Lamon sometime in the first few days of November. Lamon had just received his invitation from David Wills to be the parade marshal, but accepting this duty would prevent him from traveling to Illinois to escort his wife to Washington as he had promised his father-in-law, Stephen T. Logan. "He came to me," Lincoln explained to Logan, an old friend and former law partner, "and I told him I thought that in view of his relation to the government and to me, he could not well decline. Now, why would it not be pleasant for you to come on with Mrs. L. at that time? It will be an interesting ceremony, and I shall be very glad to see you."[40]

Lincoln's description of the Gettysburg dedication as "an interesting ceremony" set the keynote for how the event was understood by Lincoln and others; this was an event to attend, not a venue for a speech. One simple but powerful reason Lincoln thought the opportunity to be "interesting" was the prospect of seeing the site of the war's most momentous battle, one that Lincoln had once hoped might—with the fall of Vicksburg, Mississippi—bring about the end of the rebellion. Stanton's note of November 17 assuring Lincoln that the train arrangements left time to "view the ground before the dedication ceremonies" shows that this was an important consideration to Lincoln. When Lincoln got to Gettysburg he confirmed this interest by visiting the battlefield with Secretary of State Seward on the morning of the dedication.[41]

In addition to being interested in Gettysburg as a sight to be visited, Lincoln may also have considered the trip a chance for an excursion with his wife and, possibly, son, because several newspaper reports originating in Washington stated that Mrs. Lincoln would accompany Lincoln.[42] Mary had gone on several of Lincoln's trips to the Army of the Potomac, including a week-long stay the previous spring when their son Tad had also come along. As it happened, Mary did not accompany her husband to Gettysburg, undoubtedly because Tad fell ill in the days just before the dedication ceremony. Since the wrenching death of their son Willie a year and a half before, the Lincolns, and Mary in particular, had been deeply worried anytime Tad had taken sick. That Lincoln continued with his plans to visit Gettysburg even though his son was quite ill is often, and rightfully, seen as a sign that Lincoln considered the dedication ceremony to be an important event, but there is no evidence for the much later depictions of a "hysterical" Mary demanding that he not go.[43]

Lincoln's "interest" in the Gettysburg ceremony was further explained in an authoritative article in the regular column by "Occasional" in the *Philadelphia Press* and datelined November 16, Washington, D.C. "Occasional" was widely known to be Lincoln's close associate, John Wein

Forney, a political operative from Pennsylvania who owned and edited several important newspapers, including the *Philadelphia Press, Forney's War Press,* and a newspaper that was with good reason widely known as the semiofficial press organ of the Lincoln administration, the *Washington Daily Morning Chronicle.* A lifelong Democrat and one-time politician, Forney had very publicly broken with James Buchanan's administration over the issue of whether slavery would be allowed in Kansas and over the lack of official patronage for his newspapers. He supported Stephen Douglas in 1860, but after the election his seemingly genuine antislavery sentiments, and his fine sense of where power and patronage now lay, led him to become a staunch Lincoln man; among Democrats he was known ever after as "Lincoln's dog."[44]

For his part, recognizing Forney's importance and influence, in 1861 Lincoln personally intervened to support his appointment to the lucrative post of clerk of the Senate. Lincoln also guided government printing to Forney's papers. With the New York governor's mansion in the hands of Democrats, Pennsylvania was the largest Republican state and was vital to the party, to the Union cause, and to Lincoln's upcoming reelection campaign, as the state in 1864 would account for nearly a quarter of the electoral college votes needed for victory. Lincoln had been deeply concerned with the recent election there, and during the campaign he had been in almost continual contact with Forney and Governor Curtin, but he had also been very careful to maintain close ties with Curtin's rival for influence and power in the state, former secretary of war Simon Cameron. Indeed, part of Forney's usefulness for Lincoln was that the supple and personable Pennsylvanian somehow managed to be on good terms with both the Curtin and Cameron factions in the state. For these and other reasons, Lincoln frequently consulted Forney about patronage in Pennsylvania and about press coverage of the administration, with Lincoln paying special attention to the columns by "Occasional."[45]

At the time of the Gettysburg ceremony, Forney was helping Lincoln bring together a coalition of Democrats, Republicans, and others in support of the government under the banner of the Union Party, which would be Lincoln's official party label in his 1864 reelection campaign.[46] These interests intersected with the Gettysburg ceremony on November 12, 1863, when Forney met with Lincoln and introduced him to two other Democrats who had supported Republicans in the recent elections. Forney described one of them, Judge Peter Shannon of Pittsburgh, as "a democrat who has been a hero in our late Election [in Pennsylvania], and has made your name his text." Shannon was probably with Forney on the presidential train to Gettysburg, and the two even gave short speeches there the night before the ceremony.[47] We can be sure that on November 12 Lincoln and his guests talked about the ceremony, because the afternoon edition of the *Washington Daily Morning Chronicle* that day mentioned Lincoln's "intention" to "visit the battlefield of Gettysburg on the 19th of this month, when the great National Cemetery is to be inaugurated."

Forney's "Occasional" article of November 16 presumed to report Lincoln's inner thoughts and emotions about going to Gettysburg. "His solicitude for the families of the brave men who fell" was first mentioned, a patriotic cliché that also reflects Lincoln's well-documented concern throughout the war for the families of the Union dead. "Occasional" mentioned too that Lincoln decided to take part in the ceremonies because of "his deep interest in the dedication of the great cemetery," recalling Lincoln's own words to Logan: "It will be an interesting ceremony." Forney, that is, "Occasional," went on to describe the event in ways that suggest some of the reasons for this presidential interest: "A very large concourse may be expected," and "many prominent officers and civilians will take part." In particular, "Occasional" emphasized that "Mr. Everett's oration . . . will probably be the finest production of his life" and fervently praised the orator. "What a wonderful man is Edward Everett!" the article proclaimed, recalling to readers Everett's myriad services to the nation. On November 11, Forney had even written Edward Everett for an advance copy of his oration.[48] "And if anything more were necessary to make next Thursday memorable in our history," Forney continued, it would be that the statesman from Massachusetts would have "the good, the wise, and straight-forward President of the United States, Abraham Lincoln, by his side." Everett's oration was given much attention, but no speech or word from Lincoln was mentioned in this article. Forney, as usual, appears to have been well apprised of the thinking in the White House about the event; certainly he would not publish such direct characterizations of Lincoln's thoughts in the "Occasional" column unless he believed them to be in accord with Lincoln's views and purposes.

The ever-political Forney's patronage of the ceremony and Curtin's role in the decision to invite Lincoln illustrate how the mobilization and political divisions of the Civil War endowed every move by public officials with tremendous political significance, potentially affecting the very survival of the Republic, or at least, the survival of the administration in power. Lincoln's trip to Gettysburg was certainly no exception, as he recognized in his letter of November 9 to Stephen Logan explaining why he had advised Ward Lamon to accept the role of parade marshal: "I told him I thought that in view of his relation to the government and to me, he could not well decline."[49] Lincoln's remark placed the Gettysburg ceremony in the context of politics in two distinct ways: Lamon's decision about whether to accept related to the administration as an institution, but it also reflected upon Lincoln. The same reasoning would apply all the more to Lincoln himself; he, too, "could not well decline" the invitation he had received to participate. Put another way, it was in the interests of the government and of Lincoln that Lincoln should accept.

Going to Gettysburg was clearly in Lincoln's political interest in that it associated the administration with the sacrifices of the soldiers in the service of the cause they all served. Lincoln's opponents tried to use the obvious and inevitable political implications of the Gettysburg ceremony against him, arguing that he and his political henchmen were engaging in crass electioneering over the graves of the dead.[50] Shorn of its partisan edge, the accusation was justified, for Lincoln did in fact use the occasion, and virtually every other opportunity of the war, to argue for what he thought was the proper political course and the right path to the ends he had in view.

Nothing better demonstrates Lincoln's determination to link his administration to the battle, cemetery, and ceremony at Gettysburg than his attempt to bring nearly his entire cabinet with him. Seemingly all of his cabinet members received invitations from Wills at the same time as Lincoln, but it was Lincoln who took it upon himself to encourage a collective, coordinated attendance as a group. "I was invited and strongly urged by the President to attend the ceremonials at Gettysburg," Secretary of the Navy Gideon Welles wrote in his diary, and Attorney General Edward Bates noted in his diary for the day of the consecration, "The President and most of the Cabinet are gone—I could not go." Secretary of the Treasury Salmon P. Chase told his daughter in a letter dated November 18, "The President, with all the 'Heads' except Mr. Stanton & myself go to Gettysburgh today." These comments show Lincoln's expectation, even his strong desire, that the cabinet would attend more or less as a body.[51] The date of these reports and their association with the formal announcement that Lincoln would attend demonstrate that, for Lincoln, the attendance of his cabinet officers was an integral part of his going to Gettysburg. He evidently wanted to make a show of force, a united front, that would place the administration clearly behind the ceremony and its ideals, including honoring the soldiers and the heroic sacrifices of the war, and that would also bind the administration even more closely to the ideals and sacrifices that the battle, the cemetery, and the ceremony represented.[52] No wonder he was annoyed when his secretary of the treasury had not even shown up to the cabinet meeting.

Although he clearly hoped to attend the ceremony, Lincoln only finally decided that he could actually do so at what was perhaps the last possible moment, given the needs of railway scheduling and administrative arrangements. Among the news reports that suggested Lincoln very nearly did not go, or even had decided against going, one explained his decision to attend by referring to "the pressure exerted on the President." Another well-informed report stated significantly that "the President did not believe that he could leave for so brief a time even, but at the urgent solicitation of several Executives of the States so concerned."[53]

While these articles did not mention any governors by name, on November 14—that is, the Saturday of the weekend that Lincoln made his final decision to attend the ceremony—Lincoln did in fact meet with one governor: none other than Andrew Curtin of Pennsylvania. Fresh from his difficult reelection campaign, Curtin wanted to discuss patronage. "I will ask very little," he explained to Lincoln, "but you can readily imagine that in such a contest compromises had to be made." We know nothing of Lincoln's discussions with Curtin about patronage during their November 14 meeting, but a note by Curtin implies they discussed the Gettysburg ceremony.[54] Curtin does not appear to have been in a position to bring "pressure" to bear on Lincoln, but nobody needed to tell him that Pennsylvania was a crucial state and that political life of the day required building and maintaining networks of reciprocal obligations.

Whether Lincoln's decision to attend the ceremonies had more direct connections to his aspirations for reelection is an open question. Ten days after the trip to Gettysburg, Seward warned Lincoln, "The more I reflect, the less I am inclined to trust the Pa proposition. The public men of that state are queer," a mysterious reference that may relate to some bargain or deal regarding presidential or patronage machinations that had been under discussion, perhaps at Gettysburg or just after. At about this time, former secretary of war Simon Cameron, who would be at Gettysburg and who was held by many to be the true power in the state, was working to ensure that the Republicans in the state legislature passed an early resolution supporting Lincoln's renomination. Cameron was probably hoping to thwart Governor Curtin's supposed ambitions for the White House, but such a resolution also helped seal Cameron's ties to the Lincoln administration and its patronage. Then, in early January, once the resolution had passed, John Hay overheard Cameron say, "I have kept my promise." What Lincoln's side of the bargain may have been, if any, is unclear; nor is it certain that this was even related to Seward's warning against the Pennsylvania "proposition." When political movers and fixers like Cameron, Forney, and Curtin were in play, there was assuredly some deep game under way, but probably these obscure conspiracies played little or no role in bringing Lincoln to Gettysburg.[55] He usually did not take well to "pressure," but he was quick to see cold facts, such as Pennsylvania's twenty-six electoral votes, and there is also no reason to doubt that Lincoln also wished to honor the hero dead.

Whatever the basis for Curtin's arguments, it appears that, after having evidently approved Lincoln's invitation to speak, it was Curtin's "urgent solicitation" that gave Lincoln an additional reason to decide that he could leave a sick child and an unfinished Annual Message in order to go to the ceremony at Gettysburg.[56] Lincoln certainly felt pressed by the calendar. The White House announced that on Lincoln's return he would not receive visitors because of important government business—and that meant the reconstruction plan he was intending to present in his Annual Message, which he had started on Friday, November 13 and which was now put on hold for the trip to Pennsylvania, made public by the Washington press corps on Monday, November 16.

This was a ceremonial event calling for the attendance of the president, but it was not an occasion for a major speech. In the national memory, Lincoln went to Gettysburg in order to give the Gettysburg Address, but Lincoln's own testimony, by words and actions, suggests otherwise. Lincoln went, most probably, for a variety of reasons, all of them aptly summarized by his assessment that "it will be an interesting ceremony." He went because—like Lamon—he could not well decline. He went because it would be a grand, unprecedented celebration gathering a large crowd from across the Union and some of the most eminent politicians and orators of the day. He went because he hoped to console the living and commemorate the dead. He went because it was his duty. He went because he wanted to see the battlefield. He went because it promoted his political ideals and his own chances for reelection. He went because it might be a pleasant trip with his family. He went to honor those who gave everything to a cause that represented everything he believed in. But all the reasons that can be associated with Lincoln's decision revolve around his presence, not the words he might speak. Abraham Lincoln did not go to Gettysburg in order to deliver the Gettysburg Address.

In some ways, it is because Lincoln's speech was not the reason he went to Gettysburg that it became such a distinctive, even unique, statement among Lincoln's writings. The content of the speech was not determined by a particular administrative or military need or chosen to explain a policy or specific incident, which was the case for so many of Lincoln's speeches. This meant Lincoln's ideas could develop a kind of internal momentum, driven from within, by Lincoln's own inspiration. At several points in the composition process Lincoln appears to have created what he probably took to be a relatively complete or final text—and then he returned again to his words, each time adding or changing emphasis, even while speaking. This was a speech that arrived at a different destination than Lincoln first conceived; it grew and changed with each step of his eventful journey to the speakers' stand.

Lincoln's story to James Speed expressed a sense of contrast, even surprise, that a speech with such beginnings—as, for example, the chaos of the final decision to attend and the transportation arrangements—should have turned out so well as to be remarked and noted, most strikingly by the greatest public speaker of the day. One of the central wonders of the Gettysburg Address for many of its admirers in the last century and a half has been this same contrast between a purportedly haphazard composition process and the poetry of the speech—this is part of the attraction of the stories that Lincoln wrote his speech while rattling along on the train, stories that were for so long the hallmark of the Gettysburg Address in the American imagination. Lincoln was the first to sense this paradox, this fortunate turn of events that created a notable success.

Composed in turn at the White House, in Lincoln's room at Gettysburg, and even on the speakers' stand on the field of the great battle itself, the Gettysburg Address arose from the circumstances of its creation, and upon its manuscripts are imprinted the marks of its origins, including the expectations contained in an invitation sent by a small-town lawyer and the political imperatives of the national electoral calendar. By about November 16, the period of contemplation and development was done, when, as Lincoln told his old friend James Speed, "he was very uncertain whether his duties would not detain him in Washington—but was anxious to go." He would indeed attend the "interesting ceremony," and now Abraham Lincoln set about writing "some appropriate thing."

∎

TWO

The Washington Draft

Even with all the mysteries of the manuscripts, some things are certain. Sometime around the middle of November 1863, Abraham Lincoln sat down with a blank page of Executive Mansion letterhead paper before him, dipped his pen in ink, and wrote:

> Four score and seven years ago our fathers brought forth, upon this continent, a new nation, conceived in liberty, and dedicated to the proposition that "all men are created equal[.]"

These words are found in the first page of the so-called Nicolay copy of the Gettysburg Address; there is no disagreement today that that page is the earliest surviving page among the five copies of the speech handwritten by Lincoln, and that he wrote it in Washington before leaving for the dedication ceremony at Gettysburg.[1] Beyond this, however, almost everything remains obscure about the composition process in Washington when Lincoln began to write what would later be called the Gettysburg Address. Lincoln's writing of the speech in Washington has received remarkably little direct attention, having long been overshadowed by the scene of Lincoln at Gettysburg, speaking over the graves of the Union's fallen heroes, an image that for more than 100 years has provided the title for innumerable books and articles, as if it was at that moment that Lincoln first composed his words. The five surviving versions of the Gettysburg Address in Lincoln's hand each has a well-established name in the literature, and the contested history of each has been told in a variety of ways, but the text that Lincoln wrote in Washington and took with him to Gettysburg has received no such attention. This first writing, the earliest surviving element of what would become the most admired speech in American history, has not even been dignified with a name.[2] A more secure understanding of Lincoln's speech starts with its first known version, what can be called the Washington Draft of the Gettysburg Address.

In part, the relative neglect of the Washington origins of the Gettysburg Address stems from a lack of direct evidence. Unlike at Gettysburg, no one left a record of seeing Lincoln writing his speech in Washington. Yet there are four key witnesses who spoke with Lincoln about his text as it existed in Washington or who can bring their own recollections to bear on the issues: James Speed, Noah Brooks, Ward Lamon, and John G. Nicolay. Each is in some way problematic, but together their testimony reveals a nuanced, remarkably consistent, and at times surprising portrait of the Washington Draft, providing essential clues to the state of the text that Lincoln took with him on the train to Gettysburg.[3]

Even the account of James Speed, our most valuable guide, presents some difficulties when looking more closely at the Washington stage of the compositional narrative Lincoln described to him, particularly regarding the question of whether the speech in Washington was complete and finished. Speed recalled that Lincoln told him that after being invited he "desired to be prepared to say some appropriate thing" and that "the day before he left Washington he found time to write about half of a speech." Eight years after first telling this story in print, Speed confirmed that Lincoln had said that "he partially wrote it before he left Washington, and finished it up after arriving in Gettysburg."[4] Together, these accounts suggest that Lincoln first seriously put pen to paper on November 17 and that the speech was only about half finished when he boarded the train for Gettysburg. Yet other eyewitnesses will show that the story, as always with the Gettysburg Address, is somewhat more complicated.

To begin with, the testimony of the document itself suggests that the speech as written in Washington was far more than half finished and might possibly even have been a full and complete text, though certainly different from the speech as eventually delivered. As the guardian of the Lincoln papers, John Nicolay, who had been Lincoln's secretary, first published in 1894 what he called "the autograph manuscript" of the Gettysburg Address, which was not known publicly up to that point and which has since come to be called the Nicolay copy of the Gettysburg Address.[5] Yet the Nicolay copy of the Gettysburg Address is not the Washington Draft. The Washington Draft is the text as written in Washington, but only its first page survives as the first page of the Nicolay document.

In contrast, Lincoln created the Nicolay document in Gettysburg when he merged the first page of the Washington Draft with an additional second page that he wrote in Gettysburg, splicing the two very different pages together by an ungrammatical edit in pencil of the last line of the first page. Lincoln originally wrote this first page wholly in ink on Executive Mansion letterhead stationery, the only page like it among the five versions of the Gettysburg Address in Lincoln's hand, so it might be labeled the Letterhead Page for ease of reference. "This," John Nicolay affirmed in a letter of 1885, "the president wrote in Washington and brought [to Gettysburg] in his pocket."[6]

The current second page of the Nicolay document differs physically from the Letterhead Page in virtually every way, for it is "bluish-gray foolscap of large size," as Nicolay described it, "foolscap" being the term used to describe common writing paper of the day, with no printed letterhead. "This he wrote in Mr. Wills house" in Gettysburg, Nicolay flatly declared in 1885, specifying in a letter of 1894 that Lincoln wrote the second page "in my presence" on the morning of the speech.[7] It is the only page written in pencil among the five versions, so for convenience the page written in Gettysburg might be called the Pencil Page.

Reading the Nicolay document through the contexts and events provided by the witnesses and other sources allows us to see much about the Washington Draft that was previously believed to have been beyond recovery, including a better sense of whether it was only half a speech as Speed recalled Lincoln telling him. The confident and bold writing of the Letterhead Page, all in ink with no stray marks or edits, combined with its complex phrasing and ideas, reveals that it was most certainly not a first draft, and the text gives every indication of knowing precisely where it is going— if not to a full and complete conclusion, then at least very near to one. It seems highly unlikely that Lincoln first wrote the words of this entire page on November 17 as Speed implied, a day that was quite filled with a cabinet meeting, a review of troops, train arrangements, and many other matters, and this impression is confirmed by the other witnesses to the Washington Draft.

Speed told the overall story of the speech and Nicolay provided the document, but Noah Brooks gives us our best look at the speech in Washington while Lincoln was still working on it. Brooks was a journalist from Illinois who became particularly friendly with the Lincolns in the final two years of the Civil War and was even scheduled to replace John Nicolay as Lincoln's secretary in 1865, when Lincoln's assassination intervened.[8] Brooks was personally interested in the dedication ceremony, as he was listed among the "marshall's aids" assisting Ward Lamon who were to travel to Gettysburg on November 17 to help with the dedication ceremony.[9] Unfortunately, differences in wording and emphasis in the accounts by Brooks over several decades have led some to dismiss his Gettysburg story entirely, but the core appears to be sound.

Brooks in an 1878 article recalled that Lincoln had invited him to come along to a photography studio one Sunday before the ceremony, but as they were leaving the White House, Lincoln stopped and said, "Hold on, I have forgotten Everett!" He stepped back hastily and returned with "a folded paper" that Lincoln said was "a printed copy of the oration that Mr. Everett was to deliver, in a few days, at Gettysburg." According to Brooks, Lincoln brought the speech along "thinking he might have time to look it over," but he did not have the opportunity. Brooks then recounted their conversation:

> "It was very kind in Mr. Everett to send me this. I suppose he was afraid I should say something that he wanted to say. He needn't have been alarmed. My speech isn't long."
>
> "So it is written, is it, then?" I asked.
>
> "Well, no," was the reply. "It is not exactly written. It is not finished, anyway. I have written it over, two or three times, and I shall have to give it another lick before I am satisfied. But it is short, short, short."[10]

Lincoln's desire to say "some appropriate thing," as Speed recalled him saying, is reflected here in Lincoln's emphasis on the brevity of the speech, just as in his letter to Everett the day after the ceremony, and also by the concern he expressed to Brooks about covering the same ground as

Everett. Moreover, according to the 1878 account by Brooks, Lincoln was clearly taking great care with his speech, writing it over "two or three times" and creating "several draughts and interlineations" of what Brooks called "that famous address."

Lincoln's words as reported by Brooks suggest that the speech was complete or nearly so, even if not polished, for that would seem to be the only way Lincoln could be so emphatic about its length, and it is difficult to see how a "short, short, short" speech could be written several times without arriving at some sort of conclusion. This evidence of written preparation and relative completeness conflicts with Speed's seeming implication that the speech was only about half completed in Washington and was essentially started only on November 17. Yet Brooks is supported by the physical appearance of the Washington Draft, which suggests the manuscript was based upon earlier notes or drafts.

Brooks's trustworthiness has been questioned, but careful reading of his statements reveals strong evidence for his reliability.[11] For example, Everett did distribute an advance copy of his oration just as Brooks described; what is more, one of these advance copies of Everett's oration was in Washington, D.C., in the days before the Gettysburg cemetery dedication and in the newspaper office of the man vilified by Democrats as "Lincoln's dog," John W. Forney.[12] Although Everett supplied the text on the condition that it would not be published until after the ceremony, the sly Forney found a way around the problem: an editorial hailing the dedication ceremony published in his *Washington Daily Morning Chronicle* on the morning of November 19 simply lifted without attribution sentences and phrases from Everett's speech. This means that Everett's advance copy was probably received in the *Chronicle*'s office on the eighteenth at the latest, the morning Lincoln left for Gettysburg, but because Everett's advance copy could have been sent by train from Boston as early as Sunday the fifteenth, there is no impediment to its having arrived on the seventeenth or even the sixteenth. Given all these linkages, the scene as presented by Brooks of Lincoln having Everett's speech in hand before his departure becomes all the more plausible.[13]

More supporting evidence for Brooks's reliability can be found in his statement in 1895 that Lincoln quoted what Lincoln said was a line from Daniel Webster when describing Everett's Oration, "Solid men of Boston, make no long orations," a small anecdote with possibly important implications for the state of Lincoln's Washington Draft.[14] By the 1850s "solid men of Boston" was in common use, employed by Frederick Douglass, William Seward, and others to describe the New England elite, including Edward Everett himself, so Lincoln's quoting a line about "long orations" in relation to what Brooks in 1878 described as Everett's "formidable" oration fits perfectly into the larger cultural context. Moreover, Webster himself quoted the line, just as Brooks quoted Lincoln as saying.[15]

It has long been argued that Webster's nationalist "Reply to Hayne," one of the most admired examples of political oratory in the free states before the war, was the inspiration for Lincoln's phrase "government of the people, by the people, for the people."[16] Here, then, Brooks portrays Lincoln as speaking lines that Lincoln said came from Webster at the very time that Lincoln was first writing a speech that would include in its last phrase words that were also rooted in Webster. This suggests that at the time Brooks spoke with Lincoln, the idea behind the "government of the people" phrase, and probably at least a close approximation of the words, was already in Lincoln's speech. This idea and phrase is found in the last few words of the Gettysburg Address, so if the idea or words were in the Washington Draft, this might also suggest that the draft was fairly complete.

There is, however, one large problem that has prevented Brooks's testimony from being given sufficient importance for the history of the Gettysburg Address: this conversation could not have taken place at the time and place Brooks said it did.[17] Lincoln did not go to a photography studio at any time that he could also have had Everett's oration. And yet the conversation with Lincoln and the larger context appears to be reliable, given the number and variety of elements that conform to evidence that was not available to Brooks otherwise.

This puzzle is perhaps best solved by recognizing that memory (in individuals and in cultures) is a process of dynamic reconstruction of different elements, not the passive recall of a fixed image or scene.[18] Brooks and Lincoln probably did look at prints of a November 8, 1863, sitting at Alexander Gardner's studio, because a "blurred foot" photograph that Brooks described in the 1878 article was taken on that day, which Brooks said was Lincoln's last sitting for Gardner. However, Brooks probably actually visited Gardner's studio with Lincoln on Sunday, February 5, 1865, which indeed was the last sitting, when a "cracked negative" photo was taken that Brooks also wrongfully associated with 1863. It appears that Brooks in 1878, looking back fifteen years, had overlaid details about the photographs and circumstances of a 1865 studio visit upon a conversation with Lincoln from 1863, which also involved discussing photographs of Lincoln. Brooks's depicting Lincoln with an advance copy of Everett's oration raises the possibility that Everett's speech influenced the composition of Lincoln's own remarks.[19] Still, if Lincoln did have Everett's speech, it seems to have not affected the speech written by Lincoln at the time he spoke with Brooks, for Lincoln had not read it.

At some point after the speech Lincoln spoke with Brooks about it again, similarly perhaps to the way Lincoln discussed it with his son and with James Speed. At that time, Brooks gained the impression that Lincoln "did not appear to think very highly of his own speech," a comment that sounds dismissive but takes on more credibility when read next to the narrative Lincoln told Speed.[20] Given Everett's complimentary letter of November 20, and also his own sound judgment of oratory and narratives, Lincoln from the start had good reason to value his speech. But when speaking to Brooks, Lincoln might well have used language that could sound belittling of the final product, even if what he meant was only that the composition process was somewhat disjointed, just as in Lincoln's similar conversation with Speed. Yet if Brooks seems to verify Speed's depiction of Lincoln's frame of mind, his testimony suggesting the Washington Draft was fairly complete seems to differ from Speed's account. The third eyewitness can help resolve some of these differences.

The question of what Lincoln thought about his speech was a central concern of Ward Hill Lamon, who in Lincoln historiography often appears as a cross between a buffoon and a renegade.[21] He was infuriated by the postwar idealized image of Lincoln, and he carried on a sustained campaign to portray Lincoln in what Lamon believed to be his real, remarkable colors. Lamon's testimony needs to be handled carefully, but what he said about Lincoln's Washington Draft is particularly important because of his role as marshal of the Gettysburg ceremonies and his close friendship with Lincoln. They spoke several times about the ceremony, including just before Lamon made a preparatory visit to Gettysburg on November 12 and 13 and also the next week "just before" or "a day or two" before the dedication ceremony.[22]

This chronology suggests that Lincoln spoke with Lamon sometime between Saturday, November 14, after Lamon returned to Washington from Gettysburg, and his departure for Gettysburg again at 11:00 a.m. on the morning of November 17. However, Lincoln's busy morning on the seventeenth and Lamon's imminent train would suggest this conversation occurred on November 14, 15, or 16. It does seem reasonable that during this time Lamon would describe the arrangements to Lincoln, who confirmed his interest in the details of the event at precisely this time by summoning the cemetery designer to meet with him. If he and Lamon did talk sometime from the fourteenth to the sixteenth, Lamon would certainly have told Lincoln about what he saw on November 13 when he and David Wills toured the still-incomplete cemetery, with the state plots laid out and its freshly dug graves, which may well have provoked Lincoln to summon the designer. As noted, Lincoln also met with Governor Curtin on the fourteenth, which probably triggered the final decision to attend; Gettysburg was becoming an important part of Lincoln's days even before his departure on the eighteenth.

Lamon recalled that Lincoln told him "that he was extremely busy and had no time to prepare himself for it and feared he would be unable to do himself and the subject justice," which, accounting for Lamon's habitual exaggeration, conforms closely to what Lincoln later told Speed; nor does there appear to be cross-contamination of sources. A slightly different version published in Lamon's posthumous *Recollections* stated that Lincoln said "he greatly feared he would not be able to acquit himself with credit, much less to fill the measure of public expectation." According to Lamon, Lincoln then "took out of his hat (the usual receptacle of his notes and memoranda), a page of fools cap [paper], closely written and read to me, what he called a memorandum of what he intended to say." It was "in substance and I think in *haec verba* what was printed as his Gettysburg speech," using a legal term that implies an assurance of a close or verbatim transcription.[23]

Lamon is the only one of the Washington Draft witnesses who described Lincoln reading his speech, and his recollection has been challenged, but perhaps it is understandable for Lincoln to read "what he intended to say" to the grand marshal of the event who had just returned from the site of the impending ceremony and was Lincoln's best resource at that time for gaining a sense of what would be "appropriate remarks" for the event. Lamon's depiction of Lincoln as concerned about meeting expectations adds a similar but more anxious note to Speed's depiction of Lincoln as wanting to say "some appropriate thing" and to the evidence from Brooks that Lincoln was taking care with his speech and thinking about it in relation to other elements of the program, including Everett's oration.[24] According to Lamon's account, this early version of the speech on "fools cap" paper was clearly well developed by the time Lincoln read it to him, which was almost certainly before the morning of November 17.[25]

In apparently the first of several published versions of this story, Lamon went on to describe Lincoln's assessment of the speech, supposedly rendered just after the ceremony, with a typically hyperbolic quote, "Lamon, that speech won't *scour!* It is a flat failure, and the people are disappointed," and Lamon added that Lincoln "seemed more than ordinarily concerned about what the people would think of it."[26] Lamon told this story in several ways, but shorn of its Lamonian overstatement it is consistent with accounts by the others in which Lincoln is similarly concerned about how his speech might be received and expressed himself in a way that could have been understood as belittling his speech or its process of composition, perhaps more than mere modesty would demand. While it seems unlikely that Lincoln would have said such a thing after the speech, Lamon's depiction of a harried and hurried Lincoln coincides well with Speed's account. Furthermore, Lamon's account of the reception of the speech varied greatly over time, but his story of the conversation with Lincoln about writing the speech is much more stable.

Lamon's general point that Lincoln had a relatively solid draft before the seventeenth and was concerned about whether it was appropriate seems credible in its outline even when the phrasing or details sometimes inspire skepticism. It would be imprudent to rely on Lamon alone, but taken together, Brooks, Speed, and Lamon suggest that Lincoln experienced the composition of his speech as an odyssey fraught with complexity and the potential for difficulty. Still, Lamon, in contrast to Speed, presents a relatively complete text, adding further support to both the manuscript and to Brooks's statement in this regard, and it is a text that would almost certainly have to have been begun before November 17, which also conforms to Brooks's account.

Lincoln's problematic journey to the Gettysburg Address was the keynote of the last of the four eyewitnesses to Lincoln's Washington Draft, John Nicolay, in his first published account of the speech in 1890.[27] Nicolay, as much as Lamon, believed he knew Lincoln better than anyone, to such an extent that he and his literary partner John Hay often seem to be speaking for Lincoln, describing thoughts and attitudes that clearly are intended to express Lincoln's words and actions as he saw and understood them. Hay repeated with approval Nicolay's account of the speech, and while this does not make Hay an independent witness, it does show that

Hay thought Nicolay's account conformed to what Hay knew of the speech, and Hay was with Lincoln in Washington and Gettysburg through this entire period.[28]

⌐ Of course, Nicolay too was in Washington before the speech and was at Gettysburg when Lincoln created the final written version of the speech, and he proudly declared, "I was with him at the time." Nicolay strongly argued against the misconception that Lincoln first started to write his speech on the train or in Gettysburg, citing his memory of the morning of the ceremony, when he categorically stated that he saw Lincoln working with the draft that Lincoln had brought "in his pocket" from Washington. Because Nicolay so faithfully presented his understanding of Lincoln's words and perspective, his story of Lincoln's speech projects an arc from uncertainty to success that echoes what Lincoln himself told Speed. After describing the scene on the speakers' platform, Nicolay lauded, across ten pages, Everett's magnificent career and magisterial speech, which ended, he said, with "a brilliant peroration, the echoes of which were lost in the long and hearty plaudits of the great multitude." And then, Nicolay added anti-climactically, "President Lincoln arose to fill the part assigned him in the programme." Nicolay then paused, leaving Lincoln standing to give his speech, to evoke the difficult task that had been set before Lincoln, to write a speech that could "fittingly crown with a few brief sentences the cere-monies of such a day, and such an achievement in oratory."[29]

Well might Nicolay summarize Lincoln's plight: "It was a trying or-deal." Or, as Lincoln himself was quoted in a news report of 1865 when discussing his speech on the train going to Gettysburg, "the occasion was a novel and difficult one."[30] And just as in Lincoln's own narrative to Speed, in which a disjointed composition process inspired a compliment Lincoln cherished to the end of his life, so too in Nicolay's account, the peril of Lin-coln's position turned to triumph. Here, the question of Lincoln's own sense of concern with his speech merges with Clark Carr's evidence that Lincoln's invitation was controversial among the cemetery agents, for Nicolay by 1894 (long before Carr's first published accounts) clearly knew of the concerns among the organizers of the event about Lincoln's fitness to speak on the august occasion. Nicolay began with the specter of failure: "If there arose in the mind of any discriminating listener on the platform a passing doubt whether Mr. Lincoln would or could properly honor the unique occasion"; then continued to success: "that doubt vanished with his opening sentence"; and culminated in apotheosis: "one of the world's masterpieces in rhetorical art."[31]

It is quite possible that Nicolay heard about the opposition to Lincoln's speaking when he was in Gettysburg at the time of the ceremony, and it is certain that Carr spoke with Nicolay afterward—probably in the White House—and then corresponded with Nicolay.[32] At the time of the dedication ceremony, Carr, an appointed officeholder and loyal party activist, might very well have thought it to his advantage to cast himself to Hay and Nicolay, both of whom also hailed from the Illinois frontier, as Lincoln's champion against the polished easterners among the cemetery organizers, just as he did in his various accounts decades later.

Nicolay developed more fully this vision of Lincoln's difficult situation as he grappled with his role, and of Lincoln's eventual achievement, in his 1894 article in *Century Magazine* in which he first published the Nicolay text. Lincoln was "extremely busy," Nicolay wrote, and there was even "great uncertainty" whether he could attend, so that "no definite arrangements" for his journey had been made until November 17, which Nicolay could document because of his monopoly on access to Lincoln's papers. Lincoln lacked the opportunity "to even think leisurely about what he might desire to say," all themes familiar from Speed and Lamon. As if things weren't difficult enough, "there was much greater necessity for such precaution" given that Everett was "quite certain to make a long address." This remark was certainly sparked by Nicolay's knowledge of Lincoln's letter to Everett after the ceremony, cited in the article, which made the same point, but this only confirms that Nicolay was essentially parroting what he thought was Lincoln's perspective throughout his account. Nicolay also noted that Lincoln had to conform to the invitation soliciting a speech that, in Nicolay's words, "should only be 'a few appropriate remarks.'"[33] The word "only" is a significant addition, as it is not found in the original invitation, which Nicolay first published in this article. Nevertheless, it probably does express the way the letter was interpreted in the White House in 1863, when going to Gettysburg was envisioned as attending a grand event, not the occasion for a major speech.

When it came time for Lincoln to speak, Nicolay in his 1894 article again placed Lincoln on the platform after Everett's oration, as he had in 1890, but in this version Nicolay provided additional insight into the problem Lincoln faced in fulfilling his role. For many of those present, Nicolay declared, "Mr. Lincoln was there as a mere official figure-head, the culminating decoration, so to speak, of the elaborately planned pageant of the day." This, too, conforms to Carr's later statements. Nicolay, who shows remarkable interest in and insight into the expectations of the organizers, wrote that it was thought Lincoln's remarks "would consist of a few perfunctory words, the mere formality of official dedication," which explains why the crowd was "totally unprepared for what they heard," and they "could not immediately realize" the power of Lincoln's words, which were like "a trumpet-peal to the farthest posterity," echoing Lamon's more harshly phrased depiction of disappointment at Lincoln's speech, but with the added note of ultimate vindication. Of course, this same happy turn of events is found in Lincoln's own narrative to Speed. As in his other writings, Nicolay, in describing how Lincoln wrote and presented the Gettysburg Address, seemed to want to act as a kind of oracle, speaking for the martyred president, presenting Lincoln's experience as seen through Lincoln's eyes. That experience as interpreted by Nicolay included the same combination of potential disaster and happy conclusion found in Lincoln's story of his speech as told to Speed.

With the testimony of the manuscript and the four witnesses before us, there is good evidence to think that the Washington Draft was based upon earlier notes or drafts. In addition to the evidence of the appearance of the manuscript itself, we have Brooks's description of Lincoln talking about rewriting and revising, as well as Lamon's statement that the document he saw was on foolscap paper, which was obviously not the Letterhead Page. The Washington Draft also seems to have been a relatively complete text: Lamon depicts Lincoln's speech as essentially finished before the morning of the seventeenth, and Brooks provides evidence suggesting that Webster's "of the people" phrase was probably already in the "short, short, short" draft when he spoke with Lincoln.

With all this in mind, another look at the Nicolay document can help resolve the problem of the state of the text in Washington, particularly in light of the evidence presented by Speed, Brooks, and Nicolay that Lincoln wrote the speech in two distinct phases. According to Nicolay's testimony—and other evidence to follow—when Lincoln delivered his speech, he held in his hands the Letterhead Page, written in Washington, and a second page, the Pencil Page, added to it in Gettysburg. When Lincoln spoke with Speed a year after the events, then, those physical, tangible pages of the document would have represented for him, in a very direct sense, his "speech," an understanding reinforced for Lincoln when he worked with the document while rewriting and revising the speech back in Washington after the ceremony. Thus, when Lincoln told Speed a year after the event that "the day before he left Washington he found time to write about half of a speech," he was not telling Speed that he had written in Washington only half of the words of the speech that he gave at the cemetery; rather, he was saying that half of the speech given at Gettysburg, meaning half of the physical document that he held, was composed of the document that he had created in Washington, that is, the Washington Draft. This explains how the Letterhead Page as written in Washington could present such a strong image of a completed text—well developed conceptually, clearly based on earlier notes or drafts, and perfect in written form, with strong letters, bold strokes, no editing—and yet Speed could recall that Lincoln described it as "half" of a speech.

The conclusion that Lincoln was referring to "half" of the material document and not to half of the abstract words of the speech that he gave at Gettysburg is confirmed when we see the key phrase in the context of Speed's account: "The day before he left Washington he found time to write about half of a speech. He took what he had written with him to Gettysburg, then he was put in an upper room." By depicting Lincoln taking "what he had written" with him to Gettysburg, Speed very clearly was referring to the document itself, powerful evidence that Lincoln was also speaking of the document when he described what Speed referred to as "about half of a speech." This understanding conforms more fully to evidence of the document itself than does the hypothesis that Lincoln somehow stopped abruptly in midsentence with "to stand here."

While the Letterhead Page is today a "half-sheet" (roughly equivalent to a standard sheet of printer or copier paper today) the Letterhead Page of the Washington Draft was originally the first page of a single, full sheet (equivalent to a double sheet today), which when folded had four pages. This means the text continuing "to stand here" would probably have been written on the third page of this single, folded, sheet.[34] Furthermore, the argument that the "half of a speech" in Speed's account was referring to the Letterhead Page of his delivery document is supported by Lincoln's telling Brooks that "he made several changes in the manuscript of his own address after he got to Gettysburg."[35] The phrasing here makes it clear that Lincoln was referring to the document ("the manuscript") while Speed's phrasing ("a speech" or "it") is ambiguous and might be taken as referring to the words. So when Lincoln told Speed that the day before leaving he had written "half of a speech," he was saying that he had written half of the two pages of his composite delivery text; the Letterhead Page is that "half."

And not only has Lincoln confirmed that the Letterhead Page was indeed written in Washington, but on this interpretation Lincoln was also telling Speed that he wrote the second part of his speech, the Pencil Page, in Gettysburg, just as Nicolay would later describe. Like the Letterhead Page as written in Washington, the Pencil Page bears no editing, revisions, or erasures whatsoever, and, again like the Letterhead Page, its words are so complex and finished that it must have been based on prior notes or an earlier draft. Those earlier notes, that earlier draft, must have included the Washington Draft.[36] Working backward, then, at least some of the words and phrases, and some of the themes and ideas, of the Pencil Page written in Gettysburg derived from the text written in Washington that included and continued the Letterhead Page, that is, the Washington Draft. From Brooks's evidence, that draft probably included the Websterian "of the people" phrase currently found at the end of the Pencil Page. It hardly needs pointing out that all this corresponds to the Nicolay document exclusively; no other text, extant or hypothetical, could correspond so well to the record of the eyewitnesses and the events.[37]

The four witnesses and the manuscript reveal the Washington Draft to have been a fairly complete text written on the basis of notes or earlier drafts. This might suggest an extended compositional process, but here the evidence supports Speed's depiction of a late start to the writing phase, for Lamon and Nicolay similarly portray Lincoln as busy and rushed. It would make little sense for Lincoln to devote a great deal of time to his remarks when he was not sure he would be able to go, although undoubtedly in odd moments he thought about what he might say and may even have jotted a line or two; John Nicolay called this "cumulative thought."[38]

Speed's recollection that Lincoln said it was only "the day before he left Washington" that he "found time to write about half of a speech" might be literally correct if one accepts that Lincoln in referring to his "speech" meant the document he held, for there is strong evidence that Lincoln himself had identified November 17, the night before boarding the train, as a kind of deadline for getting his remarks in order. This is suggested by the fact that Lincoln took the time to schedule an unusual meeting for that evening: he wanted to talk with a gardener. Or rather, he wanted to speak with William Saunders, the landscape gardener who had designed the grounds of the Gettysburg soldiers' cemetery. Saunders recalled that it was "a few days before the dedication of the grounds" that Lincoln sent word to Saunders to come to the Executive Mansion "on the evening of the 17th (November)." This would place Lincoln's request around Monday the sixteenth, when the White House had announced that Lincoln would attend the dedication ceremony. But why call for Saunders when there was so much to do and prepare? When Lincoln had "sent word" that he wished to see Saunders, he had made a quite specific request: "He desired me to call at his office," Saunders recalled, "and take with me the plan of the cemetery."[39]

Although Saunders did not speak with Lincoln about his speech directly, the approaching dedication ceremony pervaded their conversation so thoroughly that Saunders, too, must be considered an important source for Lincoln's thoughts at this crucial moment, for it seems very probable that Saunders was the last person to speak to Lincoln about the cemetery and the ceremony before Lincoln wrote the final version of the Washington Draft.[40] Lincoln may have heard about Saunders and his design of the Gettysburg cemetery from Governor Curtin during their talk on the fourteenth or from Lamon, who had just returned from a tour of the cemetery grounds conducted by David Wills, and he also may have seen some of the brief press reports about the cemetery that appeared in October and early November, some of which reported that Saunders visited the cemetery grounds and supervised the ongoing work.

But Lincoln also almost certainly heard about the cemetery plan and its designer from John W. Forney during their meeting with Judge Peter Shannon on November 12. Forney had seen the cemetery plans during a visit with Saunders the week before at the experimental gardens that Saunders supervised in Washington for the commissioner of agriculture, and he had been tremendously impressed by them. As part of Forney's assiduous publicity for the Gettysburg cemetery, on November 5 he published in the *Chronicle* a gushing article about Saunders's design. Given the semi-official status of the *Chronicle*, Lincoln may well have seen the article. It provides some idea of what Forney may have said to Lincoln on November 12 about the Gettysburg cemetery and can provide some insights into what Lincoln probably knew about the cemetery and its dedication ceremony— and even more important, what Lincoln wanted to know—at this crucial moment in framing his remarks.

"This is and must ever be a national institution," the November 5 article said of the Gettysburg cemetery, "and the whole country has an interest in its being laid out and ornamented in a way worthy of a people who so truly honor the memories of their brave dead." The article extolled the talents of "Mr. William Saunders, one of the best and most tasteful landscape gardeners of the present day," who had just left for Gettysburg with the "beautiful drawings" of the cemetery plans "for the interesting work he has undertaken." The article waxed eloquent about the plans and "their unique beauty and picturesqueness, and their perfect adaptability to the controlling idea of a national cemetery," lamenting that "we may not be able to convey to our readers a just idea of the perfectness of his design." The article's enthusiasm probably found its way into Forney's discussion with Lincoln on November 12, even if the president did not see the article itself; at the very least, Lincoln had heard about Saunders and about the cemetery plan and wanted to find out more.

"I was on hand at the appointed time," Saunders later recalled, "and spread the plan on his office table," no doubt the same table around which the cabinet met and that can be seen in several photographs of Lincoln's upstairs office at the White House. From Saunders's description, the drawing of the cemetery layout was a large paper, probably rolled for ease of handling, and brightly colored. Saunders would certainly have selected the most beautiful of the drawings that had so impressed the author of the November 5 *Chronicle* article.[41] Saunders retained a vivid impression of Lincoln's reaction to the design, and it must indeed have been a proud moment for the Scottish landscape gardener as he spread his drawing for the president. Saunders had been deeply involved in the cemetery project for months, and his plan for the grounds arose from profound and insightful meditation on the relationship of the spatial arrangement of the graves and other features to the intended effect on the thoughts and sentiments of visitors and mourners. He was by no means an untutored gardener; rather, he was, as his St. Andrew's College education and many publications attested, a professional who sought to embody in his creations complex ideals of beauty and utility. His 1869 treatise on landscape architecture, "Landscape Gardening," evoked Eden, Babylon, and Rome to argue that gardening was synonymous with civilization. On this most crucial night of November 17, Lincoln could have had no better guide to the ideals and aspirations behind the Gettysburg cemetery.

From the way Saunders presented his plan to others at that time, it

CHAPTER TWO

seems likely that he would have carefully led Lincoln through the details of the design, relating the elements, such as the division into states, to the larger ideals of equality in sacrifice, and inviting Lincoln to imagine the view from the cemetery site across the battlefield, to contemplate walking the paths between the graves, and to behold in his mind's eye a fitting monument rising at the center of his design. "As the trees spread and extend," Saunders wrote in his 1864 report, "the quiet beauty produced by these open spaces will yearly become more striking," describing his plan as if one were actually there to experience the effect, as he probably did when speaking with Lincoln.[42]

"He took much interest in it," Saunders proudly recalled of Lincoln's reaction as they looked over his plan, and the two then had what appears to have been a thorough discussion of its form, inspiration, and meaning in relation to the larger ideals and goals of the cemetery project. Lincoln "asked about its surroundings, about Culp's Hill, Round Top, etc., and seemed familiar with the topography of the place, although he had never been there."[43] That Saunders knew that Lincoln had never yet been to Gettysburg no doubt directly reflects what Lincoln told him as the two men bent over the plan; it is an offhand comment that allows us a glimpse into this meeting of president and landscape gardener. When Lincoln, poring over the cemetery design with Saunders, "took much interest" in the cemetery and "asked about its surroundings," he wanted to gain a clearer sense of the place and its relationship to what he knew of the landmarks of the battle and the names so familiar from those anxious days of July 1863. Similarly, the consummate orator Edward Everett called upon several persons who had been to Gettysburg to tell him more about the site of the ceremony. Experienced public speakers know the importance of place and venue in framing their words, and Lincoln himself is known to have revised his speeches to account for changes in location and venue.[44] Lincoln, then, was collecting precisely the kind of information that could help him with his "remarks."

Lincoln's questions about the topography and surroundings of the cemetery also included sharp insight into the unique layout of the cemetery. "He was much pleased," Saunders wrote, "with the method of the graves," and more precisely, Lincoln "said it differed from the ordinary cemetery."[45] Lincoln knew the "ordinary" cemeteries of his day all too well. Eighteen months earlier he had buried his dear boy Willie at Oak Hill Cemetery in the Washington suburbs, with its winding paths, naturalistic landscaping, professional design, and Gothic-revival chapel, a fine exemplar of the "rural cemetery" so well evoked by Garry Wills in *Lincoln at Gettysburg*. But Lincoln was, of course, also thoroughly familiar with the more traditional town and church cemeteries that were far more common at the time; he had buried his first son, Edward, in one many years before.

Saunders's elaborate descriptions of his plan leave no doubt that he would not have been at a loss for words as he "explained the reasons" to Lincoln that the plan "differed from the ordinary cemetery." The Gettysburg cemetery was in what Saunders called the geometric style, in which "everything is architecturally accurate in its lines, perfect symmetry pervades the whole, and all parts are equally balanced." This classic equality was mirrored in the equality in death represented by the balanced layout of the graves in their state plots within the semicircular design. The Greek column and Roman arch having become the favored public architecture of the American Republic, Saunders chose well when he incorporated the symmetry of classical forms into his design for the nation's most celebrated cemetery. This geometric, semicircular "method of the graves" was the most striking feature of Saunders's plan, so unlike either the new "rural" cemeteries or the traditional cemeteries that were both so familiar to Lincoln, which no doubt explains Lincoln's perceptive remark that it "differed from the ordinary cemetery."[46]

In response to Saunders's description, Lincoln "said it was an advisable and befitting arrangement."[47] That is, according to Saunders, and no doubt prompted by the way he had described the inspiration behind the cemetery design, Lincoln complimented the cemetery plan in terms that recognized that it comported with the national vision and elevated patriotic purposes of the cemetery project. Taking a cue from Wills's letter of invitation, and judging from the accounts of the Washington Draft witnesses and from his own letter to Everett of November 20, Lincoln was sensitive to the question of what would constitute "appropriate" remarks, and Saunders described him as similarly complimenting his "befitting" plan. Lincoln's words at Gettysburg will reveal that as he spoke with Saunders—a moment when, perhaps, a version of the Washington Draft was tucked in a pigeonhole of his desk or even lay, unremarked, on the table on which Saunders had spread out his plan—Lincoln was thinking about the battle, the war, and the sacrifices so tangibly represented by the beautifully arrayed graves in Saunders's plan in relation to the larger purposes and contexts of the American nation and of democratic government.

At the end of their interview, Saunders recalled that Lincoln "asked me if I was going up to Gettysburg to-morrow." One can almost see Saunders rolling up his plan as the two brought their meeting to an end, perhaps moving to the door and shaking hands, with Saunders remembering, "I told him that I intended to be there and take up the plan. He replied, 'Well, I may see you on the train.'"[48]

Lincoln's questions to Saunders suggest that he was seeking information that would help him write or revise his speech; in the crush of events that nearly prevented him from even attending the ceremony, it was certainly not idle curiosity that prompted Lincoln to call the Scotsman to the White House for a detailed examination of the geometry of the plan, the topography of the grounds, and the "advisable and befitting" arrangement of the graves. The timing and nature of Lincoln's conversation with Saunders confirms that, as Lincoln told Speed, the evening of November 17 was the moment when Lincoln put the Washington Draft in its final form. In all, the witnesses, the text, and the events give good reason to think that it was only after his visit with Saunders that Lincoln would have had both the time and the foundation of information he wanted in order to take a last look at his remarks before leaving the next morning.

Lincoln wrote a great deal of his state papers and correspondence in the late evening or at night, when he was less likely to be disturbed by the business of the day. November 17 was certainly no exception. Surely it was then that Lincoln sat down with that full sheet of Executive Mansion letterhead paper before him, with his notes undoubtedly nearby, and wrote what has become one of the most recognizable sentences in the English language before going on to write out the rest of the Washington Draft in a clean, bold, finished-looking copy. We cannot be certain of the time or where he may have been, but the evidence from the conversation with Saunders suggests it was probably in his upstairs office sometime after Saunders bid him goodnight. The room's central feature was a large table-like desk, the same one on which Lincoln had signed the Emancipation Proclamation on the first day of that year and on which Saunders had just laid out his plan for a cemetery that would inspire another charter of freedom. A few chairs, a fireplace, portraits of the British radical John Bright and the staunch nationalist (and arch-Democrat) Andrew Jackson on the walls—a working room, with maps and papers usually piled high and a thousand details demanding attention. Today the room is called the Lincoln Bedroom, and, most fittingly, it is the formal home of the last of Lincoln's handwritten copies of the speech whose first known text Lincoln undoubtedly wrote in that room on that night of November 17, 1863.

Only the first page, the Letterhead Page, has been preserved; try to read the words as if unaware of its final phrases. It is the Gettysburg Address in its earliest surviving form, the Washington Draft, earlier even than the Nicolay document that has for too long been misidentified as the first draft:

> Four score and seven years ago our fathers brought forth, upon this continent, a new nation, conceived in liberty, and dedicated to the proposition that "all men are created equal"
>
> Now we are engaged in a great civil war, testing whether that nation, or any nation so conceived, and so dedicated, can long endure. We are met on a great battle field of that war. We have come to dedicate a portion of it, as a final resting place for those who died here, that the nation might live. This we may, in all propriety do. But, in a larger sense, we can not dedicate—we can not consecrate—we can not hallow, this ground—The brave men, living and dead, who struggled here, have hallowed it, far above our poor power to add or detract. The world will little note, nor long remember what we say here; while it can never forget what they did here.
>
> It is rather for us, the living, to stand here,

The essential mystery at the heart of all human creativity will forever prevent perfect understanding of what prompted that first sentence and the resonant words that followed. But even for this first known draft, as for the later texts, we best approach the heart of Lincoln's thought and purposes when we can see how he selected and edited and revised his own words from one text to the next. In his choices we can see his mind working and, in some ways, the issues of the war turning.

There is no known text of the speech prior to the Washington Draft for comparison, but here is another sentence spoken by Lincoln about Gettysburg, one that is unlikely ever to have been celebrated in song or recited at school functions and Lincoln Day celebrations:

> How long ago is it? Eighty-odd years, since upon the Fourth day of July, for the first time in the world, a union body of representatives was

CHAPTER TWO

assembled to declare as a self-evident truth that all men were created equal.[49]

Lincoln spoke these words on July 7, 1863, when first welcoming the glorious news of the twin victories at Gettysburg and Vicksburg that were immediately hailed as the turn of the tide of the war, and his words that night have long been recognized as a kind of first sketch of what Lincoln would say at the cemetery four months later. To those accustomed to the powerful chords of "Four score and seven years ago," the phrase "eighty-odd years" and the awkward wording of the July 7 speech sound discordant and inelegant. In those distinctions lie some of the most important elements of the story of how Lincoln in Washington first came to write the Gettysburg Address.[50] On July 7, Lincoln was speaking to a raucous victory celebration; writing in November, he was responding to an invitation to dedicate by a "few appropriate remarks" a sacred place where the honored dead of the Union's greatest victory would be honored for all time.

Comparing the sentences spoken on July 7 and November 19 demonstrates that the "interesting ceremony" at Gettysburg, as Lincoln described it in his November 9 letter to Stephen Logan, was undoubtedly the most immediate and direct element shaping how Lincoln wrote the Washington Draft that he took with him when he left the White House for the dedication ceremony. The words written in Washington were Lincoln's way of saying "some appropriate thing," as he explained his task to Speed, starting with the biblical resonance of "Four score" and ending in that first sentence with the historical authority of the "fathers." Lincoln's understanding of how to meet the expectations of the occasion were particularly powerful in shaping his speech because of the nature of the event and the double origins of the speech in both Washington and Gettysburg. This was an occasional speech, solicited for a purpose that originated outside Lincoln, and because it was not initially founded in Lincoln's desire to say any particular thing, it developed and grew in an almost organic way within the framework of Lincoln's understanding of the event and within his evolving vision of what he came to recognize he wanted to say. This is why the journey to Gettysburg, figuratively and physically, was such a powerful force in shaping the eventual text—the final speech was quite literally created as a result of reflection on and response to a specific set of events and experiences that took Lincoln from the first moment after receiving his invitation, to the speakers' platform on the battlefield.

When tracing the part of the journey that created Lincoln's words as written in Washington, the July 7 speech emerges as a crucial text that fixed certain structures in Lincoln's speech and provided essential points of departure. At a basic level, we can see just from looking at this single sentence from the July 7 speech that it provided some of the words and the rhythm of the opening sentence of the Washington Draft, as when Lincoln referred to the "eighty-odd years" since the nation's founding. During the 1850s this kind of phrasing had been common with Lincoln, as when he would mention the "seventy-odd years" since the ratification of the Constitution, so the archaic and grand "Four score" of the Washington Draft provides a clear sign that Lincoln was seeking an elevated tone. Even beyond the words, the July 7 speech also served as a rough draft of some of the ideas of Lincoln's Washington Draft.

The Gettysburg Address and the speech of July 7 share the remarkable trait that they are the only instances during Lincoln's presidency when he publicly spoke the words "all men are created equal."[51] These radical words, even more controversial in the race-conscious 1860s than in the 1770s, were the central axis of Lincoln's political life, and the Declaration of Independence was the founding text of his creed. "I have never had a feeling politically that did not spring from the sentiments embodied in the Declaration of Independence," he once proclaimed.[52] So powerful and radical was the phrase, so filled with explosive meaning, that Lincoln the pragmatic politician banished it from his public speeches during his run for the presidency; in contrast, it had been a constant refrain in the 1850s. So too, through the first years of his presidency, while he pursued a "southern strategy" of attempting to preserve the embattled Union by placating Southern Unionists and Border State moderates, he only once included this central phrase from the Declaration of Independence in a public paper: his message to the special session of Congress he had called to meet on July 4, 1861, the anniversary of the Declaration.[53]

The words "all men are created equal" are so much taken for granted in the Gettysburg Address that it has not been sufficiently recognized that there was no particular reason, in November 1863, for Lincoln to evoke the Declaration of Independence. Lincoln in November associated Gettysburg with July 4 and the Declaration of Independence because he had made the connection in the July 7 speech, remarking on the "very peculiar" coincidence that John Adams and Thomas Jefferson should have died on the same July 4 and other coincidences, such as the victories at Gettysburg and Vicksburg that seemed to Lincoln, in a celebratory mood, to be "a dispensation of the Almighty Ruler of Events." This train of thought, he said when ending the July 7 speech, was a "glorious theme and a glorious occasion for a speech, but I am not prepared to make one worthy of the theme and worthy of the occasion." Lincoln did not follow up this idea at Gettysburg, where he argued instead that "we" are responsible for assuring the success of the "unfinished work," but by linking Gettysburg and the Declaration of Independence in his mind, the July 7 speech provided the first point of departure for Lincoln's speech in November.

The difference between that point of departure and the Washington Draft reveals how Lincoln was evolving during this time when the central problem of the administration was pivoting from fighting secession to rebuilding the Union. Lincoln's phrasing in the July 7 speech reflected his deep reading in the writings of the "fathers," reading that he had undertaken to combat Stephen Douglas and the notion of popular sovereignty. The July 7 speech, for example, revealed Lincoln's earlier research into the founding era when he correctly cited the number of the signers of the Declaration. Although the newspaper report of Lincoln's words was fragmentary, it seems that Lincoln on July 7 was also paraphrasing part of a 1788 speech by Governor Samuel Huntington of Connecticut arguing for ratification of the Constitution: "This is a new event in the history of mankind. Heretofore most governments have been formed by tyrants, and imposed on mankind by force. Never before did a people, in time of peace and tranquility, meet together by their representatives, and, with calm deliberation, frame for themselves a system of government."[54]

Huntington's speech, or its many imitators over the decades, had also been used as a model by Galusha Grow for his speech upon becoming speaker of the House in 1861. More immediately, on the day of the July 7 speech the *Washington National Intelligencer* had editorialized that "Eighty-seven years have passed away since our Revolutionary fathers assembled in Continental Congress" to declare independence.[55] The point is not that Lincoln had plagiarized Grow or the *Intelligencer,* for the phrasing on July 7 partakes more of Huntington, and Lincoln had used similar words previously; rather, the key point is that Lincoln changed and adapted the basic structure of Huntington and Grow and the *Intelligencer* to make the "new event" refer not to the independence of a democratic people but, instead, to the fact that "for the first time in the world" a free people had founded a government on the principle that "all men are created equal."

The opening sentence and initial point of departure for the Gettysburg speech, then, is a kind of echo of Lincoln's merging of the meaning of the Gettysburg victory with the Fourth of July and the Declaration of Independence, which cast Lincoln's mind back to his researches in the founding era and the arguments he had developed to fight Douglas and the idea of popular sovereignty. These same concepts had also served Lincoln in the fight against secession: supremacy of the collective national will over localized interests; assertion of fidelity to the true principles of the founders; recognition of the human dignity and natural rights of the enslaved; and the moral imperative of assuring that slavery would be a limited and dwindling element in American society. Even in the early years of the war, Lincoln had not evolved much beyond these positions, first staked out more than a decade before. In the message to Congress of July 4, 1861, which mentioned the phrase "all men are created equal," Lincoln stated plainly that his "understanding of the powers, and duties of the Federal government, relatively to the rights of the States, and the people," in the South after suppressing the rebellion would be no different than it was before his inauguration.[56] That is, in the shorthand of the day, Lincoln in July 1861, and in compliance with congressional resolutions, officially sought only "the Union as it was," with no federal interference with slavery in the states where it already existed. Lincoln in these first years of the war did not deploy the Declaration as a revolutionary or transformative document; rather, his point in quoting the Declaration in 1861 was conservative: the Union better embodied the ideals of the founders than did the Confederacy, which denied not only the Declaration's assertion of equality but also refused to base its authority on "We the People."

Lincoln in the July 7 speech continued this essentially traditionalist or conservative usage of "all men are created equal." He also developed even more fully the argument that the Union represented the founders, whereas Confederate forces were instead defined as "the enemies of the declaration that all men are created equal" and secession was described as "a gigantic rebellion . . . precisely at the bottom of which is an effort to overthrow that principle that all men are created equal." This same theme of tying the Union to the ideals of the founders will be, of course, the central point of the first sentences of the Washington Draft, but here we must pause to await Lincoln's final written text to see where those first sentences would take him in the delivery text of his speech. It is not at all certain that the much more assertive and radical resolution upon "a new birth of freedom" was present in the speech as written in Washington; the changes in Gettysburg suggest that it was not. What is clear is that Lincoln continued to believe, as he wrote in 1858, that "the declara[tion] that 'all men are created equal' is the great fundamental principle upon which our free institutions rest."[57] Democracy, more than equality, still predominated in 1858 and 1861 and even on July 7, 1863; but the triple repetition of the explosive phrase in his speech that night is a sign of changes to come.

Lincoln was evolving—and the troubled, eventful composition of the Gettysburg Address signals a decisive turn in his thought, and the process was still incomplete when Lincoln wrote the final version of his Washington Draft. The mystery of the last line of the Letterhead Page provides clues to the direction of Lincoln's text in Washington, offering the potential for understanding the destination of those words from a Gettysburg Address that almost read, "It is rather for us, the living, to stand here." Lincoln edited that last line in Gettysburg, but the Letterhead Page in Washington continued beyond these enigmatic words. Most secure are the structural connections that must have existed between the known Letterhead first page and its lost text continuing the Washington Draft. The first page, for example, strongly reveals a standard structure of Lincoln's writings, of looking backward to the road traveled in the past and then taking stock of the landscape in the present.

Lincoln took this retrospective approach in virtually every important text, from his Peoria speech in 1854 to his Second Inaugural Address, and he did so too in the Letterhead Page. In all those texts, these two steps are merely the foundation for the culmination and endpoint of the speech or writing, to present a set of principles or course of action and illustrate their benefits by projecting them into the future. The Pencil Page written in Gettysburg does this too, and the pivot in the last phrases of the Washington Draft appeared to be moving in the same direction. Lincoln's mention of Webster while discussing his speech in Washington suggests that he was at least thinking along the lines that would lead to the "government of the people" idea, which forms the endpoint and culmination of the eventual Gettysburg speech. As the summit of Lincoln's political aspirations for humankind, democratic government as expressed in the first page by the "new nation" brought forth by the fathers, and perhaps even "government of the people, by the people, for the people," was probably the destination of the Washington Draft, according to the logic of the Letterhead Page, to Lincoln's habits of thought, and to the evidence of the conversation with Brooks.

Similarly, the powerful central trope in the Gettysburg Address of comparing and assimilating what "we" have yet to do in relation to what "the brave dead" and "those who died here" did do (the word "did" is even underscored in the edited Letterhead Page) was also found in the Washington Draft in both the first page and the succeeding text, as explicitly stated in the last line that ends at the page divide: "It is rather for us, the living, ..." In the text as edited in Gettysburg, the word "dedicated" inserted in pencil provides the pivot point toward the evocation of what "we" are to be "dedicated to . . . take increased devotion to . . . highly resolve . . . ." In contrast, the original Washington Draft concludes the "It is rather for us, the living" phrase with the words "to stand here," but the concept of standing with, by, or for probably structured at least the first part of the second page of the Washington Draft, just as "dedicated" structures the finished speech.

In earlier years, Lincoln had often used "stand" in relation to a duty or a moral question, most famously in the Cooper Union speech of 1860 ("let us stand by our duty, fearlessly and effectively"). Lincoln usually used the term not in a metaphorical sense but in the literal sense of standing before a crowd, or standing at a place, but when he did use the term metaphorically during the war it was almost always some variation of standing in support of the soldiers and sailors specifically or of the larger causes and purposes of the war more generally—and usually both at the same time. In this sense the association of standing by or with a duty or moral question before the war became more fixed and focused upon the soldiers and the Union cause more particularly.

After writing "to stand here" in the Washington Draft, Lincoln later, several times, used variations of the word "stand" in fairly similar formulations, which suggests that perhaps in the Washington Draft he had arrived at a formulation that remained with him even after he had removed the reference in the final version of his speech. On August 31, 1864, at a time when Lincoln despaired of his reelection, he spoke to a group of departing soldiers with words that seem like a cross between the Gettysburg Address and the Washington Draft as it may have been. "It has been your honorable privilege to stand, for a brief period, in the defense of your country," Lincoln said, and he then evoked "the struggle in which we are engaged," which he defined as "striving to maintain the government and institutions of our fathers, to enjoy them ourselves, and transmit them to our children and our children's children forever," before finally ending with an exhortation to "stand fast to the Union and the old flag."[58]

Lincoln returned to these same syntactic elements in ways that echo elements of both the Gettysburg speech and the Washington Draft when on November 8, 1864, he greeted the news of his reelection: "I give thanks to the Almighty for this evidence of the people's resolution to stand by free government and the rights of humanity."[59] The Washington Draft may have incorporated something like this exhortation to "stand" with the soldiers and "stand" with the war's largest importance, just as the Pencil Page links the devotion of the soldiers to our resolution to support "government of the people."

Lincoln included precisely such a pairing of "standing" and democratic government in his Annual Message of December 1863, which across its text understandably includes several similarities to the Gettysburg speech because it was written in the weeks bracketing the ceremony: "We do also honorably recognize the gallant men" he wrote, "to whom, more than to others, the world must stand indebted for the home of freedom disenthralled, regenerated, enlarged, and perpetuated."[60] But it was on the very morning of the Gettysburg ceremony that Lincoln gave the most tantalizing clue, and the clearest evidence, in the mystery of those enigmatic words "to stand here." Nicolay states that he was present in the "upper room" of the Wills house while Lincoln edited the Letterhead Page and finished his speech. Yet even after striking the words "to stand here" from his text, Lincoln retained them in his mind. Downstairs, as he prepared to join the parade to the cemetery grounds, Lincoln told a reporter, "The best course for the journals of the country to pursue, if they wished to sustain the Government, was to stand by the officers of the army."[61] Here, then, on the very day of the speech, Lincoln brings together the word "stand" as found in the Washington Draft with the fate of the government as found in the Gettysburg Address, while also evoking the Union's defenders, as found in both texts.

If this analysis is correct, then, the structure of the Washington Draft was not unlike that of the eventual Gettysburg Address: our "fathers" created the proposition of a government of equality and liberty; now "we" are testing it; the next step requires "us, the living" to "stand here" in some relationship with the soldiers, "living and dead." This much is certain from the existing Letterhead Page, but the evidence of the text and the eyewitnesses suggests that Lincoln in the Washington Draft went on to urge "us" not only to "stand by" the soldiers, as he said on the morning of the speech, or to "stand indebted" to them, as in the 1863 Annual Message, but to also stand with the ideals of the fathers for which they stood and died—probably including the words and idea of "government of the people." This suggests a Washington Draft that has important structural similarities to the final Gettysburg Address but whose text beyond the first page was no doubt different in many ways, including phrasing and cadence, both of which, of course, are essential in making the final version a powerful element of American memory and identity.

The speech that Lincoln wrote in Washington and did not give illuminates in new ways the Gettysburg Address he did give. The story this evidence tells should bring an end to the 150-year debate about whether writing the speech was a long belabored process or a purely spontaneous effort, while opening new areas of discussion, including the possible impact of Everett's "advance" speech. Furthermore, the eyewitness and textual evidence is definitive that the Washington Draft, only a part of which survives in the Nicolay document, was indeed Lincoln's earliest text. There is no room in this story for the Hay text, which events will show was written after the speech was given. The Letterhead Page, with its focus on the founding and its retrospective view of the Declaration of Independence, echoes Lincoln's outlook in the rough sketch of July 7, but already we can sense an evolution in Lincoln's understanding of the issues. Finally, recognizing the accurate core within the flawed testimony of Noah Brooks suggests that something like "government of the people" was from the first a central theme of how Lincoln conceived his "short, short, short" remarks, while Ward Lamon's questionable account finds surprising confirmation in the recollections of John Nicolay, who seconds, as well, the remarkable narrative of eventful beginnings and ultimate triumph that Lincoln himself detailed to James Speed.

As the Saunders conversation so clearly shows, even before leaving Washington Lincoln had become familiar with Gettysburg, not only as a battlefield but also as a ceremonial and patriotic site, created by men of vision and planned with care to inspire sentiments of sublime solemnity and reverential patriotism. Lincoln did not need Saunders to link Gettysburg and the Declaration of Independence's assertion that "all men are created equal," for he had made the association in his July 7 speech, but it seems certain that Lincoln did need Saunders and the cemetery plan in order to envision more vividly the place of his speech.[62] If, as it seems, Lincoln did work on his speech that last night in his upstairs office at the White House, it would have been Saunders's elaborate descriptions and his classical, symmetrical plan for the cemetery grounds that provided Lincoln with his most immediate image of the site and its surroundings, the graceful arcs of headstones on the beautifully colored plan perfectly "befitting" the sacred patriotism embodied in the cemetery project. That would be what Lincoln saw as he imagined himself on the platform before the people, at this "final resting place," and where we, too, "the living," have come, "to stand here."

The morning after speaking with Saunders, November 18, Lincoln may have had time to review or look over his remarks before his train was scheduled to leave at 11:30, but written revisions seem unlikely. Preparing for the journey and the press of normal business would probably not have allowed for quiet contemplation. Possibly it was decided just that morning that Mary would stay home to look after Tad and not go to Gettysburg as had been planned, as it was only at this late date that Lincoln arranged to be accompanied by William Johnson, his former personal servant in Springfield, a black man who had for a time also worked in the Executive Mansion.[63]

Lincoln that morning also appears to have worked as usual in his White House office; for example, he met at around ten in the morning with Thomas Duval, a Unionist federal judge from Texas who had refused to give up his post when the state seceded. Lincoln is sometimes portrayed as sad and depressed because of Tad's illness and Mary's alleged hysterics, but he did not seem so to Duval during their meeting. "As he was just about leaving for the celebration at Gettysburg, it was necessarily short—But it was a pleasant one," Duval wrote at the time in his diary, "I never met a man who made more favorable impressions on me than Mr. Lincoln. There is a kindness in his manner, a frankness in his speech, and such practical good sense and justice in his remarks, that cannot but be prepossessed in his favor. . . . I hope I made half as good an impression on him as he did on me."[64] This is Abraham Lincoln on the cusp of giving the Gettysburg Address, the Lincoln photographed so brilliantly by Alexander Gardner two weeks before in the famous *Gettysburg Portrait*.

Duval had come to Washington to collect his back pay, and he wanted to tell Lincoln about an idea he had for gradual emancipation in Texas, but the appointment had no particular urgency. This suggests that Lincoln did not feel he needed to take time to extensively review or write his speech, and so he was evidently content—at that point—with the state of his Washington Draft. Certainly, Lincoln had no plans to write on the train. The jarring of the cars was notorious, and in any case, he had arranged to talk politics on the way with the chair of the Pennsylvania Union Party.[65] Moreover, even aside from the overwhelming evidence for the Washington Draft, it is not credible that Lincoln would have thought he could begin his speech from nothing on the train or in a town crowded with the thousands that were expected, when he knew or could have guessed that there would be merry revelers to fend off, and a grand dinner with perhaps a dozen governors at the table, and all the peace and calm of what was taking on the aspect of a colossal patriotic festival. This was, after all, going to be "an interesting ceremony" and a grand occasion. No, the surviving portion of the Washington Draft, supported by the eyewitnesses, bespeaks a complete or nearly complete text and reflects the usual workaday crush of events exemplified by the meeting with Duval. It was only the unscheduled inspiration of the last-minute revisions in Gettysburg that created the ungrammatical and mismatched Nicolay document.

When it came time to leave for the train, Lincoln was running late but was still in good humor. The escorting officer knew him well and was not afraid to remind him that there was no time to lose. "Well, I feel about that as the convict in one of our Illinois towns felt when he was going to the gallows" replied Lincoln. "People, eager to see the execution, kept crowding and pushing past him. At last he called out: 'Boys, you needn't be in such a hurry to get ahead, *there won't be any fun till I get there.*'" The eventful experience Lincoln related to Speed, of thinking about and writing one of his greatest works, suggests that it was not merely comedic license that led Lincoln to imagine himself meeting a disastrous fate at Gettysburg, as if the speakers' stand were a gallows. With this homely story—exactly the sort of thing that made some of the event organizers question whether this uncouth westerner was a suitable choice to speak at their solemn cemetery dedication—and with the Washington Draft in his pocket, Abraham Lincoln set out for Gettysburg.[66]

CHAPTER TWO

■

THREE

A Celebrated Railway Journey

UNION SOLD. GRAVES

Lincoln stepped onto the speakers' platform at Gettysburg only twenty-four hours after leaving Washington, but the speech he held as he spoke was not the Washington Draft—all in ink, on Executive Mansion letterhead—that he had brought from the capital. Lincoln composed his words in Washington with one set of ideas, incorporated in the draft of the speech that he took with him when he left the White House. But by the time Lincoln stood on the platform at Gettysburg a day later he had traveled a long road, and because of this journey, and because of Lincoln's understanding of the meaning the battle and the war had for the Republic, the speech also reflected Lincoln's conception of the nation's journey to Gettysburg, its path across time from its founding, through its testing in the furnace of civil war, to hope for a "new birth of freedom" for the future. Like the nation's story itself, Lincoln's speech was a work in progress, even to the very moment of its presentation. Having set out the day before with his Washington Draft, Lincoln finished his journey to the speakers' stand with a revised delivery text and an altered vision that gathered all the threads of his far longer journey to Gettysburg.

The road to Gettysburg included one of the most deeply rooted moments of American memory, the famous train journey during which he was said to have composed his speech in a single burst of inspiration. As it happens, the trip to the speakers' stand at Gettysburg was indeed inspirational, but in an even more remarkable and profound sense than suggested by the popular image of Lincoln jotting his remarks on stray scraps of paper while rattling along the rails. The story of a backwoods boy who rose to the White House and summoned a majestic statement of American purpose from such ramshackle circumstances caught the imagination of a people who wanted to believe that all Americans could rise to greatness no matter their beginnings. As revealed by his words to James Speed, Lincoln—himself a proponent and symbol of that American creed—experienced and interpreted his composition of the speech in much the same way. The journey to the stand at Gettysburg, including the mythic railway trip, was an essential part of Lincoln's experience of the event and helped shape the speech he gave that day.

No contemporary account suggests Lincoln wrote anything on the train, but the train trip entered into the emerging Gettysburg myth quite early, in the immediate aftermath of Lincoln's assassination, when almost his every word and movement began to take on prophetic power and transcendent meaning. Eventually the rail journey crossed from history into memory and finally became myth, strong enough to shape personal recollections and craft new memories from the fragments of experience. The way this element of Lincoln's Gettysburg journey developed reveals the importance of precisely tracing the movement of events to better understand the porous boundary between history and memory in the creation of Lincoln's speech, each affecting the other to create legend and myth out of an ordinary railway trip to an extraordinary destination.

When Lincoln arrived at the Baltimore and Ohio rail station in Washington just before noon on November 18, he found gathered there some of those he had encouraged to attend or had invited over the previous weeks, as "no one rode upon this trip except such as were specially invited by the President himself," according to Forney's *Philadelphia Press*. This may have been literally true, as John Nicolay's printed pass may still be found in his papers, good for passage "To and from Gettysburg by Special Train, 11:30 am.," a small souvenir of an eventful time.[1] John Hay was also there, as was Charlotte Wise, Edward Everett's daughter, who was going along with her husband to see her father give what many believed would be the crowning oration of his career. There was also, inevitably, John Forney, whose incorrigible boosterism for the cemetery had done so much to keep it before the public eye. Also adding a touch of partisanship to the company was Wayne MacVeagh, the young chair of the Pennsylvania Union Party who had managed Curtin's recent triumphant reelection and whom Lincoln had invited specifically to conduct a little political business on the way to Gettysburg.

Certainly, it was a select group that left the station sometime just after noon, a microcosm of Washington, D.C., bringing with them to Pennsylvania all the cares of war and enough political intrigue to keep everyone alert for subtexts and subterfuges. In the first rank were Secretary of State William Seward, Secretary of the Interior John Usher, and Postmaster General Montgomery Blair, a political grouping that did not escape notice. "It is a little singular that [when] Mr. Lincoln goes off anywhere, it is the Conservative members of the Cabinet who accompany him," the radical *National Anti-slavery Standard* pointed out a few days later, continuing its long campaign to force Blair from the cabinet and promote the presidential aspirations of Secretary of the Treasury Salmon P. Chase. However, Blair may well have accompanied Lincoln from weakness as much as from strength, for his infamous Rockville speech the month earlier equating radicalism with "amalgamation" had brought down thunderous denunciations from Radicals like Thaddeus Stevens and others, who demanded that Lincoln force Blair to resign.[2]

Far from a cabal, the three cabinet officers who did accompany Lincoln were not even a majority of its members. Lincoln may well have been disappointed at the turnout for the trip, although having Chase along might have made for an uncomfortable journey. Chase's obvious presidential ambitions led Attorney General Bates to write in his diary the previous month, "Mr. Chase's head is turned by his eagerness in pursuit of the presidency," and Secretary of the Navy Gideon Welles noted in December, "Chase avoids coming in these days" to cabinet meetings. According to Welles, Chase's absence from Gettysburg was no great loss. "Chase's jokes are always clumsy," Welles wrote in his diary. "He is destitute of wit." Days before, Chase had decided that "imperative public duties" prevented his attendance; perhaps better stated, he had decided his presidential ambitions would be better served by remaining in Washington. For Chase, the two were one and the same, and playing second or third fiddle to Everett and Lincoln at Gettysburg would certainly not promote his interests. While Lincoln was away, Chase busied himself with drumming up support for his presidential aspirations, and with perhaps the worst timing in the history of presidential predictions, on November 26 he opined of the man who had just given the Gettysburg Address that someone of "different qualities from those the President has will be needed in the next four years."[3]

Others shared Chase's disregard for Lincoln's prospects in 1864. The assumption then was that presidents served one term, none having been reelected since Andrew Jackson over thirty years before. The *National Anti-slavery Standard* of October 24 asserted that Republican successes in the fall elections meant Chase could easily carry the free states, an open invitation to stand against Lincoln. Such calculations prompted U.S. Treasurer Francis Spinner to remark, when told that Lincoln, Seward, and Blair had gone to Gettysburg, that it was only proper to "let the dead bury the dead." Lincoln later heard the story and liked it so much he repeated it to the cabinet, but with Thaddeus Stevens as the author of the witticism.[4]

Lincoln was also accompanied to Gettysburg by half a dozen or more diplomats and foreign dignitaries, and this at a fairly delicate moment in the foreign relations of the Union. Certainly the prospect of armed intervention had receded since 1862, but even if Britain was beginning to reconcile itself to an eventual Union victory, France still sought to divide the United States in order to pursue its adventures in Mexico, orchestrating loans for the Confederacy and building several up-to-date ironclads that were obviously destined for sale to Richmond. The French minister, Edouard-Henri Mercier, who was the highest-ranking diplomat to travel with Lincoln, had close personal ties to Confederate politicians, and his occasional visits to Richmond did nothing to calm fears that he favored armed intervention. Seward's son and secretary Frederick claimed that his father thought Mercier "one of the most impudent men in history."[5]

The presence of several Italian naval officers at Gettysburg was less fraught but was similarly a way to display the strength and resolve of the Union at the celebration of the great victory at Gettysburg. The officers were in Washington as part of a goodwill tour (Italy even then was still in the midst of its wars of national unification, not unlike the Americans), and they had the good fortune to be introduced to Lincoln on Monday, November 16, just as Lincoln's decision to attend the ceremony was being made public. Possibly Seward invited them, but it may be that Lincoln himself extended the invitation, just as he invited William McDougall, a Canadian politician who would be counted among the thirty Fathers of Confederation and who was at the time the commissioner of Crown lands, roughly equivalent to secretary of the interior. Years later two men sepa-

CHAPTER THREE

rately recalled that McDougall had told them that when he was introduced to Lincoln, he was offered almost in passing a place on the presidential train. While not all the details of the accounts are reliable, according to one version Lincoln looked the tall McDougall up and down and said, "Are you a descendant of the man to whom the King said, 'Lay on McDuff and damned be he who first cries Hold! Enough!'"[6] Such informality aside, the participation of foreign dignitaries added an elevated, international, and nonpartisan tone to the president's party and was much noted in the newspapers as adding dignity and impressiveness to the occasion.

Bedecked with wreaths and flags, the three cars and locomotive in the excursion train left at 12:10 p.m. and passed quickly up the tracks toward Baltimore, taking priority over other traffic. Presidents did not then have their own rail cars, so Lincoln traveled in a Baltimore and Ohio car that had been "beautifully fitted up" and "divided into two apartments," with Lincoln usually seated in the compartment at the end of the train. Lincoln, then, was well placed to step out onto the rear platform to greet the people, as was expected whenever political notables traveled. According to newspaper reports, he was joined in his car by some of the principle members of the party, including Seward, Usher, Blair, and Provost Marshal James Fry. In such circumstances, it is understandable that there is no contemporary evidence that Lincoln worked on his speech, much less that he wrote it while jostling over the rails. Lincoln's secretary, John Nicolay, who might have been expected to help with any official business, categorically denied that Lincoln wrote anything on the train, and his assistant secretary, John Hay, similarly mentioned nothing about it in his diary, but he did note "we had a pleasant sort of trip."[7]

No doubt one of the two unnamed marine officers mentioned in the press as riding in Lincoln's car was Marine Lieutenant Henry Clay Cochrane, who many years later wrote a precise and reliable memoir that befit the brigadier general he had become. He recalled that soon after leaving Washington, he loaned Lincoln a copy of the ferociously Democratic *New York Herald,* an interesting choice of paper to hand to a Republican president. Lincoln read it for a while, laughing sometimes at "some wild guesses of the paper" about current military operations, then "he returned the paper and we began to talk," Cochrane recalled, with Lincoln "remarking among other things that when he had first passed over that road on his way to Congress in 1847 he noticed square-rigged vessels up the Patapsco river as far as the Relay House, and now there seemed to be only small craft." Lincoln must have been looking out across the Patapsco from the famous Thomas Viaduct, a 700-foot-long curving masonry span, a marvel of early railway engineering marked in 1832 with a monument placed next to the tracks by its proud builders. As a vital piece in the only rail link between Washington and the north, the bridge was heavily garrisoned, and during the war the restaurant at the Relay House stop at its northern end was as much an armed camp as it was a proper rail station.[8] Including four stops for fuel and water, Lincoln's train took just over an hour to make the 40-mile run to Baltimore, a breathtaking pace that was noted in the newspapers. Certainly it seems hardly possible for Lincoln to have worked on his speech on this first leg of the journey.

The Baltimore morning papers had announced that Lincoln would pass through the city, and "a considerable crowd" gathered about the train when it reached Camden Station on the southern edge of the city center. A delegation of officers and railroad executives entered Lincoln's car to welcome him, and the Marine band accompanying the president's party descended to the station platform to play patriotic music, but Lincoln himself appeared only briefly to acknowledge the greetings of the crowd. Meanwhile the locomotive was detached from the train and, with the ceremonies complete, tandem teams of horses laboriously pulled each of the cars with their passengers about a mile across the city up the Howard Street hill for transfer to the tracks of the Northern Central Railway.

As Lincoln's coach, now as much a city trolley as a railroad car, made its way slowly along the streets, many Baltimoreans followed along and were joined by others attracted by the commotion, and Lincoln several times appeared on the platform at the end of the car to acknowledge the greetings of those on the sidewalks. When the cars reached Bolton Station, they were attached to a new locomotive, giving time for about 200 people to gather and set up a call for Lincoln to again come out and show himself. As Cochrane remembered it, only Seward's intervention induced Lincoln to agree, but when he did he waded in with feeling, taking up two or three babies and kissing them, "which greatly pleased their mothers."[9] Then the whistle blew, Lincoln stepped back aboard, and sometime after two o'-clock the train left the city, heading northwest through fields and rolling woodlands.

Although seemingly uneventful when viewed from the outside through the newspaper record, Lincoln's passage through Baltimore created anxious moments for some inside the presidential party and may well have inspired at least unpleasant memories in Lincoln himself. In 1861, warned of an assassination plot, Lincoln had traveled incognito through the city on the way to his inauguration, and if Lincoln was able to recall his first trip in 1847, he most certainly also remembered the merciless ridicule he received after the 1861 journey when he was (inaccurately) reported to have been disguised in a Scottish cap and long tartan cloak. Lieutenant Cochrane thought that as the train approached Baltimore, Seward became visibly uneasy, and not without reason. The city remained notorious as a nest of Copperheads and secessionists, the scene of a deadly riot just after Lincoln's inauguration when a crowd had attacked a Massachusetts regiment on its way to protect the capital while it was making the same transfer across the city that Lincoln was now undertaking. The month before, a federal officer had been shot and killed in Maryland while enforcing the draft. Everyone on the train would have been well aware that the journey along the streets would require extended exposure of the president, so that on this trip "there was something of the same fear of attack or assassination" as in 1861, Cochrane recalled.[10]

Frederick R. Jackson, the officer commanding the soldiers of the Invalid Corps escorting Lincoln also experienced the journey through Baltimore as perilous. Jackson was not a man to be scared lightly, having earned the Congressional Medal of Honor for repeatedly charging a Confederate position even after his left arm had been shot away. Yet decades after the rail journey, he wrote, "It was well the President had a guard on that occasion, for an attempt was made in Baltimore, by a gang of roughs, to get into his car." Jackson recalled, "As the cars were being slowly hauled through the city by horses, the mob jumped upon the platforms. We tried to persuade them to get off, but they persisted, until I was forced to order my men to use their bayonets, and several were quite severely pricked before they would get down."[11] Although contemporary accounts depict only excited crowds anxious to see Lincoln, Jackson's recollection reveals the concerns of a man who considered himself personally responsible for Lincoln's safety as he crossed an unruly city in what was still a slave state, echoing the worries of others on the president's train. As ever, the divisions and violence of the war surrounded Lincoln, even on a ceremonial excursion.

The journey through Baltimore also brought aboard Lincoln's train more of the political divisions surrounding Reconstruction that he was confronting in the Annual Message to Congress that lay unfinished on his desk at the White House and that would find expression in his remarks at

Gettysburg. Among the officers who joined Lincoln's party at Baltimore was Robert Schenck, who had served with Lincoln in Congress when they were both Whigs and who had just won reelection to Congress from Ohio against the infamous Peace Democrat Clement Vallandigham. Lincoln had made Schenck a general, and the career politician had imposed heavy-handed military supervision over the recent elections in Maryland, forcing a loyalty oath as a precondition for voting that had outraged many in the state and attracted enormous attention nationally. Lincoln had called Schenck to the White House for close questioning and a sharp rebuke for some of his harsher tactics, yet Lincoln had publicly supported Schenck's actions over the vigorous protests of Governor Augustus Bradford, whose case was probably not helped by his earlier opposition to the Emancipation Proclamation.

Schenck and his staff had also attracted controversy, and Lincoln's personal ire, in their irregular recruitment of "Colored" regiments, threatening to upset the delicate balance of that "perplexing compound—Union and Slavery" as Lincoln called it, which up to that time had kept the border states in the federal fold.[12] Extending the emancipation strategy of bringing African Americans out of slavery and into the Union army, Lincoln in early October had issued General Order 329, one of the most radical measures of Lincoln's entire administration. When draft quotas were not met, it enforced compulsory, compensated emancipation on all slave owners, loyal or rebel, in the Union slave states. Although the Emancipation Proclamation did not cover Maryland, the enrollment (with emancipation) of slaves in Union states threatened to destroy Unionist coalitions across the border states, including Maryland and Missouri. Bradford had traveled to Washington to ask (unsuccessfully) that slaves of loyal owners be excluded; the order was so potentially explosive that at first it was not made public and did not apply to Kentucky.[13] To make matters worse, the Blair family had long been a power in Maryland and was ranged against radicals there just as it was in Washington, so that the state election recreated and heightened the battles within the cabinet and inside the Republican coalition more generally.

As critics feared, under Schenck's oversight the Maryland elections were marked by hundreds of well-documented cases of intimidation of suspected Confederate sympathizers, including the arrest of a former governor who refused the oath, and the low voter turnout cast a shadow over the Republican victory, providing evidence for Democratic denunciations of

Lincoln's tyranny. These tensions, and the fact that Lincoln had imposed compulsory recruitment of slaves on Maryland over the objections of Governor Bradford, may explain why Bradford, a conservative Unionist, arranged to travel to Gettysburg on a train organized by the Baltimore city council, which left just an hour after Lincoln's, even though Lincoln's train was scheduled to link up on its journey with a "Governor's Special" train bringing governors and state delegations to the cemetery dedication. Indeed, no local or state official greeted Lincoln at any time in his passage through the state, a measure of the controversies swirling around the administration.

Perhaps to dispel such tensions, after Schenck and other officers joined the train at Baltimore, Lincoln left the back of his coach and came forward to talk with some of the "choice spirits" in the party, swapping stories for an hour or so and "taking his turn and enjoying it very much," according to Cochrane. This presidential sociability was a defining trait of this middle segment of Lincoln's journey and was appreciated by at least one of the new arrivals, Assistant Adjutant General E. W. Andrews, who remembered that "the President placed everyone who approached him at his ease." Andrews was bringing a military band from Fort McHenry to Gettysburg, but he had also to convey to Lincoln the regrets of General William Morris that he was unable to join the party, being beset by "one of the troubles that had tried the patience of Job." Without losing a beat, Lincoln launched into an elaborate story of how a cavalry officer was cured of "a big boil where it made horseback riding decidedly uncomfortable" by being so scared by an unexpected Confederate attack that he sprang to his saddle without a thought for his affliction. "The colonel swore that there was no cure for boils so sure as fright from rebel yells," Lincoln concluded, "and that secession had rendered to loyalty *one* valuable service at any rate."[14]

Lincoln continued to be in fine form during lunch in a baggage car that had been added to the train in Baltimore and fitted out with a table and provisions. When they passed through a deep cut, rendering the car especially noisy and dim, Lincoln, sitting at the head of the table, was immediately reminded of a story about a friend back in southern Illinois who had been beset by a violent thunder-and-lightning storm while traveling on horseback though a dark night. "The traveler, although not accustomed to prayer," Lincoln said, "thought that the time had come to address his Maker, and said, 'Oh, Lord, if it would suit you equally well, it would suit me much better if I had a little more light and a little less noise.'"[15] These "leetle stories" for which Lincoln was so well known may have rankled those who sought more refined manners in their president, but Lincoln found them very helpful in forging political friendships and disarming potentially difficult situations, such as when sitting down to a meal with men whom he had severely chastised just weeks before or who were lifelong Democrats, like Andrews.

Lincoln's stories and conversation on the train revealed the same combination of frivolity and seriousness that he displayed in Gettysburg—cracking jokes with a crowd one moment, then shedding tears not long after—and that made him an enigma to many. Andrews, for example, recounted another story that shows Lincoln was thinking of the larger purposes of the journey in ways "that deeply touched the hearts of his listeners," telling of a conversation with a man who at Gettysburg was planning to visit the site where his only son had been killed. As retold by Andrews some twenty-five years later, the story is presented in words and phrases that seem unlikely to have been uttered by Lincoln, but the sentiment and central idea perhaps suggest the direction of Lincoln's thoughts.

"A visit to that spot, I fear, will open your wounds afresh," Lincoln purportedly told the man; "if we had reached the end of such sacrifices, and had nothing left for us to do but place garlands on the graves of those who have already fallen, we could give thanks even amidst our tears." This was, of course, precisely what Lincoln and the others were traveling to do, "place garlands on the graves." But as Lincoln told the man, and as he would tell the mourners at Gettysburg, that was not all that had to be done. There were still "sacrifices of life yet to be offered" and "hearts and homes yet to be made desolate before this dreadful war, so wickedly forced upon us, is over," Lincoln said, echoing the message of the speech that he perhaps carried, even then, folded in his coat pocket: there was still something "for us, the living," to do, something more, even, than honoring the dead and hallowing their graves.

How to honor those sacrifices, while still demanding and justifying others, was one of the central problems Lincoln faced in his remarks the next day. On this occasion, according to Andrews, rather than linking these sacrifices to the largest purposes of the war, as he would do in his speech, Lincoln spoke to the man in a personal vein, saying that when he thought of the inevitable sacrifices to come, "my heart is like lead within me, and I feel, at times, like hiding in deep darkness."[16] Uncharacteristic language perhaps, but not far removed from the despair Lincoln had felt when he found that after Gettysburg the Army of Northern Virginia had escaped across the Potomac and that the great victory would not lead to the destruction of Lee's army or even the end of the war, as Lincoln had hoped in the days after the battle.

It was just such a conversation about the battle and the cemetery, with the countryside of Maryland and Pennsylvania rolling by, that seems to have given rise to the myth of Lincoln actually writing his speech on the train. The first seeds of what would grow into the legendary rail journey appear to have taken root in a newspaper account of May 1865, at a time when articles were still recounting the dramatic death of John Wilkes Booth and Lincoln's funeral train had not yet reached Springfield. In an article of miscellaneous and reliable recollections of Lincoln, Richard C. Mc-Cormick, a well-connected journalist whom Lincoln in March 1863 had appointed secretary of the Arizona Territory, argued against the common misconception that Lincoln was "a slow and doubting writer." As proof, McCormick added a statement in support of Lincoln's literary abilities that is the first mention of the rail journey as an important element in the story of Lincoln's speech: "I have it from a gentleman who rode with him to Gettysburg, that upon nearing that place he asked what he should say at the ceremony on the morrow, stating that he had made no preparation whatever, and that the occasion was a novel and difficult one."[17]

The Washington Draft Lincoln carried in his pocket proves that Lincoln had made a good deal of preparation, but the small detail that Lincoln spoke of his remarks "upon nearing the place" provides a whiff of authenticity. More importantly, that Lincoln reportedly said that "the occasion was a novel and difficult one" conforms well to the later reports by the Washington Draft witnesses Speed, Lamon, and Nicolay, who confirm that Lincoln saw his task as challenging or even daunting. Already the Gettysburg myth was building, for McCormick then added, "The touching address which will forever tenderly connect his name with Gettysburg and its honored heroes, must have been written in the small hours of the morning of the day upon which it was delivered." Here again, though, McCormick's source correctly knew that Lincoln had spent the night in Gettysburg and that between the evening arrival of the train and the start of the ceremonies in the morning there would have been only a brief window for composing the speech; while this information was publicly known, placing it here in this sequence suggests the perspective of someone who had participated in these events.

Whoever the source, McCormick's brief note of 1865 explicitly stated that Lincoln did not write his speech on the train, but this clarity was lost when apparently the same story was repeated later that year in a book by the journalist and author Josiah Holland. The editor of the *Springfield [Mass.] Republican,* and later the editor of such nationally respected journals as *Scribner's Monthly* (later *Century Magazine*), Holland was not at Gettysburg, so he was seemingly relying on McCormick's note, or perhaps a common source, when he described the episode. Lincoln's "brief remarks" said more than all of Everett's pages, he declared—making a point similar to McCormick's about Lincoln's literary abilities—"yet they were written after he left Washington, and during a brief interval of leisure."[18] There is no hint of a train anywhere in the account, but the element of Lincoln writing the speech "in the small hours of the morning" in Gettysburg has been replaced by a general statement that it was written after leaving Washington.

This loss of specificity may have been crucial, because more than a year after the publication of Holland's book, another similar and very influential account moved the composition of the speech even farther from Gettysburg and toward the train. In an 1866 biography, Isaac Arnold, a politician and personal friend of Lincoln's, depicted him "while on his way from the Capital to the battle-field," and, just as Holland had noted, it was "after he left Washington" that Lincoln wrote his speech. Yet Arnold added that it was only at that time that Lincoln "was notified that he would be expected to make some remarks," a new, and of course erroneous, element in the story. Like Cochrane and Holland, though, Arnold portrayed Lincoln "retiring a short time" when "he prepared the following address, which for appropriateness, comprehension, grasp of thought, brevity, beauty, the sublime in sentiment and expression, has scarcely its equal in English or American literature."[19]

These early accounts by McCormick (1865), Holland (1865), and Arnold (1866) seem to share a common foundation, or at least they coincide, in having Lincoln writing the speech in a single, brief episode after leaving Washington. While none states that the speech was written on the train, Arnold may well have meant to suggest as much when he placed the anecdote "while on the way" to "the battle-field." Yet this could include the time in the town of Gettysburg, and if Lincoln was supposed to be on the train, it is not clear to where he might have retired—unless one assumes some appropriate arrangement of the car or the train, which is not even mentioned in Arnold's account. Harriet Beecher Stowe, for example, understood Arnold to mean that Lincoln "wrote it in a few moments, while on the way to the celebration, on being told that he would be expected to make some remarks."[20] Stowe did not mention a train, either, and if we did not know of the later train stories, we could easily envision Lincoln writing in a hotel or house where he stayed before the ceremony. Over time, a story that began in 1865 with McCormick depicting Lincoln writing his speech in Gettysburg "in the small hours of the morning" and not on the train became by 1868 a story that Lincoln wrote it "while on the way" (the exact phrase of both Arnold and Stowe), with no train in sight but with the possibility of an implication that would eventually become the story's dominant theme.

Indeed, the first unambiguous reference to Lincoln writing on the train dates only to 1882. Lincoln's secretary of the interior, John P. Usher, who was at the time the mayor of Lawrence, Kansas, said in a widely reprinted speech that "the President was expected, of course, to say something" but was quite "harried by business in Washington," a portrayal similar to that of the four eyewitnesses to the Washington Draft. Usher then asserted that Lincoln "had no time to write out any notes" and so, "on the cars, between the National Capital and Gettysburg, upon a piece of pasteboard placed on his knee, with a great crowd all around him, talking, gossiping, laughing, and chattering, he wrote the words of which Everett said, 'I would rather be the author of those twenty lines than to have all the fame my oration today will give me.'"[21]

This is the text that launched a thousand recollections and became the foundation of the enduring train-composition narrative that still haunts the American imagination. Usher added the detail of the "pasteboard placed on his knee" and stated plainly what was only a possible implication in Arnold's account, that Lincoln actually wrote on the train, but overall Usher's statement adds very little to the record. Usher rode in the procession with Lincoln to the cemetery, he sat just feet away from the man giving the most admired speech of his time, and yet he wrote and said nothing about any of this. When in 1885 Usher was asked to contribute to an important collection of reminiscences of Lincoln, his contribution told of Lincoln's disappointment that George Meade had not followed up the victory at Gettysburg, but he did not even mention being with Lincoln in Gettysburg or this anecdote of Lincoln writing the speech on the train, despite the fact that his 1882 lecture had received a good deal of comment. This silence might reasonably be taken as tacit repudiation of the earlier tale.

Usher's 1882 lecture mentioned no theme or incident that is not found in Arnold's 1866 account, which it traces exactly in the order of topics. Arnold, for example, had also mentioned the "Capital" and had also ended with a version of Everett's supposed compliment to Lincoln while on the stand at Gettysburg. The pasteboard mentioned by Usher may be a transference from an unrelated episode of seeing Lincoln writing, or it may reflect an often-reprinted anecdote from 1865 by Noah Brooks saying that it was "a favorite habit of the President, when writing anything requiring thought," to write on stiff pasteboard slips that he placed "on his knee," exactly as depicted by Usher.[22] Indeed, it is not clear that Usher intended his statement to be taken as a recollection of his own experience, for the newspaper report prefaces its summary of Usher's talk with the comment that he "gave the history of the famous Gettysburg oration," and several other anecdotes given in the article are clearly stories Usher collected over the years and not eyewitness recollections. Usher gave no indication in the lecture that he was on the train or was even at Gettysburg. It would appear, then, that Usher may well have been giving a rather highly colored summary in his own words of Arnold's statement—which was itself most probably a misreading of McCormick. Even Usher's addition of the aside "of course" when recounting that Lincoln was expected "to say something" suggests that he was contradicting Arnold's obvious error on this point.

After Usher, the scene of Lincoln writing his speech on the train became an increasingly common element of the Gettysburg story. Usher's account, seemingly a creation of the myth, even doubled back into the history of the speech, as Isaac Arnold in 1885 rewrote his account of 1866 to more clearly bring out elements that may not even have been intended at first. The new version now specified that Lincoln wrote the speech "in the cars" on his way from the White House (Usher had said "on" the cars) and even added that Lincoln asked for paper and that "a rough sheet of foolscap [paper] was handed to him, and, retiring to a seat by himself, with a pencil, he wrote the address."[23] Arnold's second edition became another foundational text of the train composition legend. It, or one inspired by it, was even echoed by Robert Todd Lincoln, who in 1885, in response to an inquiry, wrote, "My father's Gettysburg Address was jotted down in pencil, in part at least on the way to the place."[24] However, the effect of the misinformation spread by Usher and Arnold was not all negative. By the fall of 1885, Lincoln's host in Gettysburg, David Wills, had become so indignant over printed reports about the speech having been written on the train and not in his own home that he began putting his recollections in order, providing us with our best source for events inside the Wills house on the evening of November 18, when Lincoln set about revising the speech he had brought from Washington.

By the late 1880s, the mixed-up tale of Lincoln writing while on the train entered school textbooks and general histories.[25] John Nicolay and others put up vigorous opposition, but there was no stopping the legend, particularly as new press reports constantly appeared that were allegedly based on evidence from credible sources such as Governor Curtin; on closer inspection, all dissolve into garbled accounts of second- or third-hand provenance.[26] Then there were the outright hoaxes spawned by the constant need for new newspaper copy about the martyr president. An article of the late 1880s supposedly authored by Edward McPherson, former representative from Gettysburg and longtime clerk of the U.S. House of Representatives, depicted Lincoln and Everett conferring about the speech on the train, then stated that McPherson provided the scraps of paper for the immortal address. McPherson denied the story, but it continued to circulate well into the 1890s despite his denial and despite the fact that it could be easily shown that Everett was never on Lincoln's train.[27]

The train composition story grew in the telling during the increasingly hagiographic atmosphere of the later nineteenth century, reaching its mature form in "The Perfect Tribute" of 1906, Mary Shipman Andrews's touching short story of national reunion. Andrews portrayed Lincoln on the train awkwardly clutching a pencil as he bent in concentration over a torn piece of brown wrapping paper, writing a speech he thought was a failure, then later comforting a dying Confederate soldier whose last words of praise for the great speech brought reconciliation and peace to Lincoln and to the nation.[28] Andrews never intended her story to be anything more than fiction, but it was so heartfelt and fit so perfectly with contemporary themes of Blue-Gray veteran brotherhood, that it was incorporated into school texts across the nation. This fiction made the image of Lincoln writing on the train a fixture of the popular imagination for nearly a century, losing its power only gradually as the generations schooled in the 1910s, 1920s, and 1930s passed from the scene. It would be difficult to find a clearer example of the interplay of memory and history, imagination and nation. McCormick's little pebble that started the train composition avalanche no doubt correctly portrayed Lincoln discussing the ceremony and his remarks while on the train, but there is no evidence within twenty years of the event—and no credible evidence ever—that places that pasteboard on Lincoln's knee.[29]

Indeed, Assistant Adjutant General Andrews and Lieutenant Cochrane both confirm that Lincoln talked of Gettysburg on the train, with Cochrane adding that Lincoln retired to think about his speech, when "approaching Hanover Junction." This timing may well be accurate, for according to the carefully constructed itinerary, the presidential train would rendezvous there with the special train coming from Harrisburg and carrying the governors and delegations from the north. At the junction, the cars of the two trains were to be joined for the final 30 miles to Gettysburg over the "Hanover Junction, Hanover, and Gettysburg" branch line, which ran directly west from the Northern Central tracks. The grand arrival in Gettysburg on one train of the president and as many as a dozen governors had apparently been organized from Harrisburg and would have presented an impressive spectacle, but it meant that on the final leg of the journey, after Hanover Junction, Lincoln certainly could not have expected to have the time and peace to think about his speech on a train full of politicians.

Another bit of garbled evidence also suggests that Lincoln may have retired from the larger group before getting to Hanover Junction. In 1866, Francis B. Carpenter wrote that someone told him that about an hour before reaching that station, both Lincoln and Seward "had gone into the sleeping-car attached to the train, for some rest." No other source mentions a "sleeping-car," but the secondhand anecdote becomes even stranger when Carpenter gives Lincoln's alleged response after someone "intruded" upon him and said he was "expected to make a speech" to a crowd at the station: "'No!' he rejoined, very emphatically; 'I had enough of that sort of thing all the way from Springfield to Washington. Seward,' said he, turning over in his berth, 'you go out and repeat some of your "*poetry*" to the people!'"[30] Carpenter's anecdotes are generally reliable, but if this story has any claim to accuracy, it must be that Lincoln had removed himself from the company, perhaps for a moment of rest; it also expresses in dramatic fashion Lincoln's general aversion to impromptu speeches; possibly, too, the smallpox that would soon hit Lincoln explains his alleged need for rest, for he was always accounted to be as tireless as a horse. Lincoln's referring to Seward's oratorical exercises as "*poetry*" does correspond to stories told by others that Lincoln "thought Mr. Seward's style too verbose—too much like 'machine writing,'" but the story overall is so idiosyncratic that the actual event it describes may be irretrievably lost.[31]

If Lincoln did find time to think or rest—which may have been function-ally the same thing—it could seemingly only have been at this stage of the trip. He did not have long. Since leaving Baltimore at about two in the afternoon there had been lunch, storytelling, and conversation, yet it could not have been much after four when the train pulled into Hanover Junction. Contrary to the garbled report by Carpenter, there was no large crowd, nor, in the event, was the Governor's Special to be found. Trains at that time could not receive telegraph messages en route, so it is possible that it was one of the dispatches Lincoln was said to have received at the station that first informed him that the train carrying the governors had broken down along the way. The president's train would go on without them, but there was still a short delay at the junction while switching to the branch line for Gettysburg. The transfer also entailed new train personnel; David Wills, busy in Gettysburg preparing for the great day, was a director and the treasurer of the Gettysburg line, but "Captain" Abdiel W. Eichelberger of Hanover was its president, and it fell to him to welcome Lincoln at the junction.[32]

Lincoln descended from the train, and Eichelberger always said shaking Lincoln's hand was the proudest moment of his life. They stood under a great elm tree as the cars were shunted on the tracks, and Eichelberger remembered Lincoln listening intently as he told how J. E. B. Stuart's Confederate cavalry had burned the rail bridges in the area during the run-up to the battle at Gettysburg. He might have added that the station at Hanover Junction itself had been raided and a good deal of property destroyed. Eichelberger may have felt doubly targeted, as his flour and saw mills in Alabama had also been confiscated by the Confederates. The damage to the tracks at Hanover Junction was quickly repaired, and within days of the great battle the first of over 10,000 wounded soldiers passed through on the way to hospitals throughout the North. Like so many elements of the journey to Gettysburg, the tree that Lincoln and Eichelberger stood under became a repository of Lincoln's memory. When it was finally removed in 1929, the papers once again told of the conversation under the elm. The station remained, gathering memories: in 1953 John Nicolay's daughter came to dedicate a plaque marking Lincoln's visit. The station was later restored, and one could again stand on the platform where Lincoln waited before making the last stage of his trip to Gettysburg—and a way station too of Lincoln's last journey, when his body was carried back to Springfield. But the layers of memory and meaning at Hanover Junction did not detain Lincoln and Eichelberger. After a short time, the conductor called the "All aboard," and Lincoln stepped into the car with a characteristic remark, "I reckon, Captain, we don't want to be left behind."[33]

The train seems to have been running a little late all day, but the engineer on the last leg of the journey recalled assuring Lincoln that he could make up for lost time and claimed ever after to have done so. Eichelberger joined the train at Hanover Junction and confirmed that, as Cochrane also remembered, during this last part of the trip Lincoln rode in the rear coach, with Eichelberger recalling the presence of Seward and several others, including Edward McPherson, who would have been well-known to him as the region's representative in Congress. It was seemingly at this point, evidently surrounded by politicians, and "just before arriving at Gettysburg," that Lincoln "got into a little talk with McVeagh about Missouri affairs," as John Hay wrote in his diary with typical understatement. MacVeagh, the party chair in Pennsylvania, for his part recalled that Lincoln had specifically invited him along on the journey "to discuss some matters," and that could only mean politics.[34]

Lincoln had probably first met MacVeagh in September when he came to the White House to consult about Governor Curtin's reelection strategy, with MacVeagh asking Lincoln to encourage the popular Union Democrat and general Benjamin Butler to campaign in favor of the governor. After their September meeting, MacVeagh had kept Lincoln informed about Curtin's campaign, and Lincoln himself wrote to MacVeagh with military news that might affect Curtin's prospects. MacVeagh in later years had a brilliant career—lawyer, reform politician, railroad magnate, attorney general to President James Garfield, diplomat, his profile cast in bronze by Augustus Saint-Gaudens. At the time, however, he was a thirty-year-old district attorney for Chester County making his first foray into state politics. Democrats ridiculed him as a sophomoric political amateur, but he was fast becoming "the rising hope of the exuberant young Republicans of Pennsylvania," according to John Russell Young, a Philadelphia journalist and longtime observer of the political scene, and was "much sought after at county fairs and gatherings which yearn for eloquence."[35]

MacVeagh had helped secure Governor Curtin's reelection by organizing a letter-writing campaign by soldiers in the field, who could not vote absentee, urging their family and friends to vote for Curtin, "the soldiers' friend." He and other Pennsylvania Republicans (under the label of the People's Party) then pushed through a state constitutional amendment to allow soldiers in the field to vote, a vital element in Lincoln's 1864 strategy; across the nation, the 1862 congressional and state elections had been disastrous to the party in part because of the absence of so many committed Republicans at the front.[36] MacVeagh's political and diplomatic abilities may be best measured, though, by the fact that despite being a Curtin man, he courted, and in 1866 married, a Cameron daughter. Nonetheless, the perpetual Curtin-Cameron feud in Pennsylvania was a constant worry to Lincoln. Just after MacVeagh's visit to the White House in September, John Hay had gone to Philadelphia and met with MacVeagh, Butler, and others, reporting in his diary, and most probably to Lincoln, "McVeagh does not seem entirely easy about the result in Pennsylvania. He wanted everybody to beg Butler to make more speeches & specially wanted Cameron to come out strong for Curtin which he has not yet done."[37] This was at a time when Cameron was warning Lincoln that Curtin hoped to replace him as the party nominee in 1864. Although the September meeting was seemingly Hay's first acquaintance with MacVeagh, the two would be inseparable during the Gettysburg journey.

By the time Lincoln spoke with MacVeagh on the train, the Pennsylvania elections had been won, but now, as revealed by Lincoln's troubles in Maryland, the problems of Reconstruction loomed as the greatest political threat to the administration and the Union cause. Even though Missouri was technically still part of the Union, tens of thousands of Missourians served the Confederacy as guerrillas, and as in most border states, Unionists were bitterly divided between radicals who sought immediate abolition and conservatives who supported a perhaps hypothetical "gradual" emancipation. What's more, the conservative postmaster general, Montgomery Blair, and his family were a force not only in Maryland but also in Missouri, and Missouri's governor Hamilton Gamble, also a conservative, was the brother-in-law of Lincoln's attorney general, Edward Bates, himself an influential figure in the state—his son had just been elected to the state supreme court, for example. In Missouri, nearly all the problems afflicting the border states, from Maryland to the Ozarks, were bound up into one virtually intractable political conundrum for the administration.

Lincoln had been pleased that despite these divisions, the recent elections in Missouri had gone well, but he still felt beleaguered. As MacVeagh later told Carpenter, Lincoln on the train particularly lamented the attitude of Governor Gamble, who resisted enrolling blacks into state or federal regiments and who particularly disliked the compulsory emancipation imposed by General Order 329. On the train Lincoln told MacVeagh, "I do not understand the spirit of those men who, in such a time as this, because they cannot have a whole loaf will take no bread. For my part, I am willing to receive any man, or class of men, who will help us even a *little*." (Gamble returned the compliment, referring to Lincoln as "a mere intriguing, pettifogging, piddling politician.") Lincoln might just as well have been tacitly admonishing MacVeagh, who was something of a "whole loaf" man himself, but on the other side of the larder. Seemingly all the radicals in Pennsylvania not only wanted Blair sacked, but they also hoped Lincoln would remove Governor Gamble, who was well known to Keystone State politicians because he had lived in Pennsylvania before the war. MacVeagh later that day told John Forney that he had "pitched into the President coming up and told him some truths," but this assertion is belied by Hay's own assessment of the conversation; Hay noted that MacVeagh "talked radicalism" with Lincoln but only "until he learned he was talking recklessly."[38]

The controversy of the moment in Missouri had blown up because Attorney General Bates had sided with conservatives and dismissed radical federal prosecutor William Edwards "for participation in political enterprises hostile to the known views of the Executive Government of both the nation and the state," as had just been reported in the press. Radicals in Missouri and around the Union took this to be an open declaration of war by the conservatives. More generally, many radicals feared that Lincoln had been "Blairized" and would present a conservative Reconstruction policy in the Annual Message, so they were particularly troubled by Bates's suggestion that he had fired Edwards with Lincoln's approval. In contrast, talking on the train with MacVeagh, "the President disavowed any knowledge of the Edwards case," Hay wrote in his diary for November 19. Hay was paying particular attention; he had been deeply involved in Missouri issues for some time, having been before the war the sometime Springfield correspondent of the Blair family paper, the *Missouri Democrat*. Hay had also sat in on the recent dramatic and widely discussed summit meeting between Lincoln and a delegation of sixty Missouri radicals who had come to Washington to plead their case. However, Hay's account may be somewhat overstated, for, as Hay knew, Bates had indeed spoken with Lincoln about the dismissal but had assured Lincoln that "Edwards was inefficient and must be removed for that reason," not because he was a political opponent.[39]

CHAPTER THREE

Hay's account suggests that Lincoln on the train had induced MacVeagh to back down from his radical talk, but MacVeagh and the radical supporters of Edwards evidently had made an impression; a good deal of Lincoln's success came from talking moderate but leaning radical. Within days of the Gettysburg trip the press was reporting, "The President's friends are giving out that he now very much regrets the removal of Edwards of Missouri," and hinting that Lincoln felt Bates had misled him. In December, as part of longer-term evolutions in his Missouri and Reconstruction policies more broadly, Lincoln replaced the commanding general in the state with one more acceptable to the radicals. The Edwards controversy continued to roil the administration into the second week of December, when Lincoln, Hay, and other insiders were still mulling it over late into the night, wrapping it up with Blair and Bates and the factional squabbles that bound together the politics of Missouri and Maryland and the border states.[40] And so Lincoln's journey to Gettysburg rolled on, a train full of politicians, generals, and diplomats burdened with local concerns, international complications, hopes of personal advancement, and the fate of the Union, but not a train on which a president could have expected to write anything of substance, much less a ceremonial work of high rhetoric that Lincoln's letter of invitation had so clearly called for.

One last stop awaited before reaching Gettysburg, at the village of Hanover. Long before 5:00 p.m., when the president's train was scheduled to arrive, Mary Shaw Leader, the editor of the Republican *Hanover Spectator,* saw "men, women, and children going hurriedly toward the depot all anxious to get a 'good look' at the President." Here the train halted on a siding to allow passage of an eastbound train, and as soon as the cars stopped, "the people immediately massed themselves around the car containing the President, and gave him cheer after cheer, and asked him to 'come out.'" Popular tradition in the town long remembered that it was the heartfelt call of a local pastor, "Father Abraham, your children want to hear you," that finally brought Lincoln to step onto the rear platform of the car, removing his high hat and stooping to avoid the low roof. According to press reports, Lincoln took in the cheers and said, "Well, you have seen me, and according to general experience, you have seen less than you expected to see." It was one of his standard lines for such occasions but was nonetheless greeted with "a genuine hearty round of merriment."[41]

Primed by Captain Eichelberger's description of the cavalry skirmishing around Hanover Junction, and no doubt based on his own knowledge of the Gettysburg campaign, Lincoln said, "You had the Rebels here last summer, hadn't you?" and received a loud "yes" in reply. Hanover, in fact, unlike Hanover Junction, had been the scene of a sharp fight with several hundred casualties, and rebels had occupied the town. "Well," he asked playfully, "did you fight them any?" This was "a poser" according to the *Philadelphia Inquirer,* and the people "looked at each other with a half-amused, half-puzzled expression, while the long, tall form of the President leaned from the car as he waited the reply." The editor of the democratic *Hanover Citizen* heard someone say, "yes," for the citizens really had pitched in to help push back the Confederates, building barricades, caring for the wounded, and providing intelligence about the country and the movements of the enemy. For its part, the *Inquirer* reported that the awkward silence ended only when "the ladies" came forward to present Lincoln with bouquets and planted on the back of the car "a beautiful flag, the work of the fair women of the neighborhood."[42] Some of the women were probably among those who, the summer before, relieved by the retreat of the Confederates, had sung patriotic songs to rally the Union soldiers marching through the town to join the fight at Gettysburg.

"The flag deserved and received the salutations of all present," noted the *Inquirer,* and it may have been this that led Lincoln to say, according to local tradition, "I trust when the enemy was here the citizens of Hanover were loyal to our country and to the Stars and Stripes. If you are not true patriots in support of the Union you should be." This rather severe admonition does not correspond to the light tone of the newspaper reports, but whatever Lincoln said, his visit demonstrated to the people that he knew something of what they had been through in the name of the Union. Perhaps it was at this stop that a little girl with a bouquet of roses was lifted up to Lincoln, saying with a childish lisp, "Flowrth for the President!" Kissing the child, he said, "You're a sweet little rose-bud yourself. I hope your life will open into perpetual beauty and goodness." At some point during the stop, too, little Jackie Melsheimer, held up by his father, gave Lincoln an apple—such are the stories that were told and retold across the decades, along with the exact duration of the stop: eight minutes precisely. Then, "the whistle screamed, the brakes loosened, the assemblage gave one long, hearty cheer, and the car rattled up the Gettysburg Road."[43]

Six hours after leaving Washington, Lincoln's train came out of some low, wooded hills and the passengers gained their first glimpse of Gettysburg, shimmering under the moonlight in the chill November air. Lincoln had come to Gettysburg. And just as John Nicolay remembered, he arrived with his Washington Draft in his pocket, unchanged since leaving the capital. The story of Lincoln's rail journey to Gettysburg, and of the early decades of the developing train-composition myth, reveals the tendency of multiple iterations to fabricate new elements and misremember old ones until the meaning of an event can become inverted. In this case, a story of how Lincoln wrote in Gettysburg and not on the train became a story of how Lincoln wrote on the train and not in Gettysburg. It would not be the first time that Lincoln's speech would be subjected to transformation, whether speeding down telegraph lines to be printed, and misprinted, in the morning papers, or arcing across the years to become part of the permanent process of redefinition that is a hallmark of American memory and identity.

FOUR

Revisions in Gettysburg

MEADE'S HEADQUARTERS.

"The wind high and the weather threatening today," Edward Everett wrote in his diary for November 18, so he kept to his room in the Wills house, "gathering my forces for tomorrow." Still, the seventy-year-old went down to the Gettysburg station to greet the president and introduce him to David Wills. It was a characteristically polite and formal gesture by Everett, whose puritan austerity, which many mistook for lack of feeling, is suggested by his diary entry that "Mrs. Wise was in the party" accompanying the president; Mrs. Wise was his daughter. An "immense crowd" had gathered at the station, among them John Russell Young, a reporter with Forney's *Philadelphia Press,* who witnessed at around six in the evening a "straggled, hungry set" descend one by one to the platform at the station, preserved today as a museum in honor of the day Lincoln came to town. First came Forney, "in the flush of his winning manhood," who Young thought considered himself the host of this affair in his home state; "Lincoln, with that weary smile"; Seward wearing "an essentially bad hat"; John Hay, "handsome as a peach, the countenance of extreme youth," in attendance upon the president, and the rest. So great was the crush of the crowd that, according to Everett, "the president [was] extracted from the good natured pressure, with some difficulty."[1]

The crowd followed as Lincoln traveled by carriage the few blocks to the Wills home, the scene of Lincoln's written revisions while in Gettysburg. As Hay wrote in his diary, upon arrival the party "broke like a drop of quicksilver spilt." Lincoln joined Everett to be among the thirty-eight people (by Everett's count) who lodged at the Wills house, while Hay, Nicolay, the diplomats, Secretary Seward, and Postmaster General Blair went to stay at the adjacent home of Robert Harper, longtime editor of one of Gettysburg's Republican papers. Typically, no one mentioned Usher's whereabouts. Others went to one of the hotels or stayed with various residents.[2]

The town was already nearly filled to capacity with guests, many of whom must have shared the sentiments of Josephine Roedel, who wrote, "Never in my life will I have the same opportunity of seeing so many of the great men of the nation." For the most part the early evening in the town was relatively quiet as people perused the tables of relics for sale that dotted the sidewalks, found dinner and warmth by a fire, or sought accommodations in the private homes, churches, schools, and businesses that had been thrown open to receive them. After the clouds blew through, it turned into a beautiful, clear, and chilly November night, shimmering under a bright three-quarter moon. "Every house groaned with the good things of this life prepared to feed the coming crowd," a Gettysburger wrote, although some visitors grumbled that the prices charged were a bit steep.[3]

Probably fairly soon after arrival, Lincoln and the Washington dignitaries ate dinner at the Wills house, prepared by a very pregnant Catherine Wills, who would be delivered of a healthy girl, Jennie, just a month later. Decades later, Jennie spoke of a "family dinner" with Lincoln the night before the ceremony, but our only glimpse of the scene comes a year later in the aftermath of the 1864 presidential election season, during which not just Democrats had parodied Lincoln as a bloodthirsty boor.[4] Defending Lincoln's manners, Everett told a formal banquet attended by the cream of Boston society that he had dined at the home of "my friend, David Wills," surrounded by a grand company of ambassadors, officers, and diplomats, and he said of Lincoln, "In gentlemanly appearance, manners and conversation, he was the peer of any man at the table."[5]

Lincoln then spent at least an hour or two greeting and talking with the guests and visitors at the Wills house. Among the many guests whom Lincoln met that evening was a local soldier, William McIlhenny, with both his sister and his fiancée, who probably owed this special introduction to the fact that he had recently been shot through the shoulder in a skirmish around Winchester, Virginia, about 80 miles to the south. "I had my right hand in a sling at the time, and of course, had to give the President my left hand," he remembered. "I felt a little like thanking that Rebel that shot me for giving me this opportunity of meeting this great man." Everett had taken tea that day at the nearby home of Professor Martin Stoever from the college; there he heard about the bullets that had passed though the Stoevers' parlors during the battle while he ate preserves from "the famous peach orchard" where so much blood had been shed. Lincoln, too, doubtless heard many such stories as he circulated among the guests at the Wills house, which had seemingly escaped the battle unharmed but saw its own share of blood, having served as a hospital after the battle.[6]

So august was the company at the Wills house that Wayne MacVeagh, who counted as an important political player, was left to wander the town in the company of John Hay and Edwin Stanton Jr., finally getting oysters and then dinner at Pennsylvania College, just to the north of the town center. The young men—MacVeagh at thirty was the eldest—then made their way to the county courthouse, where since about eight in the evening Lamon had been presiding over a meeting of parade marshals. The trio did not stay long, instead joining up with John Forney and going back to his lodgings in the Fahnestock Building for some whiskey and politics. Hay thought that Forney, after drinking all day, "was getting to feel a little ugly and dangerous. . . . he was particularly bitter on Montgomery Blair." After hearing Lincoln on the train correct MacVeagh's reckless talk, Hay must have found it illuminating to listen as MacVeagh told Forney that on the train he had "pitched into the President." Forney replied that the president "got a good deal of that from time to time and needed it."[7] Thus did the loyal Pennsylvanians conspire to educate and manage Lincoln.

As the evening wore on, the crowds grew larger in front of the Wills home, and those gathered outside could sometimes catch a glimpse of Lincoln "walking up and down the hall" or going into the parlor. The people were mostly quiet and curious at first, according to the *Philadelphia Inquirer,* making few cries to those inside—waiting patiently, it would seem, for the well-practiced civic and political rituals of the nineteenth-century "serenade" to get under way, when important visitors would be feted by bands and merry singing and would be expected to come out and say a few words. Meanwhile, as the crowds gathered, behind the scenes the Gettysburg Committee of Arrangements was at work, gaining permission from Assistant Adjutant Andrews to serenade the visitors with music from the Fort McHenry band he had brought from Baltimore on Lincoln's train.[8]

The opening signal of the night's public festivities was the arrival in front of the Wills house at around nine o'clock of the smartly uniformed, well-drilled marching band of the Fifth New York Artillery, one of the regiments that the previous July had helped clear the Confederates out of Hanover and that had then marched on to fight at Gettysburg. Somewhere out in the crowd was Clark E. Carr, the Illinois state agent, come to see the man whom he had done so much to bring to Gettysburg. "We all," by which Carr seems to have meant the other cemetery agents and event marshals, who evidently had left their meeting by this point, "headed by a brass band, marched to Mr. Wills' house, and serenaded Mr. Lincoln."[9] The impressive band played several patriotic airs, drawing even more people to the music. "After some time," the *Inquirer* reported, Lincoln appeared on the front steps of the house, "and the long repressed enthusiasm of those in waiting immediately found vent in ringing cheers." From that point until the early morning hours, Gettysburg and its visitors abandoned themselves to a joyous, cathartic outburst, indulging in the wake before the funeral. The dedication ceremony would be a solemn commemoration of sacrifice and heroism, but the night before the dedication in Gettysburg was a sprawling celebration of Union and victory.

As Lincoln took in the music and smiled and bowed to the crowd that filled York Street, the people called their greetings to "Father Abraham." Somebody—was it one of the many Republican politicians or patronage men who had flooded into the predominantly Democratic town?—set up the cry, "Three cheers for the next President of the United States!" The *Boston Evening Transcript* reported that Lincoln "said he was happy to see so many friends here to participate in the ceremonies," a sign that the large crowds had made an impression. Reports of Lincoln's comments differ, but all agree that, perhaps carried along by the cheering crowds, he was in a friendly and playful mood, indulging in the little jokes and modestly clever wordplay that was a part of nearly all his remarks on such occasions. On the night of July 7, 1863, in the wake of the glorious news from Vicksburg and Gettysburg, he had welcomed the noisy serenading party before the White House with a good-natured rebuke for being troublesome, and then had given them a speech that mixed musing about providential design with heartfelt commendations of the bravery and sacrifice of common soldiers and sailors. But when Lincoln welcomed the equally boisterous crowd before the Wills house, his thoughts did not reach so high, and he resorted to humor and self-deprecation to turn aside the crowd.[10]

"I appear before you, fellow-citizens, merely to thank you for this compliment," he began, "The inference is a very fair one that you would hear me for a little while at least, were I to commence to make a speech." Stating this "very fair" inference to people who had been clamoring for him to show himself and give them a speech could only be taken as good-humored taunting, and the laughing, cheering crowd loved it. After setting them up, with a storyteller's timing Lincoln then knocked them down: "I do not appear before you for the purpose of doing so, and for several substantial reasons. The most substantial of these is that I have no speech to make." The reports indicate "laughter" here, to signal the crowd's cheerful acceptance of this bad news. Lincoln remained just long enough to give the crowd a parting shot. "It is somewhat important in my position one should not say any foolish things if he can help it," he explained, "and it very often happens that the only way to help it is to say nothing at all. [Renewed laughter.] Believing that is my present condition this evening, I must beg of you to excuse me from addressing you further." The *Philadelphia Inquirer* seconded the crowd's "great merriment" at these remarks, which were "delivered in the humorous manner peculiar to the President."[11] Lincoln then turned and went inside while the band led the crowd around the corner to the home of Robert Harper in order to give Seward the same treatment.

Not everyone who heard the president was amused. Decades later Reverend Junius B. Remensnyder, a Lutheran theologian who was at that time the pastor at St. James' Church on the Upper East Side of New York City, recalled that he and the "students as a body" from the Gettysburg Seminary had set up a shout for Lincoln to come out, "our calls ever growing more emphatic" as the seminarians became impatient "under the long wait we had to bear." Young Remensnyder had already served his term in the Army of the Potomac and had even glimpsed the president once the year before, when Lincoln rode beside General George McClellan in review of the army at Antietam. But in front of the Wills house "the lights were dim, and we could not see him with much distinctness." Lincoln's "sensible" little speech "was quite a damper on our spirits. We felt greatly disappointed. Our pride was somewhat humbled, and the impression made on us was rather unfavorable."[12]

John Hay, that prematurely jaded and preternaturally gifted twenty-five-year-old, was also not impressed. He, MacVeagh, Forney, and no doubt others from the drinking party at Fahnestock's, were among those who had been drawn by the music to the Wills house, but Hay noted only that Lincoln "said half a dozen words meaning nothing & went in." They remained with the crowd long enough to see Seward come out but could not hear what he was saying, with Forney and MacVeagh all the while "still growling about Blair." Nicolay joined them there, for he seems to have remained at Harper's while the three younger men had gone wandering, and they made up for lost time by going back to Forney's room and drinking some more whiskey.[13]

The fiercest critics of Lincoln's brief acknowledgment of the serenade were the editors of the Democratic and opposition press, who mercilessly exploited the opening Lincoln had given them. Perhaps purposefully confusing Lincoln's words to the crowd with the dedication service itself, the November 20 *Philadelphia Age* declared that "the country should blush with shame" at the ceremonies in Gettysburg, where Lincoln had "made a joke or two." Rising to heights of patriotic indignation, the editors lamented that "these men meet to laugh and joke and electioneer" even "with the wounded still groaning and the dead unburied. . . . It is thus that they render homage to the heroic dead." The November 23 *Pittsburgh Post* scoffed that Lincoln "said he had nothing particular to say, and accordingly said very little." Considering "the thousands of new made graves" the editors found it difficult to appreciate this, but they could explain it: "Having nothing of a political or partisan character to communicate, he felt it to be the sharpest dodge to say nothing."

This criticism served two purposes: reminding readers of the horrific toll taken by an unnecessary war and highlighting the self-serving partisanship of Lincoln and others who waged it from ambition and fanaticism (that is, abolitionism); both were standard tactics. Still, the *Post* editors hit close to the mark when they pointed out that "without any vast preparation he could have spoken a few simple and touching sentences to console the survivors of the heroic dead, and mingled his tears with theirs in sorrow for their untimely end."[14] Not only on this night but on many others like it, Lincoln passed up the opportunity to say the things that were expected—to console the sorrowful, to inspire the soldier, to fire up the partisan, to express outrage, to commiserate—things that, indeed, should perhaps sometimes have been said. But had he done so, he would not have been Lincoln.

Lincoln in his mature years was almost constitutionally incapable of making rhetorical gestures that did not have practical, material implications for policy or action. Nor was it just his personality. Given his powerful sense of responsibility for the maintenance of the Republic, Lincoln felt himself to be literally, by the Constitution, incapable of speaking without weighing the potentially disastrous implications of a misspoken word. For three years and more Lincoln had been on a knife edge. One misstatement and Britain might intervene for the Confederacy; one misstep and Kentucky or Missouri or the entire border South might fall to secession. Except for a few early misadventures in oratory, elaborate speechifying was never in Lincoln's character and under such circumstances could do more harm than good, so Lincoln tended to leave decorative addresses and rhetorical exercises to others, particularly to Seward. Lincoln recognized that "*poetry*" was useful and necessary at times, particularly, say, in the Thanksgiving Day Proclamation of 1863 written by Seward but issued over the president's name, or in the formulaic messages to diplomats and sovereigns that Seward provided for Lincoln.[15] Crafting "touching sentences" and "mingl[ing] his tears" with a crowd—legitimate weapons in the arsenal of many effective leaders—was generally not in Lincoln, but this is another reason the ceremony the next day would be such a notable exception.

After Lincoln went back into the Wills house, out in front of the Harper house Seward gave the crowd some of the red meat they wanted. In the speech that Hay could not hear, Seward grandiloquently announced, "I thank my God for the hope that this is the last fratricidal war which will fall upon the country which is vouchsafed to us by Heaven—the richest, the broadest, the most beautiful, the most magnificent and capable of a great destiny, that has ever been given to any part of the human race." But as John Nicolay noted years later when describing the speeches that night, "a certain political tension existed throughout the entire war period, which rarely failed to color every word of a public speaker, and attune the ear of every public listener to subtle and oracular meanings."[16]

Such was the case with Seward's speech to the serenaders, which was read and heard with particular attention in light of a widely noted speech Seward had given the month before at Auburn, New York, that seemed to accept the continued existence of slavery in a reunited nation. Seward's remarks to the serenade at Gettysburg had been written in advance for distribution to the press and were doubtless similar to what he would have said during the dedication ceremony had he been called upon to stand in for the president. Nonetheless, he opened with a confusing statement that led many to conclude that Seward thought Gettysburg was in Maryland or was perhaps below the Mason-Dixon line, an apparent gaffe that attracted a good deal of attention in the following days. More seriously, surprising

CHAPTER FOUR

many observers and outraging the Democratic press, the supposedly conservative Seward forthrightly attributed the war to slavery and rejoiced that "this strife is going to end in the removal of that evil." One Republican reporter among the many trying to divine who was up and who was out in the contest for Lincoln's ear thought Seward "made a speech so radical that Montgomery Blair must have shaken in his boots. It was a bold, manly stand on the side of the Proclamation of Emancipation, and indicated that there was little disagreement in views between him and the President."[17] The opposition press suggested instead that Seward knew the radicals were in the ascendant and was trimming his sails accordingly. This was not far wrong, because Seward must have known that Lincoln in his upcoming Annual Message would for the first time announce that emancipation was to be a condition of readmission to the Union: the conflict would no longer be a war to bring back "the Union as it was." Amid the ringing declaration that after the war, the nation would "thenceforth be united, be only one country, having only one hope, one ambition, and one destiny," Seward even spoke of "abolishing" slavery, adroitly packaging policy within a barrage of what Lincoln had called Seward's *"poetry."*[18]

Lincoln did not hear Seward's speech, or a speech by Forney a little later, but Pennsylvania Republican Party chair Wayne MacVeagh recalled telling him about them later that night at the Wills house. MacVeagh must have been among the visitors and guests who, according to Everett, "continued to arrive all the evening." Everett himself had looked on while "the President spoke a few words in the Evening to the multitude in the street," but he then retired to his room for some peace and quiet in anticipation of the morrow. Downstairs in the parlors, though, there was a lot MacVeagh could have told Lincoln about the serenades and the celebrating. After Seward's remarks, the company from Forney's lodgings at Fahnestock's returned there for a bit more to drink and a few songs ("Nicolay sung his little song of the 'Three Thieves,'" Hay diarized, "and we then sung John Brown") and then decided they should get up a serenade themselves. Nicolay and Judge Shannon went out to gather a brass band, while the inseparable trio of MacVeagh, Hay, and Stanton junior stayed behind to coax Forney into a speech. After so much whiskey and so much complaining about Blair, the veteran campaigner probably did not need much encouragement. "If I speak," he said according to Hay's diary, "I will speak my mind," and Hay began to fear that Forney would say something "imprudent." Forney did not disappoint.[19]

We can't be sure exactly what MacVeagh told Lincoln about Forney's sodden speech, but as MacVeagh remembered it, Lincoln "greatly enjoyed my account" of the remarks by Forney and by Seward. Though a teetotaler, Lincoln had a weakness for stories about the misadventures of harmless drunks, and given that MacVeagh had just returned from what had become a drinking party, his exposition itself may have heightened the comic possibilities of the story. Of course, in 1909 the former attorney general and respected diplomat could not tell a story of Lincoln laughing at such antics on the night before his epochal speech. After all, MacVeagh's brother was even then the secretary of the treasury, and the cult of Lincoln was reaching its apex. Still, reading between the lines, it is easy to imagine that MacVeagh's recitation itself may well have been droll, deliberately or not.

Hay's diary provides the framework for what MacVeagh told Lincoln, and as Hay described it, once the band arrived, Forney had one last drink and then went downstairs and set about "blackguarding the crowd" for not better appreciating Lincoln. According to Hay, Forney extolled Lincoln as "that great, wonderful mysterious inexplicable man," before veering into a partisan defense of his own political career since his break with James Buchanan and his apparent embrace of Stephen Douglas. "He had been for Lincoln in his heart in 1860," Hay summarized, but "open advocacy was not as effectual as the course he took—dividing the most corrupt organization that ever existed—the proslavery Dem. Party." As MacVeagh wrote later, Forney explained that in backing Douglas in 1860, "his action had really been of greater assistance to the election of Mr. Lincoln than if he had supported him" because he had thereby "induced more than twice as many voters to withhold their votes from Mr. Breckenridge than he could possibly have induced to vote directly for Mr. Lincoln." This crisp recitation of Forney's speech some forty years after the event, providing details (such as Forney having mentioned John Breckenridge) that are not found in any contemporary source, supports the strength of MacVeagh's recollections of the night.[20]

In talking with Lincoln, MacVeagh may also have developed further the campaign against Blair that he had begun on the train, because Forney, again according to Hay's diary, had ended his speech by publicly berating a certain "temporizing minister," not mentioning Blair by name, who "sets himself up in opposition to the progress of the age." "And very much of this," Hay deadpanned. Going back upstairs after this oration, John Russell Young, who was reporting the event for Forney's *Philadelphia Press*,

CHAPTER FOUR

remarked archly to Hay—always a connoisseur of impudent wit—that Forney's speech "must not be written out yet," implying that Young was certainly not going to report what Forney had said. He added, "We will see about it when he gets sober," clearly meaning that the whole thing was best forgotten. For public consumption, the *Press* report was a model of diplomatic blandness, familiar to anyone who has read the minutes of a contentious faculty meeting or United Nations summit: "Forney made a brief speech, referring to the political aspect of the campaign, and particularly to the services of Douglas to the Union. He paid a eulogy to the President, and spoke of him as one that would live in history as the savior of his country."[21]

Judge Shannon, the Pittsburgh Democrat who along with Forney had met with Lincoln on November 12, seems to have spoken in a similar vein. The Democratic *Gettysburg Compiler* characterized their speeches as "low political tirades," probably meaning that Shannon had forcefully supported Lincoln and the administration, just as he had recently done during the state elections in New York and Pennsylvania, and Hay's diary is probably accurate in stating that Shannon spoke "effectively and acceptably"— higher praise than Hay had given Lincoln's earlier effort. Edward McPherson, the current representative for Gettysburg, and McKnight, a former congressman from Pittsburgh (and no doubt part of Judge Shannon's party), also spoke, but no one seems to have noticed what they said. Unfortunately, there is no detailed account of Montgomery Blair's own remarks when, at some point that evening, he made "a short, happy speech, which was received with much enthusiasm" and proclaimed "a vigorous prosecution of the war as the determination of the Administration."[22] After having been publicly excoriated for his Rockville speech, Blair seems to have decided to stay away from policy speeches for a while.

Having finished telling Lincoln of Forney's speech, MacVeagh's later account suggests that he mentioned Seward's botched opening of his speech but that he did so quite charitably. "As we had been traveling most of the day through Maryland," MacVeagh later summarized, Seward thought they were still in "a slave state," but the crowd promptly corrected him "in excellent humor," a sign that MacVeagh was one who knew how to accentuate the positive and keep the tone light, as befit the celebratory character of the whole evening in Gettysburg. However, whereas many news reports remarked upon Seward's surprising turn to radicalism, MacVeagh emphasized instead another element of Seward's speech. In the context of his conversation with Lincoln, MacVeagh in his memoir praised Seward for his statement that "the minority should loyally accept the result of an election," which was, according to MacVeagh's summary of Seward, the "only possible basis on which free government could endure."[23]

To Forney, Shannon, MacVeagh, and the others who had just been in the trenches for Lincoln or their home-state Republican or Union tickets, the evening of the eighteenth was a kind of double victory celebration: victory of the Union at Gettysburg, certainly, but more immediately, the victory of the administration and of Republicans in the hard-fought state elections just coming to a close. Given their belief that peace Democrats in power would have called for an immediate truce, many Republicans saw little distinction between the two victories: the government was the Union, and the administration was the only guarantee of the Republic. This was no partisan delusion of political operatives. Throughout 1864 Lincoln believed that if he and the Republican Party were to be defeated in the presidential election, the Union would be dissolved.[24]

Between Forney's inebriated performance and Seward's gaffe there was plenty of reason for Lincoln to have "greatly enjoyed" MacVeagh's account of their speeches. Possibly too, MacVeagh gave Lincoln some indication of his own remarks to the crowd, when he made "a touching and most beautiful speech of five minutes" according to John Hay, strong praise indeed from one who usually affected a world-weary boredom. It must have made quite an impression, because thirty years later John R. Young still remembered that MacVeagh "gave a rattling good speech at the serenade, which I helped to cheer." "I confined myself to some words of earnest praise of General Reynolds," MacVeagh himself recalled, "who had been killed in the first day's battle, with his back to his birthplace at Lancaster and his face, as always, to the foe." MacVeagh's nice turn of phrase even when describing his speech forty years later suggests why he was such a hit at county fairs.[25]

MacVeagh had good reason to single out the death of General John Reynolds, for he was not only the highest-ranking Union officer killed in the three days of fighting, but he was also, like MacVeagh, a Pennsylvanian. The site of his death was already a point of pilgrimage for the thousands who had visited the battleground since July. "He had been very kind to me the year before," MacVeagh continued, when during Lee's move north that culminated at Antietam, MacVeagh had led a mounted company patrolling the Potomac River and all of Pennsylvania's troops had been under Reynolds's command. "I was glad of the occasion to bear my testimony to his admirable qualities," MacVeagh concluded, further adding to the likelihood that he had also taken the opportunity of telling Lincoln about his homage to Reynolds, as MacVeagh may well have known that Lincoln had offered Reynolds command of the Army of the Potomac just as Lee was again moving north in the campaign that would culminate at Gettysburg. The next day, Lincoln too would visit the area of the battlefield where Reynolds had died.

Despite enjoying his talk with MacVeagh, Lincoln still had work to do. "Soon afterward," MacVeagh recalled, "he said to me he was about to withdraw because he wished to consider further the few words he was expected to say the next day."[26] And so the evening took a new turn. The public welcome at the train station, the ceremonies of introductions and greetings at the Wills house, and the mandatory rituals of the serenade were all finished. But now, with the night already growing old, Lincoln went upstairs to the guest room prepared for him to turn once again to the "few appropriate remarks" that he had prepared in Washington.

Reconstructing how Lincoln went about the second main stage of writing the Gettysburg Address that he outlined to James Speed—understanding the revisions he undertook in Gettysburg—is in part a question of building up a detailed image of his movements and actions in order to proceed from what is known about what he did there to what can be reasonably deduced about what he wrote there. Relying for the inside story as we must on later accounts and testimonials, all of them shaped by the growing myth of the Gettysburg Address, means that our perspective too can be distorted by a kind of gravitational force exerted on the historical record by the impending speech. The mysteries of the manuscripts grew up within and alongside the cult of Gettysburg, blurring the image of events and the outline of the flow of Lincoln's ideas. Given these distortions, fixing details such as the time when Lincoln went upstairs, or the paper he was using, can provide a clearer picture and a more secure foundation for reconstructing the stages of Lincoln's revisions that created the final speech.

We can see the gravitational principle at work in the recollections of those who later told of that evening in Gettysburg, leading them to place Lincoln's speech at the center of their stories. MacVeagh's 1909 testimony that Lincoln had said "he wished to consider further the few words he was expected to say the next day" suggests either that Lincoln intended to revisit the Washington Draft or that it was unfinished. This is also the implication from Richard McCormick's 1865 secondhand newspaper report that on the train Lincoln "asked what he should say at the ceremony on the morrow, stating that he had made no preparation whatever, and that the occasion was a novel and difficult one." James Speed's summary of the story Lincoln told him fits into this same picture.

These later accounts suggest that Lincoln's impending speech may have been on his mind on November 18, but it would be a mistake to imagine that Lincoln was fixated upon it. Given the rise of the Gettysburg Address legend, it was natural that later recollections and memoirs would reflect the action of memory and mythologizing over time. Elements not directly connected to the speech tended to fall away or recede in importance, as demonstrated in David Wills's account of the night of the eighteenth, which is virtually silent on any point not directly connected to Lincoln's speech. For this reason, the memoir literature creates the impression that the speech was a larger part of Lincoln's day than was actually the case. Contemporary accounts depict Lincoln moving as could be expected through a series of predictable events: a greeting at the train station, an escorted trip to the hotel or site of the speech, sometimes a grand torchlight procession before the big event, or at least a serenade by a band, and then the event itself, often involving a procession back to the train station or to the visiting celebrity's lodgings. From the routine morning meeting with Judge Thomas Duval of Texas in the White House to his lingering in the parlors at the Wills house until late in the evening, Lincoln did not deviate from the normal course of activities in any way that suggests undue concern or anxiety about his remarks.

Correcting for the distorted image presented through the lens of memory suggests that throughout the day and evening of the eighteenth, Lincoln recognized that at some point he would want to review or revisit his speech. Still, given the restricted role assigned to him in the ceremony, his express plan to give only a "short, short, short" speech (as quoted by Brooks), and the well-developed state of the Washington Draft as written, Lincoln's actions and reported words on the eighteenth suggest little more than a prudent desire to be sure that he was satisfied with the remarks he might make as part of his role in formally dedicating the cemetery, which of course would not exclude revisions in wording or emphasis. So Lincoln's statement, recalled by MacVeagh, that "he wished to consider further the few words he was expected to say the next day" was not an exclamation of a man desperate to finish a speech but a recognition that the impending ceremony called for a "few words" that should, nonetheless, be well considered.

The timing of Lincoln's revisions in Gettysburg is crucial for understanding the nature of the text he brought with him and the changes that he may have made. Fortunately, two accounts based on information by David Wills, confirmed by MacVeagh's recollection, are clear on the essential point: Lincoln went upstairs to work on his speech only after, and not before, he was serenaded by the band of the Fifth New York Artillery at around nine o'clock. One of these sources dates to 1875 and was based on information provided by Wills, but it was actually written by Edward McPherson, who was Gettysburg's representative in Congress from 1859 to 1863 and who in 1875 was just ending twelve eventful years as clerk of the U.S. House of Representatives. Wills and McPherson were longtime friends, and in the early 1850s both had studied law under the radical abolitionist Thaddeus Stevens in Lancaster. By 1875, McPherson had been at the center of Civil War and Reconstruction politics for fifteen years, with one contemporary calling him "a walking political encyclopedia," in part because he had edited a respected series of political almanacs and handbooks. In the September 9, 1875, issue of the *Nation*, McPherson mentioned Wills and then described events in the Wills house in language that can leave no doubt that Wills was his informant, noting that Lincoln "was called out in the evening to reply to a serenade, and at a late hour went to his room" where he began to work on his speech.[27]

Lincoln had finished his reply to the serenade after nine, and allotting about forty-five minutes for Seward to speak and for the fellows at Fahnestock's to carry out their own improvised serenade, after which MacVeagh went to the Wills house, it must have been ten o'clock or so when Lincoln bid MacVeagh good-night and went upstairs to the guest room the Wills family had prepared for him. This timing fits fairly well with a second estimate given later by David Wills, stating that Lincoln went upstairs sometime before nine or ten. The broad range given suggests that Wills was reconstructing the timing from what he recalled of the events of the evening, not that he remembered the time specifically. In any event, the second account by Wills confirms the key fact from MacVeagh and the 1875 statement by McPherson that it was only after the serenade that Lincoln went upstairs and worked on his speech. This provides a firm starting point for Lincoln's written revisions that evening because the serenade can be fixed reasonably accurately by the newspaper accounts.

Wills's second estimate as to when Lincoln went upstairs was contained in his most complete account of the events that night, a carefully drafted formal statement—essentially an affidavit—that he wrote sometime around 1890.[28] By that time the rising young lawyer of 1863 had become Judge Wills, an elder in his church, a civic leader, and a leading business-man. His association with the cemetery and Lincoln's speech had no doubt helped in his ascent, just as the tourists and publicity generated by the bat-tle and the cemetery had greatly benefited the town. But in the mid-1880s Wills was dismayed by press reports, probably based on Usher's 1882 lec-ture and the 1885 version of Arnold's history, that Lincoln's speech had been written on the train and not in Gettysburg at all. In September 1885, Wills wrote to Richard Watson Gilder, editor of *Century Magazine,* saying, "I have several times seen the statement in print that Mr. Lincoln wrote his Gettysburg speech in the cars on the way from Washington to Gettys-burg." Wills affirmed bluntly that "this is not the fact" and offered to write an article demonstrating instead that Lincoln began the speech "here in my house." "He conferred with me all about it," Wills wrote. "I know all about its preparation and all he said to me about it."

A strong promoter of Lincoln's legacy, Richard Watson Gilder was an influential figure on the Gilded Age cultural scene—one of his biographers has called it the "Gilder Age"—and at that time he was just about to print a series of articles by Nicolay and Hay that would become part of their massive *History of Abraham Lincoln* (1890). Perhaps to avoid crossing Nicolay, who was notoriously jealous of his role as the guardian of Lin-coln's memory, Gilder consulted him about Wills's proposal. It is a measure of Nicolay's cramped personality that he discouraged the project, empha-sizing that only he and Hay had access to Lincoln's papers, which alone could tell the entire story. "Mr. Wills is therefore not familiar with *all* the facts," Nicolay cautioned, but rather "only *what he recollects* that Mr. Lin-coln said to him. . . . It will probably add nothing very material." Gilder did not pursue Wills's offer.[29]

Denied a public outlet for his recollections, Judge Wills nonetheless typed up a statement in multiple copies, signing many of them to attest to their authenticity. The judge knew that his recollections conflicted with published accounts by Lincoln's secretary of the interior and others, so he described only what he saw and experienced in regard to how Lincoln worked on his speech on the night of the eighteenth. "After spending part of the evening in the parlors he [Lincoln] retired to his room. He had his colored servant, William, with him," was all Wills wrote of the early evening, with no mention of the reception in his home, the serenade, or virtually any of the other events connected with Lincoln's visit that he witnessed.

It was probably fairly soon after going upstairs that Lincoln set about looking over or working on his speech, but the timing suggests he had hardly begun when he decided that he wanted to know more about the events next day, just as he had the night before during his conversation with William Saunders. It was, then, "between nine and ten o'clock," as Wills recalled in his formal statement, but it might actually have been a bit later, when Lincoln "sent his servant to request me to come to his room." Wills had anticipated and planned for greeting Lincoln at the station, providing a supper, and introducing him to the company at the house, but he could not have predicted that William Johnson would call him upstairs to a private audience with the president. It must have been a surprising and memorable moment, the first of several remarkable episodes across the later evening, a moment that, among all the myths and memories and all the eyewitness accounts and fabrications, gives us our most detailed and intimate description of Lincoln writing what will become the Gettysburg Address, and some of our best evidence for the text that Lincoln took to the speakers' stand.

Let us follow David Wills as he ascends the curved central stairway from its elegant arched entry to the second-floor landing, turns to his left, and approaches a room he knew well, a room in his own home. By the door a soldier stands guard—his name is Hugh Pacton Bigham—and inside waits the president of the United States, commander in chief of the armies of the Union, and, at that moment, a guest in the home of a small-town lawyer. The room Lincoln was using was slightly rectangular, about 20 feet by 16 feet, at the southwest corner of the house. One of the shorter walls had two windows that looked over the Diamond (the main square in Gettysburg), and the interior longer wall had a fireplace with, no doubt, a strong blaze going that crisp night. Much of the room was taken up by a high double bed with a tall, elaborately carved headboard and large posts at the foot. Beautifully embroidered towels graced the washstand. It appears to have been similar to rooms in any comfortable midcentury home. Future generations would treat it as a shrine in the cult of a man to whom, alone of all Americans, they would dedicate a temple.[30]

David Wills had worked tirelessly for nearly four months, caring first for the wounded, then for the dead, and now for the memory of the dead, creating first a cemetery, and now a ceremony, that would become a touchstone of American memory and nationhood for generations. Young Wills was an able lawyer, a successful businessman, a skilled organizer, and by all accounts a fine son, loving husband, and caring father, but it must be said that he was born under a lucky star—or at least he made an astonishing fate, which is much the same. Cemetery, ceremony, and speech, he helped make them all. Without him, there is no Gettysburg Address, words that can be said of no other man, save one. That man now sits before the thirty-four-year-old David Wills, at a common table he has used many times himself, with paper before him and a question on his mind.

"I went and found him with paper prepared to write," Wills recalled in his formal statement, or, in another version of his story, "I went and found him writing."[31] Decades later the story would circulate that Wills gave Lincoln the paper he used, but Wills never said so.[32] "He said that he had just seated himself to put upon paper a few thoughts for the to-morrow's exercises, and had sent for me to ascertain what part he was to take in them, and what was expected of him. After a full talk on the subject I left him." Whatever Wills saw and heard convinced him that Lincoln had not yet put pen or pencil to paper in earnest. Young David Wills would have been paying intense attention to his president, and he could not know what was wanted. He stood before the president in a state of anticipation and, one can only imagine, at least modest anxiety, a state conducive to perception and flashbulb intensity of memory, and David Wills saw Lincoln with paper.

If we can know what paper that was, the question of the delivery text of the Gettysburg Address is solved and we can know which manuscript Lincoln held when he rededicated the nation to a "new birth of freedom." It is astonishing but true that for more than 100 years David Wills has held the secret of the delivery text of the Gettysburg Address and has told us from the first what document Lincoln brought with him from Washington. And no one has listened. To Judge Wills in the late 1880s, the paper was the key to proving that Lincoln had not written his speech on the train, as was being reported. The paper was Lincoln's speech, and Wills adamantly affirmed and vehemently stated as forcefully as he knew how—within the bounds of judicial decorum—that the paper he saw Lincoln with that night was the same paper he saw Lincoln read from the next day. Six times in eleven sentences the good judge swore to that fact, signing the document for good measure: the paper Wills saw that night was the "immortal" Gettysburg Address.

And yet, maddeningly, in his 1890 statement Wills did not describe the paper or whether Lincoln was writing in pen or pencil. Fortunately, the 1875 note in the *Nation* by Edward McPherson, based on information provided by Wills, gives a very precise description. McPherson could only have heard this information from Wills, either orally or from an early and now lost version of Wills's own written statement. "Sending for his host," McPherson wrote, "he enquired the order of the exercises of the next day," a phrase that is found in many of the versions of the story that originated with Wills. Next, McPherson in 1875 explained that Lincoln then "began to put in writing what he called some 'stray thoughts' to utter on the morrow." This, again, is Wills's formulation and cadence in 1890: "he said he had just seated himself to put upon paper a few thoughts for the to-morrow's exercises." It is this paper that Wills in 1890 was so certain he saw Lincoln reading from the next day on the speakers' stand. The 1875 account by McPherson then added the final piece of the puzzle: "When delivered, they were read from an official letter-sheet."

"An official letter-sheet." Wills affirmed that he saw Lincoln writing that night on the "same paper" that he read from on the stand, which McPherson, following Wills, clearly stated could only have been the Letterhead Page of the Washington Draft. McPherson's 1875 summary of what Wills told him tracks the 1890 formal statement by Wills so precisely that the 1875 version can be considered to be as authoritative as Wills's signed declaration. Possibly, Wills used McPherson's 1875 statement as a basis for his own later version, but the information first had to have originated with Wills and Wills only. In 1879, McPherson would state instead that Lincoln read from the common foolscap paper of the time, further demonstrating that the description of "official letter-sheet" in his 1875 account derives from Wills; it is not McPherson's own recollection.[33] So close is the correspondence in language and structure between the 1890 and 1875 texts that of at least nine major points of similarity, indicated here in brackets, only one (point 6), differs in the order of placement:

WILLS (1890): After spending part of the [1] evening in the parlors he [2] retired to his room. He had his colored servant, William, with him. Between nine and ten o'clock the President [3] sent his servant to request me to come to his room. I went and found him with paper [4] prepared to write, and he said that he had just seated himself to put upon paper a [5] few thoughts for the [6] to-morrow's exercises, and had sent for me to ascertain what part he was to take in them, and what was expected of him. After a full talk on the subject I left him. . . . The next day I sat by him on the platform [7] when he delivered his address, which has become immortal, and he [8] read it from the same paper on which I had seen him writing it the night before. He afterward made a [9] copy of it of which I have a facsimile and have had a photograph of it taken. There are but two or three changes in this copy from that as taken by the stenographers on the day it was read from the platform.

MCPHERSON (1875): He was called out in the [1] evening to reply to a serenade, and at a late hour [2] went to his room. [3] Sending for his host, he enquired the order of [6] the exercises of the next day, and began to [4] put in writing what he called some [5] "stray thoughts" to utter on the morrow. [7] When delivered, they were [8] read from an official letter-sheet. It is uncertain whether *this* manuscript has been preserved. But when Mr. Lincoln was asked, in April, 1864, to send to the Baltimore (Md) Fair for the relief of soldiers and sailors an autograph manuscript, he sent a [9] copy of his Gettysburg Address.

The 1875 version is the first appearance of letterhead paper in any record, published or not; it is not a garbled memory of some news report or an artifact of repeated iterations, as is the case with the train composition "evidence." Indeed, 1875 was the first time there was any public discussion of the various manuscripts of Lincoln's speech, prompted by the inclusion of lines from the Gettysburg Address in the fifth edition of John Bartlett's *Familiar Quotations* that year.[34] Confirming this mention of letterhead paper, in 1882 one "Medicus" wrote in the *New York Tribune* that as a member of the chorus that sang just before the speech, he saw Lincoln read from official paper, "the printed or engraved heading, in German text, 'Executive Mansion,' and blank space for date, being distinctly observed." This report gains credibility when "Medicus" is found to be Dr. Daniel Denison Slade, a medical doctor and at that time a professor of zoology at Harvard who wrote popular traveling tales under that name. In 1863 he was a member of the U.S. Sanitary Commission stationed in Baltimore, the

city of origin of the National Union Musical Association that sang just before Lincoln spoke.[35]

Once the 1875 account by McPherson is accepted as originating in
David Wills's recollections, the delivery text problem of the Gettysburg Address is solved, even leaving aside John Nicolay's supporting eyewitness
testimony of 1885 and 1894. That is, the so-called Nicolay version of Lincoln's speech, the only one that includes letterhead paper, has to be recognized as the text Lincoln held on the stand.

However, one problem must be resolved before McPherson's description
of "official letter-sheet" can be conclusively ascribed to Wills. Why did
Wills in 1890 not describe the paper as McPherson did in 1875? Indeed,
why did Wills in 1890 provide no description whatsoever of the "immortal" document he saw Lincoln writing? The answer turns out to be rooted
in the problem of conflicting memories and intersecting friendships. Wills
did not want to be seen as contradicting accounts mentioning different paper that had by the late 1880s been published by two other witnesses: not
only by Wills's political patron and the respected war governor of Pennsylvania, Andrew Curtin, but also by Wills's friend and the former representative in the U.S. House from Gettysburg during the war, none other than
Edward McPherson himself. But proving this requires following Lincoln
and Wills and Curtin as they moved through the rest of the evening in Gettysburg and seeing their experiences the only way we can, given the sources
available: through the lens of myth and memory.

As Wills told it in his formal statement, Lincoln had summoned him to
his room that evening to discuss "what part he was to take" in the exercises the next day, "and what was expected of him." The November 2 letter of invitation had, of course, asked Lincoln "to be present, and
participate in these Ceremonies" and to "formally set apart these grounds
to their Sacred use by a few appropriate remarks," and now Lincoln, after
talking with Lamon several times, with Governor Curtin on the fourteenth,
and with William Saunders just the night before, had an opportunity to
hear directly from Wills about the ceremony and his own "part."

Here we encounter more reticence from Wills, however, for he never described in writing what he told Lincoln in their "full talk on the subject."
McPherson's 1875 version, like Wills's own 1890 text, stated only that Lincoln asked about his part in the "exercises," which suggests that Lincoln
was mainly concerned with what was expected of him that day, from the

procession in the morning to the final benediction. Yet Wills in his 1885 letter to Gilder added that he knew "all about" Lincoln's speech and "all he said to me about it," which suggests that they also discussed Lincoln's "few appropriate remarks" while reviewing "the to-morrow's exercises."

Over the years very few details surfaced about Lincoln's conversation with Wills that night, but one important and overlooked source provides crucial details.[36] In 1881 Robert S. Chilton Sr., a minor State Department official and longtime U.S. consul in Canada, described "a visit in 1868 to the famous battle-field" when David Wills told him that "in the morning after the President's arrival he rapped at his door to ascertain if he had slept comfortably, &c., and found him partially dressed and seated at a small table with a half-sheet of paper before him, upon which he had been writing in pencil."[37] Thirteen years had introduced errors into Chilton's memory, but if this scene is transposed to the night of the eighteenth, it corresponds closely to Wills's later signed statement—aside from Lincoln being "partially dressed," of course, though it would not be surprising if Lincoln had been casually attired, for Hay and others later told many stories of Lincoln padding about the White House and discussing official business in his nightshirt and slippers.

A full comparison of Chilton's statement of 1881 with those by McPherson in 1875 and Wills in 1890 reveals so many correspondences in structure, content, and vocabulary that it seems clear that Chilton had read or heard from Wills an earlier version of Wills's statement, which also must have been used by McPherson in 1875. It is otherwise difficult to explain how all three would mention, for example, that Lincoln later rewrote his speech as a donation to a charity fair in Baltimore, or how a relatively unusual word like "ascertain" could be found in both Chilton in 1881 and Wills in 1890 (it is not in McPherson's published 1875 version, so Chilton could not have found it there).[38] Lincoln's being "seated at a small table" as described by Chilton would, then, correspond to Wills's 1890 statement that Lincoln said he had "just seated himself," and the "half-sheet of paper" upon which Lincoln was writing in pencil according to what Wills told Chilton in 1868 might be the "official letter-sheet" in McPherson's 1875 version of Wills's story.

But Chilton has even more surprises. Lincoln said to Wills, as directly quoted in Chilton's account, "Come in and take a seat. I want to read to you what I have been scribbling for a speech to-day, and to get your opinion of it. It isn't long." Lincoln then "read to Mr. Wills that speech exactly as he delivered it in public a few hours later." Wills himself never mentioned that Lincoln read to him, but Chilton's story does correspond to Wills's vehement affirmation that the paper (that is, the physical embodiment of "the speech") on which Lincoln was writing was the same as that of "the speech" he gave at the ceremony.

Chilton's story, including the detail of Lincoln's talking about "what I have been scribbling for a speech to-day," is undoubtedly an imperfect memory of an authentic conversation with Wills. This is reminiscent of McPherson's 1875 text quoting Lincoln describing his speech as "stray thoughts," which Wills himself sanitized into a "few thoughts" in his 1890 version. The persistent theme of Lincoln's denigrating his speech—or at least the composition process—was of course reflected in his story to James Speed and in Noah Brooks's statement that Lincoln "did not appear to think very highly of his own speech," and for that matter, also in Lincoln's own reference to "the little I did say" in his letter of November 20, 1863, to Edward Everett. Ward Lamon, of course, was most closely associated with the idea that Lincoln thought his speech was not good enough, as when he depicted Lincoln as saying it "won't scour," but finding that theme here in Chilton's note of 1881, when the speech was rapidly rising to iconic status, is counterintuitive, adding to the impression that this same theme was indeed founded in something that Lincoln said to Wills.

Potentially the most important element in Chilton's statement is that Wills told him Lincoln "had been writing in pencil." This is the first mention anywhere that any fragment or copy of the Gettysburg Address was written in pencil (the next mention of a pencil comes from Usher's lecture of 1882 that depicted Lincoln using one on the train). This means that, just as for the "official letter-sheet" paper mentioned by McPherson in 1875, Chilton's description of Lincoln writing in pencil cannot be explained away as a false memory of garbled newspaper accounts or an artifact of repeated iteration. Chilton may be incorrect (as he was about several details), but he was reporting his own memory of what he recalled Wills having told him.

The only use of pencil in any of the five known versions of the address written by Lincoln is in the Nicolay text, which, it is argued here, Lincoln created in Gettysburg on the basis of the all-ink Washington Draft he brought with him on the train. Chilton's recollection that in 1868 Wills told him Lincoln was "writing in pencil" strongly supports the contention that it was indeed the Washington Draft as described here that Lincoln was working on when Wills spoke with him, in the process of eventually creating the document that would later be called the Nicolay text that Lincoln read from on the battlefield.

In addition to the crucial information from Chilton and McPherson about the paper and pencil used that night, the dominant note in the reports originating with David Wills is that after calling Wills to him, Lincoln quite purposefully and deliberately asked about the ceremonies and expectations for his role at a time when he was also reviewing or revising his speech. Reading backward into the analogous situation the night before in Washington, this suggests that Lincoln was indeed intending to work on his remarks after speaking with William Saunders. And still, in addition to all the other information he had on the night before the ceremony, Lincoln wanted more precise and authoritative information from the chief organizer of the entire event. This was prudent, but it also hints of some insecurity or doubt and suggests that Lincoln was particularly anxious or concerned "to be prepared to say some appropriate thing," as Speed put it in 1879, or as put more strongly by Ward Lamon in 1895, that Lincoln "greatly feared he would not be able to acquit himself with credit, much less to fill the measure of public expectation."

After Lincoln had heard what Wills had to say about the "exercises" and his part in them, Wills left him and returned to a house that was still alive with activity. Visitors like MacVeagh wandered in and out, the boisterous crowds outside gave the night an air of unsettled excitement, and the arrival of the much-delayed Governor's Special train from Harrisburg was expected at any moment. This would have created a sense of anticipation in the Wills home of further arrivals, because Wills was planning for Governor Curtin to stay at his house. By this time it must have been getting on to 10:15 p.m. or even later, and between the train journey and the festivities in the town, Lincoln had been in the public eye for twelve hours almost without respite. It is perhaps this moment, just after the departure of Wills and against a background of a house full of people, that is captured in Lincoln's comment to James Speed that after being "put in an upper room in a house," Lincoln "asked to be left alone for a time."

There was still a great deal for David Wills to do, even after the president had retired. Then, at around eleven o'clock, perhaps an hour after Lincoln had gone upstairs, the Governor's Special finally arrived, and Curtin, along with probably a dozen or more others, many of them also governors, came to the house. But just then, amid the confusion and greetings this must have entailed, William Johnson again unexpectedly appeared before Wills (or rather, it was most probably Johnson; Wills wrote only that Lincoln "sent for me again"). This night of greetings and speeches now took yet another turn. Abraham Lincoln wanted to go see his secretary of state, and he wanted to talk about his speech.

1. Lincoln in his White House office, the "Backwoods Jupiter," as John Hay once described him, standing at the center of the Civil War. He later told his friend James Speed that after receiving the invitation to Gettysburg, he was "uncertain whether his duties would not detain him at Washington—but was anxious to go—and desired to be prepared to say some appropriate thing." (Keya Morgan Collection, LincolnImages.com)

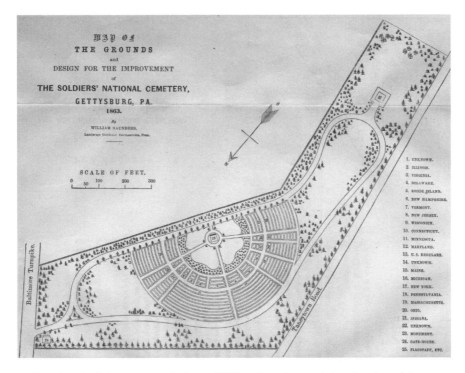

MAP OF
THE GROUNDS
and
DESIGN FOR THE IMPROVEMENT
of
THE SOLDIERS' NATIONAL CEMETERY,
GETTYSBURG, PA.
1863.
By
WILLIAM SAUNDERS,
Landscape Gardener Germantown, Penn.

SCALE OF FEET.
0   50   100   200   300

1. UNKNOWN.
2. ILLINOIS.
3. VIRGINIA.
4. DELAWARE.
5. RHODE ISLAND.
6. NEW HAMPSHIRE.
7. VERMONT.
8. NEW JERSEY.
9. WISCONSIN.
10. CONNECTICUT.
11. MINNESOTA.
12. MARYLAND.
13. U. S. REGULARS.
14. UNKNOWN.
15. MAINE.
16. MICHIGAN.
17. NEW YORK.
18. PENNSYLVANIA.
19. MASSACHUSETTS.
20. OHIO.
21. INDIANA.
22. UNKNOWN.
23. MONUMENT.
24. GATE-HOUSE.
25. FLAGSTAFF, ETC.

Baltimore Turnpike.

Taneytown Road.

2. Lincoln asked the cemetery designer, William Saunders, to bring the plan of the cemetery to the White House on November 17, 1863, the night before he left for Gettysburg. It was probably just after their close examination on Lincoln's office table of the large, beautifully colored plan and their discussion of the ideals behind the cemetery that Lincoln completed the speech that he took with him on the train the next day, the Washington Draft of the Gettysburg Address. (*Report of the Select Committee*)

Executive Mansion,

Washington,   , 186 .

Four score and seven years ago our fathers brought forth, upon this continent, a new nation, conceived in liberty, and dedicated to the proposition that "all men are created equal"

Now we are engaged in a great civil war, testing whether that nation, or any nation so conceived, and so dedicated, can long endure. We are met on a great battle field of that war. We have come to dedicate a portion of it, as a final rest-ing place for those who died here, that the nation might live. This we may, in all propriety do. But, in a larger sense, we can not dedicate—we can not consecrate—we can not hallow, this ground— The brave men, living and dead, who struggled here, have hallowed it, far above our poor power to add or detract. The world will little note, nor long remember what we say here; while it can never forget what they did here.

It is rather for us, the living, to stand here,

3. The Letterhead Page, written in Washington, D.C., probably the night of November 17, as the first page of the Washington Draft of Lincoln's speech. This page and its revisions in Gettysburg, including the phrase underlined in pencil evoking "what they did here," encodes the evidence for Lincoln's emotional and intellectual journey to the "new birth of freedom." (Library of Congress)

4. This photograph from about 1890 shows David Wills and the Wills family home, where Lincoln stayed in Gettysburg. After arriving on November 18, Lincoln had dinner and then spoke briefly to a celebratory crowd from the front door steps. He then worked on his speech for about an hour in his room (whose two windows are visible on the right above the side door), but then at about eleven o'clock he made an unanticipated visit to the house shown here immediately to the right of the Wills home to show his speech to Secretary of State Seward. Back at the Wills house by about midnight, Lincoln finished what he thought would be the speech he would give the next day. (Adams County Historical Society)

5. The Pencil Page, the second page of the Battlefield Draft that Lincoln held while speaking. After visiting the battlefield on the morning of November 19, Lincoln unexpectedly revised what must have been a completed speech by editing the Letterhead Page in pencil and adding this new second page, "but concluded it so shortly before it was to be delivered," he told James Speed, that "he had not time to memorize it." This is the first known appearance of the phrase "a new birth of freedom." (Library of Congress)

6. With the Battlefield Draft folded in his pocket, Lincoln and the other dignitaries rode on horseback in the procession to the cemetery just behind the military honor guard, shown in this photograph by the Tyson brothers, as it came south down Baltimore Turnpike from the main square. Just beyond the waiting crowd the procession turned slightly to its right to eventually enter the cemetery from the west. "The mighty mass rolled on as the waves of the mighty ocean," wrote one observer. (Library of Congress)

7. Taken on the day of the ceremony, according to photographer Peter Weaver, this photograph shows the speakers' stand just to the right of the flagpole and slightly over the crest of the hill. From this perspective, Lincoln and the procession would enter the scene from the left along the sunken Taneytown Road and then turn southeast up the central axis of the cemetery between the newly dug graves, visible here as arcs across the hillside. (Hanover Area Historical Society)

8. Alexander Gardner aligned this photograph on the gatehouse of the town cemetery and almost perpendicular to the front of the speakers' platform, with Edward Everett's tent behind. From this vantage point, the speakers would be facing away and to the left, addressing the main body of the crowd around and beyond the flagpole. Although the ceremony had been under way some time when this photograph was taken, the soldiers in the foreground still outline the space reserved for the participants in the procession. It has been claimed that Lincoln can be seen here mounted on horseback in the middle distance, but he is instead on the platform, hidden from view. (Library of Congress)

DEDICATION CEREMONY

9. This magnificent panorama by Joseph Becker shows the view from farther away but similar to that in photograph 10. It depicts the dignitaries taking their places on the platform while the rest of the parade participants enter the reserved area from the far side and pass in front of the podium. In the foreground on the Baltimore Turnpike are tables with refreshments and battlefield souvenirs for sale; the graves can be seen in the middle distance at the far right. (*Frank Leslie's Illustrated Newspaper*, December 5, 1863)

10. This photograph by Peter Weaver was taken on November 19 looking southwest from the second-floor window of the cemetery gatehouse visible in photograph 8. The flag is barely visible near the center of the image; the elevated speakers' stand, filled with journalists and participants, is to the left. On the far right in the distance can be seen the mounded graves with their temporary markers; beyond them and across Taneytown Road lies the vantage point of photograph 7. (Library of Congress)

11. This image, probably by David Bachrach, was taken directly in front of the speakers' stand and perpendicular to the opposing views in photographs 8 and 10. Like Becker's panorama, which was probably made in part on the basis of this image, it shows the dignitaries settling themselves on the platform and waiting for the remainder of the procession to enter the reserved area. (Library of Congress)

12. This detail from photograph 11 shows David Wills in his marshal's sash standing behind the seated and hatless Lincoln; Ward Lamon is still astride his horse in front of the podium. On the right, Andrew Curtin sits next to his son among the governors, and Seward, wearing the "essentially bad hat" mentioned by a journalist, is next to Lincoln. The figure looking sideways at Lincoln may be William Saunders, with Hay and Nicolay between them. Everett has not emerged from his tent. This photograph is direct testimony of the moment that created the authentic legend of the Gettysburg Address. "The tall form of the President appeared on the stand," wrote one observer at the time, "and never before have I seen a crowd so vast and restless, after standing so long, so soon stilled and quieted." (Library of Congress)

Dedicatory address of
President Lincoln

Four score and seven years ago our fathers
brought forth upon this continent a new nation,
conceived in Liberty, and dedicated to the proposition that all men are created equal.

Now we are engaged in a great civil war,
testing whether that nation or any nation
~~or any nation~~ so conceived, and so dedicated,
can long endure. We are met on a great
battlefield of that war. We are met to
dedicate a portion of it, as the final resting
place of those who here gave their lives that
that nation might live. It is altogether
fitting and proper that we should do this.

But in a larger sense we cannot dedicate,
we cannot consecrate, we cannot hallow
this ground. The brave men living and
dead, who struggled here have consecrated it
far above our power to add, or detract.
The world will little note, ~~nor~~ long remember
what we say here, but it can never forget
what they ~~have~~ did here. It is for us, the
living, rather to be dedicated here to the unfinished
work that they have thus far so nobly carried
on. It is rather for us to be here dedicated to
the great task remaining before us. that from
these honored dead we take increased devotion
to the cause for which they here gave the last

---

13. The first page of Lincoln's speech as copied and edited from the *New York Tribune*
by David Wills, which Wills and Everett then printed as the official version of Lincoln's
speech in January 1864. Lincoln used this edited, printed version as the basis for his
own later revision of his speech, during which he wrote what are today called the Hay
and Everett texts. As part of this process, Lincoln incorporated several of the
alterations by Wills and Everett into his final handwritten version of the Gettysburg
Address. (Everett Papers, Massachusetts State Historical Society)

full measure of devotion; that we here highly resolve that the dead shall not have died in vain; that the nation shall, under God, have a new birth of freedom: and that the government of the people, by the people, and for the people, shall not perish from the earth.

(18)

14. Page 2 of the handwritten copy by David Wills, crucial evidence that after a century and a half helps resolve the mysteries of the Gettysburg Address manuscripts. (Everett Papers, Massachusetts State Historical Society)

■

FIVE

The Gettysburg Draft

REBEL GRAVES

Nothing had gone right with Governor Andrew Curtin's rail journey down to Gettysburg. He and the other governors spent the better part of November 18 on a train bedeviled by a balky locomotive, but posterity is the richer for their tedious journey, for, unlike Lincoln's train, the Governors' Special was crawling with reporters who accumulated many colorful anecdotes. No one had thought to bring extensive provisions along for what was supposed to be a four-hour trip, so as the train limped into one town, there was a famished rush to inhale the meager provisions of apples, figs, and candy available at the station. Only Governor William Dennison of Ohio was reported to have "exhibited his gallantry by carrying an armful of stale ginger-cakes to the ladies car."[1]

Perhaps hunger and frustration began to tell, for one reporter noted that Governor Horatio Seymour of New York, a Democrat, could not help asking governor-elect John Brough of Ohio about the fate of former U.S. Representative Clement Vallandigham, who had been arrested and sent into exile in the Confederacy for undermining the draft. Outraged Democrats around the nation had denounced "King Abraham" and in Ohio had put Vallandigham up for governor, but Brough had won relatively easily, particularly after a Confederate raid by John Hunt Morgan had stirred up a Unionist backlash, in the same way that Lee's invasion of Pennsylvania had helped reelect Curtin. "Where is Vallandigham?" Seymour had asked "with dry pleasantry," according to the report. "'In Canada,' said Brough, laconically." Such awkward scenes were perhaps inevitable on a train overflowing with nearly a dozen governors; but among all that illustrious company, Andrew Curtin, "straight, tall, clear-faced," was picked out by one reporter as "the handsomest in the party."[2]

The trip had stretched to nine hours by the time the governors arrived in Gettysburg at around eleven o'clock in the evening, so Curtin and the others missed dinner at the Wills house and the speeches at the serenades. Curtin had brought his wife and young son to the ceremony, but the exigencies of finding lodging, even for the governor of the state, apparently required breaking up the family for the night. So crowded had the Wills house become that "at first it was proposed to put the Governor into my bed with me," Everett wrote in alarm, but with evident relief he added that Curtin "kindly went out and found a lodging elsewhere." At least Everett escaped the fate of his daughter Charlotte: the bed she and two other women were bundled into broke under the weight. "She betook herself to the floor," Everett added dryly.[3]

Before leaving the overstuffed Wills house to seek lodging elsewhere, Curtin went up to pay his respects to Lincoln, or perhaps to talk more patronage with him. In either case, the visit earned him perhaps his most enduring claim to memory, for it was then that he witnessed Lincoln writing what became the Gettysburg Address. How fitting that he should have such a moment, for it was in part his questionable reelection prospects—and a sincere desire to care for the dead—that had compelled him to appoint David Wills to do something about the crisis of death after the battle, and it was Curtin who had (it appears) approved inviting Lincoln to speak, and again, it was Curtin who had (most probably) provided the final push on November 14 that induced Lincoln to decide that he could make the journey. Curtin's information about what he saw that evening first surfaced in the summer of 1885, when an important reunion of veterans and officers from the Army of the Potomac brought him to revisit the town and tour the battlefield, which by then was already decorated with monuments. Probably at that time he also saw Wills, who was an investor in the town's developing tourist facilities and had helped arrange the event. Later that fall, Wills in his letter offering to write an article for *Century Magazine* even mentioned that Curtin could verify his account, writing, "Ex-Gov. Curtin knows the speech was written at my house as he was here at the time." Unlike Wills, however, Curtin was not at all sure that Lincoln had first started to write his speech in Gettysburg. "I saw Mr. Lincoln writing his address in Mr. (now Judge) Willis's [sic] house," Curtin confirmed to a newspaper columnist in 1888, but he then added, "He may have written some of it before."[4]

Having spoken with Wills at around ten or a quarter after, Lincoln had been upstairs about an hour or so when Curtin came to his room. During that time Lincoln clearly intended to complete or review his "few appropriate remarks" for the next day, but he could not escape other concerns of the presidency. General Ulysses Grant was expected to move into Georgia at any moment, and an attack on General Ambrose Burnside in Tennessee was much anticipated, so over the course of Lincoln's visit, Secretary of War Stanton sent the president at least four messages with news of military developments. But Lincoln was also anxious to hear about his son, or at least Stanton had reason to think so, for he specifically asked Mary Lincoln about the boy, an uncharacteristic hint of human sentiment in the formidable secretary of war and a sign that Lincoln had personally asked Stanton to send him news of Tad's condition. "Nothing from Chattanooga or any other place since your departure," Stanton telegraphed in what seems to have been his first message of the day to Lincoln. "By enquiry Mrs Lincoln informs me that your son is better this evening."[5]

It was probably a telegram from Mary herself that brought into the story of the Gettysburg Address another witness who provides a glimpse into Lincoln's revisions that night. As Curtin went into Lincoln's room, he probably passed a twenty-two-year-old sergeant posted there—indeed, it is possible that Wills knew him—named Hugh Pacton Bigham. A young man from the country who had been a store clerk before taking up arms, Bigham prospered in later years, opening his own store by 1870, eventually even serving alongside Wills as a director of the Gettysburg National Bank in the early 1890s. Indeed, all the guards at the Wills house were from Company B of the Twenty-First Pennsylvania Cavalry, recruited locally for a six-month term to confront Lee's invasion. Sergeant Bigham's younger brother was posted outside the front door. One of the soldiers of Company B recalled that the company had been specially chosen to guard Lincoln because the unit was "a particular friend of Gov. Curtin." Hugh Bigham himself later wrote, "I was asked to stand guard at the door of Mr. Lincoln's room and I was very glad of the honor."[6]

One can well imagine the intense interest with which young Bigham followed the president's every move and the watchful eye he kept on the door of his commander in chief. While he was guarding Lincoln's room, Bigham recalled, "A telegram was received and I handed it in. He thanked me and in a few minutes opened the door and said, 'This telegram was from home. My little boy has been very sick, but he is better.'" Lincoln must have been very concerned indeed to have felt compelled to share his relief with a stranger, and the story underscores again the importance Lincoln attached to the Gettysburg ceremony in the face of such anxiety. Probably the telegram that inspired Lincoln's comment to Bigham was one sent by Mary Lincoln that read, "The Dr. has just left. We hope dear Taddie is slightly better. Will send you a telegram in the morning. Mrs. Lincoln."[7] It was sent from the War Department (the Executive Mansion had no telegraph) at 9:40 p.m. and could not have reached Lincoln much before 10:30 p.m. at the earliest.

It appears that when Governor Curtin went to Lincoln's room, Lincoln was reaching a stopping point in his work on his speech and was preparing to go next door and discuss it with Seward. Possibly, however, Curtin's visit in some way triggered Lincoln's decision to see Seward, but in any case this circumstance created a confluence of memories, as Bigham, Curtin, and Wills all became involved in the visit to the Harper house. Yet none of the three mentioned the presence of the others in this episode, an illustration of the tunnel-vision effect of memory over time. Bigham, Curtin, and Wills each recollects himself as being essentially alone with Lincoln, intimately interacting with a figure who was already taking on near-mythic qualities. It was a notable moment for each of them and became more so in hindsight, but it is also important in the story of the Gettysburg Address, for Lincoln's visit to Seward the night before his speech not only allows important insights into the state of Lincoln's text that night, but it also helps explain why Wills did not mention in 1890 the "official letter-sheet" paper as McPherson had done in 1875.

In contrast to Wills's reticence, Curtin's story of the night devoted a great deal of attention to the paper he recalled Lincoln using. A letter Curtin wrote to Nicolay in 1892 describing the scene stated that Lincoln "had a very large yellow envelope on which he was writing," and in the 1888 interview Curtin said that when he got to Lincoln's room, Lincoln was writing on "a long yellow envelope."[8] These accounts are the first appearances of the famous "yellow envelope," which in later legend haunted the Gettysburg story, particularly after a garbled version of Curtin's yellow envelope story entered the schoolbooks. Usher in 1882 had mentioned only "pasteboard" on the train, but over the years a very few others also mentioned envelopes. Perhaps the most important sighting was by Noah Brooks, who wrote in 1895 that he saw Lincoln in Washington with an envelope containing Everett's oration.[9] Eighty years after the event, it was said that U.S. Representative James Ashley saw Lincoln on the train using his top hat for a desk in order to write upon a yellow envelope. One version of this highly problematic story even stated that Lincoln had Everett's oration with him.[10]

Putting these sightings together can suggest that Lincoln perhaps carried his speech or Everett's oration or both in an envelope, particularly as two of the very few pieces of evidence mentioning the envelope also bring together both Lincoln's speech and Everett's oration. The evidence is so fragmentary that firm conclusions are difficult and perhaps are not necessary in this case. Curtin's point was that Lincoln was working on his speech when he saw him that night, and that fact is not in question. Hypothetically, the existence of the envelope would support Brooks's story of Lincoln having Everett's oration; it also might suggest that Lincoln was composing his speech in Washington and preparing his journey to Gettysburg in a methodical manner by organizing his materials in an envelope, for example. Certainly, Lincoln would not have been averse to writing on an envelope if that was what was at hand at the moment; even in the White House, Lincoln wrote notes and thoughts on the back of unrelated documents and seemingly stray scraps of paper. Still, given the lack of solid evidence, nothing certain can be known about the envelope; it informs us less about the history of the address than about its mysteries.

Paradoxically, in the mature legend of the Gettysburg Address, the envelope functioned to reinforce the message that Lincoln's speech was a spontaneous work of solitary genius, written on the fly with no preparation, even though the existence of the envelope might be a sign of forethought. Yet this image in legend is not wholly inaccurate. Lincoln's preparation in Washington cannot be doubted, but the state of the text that Lincoln took to the stand on the day of the ceremony does suggest a measure of makedo, an impression reinforced by events across the evening of the eighteenth and the morning of the nineteenth. As the story of the Washington Draft has demonstrated, it is crucial to distinguish between the pressed but relatively controlled composition process in Washington, punctuated by planned events such as cabinet meetings and appointments to talk with such central figures as the cemetery designer, and the more eventful, more improvised writing activity in Gettysburg. The yellow envelope may or may not be an artifact of Curtin's memory, but whether it was real or a figment would not alter what is known, or what became a matter of belief, about Lincoln's speech.

After stating that Lincoln was writing on the envelope, Curtin's 1892 letter explained that Lincoln "took the envelope from the table" and said "he would go around and show it to Seward." It was perhaps at about this point that Wills reentered the scene. "About eleven o'clock he sent for me again," Wills wrote, making it around the time when Curtin arrived in the house. Three sentences before, Wills had similarly written, "The President sent his servant" to him for the first time, so it was probably William Johnson who again brought Wills back to Lincoln's room. This would mean that Johnson was close by during the time Lincoln was upstairs, undoubtedly taking care of the many details involved in an overnight presidential visit, moving in and out of the room, perhaps, attending to whatever was needed. He had acquitted himself well enough in Springfield to be one of the few people Lincoln brought with him to Washington, where he often served as Lincoln's barber. Johnson had gone with Lincoln to Antietam, and now here he was at Gettysburg, where he almost certainly was one of the very few who witnessed Lincoln working on the speech that would proclaim a "new birth of freedom."[11]

"When I went to his room he had the same paper in his hand," Wills recalled, "and asked me if he could see Mr. Seward. I told him Mr. Seward was staying with my neighbor next door, and I would go and bring him over. He said 'No, I'll go and see him.'" The two accounts by Wills and Curtin of the same moment clearly reveal the dilemma Wills faced when telling his story in 1890: Wills knew that when Lincoln went to the Harper house to see Seward, he took with him the "same paper" that he read on the stand the next day ("official letter-sheet," as McPherson in 1875 described it), but Curtin instead recalled that Lincoln took with him a large yellow envelope.

With his decision to go see Seward at the Harper house, Lincoln signaled that he had finished one stage in his work on the speech, ending what might be called the "evening revision," the first chapter in what turns out to be a four-part story of how Lincoln revised or completed his speech in Gettysburg that night and the next morning. Most probably this evening revision on November 18 in the upper room of the Wills house could not have lasted too much more than about an hour, from sometime just before ten until just after eleven, that is, between the time Lincoln went upstairs after speaking with MacVeagh and the time Lincoln went to visit Seward. According to the argument presented here, at the beginning of the evening revision Lincoln was working from the Washington Draft, written wholly in ink, the two leaves perhaps still joined with a fold making a "full" sheet. Its first page ended with the first line of a new paragraph that began "It is rather for us, the living, to stand here," including the final comma. The rest of the text continued after the fold onto the (perhaps still attached) second page and was probably a fairly complete or finished speech that bore structural and other similarities to the eventual speech.

After working on the speech for perhaps an hour, Lincoln reached a point that called for going to see Seward at about the same time that Curtin visited his room. This probably means that Lincoln felt he was finished or nearly so, even if some words or phrases were still problematic. Following the interpretation here of the statements by Wills and McPherson, Lincoln took with him to the Harper house the Letterhead Page. Nicolay in 1894 categorically affirmed that he saw Lincoln edit this page the next morning, which means that the text on the Letterhead Page had not yet been changed. Lincoln, then, shows no sign that night of doubting the fitness and force of the early part of his speech, from the opening chords of "Four score and seven years ago" to the tragic evocation of "what they did here." Lincoln was an amateur Shakespearean critic, a professional speaker, a sometime poet during his youth, and always a lover of language, puns, and a well-turned phrase. He must have recognized something remarkable in this page; in any case, he found nothing to alter in it that night, and rightly so, for it expressed the core vision of his life regarding the nation's founding ideals and its path of development, as well as his admiration for "those who died here, that the nation might live."

On the other hand, during this evening revision some degree of editing or new composition relating to the latter part of the Washington Draft seems certain, as that is the material that was eventually replaced by the Pencil Page. The state of the continuing text at this point is more obscure, as is the question of what this might say about Lincoln's continuing evolution across his experience of war, and his experience of Gettysburg, with all its symbolic and real implications for the fate of the nation. Ward Lamon asserted that the speech Lincoln read to him in Washington was essentially the same as what he said at Gettysburg, and Noah Brooks provided evidence that the Washington Draft included at least the concept of "government of the people." Still, it was the final part of his speech, the section in which Lincoln habitually turned to the future, that presented difficulties for him.

Possibly, and not contradicting what Nicolay later wrote, Lincoln during this time separated the two halves of the full sheet at the fold. Robert Chilton's description of Lincoln with "a half-sheet of paper before him, upon which he had been writing in pencil" could refer to an already divided Washington Draft; there was time enough to separate the pages between the moment when Lincoln went upstairs and when he called Wills to him the first time. The yellow envelope Curtin saw Lincoln take to the Harper house must remain something of a mystery. Curtin made a distinction between it and the foolscap paper he later saw, so it would appear to have been either one of the pages of the Washington Draft or an actual envelope, perhaps having contained the Washington Draft on its trip from the capital, which Lincoln also wrote upon when considering the concluding words of his remarks.

Taken together, both Chilton and Curtin present the possibility that Lincoln during the evening revision was working with several kinds of paper, which is confirmed by the eventual Nicolay text, but this would seem to complicate Wills's adamant affirmation that he saw Lincoln with "the same paper" at the end of the evening revision as he saw near the beginning (and that he saw Lincoln read from on the stand). Resolving this conundrum means asking how Wills could be so confident that each of the four times he saw the paper (early that night, just before Lincoln visited Seward, after Lincoln's return later that night, and on the stand the next day) it was the "same paper." Answering this question will also help clarify another apparent contradiction: that Wills stated that when Lincoln went upstairs he was writing his speech for the first time, and yet the existing Letterhead Page is obviously covered in writing. Judge Wills never mentioned words or writing in the context of identifying the document, which would have been obvious supporting evidence. Yet if it was merely the physical paper that distinguished what Wills saw, how could he be so sure that the paper was the same, when most pieces of paper look alike? Later that night, Curtin will see Lincoln with both a "large yellow envelope" and foolscap paper; similarly, the next day Nicolay will see Lincoln write a new page that Wills could not have seen previously. In contrast, Wills's account has Lincoln writing once, during the evening only, on paper that is easily identifiable and does not easily fit the written revisions witnessed by Curtin later that night and Nicolay the next morning—unless it was the Letter-head Page with its impressive Executive Mansion printing that Wills saw. This is the only page that Wills could have seen during each of the four sightings, the only page that was easily identifiable as unique without regard to whatever was written on it (Wills himself had almost certainly never seen a page like it), and the only page that corresponds to McPherson's 1875 summary of what Wills told him.

Furthermore, it was seemingly not only something Wills may have seen, but something he heard, that made him so certain that Lincoln was just starting his speech. "I went and found him with paper prepared to write," Wills recalled, but one could not conclude from this alone that Lincoln had not previously written any part of his speech. More conclusively, Lincoln "said that he had just seated himself to put upon paper a few thoughts for the to-morrow's exercises." This fits well with other evidence that Lincoln spoke of his remarks in a way that gave the impression that he had not prepared his speech before Gettysburg. McCormick's informant of 1865 said that Lincoln on the train "asked what he should say at the ceremony on the morrow, stating that he had made no preparation whatever." McPherson's account of the same scene had Lincoln referring to "stray thoughts," which does not suggest anything written, and only an hour before Lincoln spoke to Wills, he had said to MacVeagh that "he wished to consider further the few words he was expected to say the next day." This, and similar phrases Lincoln may have employed, could easily be understood to mean that these words did not yet exist on paper.

Lincoln's words to Wills and the others were seemingly conditional or ambiguous, phrased with his usual modesty and self-deprecation, and gave the impression that he had written very little, which of course was true: the whole speech eventually amounted to well under 300 words. Then, too, when Lincoln first spoke with Wills, he apparently had a pencil at hand (Wills said he was writing, or about to write, and Chilton, summarizing Wills, said it was pencil), and there were undoubtedly pages of foolscap about, perhaps even with a few words written in pencil. A president with pencil in hand, a page that was blank (or nearly so) that perhaps revealed the letterhead but hid the writing, and a few modest words from Lincoln would be all it took to fulfill the essential requirements of Wills's story as told in his 1890 memoir and in the summaries by Chilton and McPherson.

What is certain is that something like these elements combined to create, in the dynamic process of recollection, a vivid scene from authentic elements that nonetheless included errors of interpretation or fact. Wills saw Lincoln with paper; he affirmed it was the same as the paper he saw the next day, which McPherson in 1875, paraphrasing Wills, said was "official letter-sheet"; it simply is not the case that Lincoln first started his speech that night; it is just as certain that Lincoln had the Letterhead Page with him in Gettysburg. Taken all together, it must be that Wills saw the Letterhead Page (and possibly other pages as well) and that some mistaken combination of what Wills saw and what he heard led him to conclude something we know to be an error: that Lincoln had only first started his speech that night.

This chain of reasoning suggests that Lincoln, when he went to show or read his speech to Seward, took with him the letterhead first page, now divided at the fold so as to constitute a "half-sheet," and continuing text that was most probably written in pencil on the same large-format foolscap paper used in the existing Pencil Page. The possibility that this second page really was a "large yellow envelope" or that it was an edited second page of the Washington Draft cannot be excluded, but this second page was not, according to what Nicolay recalled of the next morning, the existing Pencil Page that is now the second page of the Nicolay document. This means that we can speak of an intermediate text created during that first part of the night, an evening text that Lincoln considered to be in a fit enough condition that, as he said to Curtin, "he would go around and show it to Seward."

The fact that it only took about an hour, during which other distractions intervened, for Lincoln to bring his text to the condition that it could be shown to Seward suggests that the revisions to the Washington Draft were relatively light. This would seem to confirm that the Washington Draft was fairly complete or finished, just as the accounts by Brooks and Lamon indicate. Similarly, throughout that night in Gettysburg the Letterhead Page remained unchanged (according to Nicolay's testimony), suggesting that the text on this first page still flowed smoothly into the following material, again implying relatively little change to the first words (at least) of the second page. Finally, the eventual speech is so tightly constructed, with multiple themes interwoven across the entire text, that it is difficult to imagine that there could have been structural or thorough changes to the latter part of the text without forcing at least a few revisions of the first page. All of this implies that as of the end of the evening revision, Lincoln's changes to the Washington Draft were relatively limited and encompassed only the material after the first page.

Lincoln had to think about the little visit to consult with Seward, and it required rather a bit of calculation and preparation to carry it off. Even if it was the nineteenth century and presidents did not have armor-plated limousines and Boeing 747s at their disposal, there were still complications for a president setting out into a night filled with celebrating, singing, raucous people who could be expected to demand speeches and grand gestures. Moreover, the arrival of the governors at the Wills house and the continued music of choirs and bands had increased the size of the crowd outside, which redoubled its calls for Lincoln and for speeches from Curtin, Cameron, Brough, and others who had just come in on the train. This caused some difficulty because Lincoln wished to avoid speaking again, so, as Curtin wrote in 1892, Lincoln "recommended that I should go to the door, and if possible keep the crowd from him, which I did." Lincoln also seems to have realized that he would need help getting through the dense gathering because, according to Bigham, "[Lincoln] asked me if I knew where Secretary Seward was stopping. I replied I did. 'Will you take me there?' I helped him on with his coat and took him to Mr. Harper's."[12] It was a small thing, perhaps, but to the end of his life Sergeant Bigham, later a bank director and pillar of the community, remembered with pride that, one night in Gettysburg, he had helped Abraham Lincoln put on his coat.

So while Curtin was dispatched to distract the crowd, Lincoln, Wills, and Bigham made their way next door. No contemporary report mentioned that Curtin spoke, but many years later the dean of the college in town was quoted in sketchy notes as saying that in his youth he had stood in front of the Wills house with a group of fellow students and that "Gov. Curtin brot word that crowd should excuse him [Lincoln]. Said he was busy."[13] It is uncertain if this is the same incident as described in the *Washington Daily Morning Chronicle,* which reported that at some point after Lincoln disappeared into the Harper house, but seemingly before he returned, the crowd at the Wills house began to grow disorderly, calling in an "irregular manner" for the governors to show themselves. Clearly, the unwritten rules of the serenade were being violated. Someone whom the reporter could not identify then came from inside to the door of the Wills house and "very cleverly caused a diversion in the noisy crowd" by telling them that "he would take them where Andy Curtin was, and they could call him out, whereupon he led them off and effected their dispersion."[14]

Lincoln's arrival at the Harpers' would have occasioned another round of introductions and pleasantries, but Wills no doubt had a great deal to do attending to a house full of guests, among them his patron, Governor Curtin, so he left Lincoln there with Sergeant Bigham. The evening at the Harper house had passed much as it had next door, except with the affable Seward as the guest of honor, undoubtedly chain-smoking cigars while talking with Andrew Cross of the Christian Commission, for example, who had worked hard to alleviate the suffering of the injured after the battle and had helped Wills in the early days of the cemetery project.[15] The Harpers had a few stories to tell of their own. On the parlor table, where Lincoln and the others could not have missed it, they proudly displayed a shell that had landed in their yard and failed to explode, and the windows and walls of their home had been damaged by bullets, one narrowly missing Harriet Harper, who was tending a wounded soldier.[16] Seward seemingly kept everyone entertained with his pithy aphorisms, leaving a vivid impression on Benjamin Brown French, a fixture in Washington since the 1830s who was helping Lamon with the event arrangements. After spending the evening with Seward, French doubted whether he had ever met anyone "whose mind is under such perfect discipline, and is so full of interesting and striking matter. . . . he is one of the greatest men of this generation."[17]

It was precisely Seward's facility with words and ideas that had brought Lincoln out into the night to consult with his secretary of state. The only glimpse of Lincoln's conversation with Seward comes from William McDougall, the Canadian politician who was probably staying at the Harper house with the other foreign dignitaries. The evidence is very late and indirect, but two men independently said that McDougall told of being invited to Gettysburg by Lincoln and of staying at an "inn" there. According to one version, after dinner Lincoln mentioned that he understood that government statements in Canada were issued after consultations among officials and then said, "Now I am somewhat like your Governor General and Mr. Seward like your Attorney General and tomorrow I have to make an important speech, so I must ask you to excuse us so we can get to work on it," and then he retired with Seward. The other version had it that, again after dinner, Lincoln "talked and swapped yarns until a pretty late hour," but this time it was Seward who "rather impatiently" reminded Lincoln that "he must come upstairs and finish preparing the speech he was to make the next day."[18] Certainly many of the details in these stories are inaccurate, but the linkage of Gettysburg, Lincoln, a dinner (no doubt the meal Everett described), an overnight journey, and Lincoln discussing the speech with Seward—even collaborating with him upstairs, away from the others—is undoubtedly grounded in an authentic recollection.

Although the content of the conversation cannot be fully recovered, there should be no doubt that Lincoln left the Wills house with the specific intent of speaking to Seward about his "remarks." Curtin stated directly (twice) that Lincoln said he was going to show his speech to Seward, and both Curtin and Wills agree that Lincoln took to the Harpers' the paper he was working on, which they both insist was Lincoln's speech. The timing and circumstances of Lincoln's visit are also telling. It is clear that the visit was improvised on the spur of the moment because not only did it happen relatively late at night, but Lincoln had to ask where Seward was staying. Wills, who as Lincoln's host might be expected to know the president's planned schedule and who had just spoken with him about the events of the next day, seemed to know nothing of the visit until the second time Lincoln called him up to his room.

It was more than just Lincoln's habitual practice of reading his writing aloud that brought Lincoln to brave the crowds whom he had done his best to avoid all evening, even taking the trouble of sending the governor of Pennsylvania out ahead as a distraction. After all, Curtin and Wills were there if Lincoln had only wanted a sympathetic audience, and there were plenty of people nearby whom Lincoln knew well from Washington if he just wanted someone with whom he was familiar. But that was not the issue. In less than twelve hours the procession to the cemetery would begin, and Lincoln had from the beginning wanted to be able to say "some appropriate thing." All the circumstances of the late-night visit suggest that something specific or pressing was wanted; this was not a casual conversation with someone who happened to be at hand. Lincoln wanted to talk about his speech with Seward in particular, and it was about something that could not wait.

Lincoln must have been relatively happy with the first part of his speech, as written on the Letterhead Page, because it was not changed that night even after the consultation with Seward. Whatever Lincoln wanted from Seward, then, was probably focused on the last part of his text, the part that was eventually discarded in favor of the foolscap Pencil Page written the next morning. This conclusion is reinforced by the most important previous instance in which Seward helped Lincoln with a speech, which was similarly in the last lines of Lincoln's First Inaugural Address evoking "the mystic chords of memory," an image suggested by Seward but given its final form by Lincoln. Given Lincoln's understanding of Seward's strengths and weaknesses as a decorative and ready writer (even if sometimes his speeches verged on verbose "machine writing") and given the textual evidence of the eventual delivery speech, it would seem that Lincoln sought Seward's opinion, and more particularly, some of Seward's "poetry," for the last lines of his own speech.

As the Lincoln scholar Douglas Wilson has suggested, it is "an intriguing possibility" that the last words of the Gettysburg Address arose similarly to those of the First Inaugural Address, with Lincoln crafting his own, unique phrases based upon an idea or word from Seward. Several observers have found similarities between Lincoln's words that "government of the people by the people for the people, shall not perish from the earth," and the conclusion of Seward's remarks to the serenaders earlier that night: "With that principle [respect for elections] this government of ours—the purest, the best, the wisest, and the happiest in the world—must be, and, so far as we are concerned, practically will be, immortal." Whatever MacVeagh or Seward himself told Lincoln about Seward's speech, copies of the prepared remarks were distributed to the press at Gettysburg, so Lincoln at almost any point that day could have read it for himself.[19]

The evidence of Noah Brooks suggests that the substantive concept or even the words in the "government of the people" phrase were present in the Washington Draft, but the last, almost wholly poetic words, "perish from the earth" may well reflect Seward's influence. He had used exactly that phrase on several occasions in the 1840s, and "perish" was a favorite with Seward, appearing in his speeches and writings of the 1850s and 1860s dozens of times. Lincoln had written the word only three times in the last ten years.[20] Lincoln wanted to show his speech to Seward for some compelling reason, and it would not be surprising if Seward had vindicated Lincoln's judgment by contributing an idea or phrase, or even a single word, to the text that Lincoln (probably) read to him. Sixty years later a story arose that Seward had said, on the stand at Gettysburg, that "no one but Lincoln could have written that speech," but this story is highly problematic.[21] With the rise of the legend of Lincoln at Gettysburg, the future might have found it heretical to suggest that the hand of another affected the creation of the iconic text, but that night when Lincoln sought Seward's advice his speech was still simply "a few appropriate remarks"; it will in fact take many hands to make the Gettysburg Address.

Even if Seward's precise contribution to Lincoln's speech is not certain, the visit to the Harper house does help establish more clearly the state of Lincoln's text that evening, but seeing this more fully entails moving with Lincoln into the next two compositional moments of the Gettysburg journey, the return to the Wills house and the final revisions in the morning. These events came directly out of the visit to Seward at the Harper house because one thing that Lincoln and Seward almost certainly discussed was visiting the battlefield in the morning before the procession to the ceremony began to form at about ten o'clock, a tour that had direct and powerful implications for Lincoln's revisions that evening and the next day.

To David Wills, who was back at his house, Lincoln appeared in the hindsight of several decades to have stayed at the Harper house only about half an hour, and decades later the retired merchant and bank director who had once been young Sergeant Bigham recalled similarly that Lincoln stayed only "a short time." These estimates probably tell more about the workings of memory than the actual passage of time because only a few days after the event Benjamin Brown French wrote in his diary that Lincoln "spent about an hour" at the Harpers' that evening, the context of his diary suggesting that at least some of that time was spent with the general company; French did not write anything about Lincoln's being closeted with Seward.[22]

By the time Lincoln left the Harper house, it must have been getting close to midnight, but people were still pressing about the front door, and to make matters worse, as Bigham recalled it, "a band of singers from Baltimore, led by Mr. Wilson Horner, asked permission to serenade the President, which was granted. They sang, 'We are Coming Father Abraham, three hundred thousand more.'" This was the "Union Glee Club" of Baltimore, which, along with the official Baltimore delegation, had arrived in town not long before, having joined at Hanover Junction the Governor's Special bearing Curtin and the other state delegations.[23] Dr. Daniel Slade ("Medicus"), who would see Lincoln reading from Executive Mansion letterhead, was probably among them. That Bigham correctly noted the choirmaster's name undoubtedly reflects the fact that several Gettysburg women sang with this choir at the ceremony the next day, leaving a strong impression in the memories of many Gettysburgers and in the written record.

The choir drew "quite a large crowd," as Bigham recalled, but just at this time, "the President came to the door, and said, 'I wish to return to my room. You clear the way and I will hold on to your coat.' It was quite dark, but we got through nicely." In another, somewhat more dramatic version, Bigham wrote that Lincoln "asked me to take him back to his room. The way was very dark and he said, 'You clear the way and I will hold your coat.' I pushed my way through the crowd to the Wills house." As seen from outside the house, a reporter for the *Baltimore American* confirmed that "a large assemblage of admiring listeners" had gathered at the Harpers' to listen to the choir, and "in a few moments the door was opened, and the President, who was about taking his departure for his lodgings, stepped out upon the steps, introduced by Mr. Harper." Lincoln bowed his acknowledgment to his visitors but declined "urgent calls" for a speech. "I can't speak tonight, gentlemen," Lincoln reportedly said, "I will see you all to-morrow. Good night." With that, Lincoln "strode off at a rapid pace, greeted with tremendous cheering."[24] Lincoln's earlier precautions in sending Curtin to distract the crowd had clearly been only partially effective.

Back safely in his room, probably sometime just after midnight or so, Lincoln evidently returned to his revisions. Wills appears to have seen Lincoln arrive, but true to his unblinking focus on the document, he wrote simply, "Mr. Lincoln returned with the same paper in his hand."[25] Several secondhand sources state that Bigham saw Lincoln at a desk or writing late at night, but to Governor Andrew Curtin goes the honor of the final word on this eventful night. In the 1888 interview, he stated that Lincoln "returned and copied his speech on a foolscap sheet." Curtin's 1892 letter, written in response to an inquiry from John Nicolay about the 1888 interview, was more forthcoming. "When I came in from the presence of the crowd of people, he had returned, and then seemed to be copying from the notes on the envelope on [onto?] the sheet of foolscap paper, and I have no doubt that was the address. I could have picked up from the table the notes that he then made, and have regretted it 1000 times that I did not do it."[26]

Not only, then, did Curtin recall that he had first seen Lincoln with a "yellow envelope," but he also saw Lincoln later copying his "notes"—some of them, perhaps, based on his conversation with Seward—onto foolscap paper. To add to the complications, Edward McPherson, who in 1875 described Lincoln reading from "an official letter-sheet," by 1879 was repeating Curtin's version instead. And, of course, if the delivery text were indeed the Nicolay document, as is argued here, then both the 1875 and the 1879 descriptions can be correct because they accurately describe the two different papers Lincoln used in making it.

All this helps us understand the difficult problem Wills faced in the late 1880s when trying to convince others that he had seen Lincoln in his house writing the speech that he read on the stand. If Wills described the paper in any way, it would conflict with accounts by one or both of his respected friends, former Governor Curtin, or former Clerk of the House McPherson. Similarly, describing ink or pencil was likely to create the same difficulty. And so, even though in 1868 Wills had mentioned to the visiting Chilton that he saw Lincoln writing in pencil ("with a half-sheet of paper before him"), and in 1875 McPherson, relying on information from Wills, stated point-blank that Lincoln read from "an official letter-sheet," Wills in his own later accounts simply excluded any description whatsoever of the document. Wills apparently decided that describing the paper or the writing implement would obscure what was for him the essential and overriding point, that Lincoln had written the entire Gettysburg Address in his house. Wills repeated that point almost obsessively in his 1890 statement, but the dilemma presented to him by Curtin's widely publicized account and McPherson's own assertions explains why Wills always used circumlocutions such as "he had the same paper" or "he carried the same paper" and never once described in any way the iconic, "immortal" document that was the centerpiece of his story.

Appropriately enough for the man who had probably approved asking Lincoln to speak at Gettysburg, Curtin's vision of Lincoln "copying" his speech onto foolscap paper is the last sign of Lincoln that night. The intrepid reporter for the *Chronicle,* still dutifully at his post in the street, reported that all became quiet at about midnight. Edward Everett confided to his diary that he went to his bed at 11:30 p.m. but that "fear of having the Executive of Penna. tumbled in upon me" kept him awake until one in the morning, although the gentle old veteran of the podium did admit that "nervousness about tomorrow no doubt had something to do with my unrest." At the Harper house the nicotine-fueled Seward seemingly kept the company lively, for B. B. French did not get to bed until one in the morning.[27] As for Lincoln, when Curtin saw him after his return from the Harpers' he was already copying his "notes," so it may be that Lincoln himself went to his rest sometime between twelve thirty and one, in rhythm with the others and with many of the good people and guests of the little town of Gettysburg. William Saunders, like so many others, found no bed available, recalling, "If we slept at all, we did so in chairs."[28]

The late-night revision in the upper room of the Wills house, then, seemingly began sometime after midnight on November 18, but there is no certain information as to when Lincoln stopped writing that night. During this time, Wills again saw Lincoln with "the same paper" and in 1892 Curtin wrote that he saw Lincoln "copying from the notes on the envelope on the sheet of foolscap paper." That Lincoln wrote after returning from the Harper house conforms to the supposition that Seward had in some way helped Lincoln with his speech. Lincoln probably recopied or reworked the closing portion of the evening draft, collating any comments or suggestions made by Seward and making other changes that occurred to him as he worked. This version of Lincoln's speech, written after the return from the Harpers', can be called the Gettysburg Draft because it was written at the end of Lincoln's evening and night in the little town.

The day was done at last, and Lincoln's speech, too. At least, Lincoln thought so—he must have. For one thing, he knew that in the morning, probably quite early, he was going to visit the battlefield with Seward. It simply would have been imprudent—hardly a Lincolnian trait—to have gone off on a tour of uncertain duration, with unexpected possible complications, on the very morning of the ceremony, unless his text was in a state worthy of the grand day and the expectations Lincoln knew he was facing. Anyone "anxious" to be there and to be able to say "some appropriate thing" would not casually leave such a speech unfinished. To the contrary, Curtin's testimony that Lincoln was "copying" his speech onto foolscap confirms that Lincoln was indeed the prudent and careful man virtually all his words and actions proclaim him to have been, writing out that night, before what he knew would be a busy morning, his "few appropriate remarks" in fulfillment of the role assigned him in the program.

After all, he had started with his Washington Draft, written out all in ink, on Executive Mansion letterhead, which he had worked on the night before in Washington, when he was thinking about what it would mean "to stand here" with the brave dead, and perhaps seeing in his mind's eye the great sacred ceremony unfolding in a classical landscape conceived by Saunders. Then, too, at the Wills house it had required only an hour upstairs to transform the Washington Draft into a fit enough state that he could present it to Seward, who never disappointed when it was a question of final words and soaring images. The improvised, late-night visit suggests that Lincoln wanted to put the finishing touches on his speech that night.

And then he followed Sergeant Bigham's coattails through the dense crowd back to his upper room. There, no doubt with a blazing fire tended by the indispensable William Johnson, he sat at the small table mentioned by Chilton and wrote in the Gettysburg Draft the words he intended to say the next day, wrote it there, in David Wills's own home, with the handsome Governor Curtin of Pennsylvania as his witness.

CHAPTER FIVE

The Battlefield Draft

UNION GRAVES.

People were up early in Gettysburg on November 19, and many had slept little, if at all, resting fitfully on church pews or tramping about the streets to stay warm, singing "John Brown's Body" and waiting for day to break. Down the same roads that four months before had brought 150,000 men in arms there came the crowds, and all day long more arrived by train and cart and horse and foot. Scattered in houses and hotels across the town, a dozen governors and some of the highest officers of the U.S. government prepared themselves, and on the street that ran past the front door of David Wills, soldiers and citizens assembled for the procession to the cemetery. Liberty Hollinger, who had just turned seventeen, was among those who had come out to see the dignitaries and join the festivities on the town square adjacent to the Wills house, "where all was excitement," she later recalled, "and everybody was having such a jolly time." From their vantage point she and her friends could distinctly see Abraham Lincoln up in a second-floor room of the Wills house repeatedly coming to the window and then "pacing back and forth" as though "engaged in deep thought."[1]

Through her cherished memory of a day in her youth sixty years before, we can almost stand with young Liberty and her friends amid the excited crowd before the Wills house, with messengers and horses and soldiers and townspeople surging across the Diamond, Odd Fellows in regalia, wounded and mutilated veterans forming the proud honor guard, the parade marshals draped in white sashes, and all the participants trying to find their places in the grand procession. Then Liberty (a Hollywood scriptwriter would blush to have invented such a name for such a moment) looked up at the window of the Wills house and saw—on the very morning on which Abraham Lincoln gave a speech that resolved to rededicate the nation to a "new birth of freedom"—that he held "a piece of yellow paper about the size and appearance of an ordinary envelope."[2]

The paper Liberty Hollinger saw, which we can take to be the delivery text of the Gettysburg Address, should have been the speech that Curtin saw Lincoln copying the night before. But here is where the compositional story Lincoln told to James Speed truly runs off the rails, for instead of using the text he had written the night before, on the morning of the ceremony itself Lincoln returned again to revising his "few appropriate remarks." By this time, Lincoln had been hoping for about two weeks to be there, participating with others in the "interesting ceremony" of commemoration and national mourning. He had prepared remarkably thoroughly since encouraging Lamon to accept the duties of marshal, talking with his cabinet, arranging train schedules with his secretary of war, inviting seemingly everyone he met, summoning the cemetery designer to speak with him, writing a draft in Washington, then in Gettysburg speaking with David Wills before settling down for about an hour to review or revise his remarks. Aside from uncertainty about whether Lincoln would be able to attend the event, which explains the initial confusion over the train schedule, the first sign of disorder, or at least of spontaneity, in the composition process was the improvised visit to Seward the night before. Even so, the matter was handled relatively quickly, and Lincoln had returned to the Wills house and set about finishing his text, "copying" it, according to Curtin. The speech was completed, and the morning visit to the battlefield awaited.

Then something happened, for the speech Lincoln wrote out the previous night was not the speech he took to the stand; it was not what would come to be called "the Gettysburg Address." There was still more to the compositional drama Lincoln narrated to his old friend. "He took what he had written with him to Gettysburg, then he was put in an upper room in a house, and he asked to be left alone for a time. He then prepared a speech," Lincoln had told Speed. So far, so good, and the record matches each step precisely. Then comes trouble: "but concluded it so shortly before it was to be delivered he had not time to memorize it." Lincoln remembered the compositional process as rushed and pressed, as running differently from the way he would have wanted or expected it to unfold, because he had run out of time.

Lincoln wanted to memorize his speech, and as the author who had labored over the lines and whose mind was quick to retain texts and phrases, it seems there should have been time to do so, even with a visit to the battlefield. The procession to the cemetery was scheduled to form at 10:00 a.m., and Lincoln was an early riser. Yet when Nicolay saw Lincoln in his room that morning, he was still writing and revising his speech and continued to do so right up to the final moments before leaving for the ceremony. It is perhaps possible that Lincoln the night before had been so cavalier as to have simply left his speech incomplete when he went to bed, but one last, immovable object blocks this avenue of explanation: the physical document that Lincoln was creating when Nicolay—and not just Nicolay—saw him writing that morning. The Nicolay document also has its tale to tell, and its testimony corroborates the eventful narrative Lincoln told to Speed and that John Nicolay tells to us.

The story of the last morning of writing the "appropriate remarks" for the dedication ceremony, on the day of the grand event itself, reveals that Gettysburg was exerting its power to alter and reshape Lincoln's understanding of what he wanted to say, even to the very moment he spoke. The experience of the town, the battlefield, the cemetery, and the ceremony— all that Gettysburg was and became for Lincoln—actively transformed his vision and became encoded in the documents themselves. The texts tell the tale—the texts, and a visit Lincoln made in the morning before the ceremony, to see the storied field of battle and the place where "our gallant and brave friend, Gen. Reynolds," as Lincoln called him, met his death.[3]

Exactly when on the morning of November 19 Lincoln met Seward for their tour of the battlefield is not known. Astronomy informs us that the sun crested the eastern horizon at 6:58 a.m., and the newspapers tell us that a cannon salute at 7:00 a.m. announced the great day, but Lincoln may have started out earlier. He would have been more than willing to rise early because, after all, assuring enough time to visit the battlefield had been a prime consideration in arranging Lincoln's train schedule, and the desire to see the sites of the battle was certainly one of the reasons he accepted the invitation in the first place. Lincoln was drawn to the battlefields of the war, and at times he even toyed with the idea of personally leading forces in the field. He visited the only other site of a great battle in the vicinity of Washington that could be reached with safety, the field of Antietam, where he met with McClellan in October 1862. He also went several times to the forts around Washington when the defenses were threatened and where he came under fire from Confederate sharpshooters. In May 1862, he even took a hand directing field operations around Norfolk, Virginia, during one of his visits to the Army of the Potomac, and of course, at the end of the war, Lincoln spent nearly two weeks with Grant's army closely monitoring the attack against the faltering Confederates and visiting battlefields upon which still lay the dead and dying.

The precise itinerary and timing of Lincoln's battlefield tour may have been decided only the night before. When he went to the Harper house to see Seward, Lincoln had already spoken with Wills about the "order of the exercises" and could have learned enough about the morning's schedule so that he could make concrete plans about visiting the battlefield with Seward. Then too, if MacVeagh did mention to Lincoln that evening his own "words of earnest praise" about General Reynolds to the serenaders that evening, it would have rekindled or reaffirmed Lincoln's original intent to see the battlefield. Wills or others would have been able to tell Lincoln that the site of Reynolds's death, which was already becoming a point of pilgrimage, was only about a mile from the house—but in a different direction from the planned procession to the cemetery.

The route of the procession made a separate battlefield visit a necessity if Lincoln was to see the site of Reynolds's death, which had been prominently featured in engravings in *Harper's Weekly* a few months before. In addition, "Lincoln's photographer," Alexander Gardner, had photographed what he said was the site, and it was featured in the catalog of photographs that were probably on display when Lincoln had been photographed at the gallery on November 8.[4] But Lincoln would not need Gardner's photographs or the engravings in *Harper's* to be reminded of Reynolds's fate. Lincoln knew him, and knew of him, corresponding with Curtin about Reynolds's taking up the defense of Pennsylvania during the Antietam campaign of 1862, when Curtin feared the Keystone State was to be invaded. Most important, Lincoln had called Reynolds to the White House to personally offer him command of the Army of the Potomac in June 1863, just as Lee was moving north in the invasion that brought about the great battle at Gettysburg.[5] Reynolds, a fierce battlefield commander, sidestepped the politically demanding position, instead recommending Meade, who was eventually appointed.

Thus, instead of directing the Army of the Potomac from behind the lines, Reynolds was in front of his troops on July 1, when Confederates on the first day of the battle overwhelmed Union forces to the north and west of Gettysburg. There, while attempting to seize a wood lot dominating a crucial road into town, Reynolds was shot from his horse, the highest-ranking officer of either side to die in the battle. Lincoln was quickly informed, and on July 2, seeking news, he telegraphed an inquiry to General Schenck in Baltimore. Just after seven in the evening came the reply: "Two of Reynolds staff passed through with the body." Lincoln's personal acquaintance with Reynolds, and the notoriety of his heroic death, no doubt helps explain why, when Lincoln and Seward toured the battlefield on the morning of November 19, they went straight to "the ground around the Seminary," the area where Reynolds died, as Seward was overheard by a reporter describing it on the day of the dedication ceremony itself.[6]

Reynolds's body was taken by special cars provided by the Pennsylvania Railroad for public viewing in Baltimore and Philadelphia, a grand procession, and then burial in his hometown of Lancaster, Pennsylvania, and so he is not among those buried in the cemetery dedicated by Lincoln. For months after the battle, Reynolds's biography and heroic death were retold in the daily and periodical press, and the publication of Matthew Brady's photographs of the site led the *New York Herald* to assert, "The wheatfield where Reynolds fell—a spot rendered sacred and truly memorable—cannot fail to be always attractive to the patriot in civil or in military life." Emily Thatcher Souder, who had traveled to Gettysburg immediately after the battle to care for the wounded, was among the many who returned to join the dedication ceremonies and revisit the scenes of July. "We rode to Seminary Hill," she wrote in a letter, "and saw Lee's headquarters and the spot where General Reynolds fell." Her itinerary was common. "The first place usually visited is Seminary Hill," reported the *New York Herald* in one of the innumerable descriptions of the battlefield telegraphed by the reporters who had come to Gettysburg with Lincoln. The battlefield was an impressive, astonishing sight for many of them, who had reported the war from newsrooms in Boston, Columbus, Philadelphia, or New York and now were walking the ground upon which had been fought the largest battle in the history of the Western Hemisphere. "The fields are dotted with graves, the houses are riddled with shot and shell, and the fences and trees show signs of the rain of missiles," wrote the *Ohio State Journal*. The magnitude of the violence, the sheer scope of the conflict, struck all who visited that November, as it must have struck Lincoln. "The spot upon which we stood was, even yet, grim and ghastly with the mute memorials of strife and carnage," the *Journal* continued. The *Cleveland Plain Dealer* noted, "Soiled fragments of uniforms, in which heroes had fought and died, remnants of haversacks and cartridge-boxes and other mementoes of that terrible conflict still lay strewn about, while, still lower down the hillside, is seen remains of the artillery horses." Another visitor that week reported finding a skull amid the rocks of Round Top.[7]

At the time, the tombs of the many Union soldiers still to be reinterred at the Soldiers' Cemetery and all the graves of the Confederate soldiers punctuated the landscape. Often recognizable only by a mound of earth, the graves were sometimes marked by a wooden board or other improvised device. These, and the remnants of the tombs of those who had already been reinterred, served as the monuments to the dead, while rifle pits and earthworks etched the lines of battle upon the landscape. Visitors followed the signs of battle, consulted maps, or were told stories by the many soldiers who had been in the fight and were now returning to honor their comrades or by Gettysburg residents reliving the days of fear and doubt. Like the stations of the cross, the elements of a circuit were already taking shape, from the town, west to the Seminary, south to Little Round Top, and back again to the apex of the battle on Cemetery Hill, not yet marked as the high tide of the Confederacy but already celebrated as the scene of the final battle, the doomed attack that was already becoming known as Pickett's Charge.

Into this emerging landscape of memory stepped Abraham Lincoln on the morning of November 19. General Schenck was later reported to have said that he saw Lincoln in a carriage that morning with three or four people, but he provided no details. Possibly this accounts for a late, secondhand account in which Canadian politician William McDougall was said to have described traveling with Lincoln to the ceremony over the battlefield on "buckboards," a kind of open wagon. However, on the way, Lincoln was also said to have torn his speech up and then given his speech extemporaneously, so the "buckboards" of the story may be equally fictional. On the other hand, William Tisdale, of the Eleventh New York Cavalry and one of Lincoln's bodyguards in Washington, provided plenty of details some sixty years later, but his evidence appeared so long after the event that it is difficult to credit the report, even if there is nothing impossible about it. "Lincoln went over the ground on horseback. I went with him," he recalled. "The horses were from a cavalry regiment. He had a big horse, 16 hands high, with a regulation saddle. An officer furnished him with his horse and one of the men furnished mine." This seems more likely than Schenck's carriage and corresponds nicely to the rather unusual attention given Lincoln's equestrianship at the time, and also to Tisdale's posting in the cavalry. This note of authenticity is undermined by the generic statement that Lincoln "went over the grounds to Pickett's Charge and different places," but here again Tisdale added a seemingly genuine detail, that "debris of the fight were all around, guns, dead horses."[8]

A description of a visit on November 18 to the woods where Reynolds was killed reveals the stories of valor and sacrifice that were being told on the ground in Gettysburg when Lincoln was there, focusing memory and recognition particularly upon this son of Pennsylvania. At Willoughby Run, a small stream just below Seminary Ridge, the visitors paused while their guide told them, "The rebels were in the woods yonder, and as we were pressing them very hard, they made a terrible fight. Our boys had come around the town, and marched right over the ridge in line of battle. They did their best, but were not strong enough, and the line seemed to waver and tremble." This description conforms so well to the accounts of Reynolds's death given to his sisters by his aides that the guide may well have been one of the officers involved. "The General, who was always moving around, and who did not mind the bullets any more than if they had been leaves from the trees, rode right across the field urging his men, and trying to get them ready to charge the woods." Then came the moment that Alfred Waud, the great illustrator for *Harper's* who was at Gettysburg during the battle, would immortalize in a print titled *Death of Reynolds,* and that the well-informed guide at Gettysburg described to the visitors in November. "One of the regiments came up too slowly, and he turned around to beckon it on when a ball struck him, and he fell into that little hollow. He did not speak, but was carried away to a building yonder, where he died." Reynolds had three entire army corps under his direct command but was killed leading a single regiment into battle, perhaps 50 yards from the Confederate line. The guide was so certain of his story that he could even point out the precise spot on the ground where Reynolds fell, demonstrating further the level of detail and knowledge available to visitors at the time of Lincoln's visit.[9]

What stories Lincoln may have heard about the death of Reynolds when visiting "the ground around the Seminary" with Seward cannot be known, but a small clue confirms that Lincoln did indeed visit the site that Brady and *Harper's* and his own favorite photographer, Gardner, had helped make famous. Perhaps an hour or so after his battlefield tour, while Lincoln was on his horse in the main square at Gettysburg waiting for the procession to begin, a reporter for the *Washington Daily Morning Chronicle* happened to overhear him say, as he looked about what the paper called the "fair prospect," that Lincoln "had expected to see more woods." Certainly, Lincoln did not mean he expected to see woods in the town, around the Diamond, nor could he be referring to the scenery visible through the train windows under the moonlight of his arrival the night before. If Lincoln expected but did not see more woods at Gettysburg, it could only be because he had just visited the battlefield. Almost as certainly, he was referring to the woods in which Reynolds was killed, which were popularly known as McPherson's Wood because they were associated with Edward McPherson, the Gettysburg representative in Congress who had ridden up on the train with Lincoln. Reports of Reynolds's death had placed the site in the woods or at the edge of the woods, and very often in "McPherson's Wood." Waud's engraving, based on information provided by Reynolds's aides, portrayed Reynolds's being shot from his horse in the woods, and the photographs of Brady (and the purported photograph by Gardner, which Lincoln may have seen during his visit of November 8), although mentioning farm fields in the description, still show woods beyond the immediate foreground.[10]

Of course, other noted episodes of the battle occurred in woods, for example on Culp's Hill or Little Round Top, sites Lincoln had mentioned to Saunders two nights before, but these areas were indeed heavily wooded; Lincoln could not have visited them and been surprised at not seeing woods.[11] The place where Reynolds was shot, however, was a second-growth woodlot set among expansive, cleared fields dotted with farmhouses; it best fits his comment, which testifies not only to Lincoln's connections with Reynolds but also to the common description of the event and the physical condition of the site itself. Just as in his conversation with Saunders two nights before, Lincoln has revealed that he had already walked in Gettysburg in his imagination; he knew "the topography of the place," as Saunders had noticed. A little comment, an aside reported by chance, that "he had expected to see more woods," reveals that Lincoln had already seen this place in his mind's eye and that while he wanted to know others' expectations of him, he too had developed his own expectations of what he would see and experience at Gettysburg.

Now, having imagined what it would be like "to stand here," as he had written on the Letterhead Page in Washington, Lincoln was on the very ground where Reynolds, "our gallant and brave friend," had died. From Seminary Ridge the bare trees of a Pennsylvania November allowed a wide view of Gettysburg in its valley about a mile to the east, with its steeples, cupolas, wood-frame houses, and fine brick and stone masonry buildings, normally a picture of rural calm, now filled with 10,000 visitors and more. Lincoln would have known all about the Lutheran Seminary before him, as it was notable in the reports of the battle for having served as a lookout position for each army in turn until finally it was regained after the Confederates retreated, leaving hundreds of wounded and piles of bloody limbs in its buildings and grounds. At the time of the cemetery dedication, the steward of the seminary was happy to tell visitors, like a reporter for the *Cincinnati Daily Commercial,* the "thousand tales of war and its incidents" that clustered around the building, which "for all time will make it a celebrated spot for the pilgrim to the battle ground."[12] Lee's headquarters, another celebrated site, was a modest farmstead on the road close by.

As Seward and Lincoln viewed the "ground around the Seminary," to Lincoln's right as he looked toward the town lay the fields where, at about the time Reynolds was directing the troops, soldiers saw coming toward them from the town a solitary figure, dressed in a top hat and a threadbare blue swallowtail coat last fashionable in the 1820s, and carrying an antique flintlock musket. It was old John Burns, soon to be celebrated as the only civilian to take up arms to defend the town, who fought alongside several regiments all day until three wounds and the Union retreat led him back home again. Lincoln may not have known that Burns had fought in this area, but he certainly knew of Burns's exploits, which had made him instantly famous everywhere anyone in the Union could read, but Burns would be one of the guests on the stand at the ceremony, and later that afternoon Lincoln would make special efforts to meet the heroic old veteran of 1812, the Mexican War, and now, the war for the Union.[13]

Possibly, as Tisdale mentioned, Lincoln and Seward visited other parts of the battlefield as well, but time was passing. Going back into town, Lincoln and Seward would have seen more clearly in the full morning light the bullet holes and battle damage in the buildings, fragments of knapsacks and uniforms, and a hundred other signs of the desperate struggle that many were calling the turn of the tide in the war. The night before, Lincoln had undoubtedly heard stories of bullets and shells tearing through walls and narrowly missing, or sometimes hitting, people in their homes, perhaps as he turned over in his hand the unexploded shell so proudly displayed on the parlor table of the Harpers' home. As the sunlight grew stronger, Lincoln himself would have been able to see and feel more fully the violence and sacrifices and heroism of the deadly struggle.

When Lincoln returned to the Wills house, something—the memory of Reynolds's death, perhaps, or the sight of the battle damage, or simply his further meditation on the meaning of the sacrifices so palpable and real at Gettysburg—altered his vision and inspired him to revisit the speech that he had written out the night before. This experience too became part of his speech. Much of the power of the words Lincoln spoke at Gettysburg derives from the way they crystallized and concentrated what Lincoln was thinking and feeling about the war and the sacrifices made in the name of the great task. Lincoln spoke for the Union, but the speech also spoke for Lincoln's mind and heart; his speech registered the anguish and aspirations of millions—its canonization proclaims this fact—but it also encoded the thoughts and feelings of Lincoln himself as he thought about it, as he wrote it, and as he spoke it. Lincoln's visit to "the ground around the Seminary," his experience of the battlefield, was the last scene enacted by Lincoln before his final draft of what would become the Gettysburg Address. It was the last, and perhaps the most fitting, element of the journey that created the words Lincoln carried with him to the cemetery, the Battlefield Draft.

Lincoln was already at work on the revisions that created this document when Nicolay arrived from the Harper house "to report for duty" sometime after breakfast. This "final writing" occupied "about an hour," Nicolay estimated, because "it is not likely that Lincoln left the breakfast table before nine o'clock," and the procession began to form at ten.[14] Nicolay thus indicated that he did not know when Lincoln set about working on his manuscript that morning, but he did know that when he arrived at the room, Lincoln was working on it and that he continued to do so until leaving for the ceremony. This, more than the revisions of the night before, corresponds to what Lincoln later told Speed, that he "concluded it so shortly before it was to be delivered he had not time to memorize it."

Lincoln had another witness to his work that morning: James A. Rebert, another of the hometown soldiers from Company B of the Twenty-First Pennsylvania Cavalry that had been detailed to guard the president. Rebert's father was the sheriff, so the family may have counted for something in the area; local tradition had it that the family owned the horse that Lincoln rode to the cemetery. In 1863 Rebert was only about eighteen years old, but he appears to have had the confidence of his peers because he was promoted to full sergeant in the spring of 1864. After the war he owned a store for a time and farmed; in the years before his death in 1907 he was selling insurance in Harrisburg. Rebert's statement was not published until 1917, but when he wrote it in 1891, he was about forty-seven years old, the married father of four children, and living in Philadelphia.[15]

"On the morning of the 19th I was detailed as orderly to President Lincoln, who was a guest of Judge Wills," Rebert recalled. "About 9 a.m., I was sent to the room directly above Judge Wills's office, occupied by the President at the time." Obviously, Rebert was familiar with "Judge Wills's office" in his home, although Wills only became a judge in 1874. Perhaps in later years the men had discussed what they had seen, but if so, it did not prevent Rebert from telling a story that differed, or at least offered nuance, to the story Wills told. "He requested me to wait a few minutes until he finished his writing, which I found him engaged in on entering the room." If it really was nine, Nicolay probably had not yet arrived, but it is possible that the familiar workings of tunnel-vision memory led Rebert to simply omit Nicolay and that the two were describing essentially the same scene.[16]

While waiting, Rebert evidently had some time to watch Lincoln at work because his description is quite precise. Here, then, is how the middle-aged Rebert remembered what his younger self had seen, when he had not yet been six months a soldier, as he stood by in that "upper room" and waited for his orders from the president of the United States: "He had several sheets of note paper in front of him written in pencil, and several that he was just finishing. Both looked more like notes for reference than articles for publication. He wrote an order for me to deliver to Marshal Lamon, of Washington, D. C.," Rebert concluded, "whose headquarters were at the Eagle Hotel." At the time, "note paper," while not so clearly defined as foolscap or "letter-sheet" paper, most often referred to any good-quality paper used for writing a letter.

From Rebert's description, it appears that Lincoln was copying or referring to the sheets of note paper "in front of him" while he was writing. The night before, Wills had seen Lincoln writing in pencil, according to what he told Chilton in 1868, and Curtin had also seen Lincoln "copying from the notes on the envelope" onto a "sheet of foolscap paper," so Rebert's combination of pencil and several sheets of "note paper" matches well with the descriptions of the work Lincoln had done the night before. In contrast, the Washington Draft was (presumably) written all in ink. Lincoln, then, was apparently not recopying or revising directly from the Washington Draft that morning; rather, he was revising or copying the latter section of the speech that he had written or edited the night before during the evening and late-night revisions.

Just as important is the small detail Rebert then mentioned, that "after finishing them he folded them all together and placed them in his pocket." This, and Rebert's entire account, tends strongly to the conclusion Lincoln was working on his speech.[17] Lincoln knew, for example, that he would be returning to the Wills house after the ceremony when he could retrieve any document that he cared to leave behind, but this evidently was a document Lincoln wanted to keep with him. Many eyewitnesses will testify that Lincoln on the stand produced his speech from his coat pocket. There is no extant writing by Lincoln in Gettysburg that corresponds to anything like what Rebert described except the Pencil Page. Even though Rebert was writing before Nicolay had published his recollections, Rebert's depiction of Lincoln as writing on the morning of the nineteenth, writing in pencil, and folding the pages corresponds perfectly to Nicolay's description of how Lincoln created the delivery text, which bears the marks of being folded in thirds, as if to fit in a coat pocket. Overall, the fact that Rebert's account conforms to the document (which had not yet been published), the context, and the accounts by Wills, Curtin, and Nicolay is powerful evidence that Rebert had just witnessed Lincoln finishing his speech—or witnessed him working on his speech, if this all took place before Nicolay arrived.

For his part, Nicolay described Lincoln in his "final writing" that morning using a pencil to edit the Letterhead Page, making Nicolay the third eyewitness to state that Lincoln wrote in pencil in Gettysburg (along with Wills through Chilton, and Rebert). Two of these refer specifically to the morning of the nineteenth, evidence that Lincoln that day was working on or creating the Pencil Page (the only page in pencil among the handwritten versions), but Nicolay's memory may have been shaped in part by his familiarity with the document. Taking up the Gettysburg Draft he had worked on or created the night before, Lincoln discarded its second page. Nicolay did not describe this initial step, but there must have been a second page by this point, if only because Curtin had seen Lincoln copying his speech onto foolscap paper the night before. Moreover, Lincoln that night had worked on his speech for an hour or so, and since there are so few changes to the first, Letterhead Page during his revisions, Lincoln must have been working on the second part of his text almost exclusively.

And yet, on the morning of the nineteenth, revising only the second page was not enough; this new revision, undertaken after the visit to the battlefield and most probably unplanned, did not only call for creating a wholly new second page; it also required moving more deeply into the first page Lincoln had brought from Washington than had the revisions of the night before. Turning then to the first page, the Letterhead Page that had remained inviolate to that point, Lincoln, as Nicolay described, crossed out in pencil the words "to stand here" and added above them "we here be dedica" with no hyphen. The second, Pencil Page, on foolscap paper, then begins, "ted to the great task remaining before us," so that the final version of the edited text reads ungrammatically across the two pages: "It is rather for us, the living, we here be dedica // ted to the great task remaining before us . . . ."

Nicolay's 1894 account of this revision in *Century Magazine* seconds a letter Nicolay had written to Gilder in 1885 stating similarly that "I was with him at the time" that Lincoln wrote the second, Pencil Page. Nicolay again wrote in a letter to Wills in 1894 that Lincoln finished writing the speech "in my presence." Nicolay's account was based on what he remembered and on the documents in the Lincoln papers available to him, but he knew this was not the whole story, as he indicated by carefully stating that this was how "on the morning of the nineteenth," Lincoln "finished his manuscript."[18] In this way, Nicolay pointed out that he did not know when Lincoln began his revisions, either that morning or the night before. But this was the moment, according to Nicolay, that he saw Lincoln create the delivery text, or Battlefield Draft, that Lincoln took with him to the cemetery and read from later that afternoon.

Nicolay was probably correct in suggesting in his *Century* article that Lincoln had meant to write "for us, the living, to here be dedicated" rather than "we" here be dedicated, an example of the kind of mistake one can easily make when copying or revising one document while referring to another text—exactly as Rebert depicted Lincoln doing that morning. Anyone can make a mistake copying text; the real significance of this ungrammatical interposition is that it was not corrected, which suggests this was a very late change indeed. Had this infelicity been perpetrated the night before, it surely would have been caught and rectified in the morning as Lincoln reviewed his remarks. This edit might really have been made just before leaving for the ceremony, as Nicolay stated, and just as Lincoln told Speed, when he said he "concluded it so shortly before it was to be delivered he had not time to memorize it."

While there is no evidence that Nicolay knew of Rebert's memoir, Nicolay did know about the recollections by David Wills and Andrew Curtin, yet he chose to not mention them. This reticence has frustrated and irritated generations of researchers, who have sometimes called Nicolay's motives into question, and has led some to discount his specific, documented, and precise eyewitness testimony. But Nicolay had good reason not to mention the accounts by Wills and Curtin.[19] According to Wills, Lincoln had first started his speech in Gettysburg the night of the eighteenth, but there is overwhelming evidence that Lincoln wrote at least some of his speech in Washington. Nicolay knew this from his own recollection, confirmed for him by James Speed and by his reading of the document itself. In addition, Wills asserted that the document Lincoln was working on during the night of the eighteenth was the delivery text, but Nicolay knew, again from personal recollection of the morning of the nineteenth, that Lincoln created the second page of the delivery text that morning.

Moreover, Curtin's descriptions of "a very large yellow envelope" on which Lincoln was writing and of Lincoln's "copying from the notes on the envelope on the sheet of foolscap paper" on the night of the eighteenth were not supported by Nicolay's understanding of the documentation or by anything Nicolay himself knew. And so Nicolay carried out the philosophy he outlined in a letter to Wills in 1894 where he noted, "How liable we all are to error in our recollections," concluding, "All that any of us can do is to honestly state our impressions and the written contemporary record is the only reliable arbiter of differences."[20] David Wills had adopted a similar strategy in his own 1890 account, describing what he remembered but not mentioning Curtin's recollections, which he knew of in the mid-1880s, at the very latest.

For Nicolay, who alone had daily access to Lincoln's papers, this approach of relying on documents had clear advantages, and his unique access (in addition to a personality that led him to be once described as "a grim Cerberus of Teutonic descent") helps account for his aggravating tendency to imply that he alone knew the truth.[21] In his 1894 *Century* article, Nicolay followed his own advice about how to work around divergent memories, but his willingness to contradict Judge Wills demonstrates his confidence in his recollections and in the documentation. Arguing counter-factually: had Nicolay no memory of Lincoln revising his text on the morning of the nineteenth, he could very easily have agreed with Wills that Lincoln finished (but did not begin) his speech the night of the eighteenth. Nicolay had been on the train, so he felt confident in denying even the possibility that Lincoln wrote part of his speech in the cars. Nicolay was with Lincoln the morning of the nineteenth, so he gave his recollections of those revisions, even though his story contradicted that of Wills, because he had the documentation to support his memory. He said nothing of the night of the eighteenth because he was not there and because he found no documentation of any such revisions.

Nicolay also suggested to Wills a seemingly accurate way that both their accounts could be correct, writing in 1894, "Perhaps Mr. Lincoln in the evening only made hasty notes of the closing portion of his address, which he copied more deliberately in my presence in the morning." That is, while he avoided Wills's key point, that Lincoln had started his speech in Gettysburg, Nicolay thought it quite possible that Lincoln had worked on his speech the night of the eighteenth. Indeed, it appears that Nicolay was prepared to believe that Lincoln in the morning "copied" the Gettysburg Draft created the night before. This corresponds precisely to the scene depicted in Rebert's recollections. Nicolay's suggestion that Lincoln may have been working from "notes" made the night before means that this hypothesis would also conform to Curtin's accounts of seeing Lincoln revising and copying the speech that night, whether Curtin's "large yellow envelope" is included or not. Overall, Nicolay, a man with undoubtedly many flaws, should not be accused of willfully misleading posterity or deliberately obscuring the truth when he was merely describing his memory and the documentation, even if in his characteristically irritating manner.

Nicolay's identification of the Nicolay text as the delivery document is unassailable from the standpoint of the events and contexts surrounding Lincoln's composition in Gettysburg, from the paper mentioned by Wills (as reported by McPherson) through the pencil mentioned by Rebert and Wills (as reported by Chilton). None of this corresponds to the hypothesis of the Hay text as the delivery text or to the supposition of a hypothetical lost delivery text. Accepting some other text than the Nicolay as the delivery text requires ignoring almost all the evidence about the events and contexts surrounding the manuscripts and how Lincoln wrote them. The only arguments advanced for another document besides the Nicolay as the delivery document are textual in nature, meaning that similarities and differences in words in the various documents are interpreted in such a way as to create sequences of texts that supposedly exclude the Nicolay as the delivery text. The Hay text, for example, has often been put forward as the delivery text because it is closer in words to newspaper and other reports of Lincoln's spoken words than is the Nicolay document.[22] But in the story of how Lincoln wrote his speech in Washington, finished it in Gettysburg, and then delivered it on the battlefield, there is simply no place for the Hay text. Further along, the history of Lincoln's post-speech revisions will amply demonstrate that the Hay text did not even exist at the time of the speech.

In part because the Hay text cannot be easily made to fit into the story of Lincoln's delivery text, several of the best-known and most respected scholars of the speech today argue instead for a nonextant, hypothetical delivery text that is asserted to have been similar in wording to the newspaper reports of Lincoln's spoken words.[23] Adding a hypothetical text into the story only compounds the difficulties, however, as can be seen most clearly in the fact that the two most prominent exponents of this approach disagree on the content and nature of the alleged lost document. All of this demonstrates that there is good reason for the editorial principle of parsimony: the simplest explanation that includes all the relevant information is preferred. In the case of the Gettysburg Address, now that the full story of the creation of the delivery text has shown that nearly all the contextual and historical evidence favors the Nicolay document, the only reason for doubting the Nicolay text as the delivery text is that it differs from the reports of Lincoln's spoken words. The solution is simply to recognize that Lincoln spoke some words that differed from his text and that in the absence of recording devices the words that were reported can only be taken as an approximation of what Lincoln said. The story of how Lincoln gave his speech that day will confirm this analysis.

In sum, the morning revision in the upper room of the Wills house that created the final delivery text version of the Nicolay document lasted perhaps an hour or so on the morning of the nineteenth after Lincoln returned from visiting the battlefield, the first part (at least) witnessed by Rebert at around nine o'clock, when Lincoln "had several sheets of note paper in front of him written in pencil." Nicolay was present during the "final writing" in the time before leaving for the procession some minutes before ten. This Battlefield Draft, with its first, Letterhead Page in ink and its second

Pencil Page, is the written culmination of Lincoln's journey to the speakers' stand at Gettysburg; it was the document Lincoln held while looking out over the graves of the cemetery to the hills made famous by the battle of July. The Battlefield Draft's very structure brings together the two threads of the history of the speech, in Washington and in Gettysburg; it perfectly encodes its origins and Lincoln's evolving vision for his speech.

The story of the Battlefield Draft can also be recovered by a kind of editorial archaeology, digging down through the existing Nicolay document to the substratum texts upon which it was created across Lincoln's composition process in Washington and Gettysburg. All together, the revisions in Gettysburg to the Washington Draft probably did not take four hours overall, and may have taken a good deal less than three, but of course during this time Lincoln was also busy with telegrams, governors, and other distractions. This was a continuous process of production and thought, creating an evolving text whose state can be fixed at certain milestones:

1. The Washington Draft, two pages of text written in ink, perhaps on a joined, folded, full sheet of Executive Mansion letterhead paper, only the first page of which survives as the Letterhead Page. This draft was undoubtedly created on the basis of notes or a prior draft that no longer exists, probably in the four or five days before the speech; it was very probably given its final form at the White House on the night of November 17.

2. The evening revision that Lincoln showed or read to Seward on the night of the eighteenth, consisting of the unedited Letterhead Page and, probably, a second page in pencil on foolscap paper, or perhaps the second page of the Washington Draft edited in pencil.

3. The late-night Gettysburg Draft created after Lincoln consulted with Seward and before Lincoln retired on the night of the eighteenth. This consisted of the unedited Letterhead Page and, most probably, a new page written in pencil. Less probably, the second page was merely the second page of the Evening Gettysburg Draft with further text or edits. Lincoln probably prepared this Gettysburg Draft as his delivery text.

4. The Battlefield Draft, or delivery text, also known as the Nicolay document, consisting of the edited Letterhead Page spliced to the Pencil Page, which was created on the morning of November 19 in the manner described by Nicolay as seconded by Rebert and which

was probably based in part on the now discarded later part of the Gettysburg Draft created the night before.

The delivery text that Lincoln carried to the stand may aptly be called the Battlefield Draft because he held it when speaking at the cemetery, but it is also a fit title because it was created in the immediate aftermath of Lincoln's visit to "the ground around the Seminary" where Reynolds had died that first day of battle. This enigmatic text reveals its secrets only when placed against this backdrop of events and compositional moments. With a completed, finished text now in hand, we can see that Lincoln in Gettysburg incorporated into his speech a new element that is not found in the Washington Draft.[24] The last thing Lincoln did before leaving for the ceremony was not to memorize a speech he already had written; instead, he rewrote a speech that was already completed. Or rather, he rewrote and revisited part of that speech.

Through the early and late-night revisions, it was clear that Lincoln found no fault with the first page of his speech. The lack of changes to the powerful opening phrases and prose poetry of the Letterhead Page affirms that he knew those words would meet the test of expectation. Then, after the greetings and the serenades and the consultation with Seward, he had arrived at a text that had built upon and completed "Four score and seven years" and the insight that the "brave men, living and dead" had already hallowed the ground beyond "our" power to do so. The late-night Gettysburg Draft had, like the Washington Draft, included Lincoln's habitual survey of past and present, which at the end of its first page and at the start of a new paragraph were making a transition to some statement about the next step, when he wrote, "It is rather for us, the living, to stand here," having already evoked what "they did here." Already, then, the central we/they trope was well developed, and no doubt persisted into the second page, just as it had in Washington. Lincoln was also probably still working with the words or concepts that led to his paraphrase of Webster evoking "government of the people." Yet Lincoln's revisions in Gettysburg reveal that whatever the state of the second page of the Washington Draft, he was still having difficulty seeing the next part of the story he had outlined.

These last words, at least, did not come to him easily. As he told Brooks before leaving Washington, "It is not exactly written. It is not finished, anyway. I have written it over, two or three times, and I shall have to give it another lick before I am satisfied. But it is short, short, short." One of

CHAPTER SIX

these drafts, largely finished but still in progress, had become the Washington Draft, and the composition process continued across the revisions he made while in Gettysburg: all of it concentrated only and exclusively on what must have been a prospective, forward-looking conclusion for his speech. On the very morning of the ceremony, with a complete draft from the night before in hand, he once again returned to the words and ideas that could, in the proper balance of elevated language and clarity of purpose, speak to the future that was being made by the death of Reynolds and the sacrifices of all those fighting for the Union.

What exactly led Lincoln to take up his pencil one last time, perhaps only an hour before leaving for the ceremony, cannot be known with certainty. But it must have been a compelling, powerful idea or inspiration that led him to rewrite and revise his speech so near the event when for weeks he had felt that if he went to Gettysburg he would want to say "some appropriate thing." We can know, however, the impulse and direction of his thought, for once again the texts tell the tale. The effect of Lincoln's ungrammatical and last-minute revision that morning was twofold. It removed the image and concept embodied in the words "to stand here," and it added the image and concept of the words "here be dedicated to," a change that is the pivot point of the transition between the Letterhead Page written in Washington and the Pencil Page written in Gettysburg.

In this disjuncture between the Letterhead Page and the Pencil Page, we can read the moment of crisis of Lincoln's journey. Lincoln himself provided one possible answer as to why he came to realize that "to stand here" should be removed: he occasionally employed "stand" in a negative sense, as when berating Louisiana Unionists: "Why did they not assert themselves? Why stand passive?" Similarly, in the letter to Erastus Corning justifying the arrest of the Peace Democrat Clement Vallandigham, Lincoln wrote, "The man who stands by and says nothing, when the peril of his government is discussed, can not be misunderstood."[25] In both examples, the verb "to stand" meant to allow or collaborate in wrong by inaction, to "stand by" or to "stand passive."

Even Lincoln's positive use of the verb "to stand" in formulations that are clearly cognates of his use in the Washington Draft were essentially passive or static: "to stand . . . in defense" or "stand fast" or "stand indebted."[26] Most proximate was his statement to a journalist the very morning of the speech that newspapers should "stand by" the officers of the army, which signals that the original text had invoked support for the armed forces, as was Lincoln's habit during the war when employing variations of the word "stand."[27] And yet "stand by" is the same phrase Lincoln used when excoriating Vallandigham, a usage that places the word in a highly negative context. From this perspective, "to stand here" was perhaps too ambiguous and was almost certainly too passive for the new vision that Lincoln incorporated into his speech that morning; clearly, Lincoln found it inadequate.

It is not possible to know whether the Pencil Page, created at the same time that he removed "to stand here," was also more active, dynamic, or assertive than the text it replaced, but in its existing state it certainly is a page full of forceful verbs and powerful forward momentum. In one sentence, the entire nine and a half lines of the page describe how it is that "us, the living" are to pursue the "great task" remaining:[28]

1. that, from these honored dead we take increased devotion to that cause for which they here, gave the last full measure of devotion—
2. that we here highly resolve these dead shall not have died in vain;
3. that the nation, shall have a new birth of freedom, and
4. that government of the people by the people for the people, shall not perish from the earth.

All these dynamic events or resolutions are keyed to the new "we here be dedica // ted" that Lincoln added in pencil when he crossed out "to stand here." This is not to say that they were not possibly also linked initially to the earlier "to stand here" phrase, but rather that the new conception of the last lines made a new connection, one that was important enough to entail revisiting and revising a previously untouched first page of a text that must have been whole and complete by this late date, the very morning of the ceremony.

The function of striking out "to stand here" was to arrive at the word "dedicated"; this was where Lincoln knew he was headed as he revised the Letterhead Page to better suit the destination he had in mind for his new second page that morning. For Lincoln, "dedicated" was an unusual word. He had first used it or a variant in this sense when writing to his old friend Stephen Logan on November 9 about Lamon's invitation to preside over the procession "on the occasion of dedicating the Cemetery at Gettysburg."[29] After that morning in Gettysburg, aside from his copies of the speech, he never wrote the word again. Yet on this one page, the Letterhead Page as written in Washington, he used the word four times, and now on the morning of the speech he added another, writing this one, remarkable word five times in fewer than 170 words—and, on the stand, under the power of the moment when he stood before the graves of the dead, he would add a sixth.

"Dedicate" and "dedicated," then, were already central themes and organizing principles of the speech Lincoln brought from Washington, and now, after his visit to the battlefield, he was embarking on what must have been an unexpected revision, reinforcing and redeploying the term, but for a new purpose. The Letterhead Page written in Washington, with its iconic opening chords of "Four score and seven years ago," was closely tied intellectually and verbally to the July 7, 1863, serenade and to the July 4, 1861, message to Congress, both deeply bound up with questions of the Constitution and the founding era as posed by secession. Lincoln's first use of "dedicate" or "dedicated" occurs in the first sentence of that page and refers to the past, when "our fathers" dedicated the nation to the proposition that "all men are created equal." The next three instances of the word refer to the immediate present, when the nation "so dedicated" is being tested and when "we" have come to dedicate "a final resting place" for "the brave men." There should be no question where this new, fifth written usage of the word "dedicated" is heading in this historical and intellectual development: to the measures that "us, the living" are urged to undertake in the future.

Not only, then, is Lincoln's final sentence active, emotive, and eventful, but it is also oriented to the future, to what must be done to ensure that the sacrifices achieve the great aim in view. By adding a fifth written "dedica //ted" that literally joins the two, very different, pages across the word, Lincoln in Gettysburg was highlighting a central theme by returning to a word that had already provided a structural element to his thought and his conception of the issues within the Washington Draft. Repeating the same word, the same concept that he had associated in his first sentence with the "fathers," who first dedicated the nation to its ideals, and to the brave dead of the present day, who had dedicated the sacred ground by their sacrifice, invested the "great task" still before the living with greater authority. Our task was not unlike theirs and was to continue theirs. This association by repetition sealed the essential unity of the national enterprise embodied in Lincoln's vision of the Union cause, from the founding to the future. Dedication in the past, present, and future binds together the "fathers," the "brave men," and "us" in a common goal of supporting democratic government, freedom, and equality. At Gettysburg, Lincoln did not only construct a national memory of immortal words; he was also helping build the great myth of the Cause Victorious. This was a politically charged and ideologically committed position, staking a radical Unionist claim to define the nature of the American nation.

The evidence for the Washington Draft, particularly Lincoln's conversation with the cemetery's designer, William Saunders, suggests that, in Washington, Lincoln had imagined himself standing in the landscape of Gettysburg, the battlefield around him, the graves in ordered arcs across the hillside. "To stand" in a place, as Lincoln was imagining doing when writing in Washington, is a state of existing. Even when employed metaphorically, it is almost inevitably static; it is a status. Dedication is felt; it is an emotion. Lincoln returned to that emotion when he came back from actually walking "the ground around the Seminary," as Seward described it, and seeing the village in its valley. He was coming to a new understanding, a different vision, that needed expression.

This new vision compelled Lincoln to make another change to his speech at some point, perhaps before rising from the small table in the upper room in order to join the procession or while pacing the floor as Liberty Hollinger watched from the Diamond outside. Truth to tell, this change may have been made the night before, but it has the appearance and fits the logic of Lincoln's revisions in pencil that morning, for it is the kind of change that one makes when one is preparing to stand and speak. It may be that at this time, Lincoln looked over his text, perhaps trying to commit it to memory, as he told James Speed, and to rehearse and review how he would speak his lines and play his "part" or role in the grand pageant that was about to unfold on the cemetery grounds. As he did so, something struck him, and with his pencil he underlined one word, and one word only. "The world will little note, nor long remember what we say here; while it can never forget what they <u>did</u> here."

"What they <u>did</u> here." This small change captured what Lincoln at that moment wanted particularly to convey with that word in that passage and in the speech.[30] Lincoln's sense of the reality and the importance of what the brave men had done at Gettysburg must have been very strong in the upper room that morning on the cusp of going downstairs to ride out to the cemetery. Lincoln could not shed tears simply to console, would not speak words simply because they were expected, and was seemingly unable to bring himself to rally enthusiasm with mere words. Action and policy, the end in view and the larger purpose—these were what motivated Lincoln and brought him to think and write and speak in ways that helped win the war and assure the survival of the Union. What he had thought about as he talked with Saunders, as he looked over the depictions of where Reynolds had died, and as he imagined himself in that place had now become what he was experiencing and feeling in a town filled with celebration but also surrounded by a landscape of sacrifice and death; the evidence was everywhere.

Already, the night before, he had revisited his speech as planned, incorporating in unknown ways his continued evolution toward ideas and a vision that was still taking form. Yet after consulting with Seward that night and completing, as he must have thought, the finished version, in the morning a new revision was sparked by something unexpected, seemingly by a vivid experience or insight. The text written in Washington rings with clarity and intellectual power, its multiple themes converging and reinforcing each other so strongly on the first page alone that the second must have continued these to conclusion, or very nearly. But that Washington Draft did not reach the same conclusion he reached as he took the stand in Gettysburg; the second part of his Washington Draft no longer suited; the late-night Gettysburg Draft, almost certainly a complete text, on the morning of November 19 now seemed inadequate.

This culmination of his speech is what brought Lincoln, or perhaps forced Lincoln, to imagine the future of the Republic of the "fathers" in a way that he had never done before. The fate of the Union was the dominant political question of the war, of course, but it presented new aspects in the fall of 1863 that made this period of time, indeed made this journey to Gettysburg, a pivot point of the war. Lincoln himself recognized the importance of this time in his Annual Message to Congress of December 8, 1863, the nineteenth-century equivalent of a modern State of the Union address. Lincoln reportedly said he began working on his Annual Message on Friday, November 13, and the core of his message was substantially finished by November 25, when Secretary of the Treasury Chase wrote to Lincoln expressing his support.[31] Indeed, Lincoln's primary concern in mid-November was not his words at the dedication ceremony but rather the formulation of this coherent Reconstruction policy and its presentation to Congress and the nation. Thus it happened that the Gettysburg Address, which became Lincoln's most admired and profound statement of national purpose, was written at precisely the same moment that he formulated his most far-reaching and important statement of Reconstruction policy outlining the future of the Union. This timing was not a coincidence; the two statements sprang from Lincoln's deliberations about the same problems.

Written during the two weeks surrounding the journey to Gettysburg, Lincoln's Annual Message forthrightly asserted that the moment had come for a more comprehensive and long-range plan for Reconstruction, and that meant placing his new policy within the story of the nation's development. "When Congress assembled a year ago, the war had already lasted nearly twenty months," he began in his customary manner of looking backward as a first step forward.[32] He then presented a remarkable summary of late 1862 as a time of peril and difficulty, from the results of the recent elections to threats of foreign intervention. In Lincoln's accounting, these problems were merely the prelude to the greater crisis of 1863, when "the policy of emancipation, and of employing black soldiers, gave to the future a new aspect, about which hope, and fear, and doubt, contended in uncertain conflict." Lincoln even added that "for a long time it had been hoped that the rebellion could be suppressed, without resorting to it [emancipation] as a military measure." This can be read as an admission that Lincoln did not want to bring about emancipation, but he was referring specifically to emancipation "as a military measure," which he knew would be opposed as unconstitutional. Lincoln's point was that if he were forced to resort to a constitutionally questionable presidential decree of emancipation, "the crisis of the contest would then be presented."[33]

Having led us in this passage to contemplate the fearful "crisis of the contest," Lincoln in his Annual Message followed it with one of his classic sentences, similar in its finality to "And the war came," which would so powerfully punctuate the Second Inaugural Address. "It came; and, as was anticipated, it was followed by dark and doubtful days." Just as in the Second Inaugural, this sentence signals a transition away from difficulty and toward resolution. "Eleven months having now passed," he wrote in the first draft of his Annual Message, "we are permitted to take a new review."[34] Lincoln then returned to each of the problems that had made 1862 and early 1863 such "dark and doubtful days," in each case finding a wholly changed dynamic. The elections of 1863, the attitude of the European powers, the opening of the Mississippi after Vicksburg, the movement in states from Maryland to Arkansas toward emancipation, and particularly the successes of black troops, "as good soldiers as any," collectively led him to develop a new vision of the pattern of events. "Thus," he concluded, "we have the new reckoning. The crisis, which threatened to divide the friends of the Union, is past."

So now the future beckoned, and Lincoln then presented his Reconstruction policy, the plan by which the administration would recognize state governments created on the basis of the votes of at least 10 percent of the voters of 1860 who had taken an oath to support the Constitution and the Union. But the cornerstone of the new policy, as Seward hinted in his surprisingly radical speech to the serenaders at Gettysburg the night before the ceremony, was that the administration would accept only states that prohibited slavery, thereby removing the potential issue of courts overturning the Emancipation Proclamation: there would be no reunion with slaveholders; the reconstructed Union would not be the Union as it was. A "new aspect" to the future, a "new review" of the course of events, a "new reckoning" about where the issues now stand—in the Annual Message, Lincoln explained how and why he came to a reimagined, reformulated, and renewed understanding of the war and its meaning.

The triumphs and disasters of 1863 had led Lincoln toward a more complete and expansive set of policies beyond mere military emancipation. Most important, as Lincoln stated directly in the Annual Message, were the consequences that flowed from arming and deploying formerly enslaved blacks. From the declaration of equal protection of all citizens, black and white (July 30, 1863), to compulsory manumission with compensation for slaves drafted (October 1863), to the promise of equal pay for all soldiers (in the December Message), to support for voting rights in some states (December 1863–March 1864), Lincoln's policies starting in the summer of 1863 went beyond emancipation as a military policy and began to envision the reality that the new nation born of the war would include blacks and whites coexisting in a single society. In the new reckoning, this new society would be founded upon equal rights before the law for whites and blacks.[35] It was at Gettysburg—and so far as we know, on the very morning of the ceremony—that Lincoln at last found a way in his speech to express most fully and poetically the "new review" that he was coming to see in the last half of 1863, since Vicksburg and Gettysburg had signaled the turn of the struggle.[36] In his speech, Lincoln expanded the "new reckoning" on the course of war outlined in the Annual Message and magnified it to the scale of the nation's trajectory since its founding.

Throughout his revisions Lincoln had had trouble with the last part of his speech, the prospective, forward-looking conclusion, but that changed after he had been to the battlefield and seen the ground that was soon to be consecrated to the fallen. It was then that he recognized that the passivity of "to stand here" in the Washington Draft was unsatisfactory in comparison to "what they did here." All those words had been written in Washington, when the founders of July 4 had dominated his vision, but the crucial, revealing underline in pencil presents clear evidence that it was at Gettysburg that the power and meaning of "what they did here" fully struck Lincoln. Then it came together in a moment of thought and feeling, a final push, confirmed in Lincoln's own telling to James Speed as a memorable, eventful process, completed only at the very last moment, as the text itself reveals. That morning, not only did Lincoln (probably) add the emphasis to that word as he was planning to speak it, but he also discovered in a fifth written repetition of the concept of "dedication" the path toward his final delivery text, and of a more assertive, active, and emotionally powerful vision in the final sentence.

Conjoined, ungrammatical, and, most important, uncorrected hybrid that it is, the Nicolay document, with its splice across that fifth "dedica // ted" linking the Letterhead Page of Washington to the Pencil Page of Gettysburg, is the first known appearance of this larger, new formulation, founded in a powerful sense of the devotion and sacrifices of those—Reynolds among them—who had died for the Union, a vivid realization that inspired Lincoln to express his vision of the purposes and meanings of the war and of the American experiment in the most expansive, assertive, and committed language he possessed. On the morning of November 19, 1863, as the crowds were gathering in the Diamond below, and with young Liberty Hollinger looking on, Lincoln dedicated and rededicated himself and the nation to achieving something that went beyond the work of the fathers. It was the "new birth of freedom," and it is found for the first time in the penciled words of the Battlefield Draft of the Gettysburg Address:

Four score and seven years ago our fathers brought forth, upon this continent, a new nation, conceived in liberty, and dedicated to the proposition that "all men are created equal[.]"

Now we are engaged in a great civil war, testing whether that nation, or any nation so conceived, and so dedicated, can long endure. We are met on a great battle field of that war. We have come to dedicate a portion

CHAPTER SIX

of it, as a final resting place for those who died here, that the nation might live. This we may, in all propriety do. But, in a larger sense, we can not dedicate—we can not consecrate—we can not hallow, this ground—The brave men, living and dead, who struggled here, have hallowed it, far above our poor power to add or detract. The world will little note, nor long remember what we say here; while it can never forget what they did here.

It is rather for us, the living, ~~to stand here,~~ we here be dedica //

ted to the great task remaining before us—that, from these honored dead we take increased devotion to that cause for which they here, gave the last full measure of devotion—that we here highly resolve these dead shall not have died in vain; that the nation, shall have a new birth of freedom, and that government of the people by the people for the people, shall not perish from the earth.

CHAPTER SEVEN

■

"What They <u>Did</u> Here"

ROUND TOP MOUNTAIN

With the Battlefield Draft in his coat pocket, Lincoln on the morning of Thursday, November 19, stepped from the Wills house into the crowded street and was greeted with such a cheer and welcome that the *Philadelphia Press* described him as "half blushing amid the intense ardor." In his later memoir, John Russell Young, who had probably written that account thirty years before, similarly remembered, "We gathered about the house where Lincoln resided, and waited—led horses restlessly in attendance. The President came to the door, a fine flush and smile coming over his face at the rude welcome." One person called out, "Give me your hand, Mr. President"; another, "Good morning, Mr. Lincoln"; and one simply, "Abraham." Thousands had traveled, often hundreds of miles, for this day, and the people of Gettysburg and its environs had been anticipating it for months. "My father who was a Republican and who had voted for Lincoln in 1860, said, 'We will go to hear him,'" William Storrick remembered, and so he had a story of meeting Abraham Lincoln out in front of the Wills house that he could tell to the end of his days.[1] David Wills and the cemetery agents had invited Lincoln in order to give more prominence to their grand patriotic celebration, and the attendance of hundreds, or even thousands, who had come especially to see Lincoln vindicated their gamble, even aside from the "few appropriate remarks" they had solicited, almost in spite of themselves.

"Such homage I never saw or imagined could be shown to any one person as the people bestow upon Lincoln," Josephine Roedel wrote in her diary. She had traveled from Virginia to visit family and friends and was only there by happenstance, but she still noted, "The very mention of his name brings forth shouts of applause. No doubt he will be the next President, even his enemies acknowledge him to be an honest man." As Roedel's diary demonstrates, the greetings that followed Lincoln everywhere did not need to be exaggerated by the predominantly Republican press corps, for it expressed genuine support and admiration for Lincoln among the thousands who had come to the little town. The soldiers, families, officeholders, veterans, politicians, and common folk who had made the journey needed no prompting to show their devotion to the Union and its fallen heroes, and they seemed eager as well to show themselves to be friends of Lincoln. Roedel's diary, seamlessly moving from the accolades for Lincoln to his reelection prospects, also nicely illustrates the pervasive political and even partisan atmosphere of the celebrations, which was obvious to every person on the street and is apparent in virtually all the press reports. Just as for the serenades and speeches of the night before, the unprecedented popular mobilization and high political tensions of the war pervaded every movement and action of the players—not in spite of the grand, patriotic celebrations but because of them. Opposition papers like the *New York World* could not deny the ardor of the crowds, so they complained instead that their noise and enthusiasm "seemed in bad taste and out of place."[2]

When Lincoln appeared, a barely controlled chaos reigned on the Diamond while the procession slowly took shape. An honor guard of some 1,200 soldiers and wounded veterans of the Invalid Corps would precede Lincoln and the other dignitaries of the first rank, who were to ride horseback the mile or so to the cemetery. Civic groups, state delegations, and common citizens would follow. Many of the cabinet members and governors were already astride their horses, and Lincoln himself immediately mounted what one reporter called a "splendid black steed." One of the four reporters dispatched by Forney's *Washington Daily Morning Chronicle* admired the way Lincoln "steadily mounted his horse," but even so, he was not done kissing babies, as he had done the day before. Reverend William Dickson of Chambersburg, Pennsylvania, later recalled seeing a man hold up to Lincoln his little girl, dressed in white—no doubt her Sunday best. "Lincoln reached out his long arms," according to one summary of his story, "lifted the child to a place on the horse before him, kissed her, then handed her back to the happy father."[3]

In his long black Prince Albert coat, silk top hat with the ever-present black band of mourning for his son William, and white gloves, Lincoln astride his horse was "the tallest and the grandest rider in the procession, bowing and nearly laughing his acknowledgements." He was quickly "besieged" by an eager crowd, "thronging around him, and anxious for the pleasure of taking him by the hand, while he sat pleasantly enjoying the hearty welcome," according to "J. H." writing in the *Chronicle*, who was probably John Hay. This might have gone on for some time, but the parade marshals, "having mercy upon his oft-wrung arm and wearying exertions, caused the crowd to desist and allow the President to sit in peace upon his horse." Charles Hale, Edward Everett's grand nephew, writing in his family's *Boston Advertiser* agreed that Lincoln "seemed grateful to the marshal who came to his rescue and drove back the crowd." At some point, perhaps just as the procession was about to move, Liberty Hollinger remembered, "The band began to play and Mr. Lincoln's horse became excited and pranced around quite lively. It seemed to amuse the President, and then that sober, sad-faced man actually smiled." The noble, splendid charger turned out to be "a mettlesome steed," according to the *Boston Journal,* but luckily, another reporter added, Lincoln's "awkwardness, which is so often remarked does not extend to his horsemanship."[4] The years riding the court circuit in Illinois attested to that.

"At ten o'clock the procession was formed and began to move," Harvey Sweeney, a butcher in the town, wrote to his brother just over a week after the ceremony. "This was a grand and impressive sight. I have no language to depict it and tho' the mighty mass rolled on as the waves of the mighty ocean, everything was perfect order." To Sweeney, as to so many others, in this "living sea" of soldiers, dignitaries, and officials, "the greatest of the great men that honored this occasion was President Lincoln. . . . Like Saul of old he towered a head taller than any man." The *Cincinnati Daily Gazette* agreed that the procession made "a splendid appearance." "As the procession passed the low muffled sound of a canon echoed through the streets of the village and was reverberated from the surrounding hill," the *Philadelphia Inquirer* reported, and the *Indianapolis Daily Journal* described "long glittering lines of troops, headed by Generals with dashing staffs and interspersed with scarlet-plumed bands."[5] A dozen governors (eight current, three former, and one elect, accorded equal honors), three cabinet secretaries, a half dozen foreign ministers and officials, and a dozen or more bemedaled generals graced the procession. The Baltimore city councilmen, who had not welcomed Lincoln to their city, made quite an impression, each wearing red, white, and blue ribbons and a "handsome silver model of the celebrated Baltimore monument" to George Washington on their lapels. Some of the parade marshals and cemetery agents rode behind Lincoln in bright yellow or white shoulder sashes and matching gauntlets. The members of the cabinet rode in line with Lincoln much of the way, although Seward had gotten a late start and had to ride hard to catch up with the president's party.[6] David Wills probably rode with the marshals, but he went unremarked in the accounts of the day, unjust neglect for the indefatigable force behind both the cemetery and the ceremony.

Along the route houses displayed flags or were draped in mourning, and people lined the streets and leaned out of windows. Historian William J. Frassanito has recreated the scene through the images of local photographers, the brothers Charles and Isaac Tyson. They knew the best place to capture an image of the procession, a spot slightly elevated at the foot of Cemetery Hill where the procession would turn to its right in order to circle around and enter the cemetery from the west, by way of Taneytown Road. Henry Eyster Jacobs, son of a professor at the local college and a recent graduate himself, had also carefully selected that spot. Forty years later, after the young student had become dean of the Lutheran Seminary at Mount Airy, he recalled that when "looking on the front of the procession, the cheers of the crowd lining the sidewalks told me of the approach of the President. On all sides he was greeted with enthusiasm," which Lincoln acknowledged by "appreciative smiles and continual bows." Then the soldiers turned, Lincoln came into unobstructed view, and the Tysons opened the lens. "He towered above everyone," Jacobs recalled, "and his gigantic proportions seemed to be magnified by the shape of the odd high silk hat that he wore." And that is just the scene in the remarkable image the Tysons captured, a mass of spectators and soldiers marching toward the camera, filling Baltimore Street back into the distance toward the town center, and in the midst of them all, flanked by a marshal (probably Ward Lamon) in a white shoulder sash, there stands out a large figure in a top hat, sitting tall in the saddle.[7]

Wills and the cemetery agents had planned for large state delegations and thousands of local citizens to follow Lincoln, a customary part of such processions, which were sometimes measured in miles. But Clark E. Carr, the doughty Illinois agent, was disappointed in the small turnout, "as most of the people chose to go out by themselves over the battlefield and through the cemetery." This disillusionment, a foreshadowing of larger disappointments to come, was shared by the jaded John Hay. "I got a beast and rode out with the President's suite to the Cemetery in the procession," he noted in his diary. "The procession formed itself in an orphanly sort of way & moved out with very little help from anybody." John Russell Young, who shared Hay's jaundiced eye, also recalled, "The procession from the town was a ragged affair, we all seeming to get there as best we could." Even the reliably boosterish Charles Hale in the *Boston Advertiser* reported that the procession was somewhat small because so many had hurried to get a place at the cemetery.[8]

The differing perceptions of the parade (august or orphanly; immense or disappointing) and of the day more generally remind us that everyone experienced these moments in unique ways. Smiling, laughing, kissing children, and adeptly handling a mettlesome horse, Lincoln was clearly caught up in some of the excitement and revelry of the early morning on the Diamond and the first stages of the procession, which seemed to continue the atmosphere of celebration of the night before. Yet as the procession approached and then entered the cemetery itself, a more solemn and reverential tone can be discerned. The *Washington Daily Morning Chronicle* reported that as Cemetery Hill rose ever nearer before the participants, they could see increasing signs of the battle. "Houses are dotted with musket balls, the marks being still fresh and ragged." The ground here had been repeatedly scoured for relics, but small fragments of shell or remnants of uniforms could still be seen almost everywhere. Then, as the procession moved south down Taneytown Road to the western side of the hill—the side attacked so ferociously on the titanic third day of the battle—the cemetery came into full view, and the procession marched up the central axis of the semicircle, with the mounded graves on either side. "The graves are fresh, for they are newly made, marked as yet, at head and foot, only by bits of board stuck in the ground" one reporter noted; another thought the long, curving mounds had the appearance of "garden beds" but then hastened to add that the soldiers were indeed buried individually. The few bare trees did not impede a panoramic view of the site and the valley and hills of the battlefield all around. The cemetery was not yet enclosed by a wall or barrier, but the graves themselves set this place apart as a sacred precinct, commanding silence and a reverential bearing worthy of the impending ritual consecration. "One could not approach the Cemetery itself without feeling deeply sobered and subdued," as "J. H." reported in the *Chronicle*.[9]

While no doubt some were unmoved by the scene, many others felt deeply that a sacred ceremony was unfolding before them in a great outpouring of national mourning; Lincoln would reveal himself to be among them. Emily Souder, who had served in Gettysburg as a volunteer nurse and had returned for the ceremonies, experienced the procession as a rite of sacred mourning, as so many felt it to be, and especially when standing before the temporary wooden crosses and improvised headboards over the mounded graves. "As the hour approached," she wrote days later, "the sadness of recent bereavement seemed to rest upon every heart. Soon we heard the sounds of funeral marches. Then came the President, easily distinguished from all others." No longer smiling and laughing, Lincoln appeared to Souder "as chief mourner."[10]

Up on the hill, many journalists were already at the desks set aside for them on the platform when they heard the music of the bands rising up to them. "The grand procession is moving out toward the point we occupy," Isaak Jackson Allen reported in the *[Columbus] Ohio State Journal*. "Mr. Lincoln's tall and upright figure becomes commandingly conspicuous, and is the observed of all observers." A flag flew from an enormous pole in the center of the semicircle of graves, where a tall monument stands today. Perhaps to prevent the crowd from trampling the graves, the platform was situated southeast of the flagpole, in a vacant section of the town graveyard adjacent to the new cemetery. Soldiers formed a cordon or hollow square extending perhaps 200 yards around the platform, creating an area reserved for the participants in the procession. Although tickets were issued for the favored ones who would sit on the platform, there were too many people and not enough space, so even some of the notables had to content themselves as groundlings. This was not much of a loss, according to the hostile *New York World*, as those with places were forced to sit on "a miserable, rough platform, without even an awning to shelter them," and many had to stand. David Wills and General Darius Couch, who commanded the participating soldiers, had also followed common practice and designated an area to the right of the stand exclusively for "the ladies"; one newspaper reported that 2,000 women attended the ceremony.[11] The platform faced north and west so that although the flagpole was within the reserved area, most of the crowd would stand to the east and north of the center of the new soldier's cemetery.

A salvo of salute was fired when Lincoln first arrived at the cemetery, but so many people had come up to the cemetery early and were crowding in upon the cordon of soldiers that the procession had some trouble getting through. Eventually, Lincoln was able to ride up to the platform, which was said to have been about 3 feet high. Perhaps to express the dignity of the occasion, Lincoln stepped to the platform at a slow, measured pace and found his assigned seat between the places reserved for Seward and Everett. "No chair of state was there for the Chief Magistrate of the Republic, but an old, dingy, uncushioned settee, was the seat of the chief dignitaries of the nation during the exercises of three hours," according to a cranky reporter in the *Cincinnati Daily Gazette*, who dispensed much ink bemoaning the arrangements, from train schedules to overnight accommodations.[12]

All the men took their hats off when Lincoln appeared, and there may have been a smattering of applause. Oddly, the *Boston Journal* seemed to think this funerary rite called for a rousing cheer, complaining that the crowd in front of the stand was "orderly but phlegmatic and undemonstrative. . . . There was much less waving of handkerchiefs and other marks of enthusiastic feeling" than in New England. The main Associated Press report, reprinted across the Union the next day, more tactfully noted that Lincoln was received "with the respect and perfect silence" appropriate to "the solemnity of the occasion." Our disgruntled Bostonian snidely noted that Lincoln "stepped forward to acknowledge the salute by one of *his* most *graceful* bows." Seemingly, Lincoln's proficiency with horses did not extend to such niceties, but "soon all was hushed, and for about fifteen minutes the multitude stood in perfect silence in close observation of the Chief Magistrate."[13]

While the rest of the procession entered the reserved area, the spectators and participants took in the sweeping views and made small talk. A band played a funereal dirge; according to one reporter, it "echoed back from the wooded sides of Culp's hill as if it were ghostly participating in the solemn ceremonies." David Tod, the soon-to-be-former governor of Ohio, sought out Lincoln and in "a hearty and cordial manner" said to him, "Mr. President, I want you to shake hands with me," to which Lincoln was reported to have responded just as cordially. Tod then introduced John Brough, the incoming governor, to Lincoln and then to Seward, who remarked, "Why, I have just seen [ex-] Governor Dennison, of Ohio, and here are two more governors of Ohio—how many more Governors has Ohio?" This was also when, in response to Tod saying he had called on both Seward and Usher that morning but had found Seward not at home, Seward explained, "Yes, sir, I visited the ground around the Seminary this morning, and Mr. Lincoln joined me." Seward then continued, "Well, Governor, you seem to have been to the State Department and to the Interior, I will now go with you to the Post Office," and then turned to introduce Tod and Brough to Postmaster General Blair.[14] Even if not the most impressive of witticisms, this quickness with words helps illustrate further why Lincoln had wanted the night before to consult with Seward about his speech.

All the players had taken their places, but Everett was not to be found. He had arrived in plenty of time, traveling in a carriage with Reverend Thomas H. Stockton, who was to lead the opening prayer, and the college president, Reverend Henry Baugher, who would give the closing benediction; the pregnant Mrs. Wills joined the three elderly men. Upon arrival they found behind the speakers' stand a tent, which Everett had requested, outfitted with a "pot-de-chambre" covered discreetly with a newspaper. "Into this tent, thus arranged, I was ushered with 8 or 10 men & women," he noted wryly; "they, by degrees, comprehended the nature of the position, & left me alone." Only after this awkward episode did a delegation of four governors conduct Everett to the platform to sit "at the President's right hand," as Everett wrote, carefully noting the honor accorded to him as the speaker of the day. Just as carefully, Everett recorded that one of the governors who escorted him was Seymour of New York, who was the only prominent Democrat to take part in the ceremonies and was, from John Russell Young's recollection, barely tolerated by the Republicans who had taken control of the little town. "These were stern days, my friends," Young explained. "There was a Puritan spirit abroad, and you can imagine the feeling with which a company of Roundheads would have welcomed a prince of the Cavaliers."[15]

Just after noon, and half an hour or more after Lincoln had first reached the stand, the last notes of the dirge faded away and Reverend Stockton stepped forward, introduced by Ward Lamon. "At this moment the scene was the grandest we ever witnessed," wrote the reporter for the *Philadelphia Daily Evening Bulletin*. "Here was the holy spot where fell our heroes and where their bones lie buried. On the platform was the representative of the loyalty and courage of the Republic, surrounded by genius, military daring, and civic distinction." Republican hyperbole and "patriotic gore," perhaps, but we do the past injustice if we dismiss its naive devotion without recognizing the real power of such moments to create enduring landmarks of meaning.[16] Stockton's affecting prayer opening the event was the single most emotionally powerful moment in the contemporary accounts. For many at the time it summed up and expressed the sentiments of the day, and for us it helps explain the impact of the words and ideas proclaimed from that platform at the dawning moments of the legend of Lincoln at Gettysburg.

The good reverend, several times chaplain of the U.S. House of Representatives, was recognized as one of the most outstanding preachers in an era of remarkable oratory, and he gave "a prayer such as only he is capable of," according to the *Chicago Tribune*. "Never was a man selected for any service so fit in every respect to perform it. There the reverent gentleman stood, looking as if he himself was one of the brave dead, whose graves were spread out before him, just risen from the tomb to invoke the God of nations and liberty." Stockton's sepulchral appearance lent authority to his pronouncements: "The most unearthly face out of the grave; absolutely colorless; the lips as white as the wasted cheek," noted the *Cincinnati Daily Commercial*. Even more striking was his intonation. John Russell Young, who in the 1870s toured the world with Grant and later served as ambassador to China, recalled that Stockton "could produce effects with his voice that I have heard in no other speaker but Gladstone."[17]

"By this Altar of Sacrifice, on this Field of Deliverance, on this Mount of Salvation," Stockton declared, each word associating the Union dead with God's divine plan, the enemy had come to "cast the chain of Slavery around the form of Freedom." Then, "from the coasts beneath the Eastern star, from the shores of Northern lakes and rivers, from the flowers of Western prairies, and from the homes of the Midway and the Border," came others, "to die for us and for mankind." The allusion to the Christlike sacrifice of the Union soldiers would have been clear to all. Rendered in the richest cadence of holy ritual, the prayer played upon powerful themes of religion, nation, sacrifice, and devotion. Too much so for some tastes: forty years later, Wayne MacVeagh could still recall sitting on the speakers' platform next to the young John Hay, who ironically smirked that it was "the finest invocation ever addressed to an American audience."[18]

Lincoln, and thousands of others, had a different response. For them, this ritual invocation linking the graves before them to the sacred cause of nation and God played upon heartfelt emotions. "We come with the humility of prayer," Stockton intoned, "with the pathetic eloquence of venerable wisdom, with the tender beauty of poetry, with the plaintive harmony of music, with the honest tribute of our Chief Magistrate, and with all this honorable attendance: but our best hope is in thy blessing, O Lord, our God!" As Stockton led those gathered to the culmination of his prayer, the emotions of the moment began to tell. Reverence for the dead; compassion for the wounded; consolation for the living; and, at last, hope of a greater triumph yet to come in the resurrection to eternal life and the victory of a sacred cause:

> As the trees are not dead, though their foliage is gone, so our heroes are not dead, though their forms have fallen. In their proper personality they are all with Thee. And the spirit of their example is here. It fills the air; it fills our hearts. And, long as time shall last, it will hover in these skies and rest on this landscape; and the pilgrims of our own land, and from all lands, will thrill with its inspiration, and increase and confirm their devotion to liberty, religion, and God.

And when the gaunt, sepulchral reverend, with all the skill of a practiced artist and all the power of his holy office, ended with the ritual recitation, "Our Father, who art in heaven, hallowed be thy name," he was joined in the Lord's Prayer by thousands, many of them "attesting by tears that would not be repressed that their souls were penetrated." It was, the impressed reporter for the *Cincinnati Daily Gazette* declared, "truly the nation's invocation to the God of life, of love and of liberty." Lincoln too, "united in this adjuration in all the simplicity of his soul," according to the report, "and the falling tear declared the sincerity of his emotion." At this moment, according to the *Baltimore American,* "the President evidently felt deeply and along with the venerable statesman and patriot, Hon. Edward Everett, who was by his side, seemed not ashamed to let their sympathetic tears be seen."[19]

Lincoln's revisions that morning had already demonstrated the impact of the battlefield, and now, at the cemetery, the carefully crafted rites of mourning and commemoration were coming home to him ever more fully. Stockton's prayer, overwrought and overlong as it may have been, expressed and exalted the sentiments of many who stood silently with heads bowed or who spoke the ancient words of devotion and consolation. "Many were in mourning," as "J. H." of the *Washington Chronicle* noted from the stand, "and the upturned tearful eyes of those who were near, indicated too plainly that to them the dedication was a sad pilgrimage also."[20] Lincoln's tears linked him in sympathy with the assembly, a communal affirmation of shared values, common sacrifices, and united purpose. Against the backdrop of a longer reflection on the meaning of the battle and the war, the celebratory wake of the night before, and the high spirits as the procession gathered that morning, this tearful and reverential response to the rituals and ceremonies of the day added a new element to Lincoln's experience of Gettysburg. This, in turn, will become one inspiration for the last, additional elements of Lincoln's speech.

After Stockton sat down, the Marine Band played "Old Hundredth," known also as the Doxology, the familiar strains of the sacramental music continuing the ceremonial tone. Then Ward Lamon introduced the Honorable Edward Everett for the central rite of the day, the grand oration. Since that time, it has become traditional to compare Everett's oration to Lincoln's address, always to Everett's detriment. The trope of a speech of two minutes that eclipsed an address of two hours is only one of the many paradoxes and ironies that has driven a large part of the Gettysburg legend in American memory, similar to such themes as its unlikely origins on a rickety train or the alleged disappointment of the audience in response to Lincoln's masterpiece. Yet we must distinguish between the experience of those in attendance and the impressions of those writing in the days and decades afterward. "Mr. Everett's clear and perfectly modulated voice," reported the generally unfriendly *New York World,* gave his words "far more of the thrilling 'air of eloquence' than will appear to those who read them in the newspapers."[21] Because Everett's oration had been sent out beforehand, editorials and commentary in newspapers were often based on the printed words and did not reflect the often very favorable accounts of the oration written by the reporters and others who actually heard Everett speak. In this, as in so much else, Everett's oration contrasts with Lincoln's speech, whose words were ever more appreciated by those who read them.

"Upon rising," reported the *Cincinnati Daily Gazette*, "the orator turned to Mr. Lincoln, and making a low bow, said: 'Mr. President.' Who recognized him with: 'Mr. Everett.'" Everett then "turned to the multitude, and stood in silence, observing the people and contemplating the exquisite picture spread out before him." At age sixty-nine, Edward Everett in 1863 was at the pinnacle of his career as a respected orator after a life that spanned virtually the entire history of the young Republic; he once remarked that he had corresponded with every man who had ever been president of the United States except George Washington.[22] The first American to receive a Ph.D., former professor of Greek, president of Harvard University, five-term member of the House of Representatives, four-term governor of Massachusetts, minister to Great Britain, secretary of state, and U.S. senator, Everett had attained nearly every honor the nation could confer. He had departed from the Senate in 1854 under something of a cloud, however, for he had not attended the climactic vote on the Kansas-Nebraska Act, and his failure to cast a "no" vote had so incensed many of his constituents that he resigned, citing ill health.

In truth, Everett by the mid-1850s was a man without a party, but the war had ended the apparent contradiction between slavery and union that had paralyzed him. A hesitant candidate for vice president in 1860, Everett overcame his doubts about the uncouth westerner who had been elected and rallied strongly to the cause, eventually even becoming one of Lincoln's official electors in 1864. In the months before his death in January 1865, he was once again hailed and feted by all of Boston for his services to Massachusetts and the Union. His diary reveals that as he stood on the platform at Gettysburg after nearly two months of preparation, he knew he was giving perhaps the culminating speech of a long and illustrious life. "Standing beneath this serene sky," he began, "overlooking these broad fields now reposing from the labors of the waning year, the mighty Alleghenies dimly towering before us, the graves of our brethren beneath our feet, it is with hesitation that I raise my poor voice to break the eloquent silence of God and Nature."[23]

Famously, Everett's introduction compared the occasion to the rites performed at Marathon for the Greek heroes who had turned back the Persian invasion, elevating American history to the exalted status accorded the ancients and quite consciously assigning to the Union the role of Athens in its glory. Several phrases in this opening section of his speech seem to run in parallel with Lincoln's remarks, as when Everett said, "We have assembled" to pay tribute to "those who nobly sacrificed their lives, that their fellow-men may life in safety and honor," and then immediately described the cemetery as their "last resting-place." Lincoln, of course, similarly wrote in the Letterhead Page created in Washington, "We have come" to the "final resting place for those who died here, that the nation might live." It is also true that phrases like these were quite common at the time, so the question of how much Lincoln may have been influenced by Everett's oration will always be intriguing.

Everett devoted the first hour of his speech to a detailed account of the Gettysburg campaign, trying the patience of some listeners, but his courtly appearance and masterful presentation inspired admiration even from those who found this description of the battle tedious. "Mr. Everett shows no signs of decay other than his whitening hairs and deepening lines on his face," the *Cincinnati Daily Commercial* noted, "and you can not help thinking all the while that to his many rich mental endowments, Mr. Everett adds the immense advantage of a perfect form and a face absolutely handsome." Then too, "there is the gesture, once observed, never to be forgotten, when the orator rises to some climax, and the arms outspread, and the fingers, quivering and fluttering, as one said, like the pinions of an eagle, seem to rain down upon the audience the emotions with which they vibrate." The admiring *Chicago Tribune* noted, "The most appreciative listener was Old Abe himself. He seemed to be absorbed in attention so profoundly, till the spell was broken by a mistake of the orator in saying Gen. Lee, when he should have said Gen. Meade, which mistake caused the President to turn to Seward and with a loud voice say, 'Gen. Meade,' but the orator seemed not to hear it." The *Cincinnati Daily Gazette* added that when Lincoln issued "a still louder correction" to the same mistake a few moments later, Everett "turning around, bowed very low, acknowledging the error, and apologizing for it."[24]

Like many, Lincoln was carried along by Everett's artfully crafted performance, most visibly when Everett spoke of the carnage of the battlefield "at the close of the terrible conflict." But then, Everett added, "Scarcely has the cannon ceased to roar, when the brethren and sisters of Christian benevolence, ministers of compassion, angels of pity, hasten to the field and the hospital, to moisten the parched tongue, to bind the ghastly wounds, to soothe the parting agonies alike of friend and foe, and to catch the last whispered messages of love from dying lips. 'Carry this miniature back to my dear wife, but do not take it from my bosom till I am gone.' 'Tell my little sister not to grieve for me; I am willing to die for my country.' 'O that my mother were here!'" These wrenching scenes were then sealed by a quotation from the Gospel of Matthew, assuring the "angels of pity" of their final reward to come. "Forget not WHO it is that will hereafter say to you, 'Inasmuch as ye have done it unto one of the least of these my BRETHREN, ye have done it unto me.'"

It was a moment of high Victorian sentiment. "At that point where the sufferings of dying soldiers were recited scarcely a dry eye was visible," the *Boston Journal* reported, "the President mingling his tears with those of the people."[25] The next day, during their exchange of complimentary letters, Lincoln specifically commended Everett's "tribute to our noble women for their angel ministering to the suffering soldiers" and declared that it "surpasses, in its way, as do the subject of it whatever has gone before." Lincoln was still moved by Everett's words a year and a half later when a visiting delegation presented him with a vase of dried leaves gathered on the Gettysburg battlefield. Everett had passed away just a few weeks before, and a newspaper quoted Lincoln as recalling that "a most graceful and eloquent tribute was paid to the patriotism and self denying labors of the American ladies, on the occasion of the consecration of the National Cemetery at Gettysburg, by our illustrious friend, Edward Everett." Lincoln added, "I wish you to read, if you have not already done so, the glowing, and eloquent, and truthful words which he then spoke of the women of America."[26]

Lincoln's deeply felt response to Everett's depiction of suffering soldiers and ministering "angels of pity" underscores how important it is to recognize the emotional impact of the place and the moment on those who experienced the consecration ceremony. The *Philadelphia Public Ledger* declared that this homage to American womanhood "produced as decisive effect upon the audience as any part of the address" and that "many a manly face stooped to wipe away the unbidden tear."[27] In contrast, editorials and accounts written by those who had merely read Everett's oration rarely mention this passage. Yet for many of those who actually heard the oration, this was an affecting and powerful moment, as Lincoln's tears and his later references attest.

Lincoln also displayed himself greatly interested in Everett's refutation of Confederate arguments justifying secession. The polished and urbane Everett spoke of the rebellion more harshly than Lincoln ever did, castigating secessionists as "criminals" and "traitors," vilifying them for selling into slavery free men captured during the invasion of Pennsylvania, and denouncing Confederate political theory as self-serving hypocrisy. To demolish these "wretched sophistries," Everett cited the constitutional stipulation that state officials "shall be bound by oath or affirmation to support the Constitution" in order to dismiss secessionist arguments for state sovereignty, concluding derisively, "It is a common thing, under all governments, for an agent to be bound by oath to be faithful to his sovereign; but I never heard before of sovereigns being bound by oath to be faithful to their agency."

Everett's attack on "the extreme 'States Rights' party" seemed to give "great satisfaction to Mr. Lincoln, whose recent tears now gave way to a pleasant smile," Charles Hale reported in the *Boston Advertiser*. Hale gave more details in a letter several days later to his brother Edward Everett Hale, noting that Lincoln "was visibly pleased with the oration and at one passage slapped Seward who sat next to him on the thigh."[28] The *Cincinnati Daily Commercial* also saw Lincoln several times smiling "as some forcible remark of the orator arouses him, and once he placed his hand quickly on the shoulder of the gentleman on his left [Seward] and spoke an approving word." Lincoln was so taken with this part of the oration that he also mentioned it in his letter to Everett the next day, writing, "The point made against the theory of the general government being only an agency, was new to me." Indeed, Lincoln wrote Everett that he thought it "one of the best arguments for the national supremacy."[29]

As Everett began his final peroration, he employed his considerable skills to touch one last time the hearts of his listeners and to call forth one final time the noble sentiments of love of the Union and commemoration of the dead. "God bless the Union," he declared; "it is dearer to us for the blood of brave men which has been shed in its defense." Returning to the surrounding landscape and classical allusions of his first sentences, Everett evoked the fields "where the noble Reynolds held the advancing foe at bay, and, while he gave up his own life, assured by his forethought and self-sacrifice the triumph of the two succeeding days," and he rolled on, building tension and momentum across a sentence of over 150 words that mentioned some of the same hills that Lincoln had spoken of when looking over the cemetery plan with William Saunders two nights before: "Seminary Ridge, the Peach-Orchard, Cemetery, Culp, and Wolf Hill, Round Top, Little Round Top, humble names, henceforward dear and famous,— no lapse of time, no distance of space, shall cause you to be forgotten." For Everett, who the previous day had sampled preserves from the bloodied Peach Orchard; for Lincoln, who that morning had visited Seminary Ridge with Seward and seen the place where, as Everett declaimed, "the noble Reynolds held the advancing foe at bay"; and for the entire assembly, who saw these sites spread before them on that fall day, these were no longer merely names in texts or maps; they were as present and real as the graves at their feet. "The whole earth is the sepulcher of illustrious men," Everett intoned, quoting a line attributed to Pericles. Pausing, and raising his voice into solemn, measured emphasis, "All time," he continued in the most memorable words of his oration, "is the millennium of their glory."

Applause and congratulations greeted the conclusion of the grand oration. "After I had done," Everett wrote in his diary, "the President pressed my hand with great fervor, & said 'I am more than gratified, I am grateful to you.'"[30] Everett revealed this same vanity about Lincoln's compliments the Sunday following, when he brought to church Lincoln's letter of reply to his note of November 20, in which Lincoln had praised his oration. On the church steps, he happened upon his young grand-nephew Charles Hale and read the letter to him, just as Lincoln had showed Judge Holt and his son Robert the letter Everett had sent him, each man impressed with himself for having impressed the other.[31] It was "a masterly effort," Benjamin Brown French recorded in his diary, and it reminded him of hearing John Quincy Adams's great eulogy of Lafayette thirty years before. French's own "Consecration Hymn" would be sung next, just before the president's speech.

Toward the end of Everett's oration and during French's hymn, Lincoln appeared to grow nervous, recalled Henry Eyster Jacobs, the young collegian and later seminary dean. Jacobs had hurried up to the hill after seeing Lincoln in the procession where he had been photographed, and eventually he was able to move right up to the stand because the crowd had thinned a bit during the nearly three hours since the parade had first arrived at the cemetery. "His mind evidently was not on what Mr. Everett was saying, but on his own speech. He drew from his pocket a metallic spectacle case and adjusted a pair of steel glasses near the tip of his nose." Then, reaching into "the side pocket of his coat," Lincoln produced what Jacobs recalled as "a crumpled sheet of paper," which he "carefully smoothed and then read for a few moments." Lincoln then put the paper back in his pocket, suggesting to Jacobs that Lincoln intended to speak from memory. Isaak Allen of the *Ohio State Journal* also recalled seeing Lincoln take a paper from his pocket and then put it back. Like many, Jacobs thought Lincoln appeared sad or solemn. The reporter for the *Cincinnati Commercial* also described Lincoln on the stand as having "a thoughtful, kindly, care-worn face, impassive in repose, the eyes cast down, the lips thin and firmly set, ʃthe cheeks sunken, and the whole indicating weariness, and anything but good health." It was "a Scotch type of countenance, you say, with the disadvantage of emaciation by a siege of Western ague."[32]

In fact, Lincoln would later tell French that he began to feel ill at Gettysburg and "came home sick" with the smallpox that, when it fully developed, kept him confined to bed for the better part of ten days in late November and early December. The very afternoon of the ceremony a reporter saw Lincoln "sweating" and looking "discouraged," and another observer recalled Lincoln as "listless." Wayne MacVeagh much later recalled that on the train back to Washington, Lincoln "was suffering from a severe headache, and lying down in the drawing room" of the special railcar, "with his forehead bathed in cold water." Upon arrival in Washington, Lincoln went to bed complaining of "pain in head and back, fever and general malaise."[33] Abraham Lincoln, when he gave the speech that helped raise him to near-demigod status in the popular imagination, may well have been feeling tired, achy, and feverish.

With the end of the hymn, "there is a rustle of expectation and a visible attempt to get nearer the stand, as one sees by the surging tumult on the outskirts of the crowd," wrote the reporter for the *Cincinnati Daily Commercial* from his refuge on the platform. Clark E. Carr recalled "the usual craning of necks, the usual exclamations of 'Down in front!' the usual crowding to get places to see, and much confusion." Given the disagreements and discussions about whether Lincoln was to speak, Carr and the other cemetery agents, Wills among them, must have been wondering whether Lincoln would be able to provide the "few appropriate remarks" they had compromised upon. William Saunders sat close by, as did the cabinet secretaries and diplomats and dignitaries; John Hay, with Wayne MacVeagh near enough for snide whisperings; and John Nicolay, who had just seen the finishing touches put on the delivery text. Andrew Curtin too, with his young son at his side, was photographed on the stand in the midst of the governors and politicians and patronage men—Simon Cameron, the semi-disgraced former secretary of war and still the kingpin of Pennsylvania politics, and the isolated Seymour of New York, who braved the Republican crowds. And there, behind them all, could also be descried the "dark unmistakable figure of Forney," according to our sharp-eyed Cincinnati reporter. Just two weeks before, during a campaign swing through New York, Forney had called Seymour "a traitor worse than Vallandigham," and now here they were, sharing the stand as Lincoln prepared to give his remarks among that "singular and remarkable group of men, whose names are imperishably connected with the momentous events of the last three years."[34] Over the coming decades, these well-connected participants, many of them still at the beginning of long careers as opinion makers in newspapers, elective office, veterans' groups, church pulpits, and fraternal organizations, would be one reason why this speech would not be forgotten.

Other signs were also favorable. As Ward Lamon stepped forward to move along to the next line in the program, "Dedicatory Remarks by the President of the United States," it may have been a bit after two o'clock. The early morning clouds had burned away, and the temperature must have been nearing its high of 52 degrees. "The sun never broke to life and warmth on a fairer fall day than this," wrote "J. H." in Forney's *Washington Chronicle,* declaring it "one of the most beautiful Indian Summer days ever enjoyed." Two weeks before, Lincoln had counseled Lamon that "he could not well decline" to serve as marshal of the day, and now Lamon was introducing Lincoln for his part in what Lincoln had guessed would be, in what turns out to have been astonishing understatement, "an interesting ceremony."[35]

Lincoln at Gettysburg: He rose and was greeted with a hurricane of applause—or maybe there was complete silence. He rose and said he had only just been told he should say some words—or he perhaps had been laboring on his speech since mid-October. He held no paper—or he may have held several folded pages so close to his nose that his face could not be seen. Like the number of versions of Lincoln's words that day, the different descriptions of Lincoln at Gettysburg can be multiplied to exhaustion. About 10,000 people saw Lincoln, and many hundreds, perhaps thousands, heard him, and with the rise of the legend by the 1880s, virtually all of them could be guaranteed an audience or newspaper article by telling the story.

No detail was considered too trivial. Sixty years after Lincoln took off his hat for the ceremony, an obituary would record the death of a man who claimed to have held it that day. A century and a half later a family told the story, passed down through generations, that a distant grandmother had worn a cape while hearing Lincoln speak; a descendant wore it to see Barack Obama inaugurated, adding another layer of meaning to this personal memory that has now become another thread in our national identity.[36] And so the stories were told again and again over the years, increasing the likelihood of alterations with repetition but also deepening the meaning and power of the event. Over the decades the transformations of memory fractured the image of Lincoln speaking into pieces that were then reassembled into well-worn patterns. But these details matter because what Lincoln said and did on the stand, how he moved and spoke, how his words and his image become incorporated into the memory and identity of a nation, enable us to understand this improbable story in all its complexity.

It turns out that Lincoln was met neither by a storm of adulation nor by reverential silence, but by both measured applause and respectful attention, as befit his station and the occasion. Of course, Forney's *Chronicle* reported, "The President then appeared at the foot of the platform, and upon being introduced by the Marshal, was vociferously cheered by the vast audience," and the Republican *Philadelphia Inquirer* went so far as to describe "the most enthusiastic cheering." These forthrightly partisan papers may have exaggerated, but even the more restrained *Boston Journal* reported that Lincoln's reception was "quite cordial," the report coming from the same reporter who had just complained about the phlegmatic crowds in Pennsylvania.[37]

The *Cincinnati Daily Gazette* had thought Lincoln's earlier bow to the audience less than graceful, but its report of his speaking made no such complaint, saying he "read in a modest, unpretending style." Indeed, contrary to some later depictions, there are no contemporary descriptions of Lincoln as awkward or ungainly when he came forward to speak. John Hay, a friendly but discerning critic, noted in his diary, "The President in a firm free way, with more grace than is his wont said his half dozen lines of consecration." The handsome Governor Curtin recalled that Lincoln "rose and presented himself in a most dignified manner, becoming a President of the United States. He pronounced that speech in a voice that all the multitude heard. The crowd was hushed into silence because the President stood before them." The *Philadelphia Evening Bulletin,* among others, agreed that Lincoln "was heard at a great distance." All these witnesses were on the platform near Lincoln, but at the outer limits of the crowd, many could not hear or become fully engaged in the proceedings. One soldier in the cordon around the crowd beyond earshot of the stand wrote to his sister, "President Lincoln made a very short speech, not over (if it was) 15 minutes" and thought that Seward "made a few remarks," which is not true but shows how uncertain many could be about what was happening up on the platform. One reporter for the *Indianapolis Daily Journal* had arrived late and was reduced to watching with the groundlings. "The great surging crowd around the stand, and spreading down the slope almost to the line of graves," he complained from somewhere out in the audience, "made it impossible for anybody but those closest to see or hear."[38]

Lincoln was, of course, accustomed to speaking to great gatherings in the open air. Carr, who had helped convince the cemetery organizers to allow Lincoln a place on the program because he had often heard him on the stump, must have been listening with more than average interest. He knew his judgment was on the line, for nearby sat the unnamed "discriminating listener" among the event organizers, as Nicolay and Hay put it later, who doubted "whether Mr. Lincoln would or could properly honor the unique occasion." Carr recalled thirty years later that Lincoln "waited patiently for the audience to become quiet, and there was absolute silence while he spoke. He began in those high, clarion tones, which the people of Illinois had so often heard, to which he held to the close. His was a voice that, when he made an effort, could reach a great multitude, and he always tried to make every one hear." It was "a clear, ringing voice" Carr recalled; "a clear, full voice," Charles Hale wrote in the *Boston Advertiser*; "a clear, sharp voice" according to the *Philadelphia Evening Bulletin*.[39]

In his younger days Lincoln had attempted some extravagant oratorical gestures, but as president he spoke plainly and simply, aiming for dignity more than fireworks. Still, over the decades in courtrooms and in meeting halls, he had learned a good deal about how to get a point across. Just a few months before, he had sent a letter justifying his policies to a mass meeting in Springfield, advising his friend James C. Conkling, "You are one of the best public readers. I have but one suggestion. Read it very slowly." At Gettysburg he took his own advice, speaking "with great deliberation," according to the official report of the Massachusetts cemetery agents, among whom was Charles Hale, listening closely both in his official capacity and as a reporter for the family paper.[40]

Press reports provide the most immediate guide when reconstructing the iconic scene of Lincoln at Gettysburg. Hale's report in the *Boston Advertiser* noted that Lincoln's speech "created a most favorable impression" and was "emphatically the right words in the right place." The *Cincinnati Daily Gazette* added that it was "a perfect thing in every respect, was the universal encomium." Mary Shaw Leader, who the day before had seen Lincoln at the back of his train accept bouquets from the women of

Hanover, wrote in her newspaper, the *Hanover Spectator*, "Then our great President began to deliver a remarkable speech." The delegates from the city of Boston a few weeks later declared, "Perhaps nothing in the whole proceedings made so deep an impression on the vast assemblage, or has conveyed to the country in so concise a form the lesson of the hour, as the remarks of the President"—grand praise, given the power of Stockton's opening prayer, and the impact of Everett's depiction of the "angels of pity" tending the wounded. Such assessments are plentiful and go beyond what mere partisanship would dictate, but the testimony of Lincoln's political opponents is perhaps even more telling. The *Philadelphia Age* was the only opposition paper in the city, but it was forced to admit, "The speech the President made is the best he has ever made." Similarly, the unfriendly *New York World* noncommittally noted that Lincoln's speech was "brief," yet it then added that it was "calculated to arouse deep feeling," a sure sign that the speech had indeed aroused the deep feelings of many.[41]

Combining fragments of information from multiple contemporary sources can verify the essential accuracy of these depictions, but the thread of the moment can be lost. Fortunately there are a few contemporary accounts that bring together the disparate elements of the scene in a relatively holistic and verifiable manner. One of them is the remarkable article in the *Cincinnati Daily Commercial* of November 23 that provides perhaps the single most complete contemporary account of the day, giving in one sentence a thumbnail sketch of the scene:

> The President rises slowly, draws from his pocket a paper, and when the commotion subsides, in a sharp, unmusical, and treble voice, reads the following brief and pithy Dedicatory Remarks.

The point of view here is from the platform itself, expressed in the crisp tone of a professional journalist who had seen it all. The "sharp, unmusical" comment, in particular, lets us know that this is not the vision of a mere partisan (Forney's *Chronicle* might qualify) but of a journalist—Republican, to be sure—exercising discernment and judgment. This reporter admired Lincoln's remarks but clearly was not filled with transcendent awe. Eyewitnesses and later generations will fill in more details, many of which can be questioned, but the foundation provided by the report of the *Cincinnati Daily Commercial*, verified by numerous contemporary sources, is secure and unimpeachable.

As this example shows, the vision of Lincoln at Gettysburg in much of the contemporary press is predominantly of a fine—and even very fine—speech on an exceptional occasion. On either side of this balanced vision are two perspectives that over time contended for dominance in the myth of Gettysburg. The first to emerge, at the very time of the event itself, was a more emotive and affective vision of the scene, with Lincoln being increasingly depicted as tearful or racked with emotion and the crowd as responding in mighty unison, a vision of collective resolve and dedication to the ideals of the Union that are asserted as the ideals of the nation. This conforms to the postwar rise of the myth of the Cause Victorious, the sentimentalized image of the Union cause that dominated Civil War memory in the North and among Unionists.

On the other hand, in the late 1870s, Ward Lamon's assertions that no one at the time recognized the merits of the speech, and that Lincoln himself was disappointed, created an alternative trope of an affectless, uninspired, or uncomprehending crowd. Clark E. Carr's story that Lincoln's invitation was an afterthought fits seamlessly with this vision, and Carr and Nicolay, as we have seen, agreed that the brevity of the speech left some of the organizers on the stand disappointed. The point was not to denigrate the speech but to elevate Lincoln to a unique position as a giant who alone had understood the largest questions at issue and had had the genius to express truths that only the unfolding decades would reveal to others.

Both views, then, are part of the rising cult of the Gettysburg Address through the early twentieth century, but they arrive at that veneration from different directions. Of the two, the trope of disappointment or incomprehension at the speech requires little analysis and presents few mysteries. It can be made to correspond well with the favorable but measured tone of most of the contemporary record, even if there are no contemporary accounts that plainly state disappointment or incomprehension at Lincoln's words (as distinct from opponents who mocked them). In addition, the emergence of this thread with Lamon provides clear milestones and paths for development that can be followed relatively easily in the record of the 1870s and beyond.

More intriguing, and more in need of fuller development, is the rise of the affective and emotional vision that becomes, perhaps, the dominant image of a sentimentalized Lincoln declaiming universal truths before a vociferously adoring audience. This trope has a thousand threads, emerging gradually by so many paths that its connections to the contemporary record have always been a puzzle. It seems, however, that for some of those standing before Lincoln and sitting on the platform behind him, the scene of Lincoln rising to speak upon the great battlefield, on such an occasion, and such a day, was powerfully resonant. For these participants, the procession, the speeches, the graves, the memories of the battle, the larger backdrop of a desperate war, and, very often, the personal experience of loss and tragedy in the bloody struggle made up an essential but invisible element in the moment. Just as valid was the experience of Sarah Abercrombie, the young daughter of a general, who in later years claimed to have sat on the platform not far from Lincoln. She said she could remember nothing of the speeches because she was thinking only of the dashing young hero whom she had just met and who after the war would become her husband. Similarly, the journalist John Russell Young would recall being unimpressed with the speeches and instead being very much concerned about the plight of a photographer who failed to get a good picture of the scene.[42]

It is not surprising that two people can provide different pictures of that moment, but one of the most remarkable aspects of the Gettysburg legend is that we can see it being born before our eyes in the words and memories of many of those who stood there with Lincoln. Exaggerated and intensified by its association over time with the myth of the Cause Victorious, the emotive vision of Lincoln at Gettysburg rapidly became one of the central themes in the emerging memory of that moment, in depictions of the great war president of the Union giving a beautiful and moving speech that perfectly captured the tragedy and aspirations of a terrible war—because this was how the moment was lived by some who told the tale.

One undeservedly neglected account incorporates these elements while providing the single most complete, evocative, and reliable contemporary depiction of Lincoln on the stand at Gettysburg. It is a letter published in the November 30, 1863, *Eaton, Ohio, Register,* written not by a journalist but by Robert Miller, who in 1860 (at least) was the district attorney of Preble County, Ohio, and a leading figure in military recruitment and administration in the county.[43] Unlike the reporter for the *Commercial,* Miller evidently saw the event as most people saw it, looking up at the platform from the crowd, and he was particularly attentive to how the people responded to Lincoln's words:

The tall form of the President appeared on the stand and never before have I seen a crowd so vast and restless, after standing so long, so soon stilled and quieted.

Hats were removed and all stood motionless to catch the first words he should utter, and as he slowly, clearly, and without the least sign of embarrassment read and spoke for ten minutes you could not mistake the feeling and sentiment of the vast multitude before him.

I am convinced that the speech of the President has fully confirmed and I think will confirm all loyal men and women in the belief that Abraham Lincoln, though he may have made mistakes, is the right man in the right place.

Both Miller and the reporter for the *Commercial* noted the silence that settled upon the scene, but Miller presents a clearer image of Lincoln's demeanor as well as of the response of the crowd. It may be that as an elected official, Miller, like so many of the local notables, officeholders, and politicians who had come from around the Union to attend the ceremony, was also attentive to the audience as potential voters and patrons. Miller astutely managed to promote Lincoln's reelection ("the right man in the right place") while showing skeptical voters that he himself was no Republican puppet. With good reason: his county was in the heart of Ohio's Copperhead regions, part of Clement Vallandigham's former congressional district. Many believed that only some quick gerrymandering had secured the defeat of the notorious Peace Democrat in 1862 by Robert Schenck, who had come up to Gettysburg on Lincoln's train and who had caused so much trouble in Maryland. Miller's voters were not reliably Republican, in other words, but he deftly used Lincoln's speech as evidence of popular support for Lincoln and to confirm and justify his own support for the administration, even if it had made "some mistakes." Miller even suggested that Lincoln's speech itself helped promote the war effort, in addition to constituting an argument in favor of Lincoln's reelection. This is rather a load for one brief speech to carry, but Miller obviously thought it was no ordinary speech.

Miller's testimony, among others, demonstrates that Lincoln's words, spoken slowly and clearly—businesslike, one reporter said—resonated with at least some in the crowd, but there is one contemporary source, the November 23 edition of the *Ohio State Journal*, that so fully expresses the affective and emotional elements of that moment that it may be considered the epicenter of what would become the dominant image of a transcendent Lincoln at Gettysburg. This is not to say that all emotionally laden representations are descended from this account; unlike the (untrue) legend of Lincoln writing on the train, which has a fairly clear point of origin and path of diffusion, there are multiple streams that make up the tradition of Lincoln at Gettysburg because there were thousands of witnesses. Rather, this report brings together better than any other single account most of the elements, found in a variety of other contemporary sources, of what would become the collective cultural production that is the legend of Lincoln at Gettysburg.

The article was written by Isaak Jackson Allen, former president of a small Ohio college, judge, superintendent of Cincinnati schools, and then for two or three years during the war the editor of the *Ohio State Journal*. Allen's support for Lincoln and his connections in the Republican Party would soon win him the U.S. consulate at Hong Kong, after which he returned to Ohio and to his legal practice. Here is how he experienced Lincoln's speech:

> President Lincoln rose to deliver the Dedicatory Address. Instantly every eye was fixed and every voice hushed in expectant and respectful attention. . . .
>
> The President's calm but earnest utterance of his brief and beautiful address stirred the deepest fountains of feeling and emotion in the hearts of the vast throng before him; and, when he had concluded, scarcely could an untearful eye be seen, while sobs of smothered emotion were heard on every hand.

Allen's emphasis upon the dramatic impact of Lincoln's words has struck some as the insincere flattery of an office seeker.[44] His biography suggests instead that Allen was a professional and an educator more than a hack newsman; moreover, he claimed in his manuscript memoir to have been surprised by his unwanted appointment as consul. Allen may have had a sense of drama and was certainly partisan, but there is no convincing reason to think that he did not live that moment as he wrote it; that moment for Allen included a "stout, stalwart officer" next to him, "the empty sleeve of his coat indicating that he had stood where death was reveling":

And as the President, speaking of our Gettysburg soldiers, uttered that beautifully touching sentence, so sublime and pregnant with meaning— *"the world will little note, nor long remember what we here SAY, but it can never forget what they here DID"*—the gallant soldier's feelings burst over all restraint, and burying his face in his handkerchief, he sobbed aloud while his manly frame shook with no unmanly emotion.

A moment later, Allen added, the captain "lifted his still streaming eyes to heaven and in low and solemn tones exclaimed, *"God Almighty bless Abraham Lincoln!"*[45]

A difficult scene for a postheroic world to credit, but plentiful evidence demonstrates that many people cried during the ceremonies. David Wills in his official report, and many others besides, mentioned the wounded veterans who attended and wrote, "During the exercises their bronzed cheeks were frequently suffused with tears." This reverential theme was taken up by the hyperpartisan *Philadelphia Press* in an article datelined Gettysburg, November 19, the first publication to call Lincoln's speech "immortal." On November 25 the *Philadelphia Press* proclaimed that the nation was doubly honored at Gettysburg, by the battle and by the ceremonies at the consecration: "It might be, as the law was given from God, and came down from Sinai, so an immortal spirit came from the hill of the dead. . . . Certainly the occasion was sublime; certainly the ruler of the nation never stood higher, and grander, and more prophetic. On that historic height it was proper that he should utter words such as these: The world will little note . . . ," continuing on to quote the rest of the sentence.[46]

Much later, Clark E. Carr, who thought the speech disappointing, would still say that the phrase "little note, nor long remember" was "the only one in which the president manifested emotion," adding, "There was a tremor in his voice which I can never forget." The report by "J. H." in the *Washington Daily Morning Chronicle* of November 21, which was probably written in large part by John Hay, also thought that while speaking, "the President sensibly felt the solemnity of the occasion, and controlled himself by an effort." And the *Philadelphia Public Ledger* of November 23 mentioned almost in passing that the events of the day and "the short, modest, fitting address of the President of the United States produced tears at times, and at times every other emotion as only the highest eloquence can," and it then summarized several passages from the speech, adding its own emphasis to that much-noted passage "*Words* would soon be forgotten, but what they *did*, never."[47]

"My own emotions may perhaps be imagined," Major Azor Nickerson recalled thirty years later, "when it is remembered that he was facing the spot where only a short time before we had had our death-grapple with Pickett's men, and he stood almost immediately over the place where I had lain and seen my comrades torn in fragments by the enemy's cannon." Nickerson himself had been pierced through the arm and lung during that cannonade of July 3 and had been left for dead, but he rose from the battlefield; the torn limbs, clothing, and debris of war lay all around him, just as reminders of that day still littered the ground when he returned to hear Lincoln speak on November 19. "I thought then, and still think, it was the shortest, grandest speech, oration, sermon, or what you please to call it, to which I ever listened. It was the whole matter in a nutshell, delivered distinctly and impressively, so that all in that vast concourse could hear him."[48]

This matter-of-fact description of Lincoln's manner and delivery was just the introduction to Nickerson's own experience of Lincoln's words. "Think, if you please, how these words fell upon my ears: ' . . . We are met on a great battle-field of that war . . . ,'" quoting Lincoln's words and culminating with that line that was the most noted by those who heard the speech, "The world will little note . . . ."

> If at that moment the Supreme Being had appeared with an offer to undo my past life; give back to me a sound body, free from the remembrance even of sufferings past, and the imminence of those that must necessarily embitter all the years to come, I should have indignantly spurned the offer, such was the effect upon me of this immortal Dedication.

This testimony surely reflects the legend of Lincoln Transcendent, thirty years in the making by that time, but the legend grew from such kernels of experience, whose traces in the evidence of the day can still be found.

The same is true of evidence from 1866 presented by Major H. T. Lee, a staff officer who had been on the ground at Gettysburg and had transmitted Reynolds's call for reinforcements the very morning that Lincoln's "gallant friend" had been shot through the neck and carried away to die in a barn. Lee, like Nickerson, had stood before the speakers' stand and heard Lincoln's words. Then, after the war, he had returned from Antietam and Chancellorsville and Gettysburg to his alma mater at Lafayette College, not far down the road from the cemetery, to teach rhetoric and "physical culture" to an entering class of veterans and farm boys. In 1866 Professor Lee returned again to Gettysburg to stand on the foundations of the monument then under construction at the center of the national cemetery—a stone's throw from the platform where he had heard Lincoln speak—and on a July evening he recited Lincoln's speech to a convention of school-teachers and the assembled people of Gettysburg, some of whom must have also heard Lincoln three years before.[49] Setting the scene, he added further color to the emerging image of Lincoln at Gettysburg:

> Then Lincoln arose, his face seamed and furrowed with marks of care, his eyes moist with tears, and in a voice tremulous with the deepest emotion, he pronounced in his simple and unaffected manner, the Speech of that memorable day.
>
> There was not a dry eye in the vast assemblage, and from the loud sobs that interrupted the President during some parts of his address, it was at times impossible to hear what he had to say.

Major Lee, speaking before an assembly of eyewitnesses, himself an eye-witness and participant in both the battle and in the cemetery dedication, was certainly in 1866 also a willing participant in constructing the legend of both and in creating the larger myth of the Cause Victorious. One sees here a core of elements found in the *Cincinnati Commercial* and in Miller's letter, but the traits of Isaak Allen's *Ohio State Journal* version are becoming stronger, exaggerated by devotion to a martyred president and to the glory of the Union cause. But Lincoln had indeed cried at Gettysburg when Stockton had intoned the ancient creed of submission to the all powerful will of God and when Everett had portrayed the merciful women of the Union tending the wounded and the dying, and he had even, according to "J. H.," only controlled himself with an effort when speaking.

On this scale of mythogenesis none can surpass the testimony of Wayne MacVeagh. Sitting next to John Hay evidently did not distract him from the scene, because forty years later he provided one of the grandest examples of the myth of Lincoln at Gettysburg:

As he came forward, he seemed to me, and I was sitting near to him, visibly to dominate the scene, and while over his plain and rugged countenance appeared to settle a great melancholy, it was somehow lightened as by a great hope. As he began to speak I instinctively felt that the occasion was taking on a new grandeur, as of a great moment in history, and then there followed, in slow and very impressive and far-reaching utterance, the words with which the whole world has long been familiar.

As each word was spoken it appeared to me so clearly fraught with a message not only for us of his day, but for the untold generations of men, that before he concluded I found myself possessed of a reverential awe for its complete justification of the great war he was conducting, as if conducted, as in truth it was, in the interest of mankind.[50]

Certainly, decades of toasts and after-dinner speeches had refined MacVeagh's presentation and created a variety of phrases ready to hand for any occasion that the former attorney general and diplomat might face, but here is young MacVeagh, speaking in that terrible spring of 1864, when in two weeks the Union suffered more casualties than at any other time of the war, and the next month would bring the battles of the Wilderness, Spotsylvania, and bloody Cold Harbor.[51] In late April, at the Pennsylvania state party convention, MacVeagh took part in another and perhaps equally vital struggle, the fight to renominate and reelect Lincoln. The report in the *New York Times* is fragmentary and broken, but the echoes of that November day not six months past can still be heard:

Wayne McVeagh said the American People could not be led by any man, but now at the end of three years of fire and crimson, of heart throes and civil war, this awkward, unlettered, ungainly man, the scoff of European tyrants and traitors at home, has come out the choice of the people.

Gettysburg was greater, under God, than Marathon. We are here again to take care, if need be, of our lives, that government for the people, and by the people shall not fail.

This was, perhaps, the first time that Lincoln's words were used in a political or patriotic speech to fire enthusiasm and evoke the great cause of the nation, and that honor goes to Wayne MacVeagh, district attorney of

Chester County and the manager of Curtin's reelection campaign, who had "told Lincoln some truths" on the train to Gettysburg but who also, just three weeks prior to speaking at the state party convention, had learned that his own brother had died of wounds inflicted in battle. This mixture of political calculation, lofty patriotism, and personal loss perfectly expresses the recipe that created the legend of Lincoln at Gettysburg for many who heard Lincoln speak, his words resonating with their own experience of the despair and exaltation of the war. For MacVeagh and Nickerson and Major Lee and Robert Miller, and for Isaak Allen and the stout officer next to him, too, this was a legend that was rooted in their experience of the moment that Abraham Lincoln stood before them, an experience that the contemporary record verifies as legitimate and authentic.

But there is one last piece of evidence to consult, direct from the source, near the bottom of the Letterhead Page, underlined in pencil:

> The world will little note, nor long remember what we say here; while it can never forget what they <u>did</u> here.

Lincoln had underscored that point in his text perhaps that very morning, after returning from the battlefield, when a renewed sense of the moment and the reality of the battle and the stakes had compelled a new revision—part of the new reckoning in his understanding of the war and of the nation—and had also compelled him to mark the exact point that Isaak Allen would then strike upon as the moment when that scarred veteran's emotions "burst over all restraint" in tears that could not be suppressed. Allen did not choose that moment to make a craven play for a patronage post; it was Lincoln who had chosen to literally underscore that word and that passage because he had felt and understood something in that passage that he needed others to feel and understand. His success can be measured in the many citations of that phrase—quoted more than any other part of his speech—in the immediate weeks and months afterward.

The end of the war would erode the evocative power of this passage in favor of more abstract phrases on the larger issues at stake in the struggle and at the core of American identity, but for contemporaries this phrase spoke most deeply to their hearts and their sense of the tragedy and majesty of those who died for the cause of the Union. And it started with Lincoln himself recognizing that this was the passage and the word upon which his speech turned emotionally and intellectually, moving from the sacrifices of the soldiers whose graves lay at his feet to the great task that still lay ahead to assure the victory of their cause. Some in the crowd stood unmoved; many could not even hear him. But for some, this was the most powerful moment of Lincoln's speech, the moment of the birth of the authentic legend of Lincoln at Gettysburg.

As for Lincoln himself, if at Gettysburg he gave the "best speech he ever made," if it was "perfect in every respect" and "a remarkable speech," spoken in a "calm and earnest voice," yet "with more grace than is his wont," and if he "controlled himself by an effort" and "you could not mistake the feeling and sentiment of the vast multitude" and stalwart soldiers felt "no unmanly emotion," it was because thinking about the war and the battle, enduring the generals and wrangling with the politicians, and putting every waking moment into the struggle for the principles he raised above all things had moved him to write and speak words that would be inscribed in stone and recited by generations. Yet it was not just thought and reflection that made his words. The same emotional and assertive vision of commitment in the fifth and final written "dedication" that earlier that morning had replaced the passivity of the Washington Draft's "to stand here" and that had crafted the final wording of the forceful resolutions of the new Pencil Page was now, on the stand, as he spoke, moving Lincoln to express his vision in ways that many found remarkable and some found moving and beautiful.

From that moment one element of the legend would grow. Time would transform and distort the legacy, but no matter how deep the sediments of memory, there is, under it all, in that moment on the stand at Gettysburg, the central truth of an event whose essential shape, visible in the arc of contemporary texts, validates the distortions of time and repetition. Lincoln's experience of Gettysburg, including his visit to the battlefield and the tearful emotionalism of the ceremonies, inspired him not only to give his written text its final form that morning but also to then give his spoken words their ultimate expression while he stood there on the speakers' platform in that justly iconic image of Lincoln at Gettysburg. It was then that he fully imbued the written text with his own deeply felt commitment—his own dedication—to the cause of democratic government, freedom, and equal rights, in the name of those who had given everything one can give, in the name of what they <u>did</u> there.

CHAPTER EIGHT

"My Remarks at Gettysburg"

Just as each person experienced the moment of Lincoln at Gettysburg in unique ways, so too did everyone hear a different speech. Over time, the sheer number of different versions of Lincoln's speech in circulation would be a key part of the myth—the question of what exactly he said and wrote adding another theme to the mysteries of the manuscripts. Still, upon three secure pillars we can reconstruct Lincoln's speech in all its complexity: the delivery text, the spoken words, and Lincoln's final revision that he wrote after the speech when preparing his words for publication. In the spaces between these three differing versions we can best approach Lincoln's final moments of composition, the creative performance and reading of what Lincoln referred to in a letter to Everett as "my remarks at Gettysburg."[1]

With a secure delivery text established, the first task is to determine which of the early reports of Lincoln's spoken words, virtually all of them from newspapers, are independent or reliable guides and which are merely corrupted copies of each other, because telegraphic variations in transmitting one text can create the appearance of distinct reports of Lincoln's spoken words. Not only did the telegraph require transcription into Morse code and back to words, introducing potential human error, but weather, insulation, distance, the adjustments of the sending and receiving apparatuses, and many other elements affected the accuracy of transmission. On November 20, when Lincoln's speech was first published, there were already quite literally as many versions of Lincoln's remarks in circulation as there were newspapers that printed them. Newspaper readers of the mid-nineteenth century accepted some variations in wording as unavoidable, the inaccuracies of telegraphic communications being one of the running jokes of the time.[2]

The versions in the *Washington Daily Morning Chronicle* and the *Chicago Tribune* have each been held up as possibly independent texts, for example, but both turn out to be variations of the standard Associated Press (AP) version of Lincoln's words that other papers published. That each mile along the telegraph line introduced new errors can be seen by comparing Lincoln's words as printed on November 21 in papers at different distances from Gettysburg, in this case, the *Chicago Tribune* (ChiTb21) and the *Pittsburgh Gazette* (PitGz21), both of which were printing the version of the AP report that was sent to the Western Presses association of newspapers beyond the Appalachians:[3]

PitGz21:   are created equal.   ["Good, good,"   and applause.] Now we
ChiTb21:   are created equal by a   good God,   and [applause] now we

One version has Lincoln invoking the authority of the Almighty to uphold the declaration of human equality; the other reports the shouts of a crowd.

In the East, newspapers almost exclusively published the AP version of Lincoln's speech, but with the inevitable telegraphic variations, each city's version of Lincoln's speech has its own genetic code, marked in most cases by unique combinations of mutations. The *New York Tribune* version has generally been considered the best AP report of Lincoln's spoken words, following a commonsense understanding of how the AP system worked, because most AP stories were sent from the central New York offices; reports that originated elsewhere would be sent to New York for distribution. However, when AP reports were sent to New York, they would also be picked up by newspapers that happened to be situated on telegraph lines along the way. Philadelphia papers, for example, would not wait for news from Washington to reach New York and then be redistributed but would access the messages as they came north out of the capital.[4] This standard practice was followed in the case of the Gettysburg ceremony, as attested by the changes in the AP text as it traveled outward from Gettysburg. For example, the "poor" in "our poor power" in Lincoln's written delivery text is found in newspaper reports beyond the Appalachians and south of New York but is not found in New York papers or to the north. Such evidence shows that the long-dominant New York AP version is merely another variant of the text as telegraphed from Gettysburg.

Fortunately, because telegraphic variations behave like mutations in DNA, with earlier changes being repeated by later copies, it is possible to trace texts backward in time and space to a point of common origin. Because Gettysburg had no daily papers, this can bring us back only to newspapers telegraphically closest to Gettysburg to the north, east, and south (there was no direct westward line) that published Lincoln's speech: the *Harrisburg Daily Telegraph* (HarrbDT20), the *Philadelphia North American* (PhilNA20), and the *Baltimore American* (BaltoAm20).[5] Collating the newspaper versions printed closest to Gettysburg but in different telegraphic directions offers the possibility of reconstructing the AP text of Lincoln's speech as it was sent out from Gettysburg, not as chance or error happened to have created it after it traveled down any particular line.[6]

The three versions are remarkably similar, with only 6 word differences among their more than 800 words, 4 of which can be easily dismissed as obvious telegraphic or printing idiosyncrasies. This leaves the only real difference between the three texts as a choice between "that Governments" or "that the government." The original AP report, which might be called the UrAP in homage to the long-standing quest of biblical scholars to reconstruct the original "urtext" of the Christian and Jewish scriptures, could easily have been a mixture of the three texts, but it so happened that in comparing each case of variation, Lincoln's speech as given in the *Philadelphia North American* (including "that the government") appears to be the closest approximation of the AP version as it was telegraphed from Gettysburg on the day of the speech.[7]

As arguably the best version of Lincoln's spoken words, the question of exactly how the AP report was created has been under discussion since the 1880s. The standard story was created in the 1930s by William Barton, an unreliable researcher but able writer, who selectively quoted and misquoted the reminiscences of a reporter named Joseph Gilbert. In 1917, Gilbert, who was then in his eighties, had dictated to his daughter a statement for presentation at a conference of journalists stating that he was the reporter designated to take down Lincoln's words at Gettysburg. In the event, Gilbert stated that he was so struck by Lincoln's "intense earnestness and depth of feeling" that he stopped making notes of the speech. Barton then stated that, to fill out his fragmentary transcription of the speech, Gilbert received the manuscript from Lincoln, meaning that the AP report was actually a copy, or partial copy, of Lincoln's delivery text.[8]

Consulting Gilbert's account directly reveals a very different story than the one told by Barton and shows a wholly different origin for the AP report of Lincoln's spoken words.[9] In Gilbert's actual account, after stating that he stopped taking notes, Gilbert made no mention of a Lincoln manuscript; instead, Gilbert changed topics and went on to describe the larger story of the speech, including a number of episodes that he could not have witnessed; nor does he claim to have witnessed them, for he was merely rounding out the story and filling in the background. Throughout this and other passages, Gilbert (or his daughter) often copied word-for-word and without attribution from the previously published memoirs of John Russell Young, whom Gilbert had known during the Civil War when both worked for Forney's *Philadelphia Press*.[10] It was in this later section of historical summary that Gilbert ended his treatment of Lincoln's speech with still more unacknowledged repetition of Young's memoir (points of comparison added for ease of reference):

> Gilbert (1917): Before the dedication ceremonies closed the President's [1] manuscript was copied, with his permission; and as the press [2] report was made from the copy no [3] transcription from shorthand [4] notes was [5] necessary
> Young (1901): I did not write the [2] report which appeared in the *[Philadelphia] Press*, as the [1] manuscript had been given to the Associated Press, and the [3] transcription of my [4] notes was not [5] necessary.

That is, Gilbert's suspiciously passive statement should not be taken as his own recollection of his own act, as it has generally been understood since the 1930s when Barton misquoted and misinterpreted Gilbert's statement. Barton's account and related confusions have colored virtually every aspect of the story of Lincoln's speech. If, as Barton asserted, the AP report were simply a copy of Lincoln's delivery text, then the Nicolay text would not be the delivery text (the differences are too great between it and the AP report), and the AP report would not be Lincoln's spoken words.[11] The contextual and historical evidence, however, strongly argues that the Nicolay was indeed the delivery text, which in turn would mean that the AP report cannot be a transcription of the delivery text. From this knot of interconnected apparent contradictions springs much of the confusion about the delivery text and a good deal of the motivation for putting forward a hypothetical, nonextant document or the Hay text as the delivery text instead of the Nicolay.

Fortunately for the story of Lincoln's speech, Gilbert's actual account of the AP press report is very different from that presented by Barton. Far from claiming to have been responsible for the AP report, Gilbert stated instead that he did not transcribe the speech, and he then, in a different section of his account, merely summarized John Young, who was similarly careful to deny having anything to do with the press reports of Lincoln's words.[12] Nor should Young's statement that the manuscript of Lincoln's speech "had been given to the Associated Press" be considered an eyewitness revelation. Young mentioned a few pages earlier in his memoir that at Gettysburg he had pestered John Hay for a look at Lincoln's manuscript but that Hay knew or would say nothing about it. If Young had had direct knowledge of the manuscript he would have said so. Instead, Young's passing reference to the manuscript here was most probably a restatement of a common assumption among journalists. In 1887, for example, a *New York Times* reporter who had been at Gettysburg denied taking down Lincoln's speech or seeing the manuscript but gave his impression that Lincoln's delivery text may have been "handed over to the reporter for the Associated Press, as is usual in such cases."[13]

Neither Joseph Gilbert nor John Young nor the *Times* reporter claimed to have personal knowledge of the alleged copying of Lincoln's manuscript, nor did they claim to have created the AP text. Taken together, their accounts exhibit a circularity that strongly suggests there is no substance to the story that the AP report was based on Lincoln's manuscript. This pattern is not unlike the effect of repeated iterations of the Gettysburg legend more generally, which can create an echo-chamber effect so that details and elements appear to be rooted in several sources; in reality, though, everyone is merely repeating incorrect versions of what they think someone else said or wrote.

Who then, did prepare the version of Lincoln's spoken words as published by the AP? At the time, the main function of the AP was to redistribute news reports originated by one of the seven main New York papers that dominated the association, thus avoiding wasteful duplication. It appears that at Gettysburg the *New York Tribune* was responsible for preparing the AP report because the reporter who sent Lincoln's speech to the Western Presses association used the *Tribune* text specifically, identifiable by its punctuation.[14] The archives of the *Tribune* reveal more than a little discussion over whom to send to cover the Gettysburg event, which may be further evidence that the editors knew their report would provide the AP text. In the end, they decided to send a twenty-one-year-old staff reporter, John I. Davenport, seemingly because he was particularly adept at short-hand.[15] However, when the *Tribune* printed Lincoln's speech on November 20, its report was simply the brief AP article beginning with the words "The ceremonies attending" that had Lincoln's speech and that was published by many other papers. A longer article signed by Davenport and also datelined Gettysburg, November 19, was published in the *Tribune* on the twenty-first, and it too contained essentially the same AP version of the speech. This means that either the *Tribune* did not use Davenport for his shorthand expertise, or that Davenport was the one who transcribed Lincoln's speech for the *Tribune*'s article on the twentieth, which became the AP text, and that the speech was then republished in Davenport's signed article on the twenty-first.

Other evidence confirms that Lincoln's delivery text was not copied and that some reporters (no doubt including Davenport) instead made verbatim notes of Lincoln's words in shorthand and in longhand.[16] Perhaps most authoritatively, James Speed wrote in his 1879 statement that Lincoln told him he did not have time to memorize his speech and then immediately added, "After the speech was delivered and taken down by the reporters, he compared what he had actually said to what he had written, and the difference was so slight he allowed what he had said to remain unchanged." Events suggest that this comparison took place after Lincoln had returned to Washington, when he undertook exactly the comparison Speed described; but in any case, Lincoln's central point to Speed was that when he compared the newspaper version to his delivery text, he noticed differences between the two, and Lincoln, the best authority on the topic, was quite clear: the press version reflected what he had said, not what was written in his delivery text. This contradicts Barton's interpretation of Gilbert's story, and in fact neither Gilbert nor Young nor any other reporter ever stepped forward to claim to have spoken with Lincoln about his "immortal" speech. In addition, John Nicolay, who was a kind of de facto press secretary for Lincoln, stated point-blank in his *Century* article that the speech "was taken down in short-hand by the reporter for the 'Associated Press.'"[17]

Whether or not it was Davenport who made the AP transcription of Lincoln's words, almost all the reports from Gettysburg relied on the AP for their account of Lincoln's speech; only a handful of press reports may have been prepared independently in part, but obvious errors in all of these make it difficult to identify any one—or even any particular passage within them—as authoritative, and many show signs of being combinations of several other versions.[18] Among these possibly semi-independent versions, a summary in the *Cincinnati Commercial* of November 21, 1863 (CinCm21) is the most complete, though it may have been prepared in part on the basis of the Western Presses AP variant. It is bracing to think that if an expert in shorthand working for the AP had not taken down Lincoln's words, then this text might have been thought of as Lincoln's "few appropriate remarks" at Gettysburg:

He said, in substance, that ninety years ago our fathers formed a Government consecrated to freedom, and dedicated to the principle that all men are created equal, and that we are engaged in a war testing the question whether any nation so formed can long endure and come to dedicate a portion of a great battle-field of that war to those who had died that the nation might live. He could not dedicate, consecrate or hallow that ground, for it was consecrated above our power to add or detract. The world would not long remember what was said there, but it could never forget what was done there, and it was rather for it to be dedicated on that spot to the work they had so nobly carried forward that they might not have died in vain, and that Government for and of the people, based upon the freedom of man, may not perish from off the earth.

By far the most important nonnewspaper text for determining Lincoln's words is a version put forward by Edward Everett's grand-nephew, Charles Hale, who from the beginning had been concerned about the accuracy of the newspaper accounts of Lincoln's speech, complaining in his *Boston Advertiser* article of November 23 that the version printed in the papers had "suffered somewhat at the hands of the telegraphers." In the official report of the Massachusetts cemetery agents printed in early 1864, Hale gave what he claimed were "the words actually spoken by the President, with great deliberation."[19] Still, the 1864 Hale text reproduces a few variations of the AP text associated with Hale's hometown of Boston, which, combined with its late publication date, strongly suggests that it was edited or completed with reference to another text. Although valuable, Hale's transcription, the Hale64, cannot be taken as wholly independent.[20]

Overall, the AP report (reconstructed here in its original form as the UrAP) and the Hale64, which have generally been recognized as the two texts closest to Lincoln's spoken words, differ in only seven words between them, and all the differences are quite trivial in themselves, such as the placement of a "here" or whether Lincoln said "the" before "government."[21] Comparing these seven instances of variation to the other texts that may have some claim to being independent supports the UrAP wording in every instance. Thus, not only is the original UrAP—which by chance turns out to be the exact words of the *Philadelphia North American* version—the best approximation of Lincoln's speech as telegraphed from Gettysburg, but it also appears to be the best guide to Lincoln's spoken words.

No other version of Lincoln's spoken words can match the authority of the original AP version as reconstructed here: it was published immediately, it was prepared by a reporter expert in shorthand, and it was validated by Lincoln himself, who, according to what he told Speed and according to the evidence of his later revisions, recognized that the press report represented his spoken words and not his written text:

The Reconstructed AP Report of the Gettysburg Address (UrAP)

Four score and seven years ago our fathers brought forth upon this continent a new nation, conceived in liberty and dedicated to the proposition that all men are created equal. (Applause.) Now we are engaged in a great civil war, testing whether that nation, or any nation so conceived and so dedicated, can long endure. We are met on a great battle field of that war; we are met to dedicate a portion of it as the final resting place of those who here gave their lives that that nation might live. It is altogether fitting and proper that we should do this, but in a larger sense we cannot dedicate, we cannot consecrate, we cannot hallow this ground.[¶]

The brave men, living and dead, who struggled here have consecrated it far above our poor power to add or to detract. (Applause.) The world will little note, nor long remember, what we say here; but it can never forget what they did here. (Applause.) It is for us, the living, rather to be dedicated here to the unfinished work that they have thus far so nobly carried on. (Applause.) It is rather for us here to be dedicated to the great task remaining before us; that from these honored dead we take increased devotion to that cause for which they here gave the last full measure of devotion; that we here highly resolve that these dead shall not have died in vain. (Applause.) That the nation shall, under God, have a new birth of freedom, and that the government of the people, by the people and for the people, shall not perish from the earth. (Long applause.) [¶]

Having securely established the Nicolay document as the Battlefield Draft, and having shown that the original AP report is our best evidence for Lincoln's words as spoken, one last text of Lincoln's speech is required to fully encompass the moment that Lincoln spoke: Lincoln's final revised text. This last version will allow us to bracket Lincoln's spoken words chronologically, textually, and conceptually between the Battlefield Draft and his post-speech revision. And here is where Lincoln's handwritten version today called the Hay document finally plays a role. The proposition that the Hay was a pre-Nicolay draft written in Washington before the speech has not been seriously suggested for more than half a century.[22] The history of the Nicolay document presented here shows that the Hay cannot be the delivery text itself. If the Hay is not a prespeech text, then, logically, it can only be a post-speech version, and its history and the story of its origins confirm this conclusion.

Because it was long thought that there were no sources or evidence for the history of the Hay text, its riddles have generally been approached from a purely textual perspective, by counting words and variations, an approach that has failed to resolve the issues. Yet since before the first publication of the Hay text in 1909, the answer to its origins—and indeed, the answers to many of the mysteries of the manuscripts—has been carefully preserved in the papers of Edward Everett. However, just like the evidence of David Wills (through McPherson) confirming that the Letterhead Page was the first page of the delivery text, the evidence in the Everett papers about the Hay text required the full history of Lincoln's speech in order to be fully intelligible.

In Everett's well-organized, extensively researched papers is the document that is the origin of the Hay text, written in the hand not of Lincoln but of David Wills: a full, word-perfect copy of Lincoln's speech as it would be printed in the official publications of the dedication program by Edward Everett and David Wills, complete with page numbers for the prospective publication by Little, Brown and Company of Boston.[23] Everett's correspondence indicates that Wills sent him this document and most of the other materials for publication by about January 9, 1864. The wording of this document in the handwriting of David Wills confirms the accuracy of his later statement: "I did not make a copy of my report of President Lincoln's speech at Gettysburg from a transcript of the original, but from one of the press reports."[24] More specifically, David Wills sent to Everett for publication a copy (with four words changed) of Lincoln's speech as it was printed in the *New York Tribune* on November 20 (NYTrib20).[25]

Wills's handwritten version, intended for printing, which we can call the DWills text, is the final fact that confirms Lincoln wrote the Hay text after the speech. The story is somewhat complex (which is why this part of the mysteries of the manuscript has been so troublesome for so long), so it is essential to establish the basic sequence of events that led to Lincoln's final post-speech text, the "Bliss" version that is usually meant today when referring to the Gettysburg Address:

> November 19: Lincoln speaks at Gettysburg using the Nicolay document as the delivery text.
>
> November 23: David Wills requests "the original manuscript" of Lincoln's speech, "to be placed with the correspondence and other papers" relating to the ceremony. As Wills later stated, Lincoln did not send a manuscript, probably because beginning on this day smallpox confined Lincoln to bed for the better part of ten days, and John Nicolay was away from Washington at the time.
>
> January 9: By this date Everett had received the DWills text now in Everett's papers; textual evidence demonstrates that David Wills had made this by copying, with four word changes, the AP version of Lincoln's speech as published in the *New York Tribune* on November 20. Edward Everett then had the exact words of the handwritten DWills text printed by the Boston publisher Little, Brown, along with his *Oration,* on or about January 31, published to benefit the fund to build a monument at the Gettysburg cemetery. David Wills also printed the exact words of the DWills text in his official report to the state of Pennsylvania in March 1864.

January 30: Everett wrote Lincoln that he would soon send what he called the "authorized edition" of the Gettysburg speeches (that is, the Little, Brown printed version). In the same letter, Everett made an unrelated request for "the manuscript of your dedicatory remarks, if you happen to have preserved it" so that he could include it, along with the manuscript of his own *Oration*, for sale at a charity fair.

February 4: Lincoln wrote Everett thanking him for sending the printed version of the speeches and added, "I send herewith the manuscript of my remarks at Gettysburg, which, with my note to you of Nov. 20th you are at liberty to use for the benefit of our soldiers, as you have requested." This handwritten version by Lincoln is today known as the Everett version.

Mid-February: George Bancroft, on behalf of John Pendleton Kennedy and Bancroft's stepson, Alexander Bliss, requested from Lincoln a handwritten copy of his speech to be engraved for inclusion in *Autograph Leaves of Our Country's Authors* (1864) to be published for the benefit of sailors and soldiers.

February 29: John Nicolay sent the Everett text and Lincoln's February 4 cover letter to Edward Everett, who sent his thanks on March 3.[26]

Nicolay also on this day sent George Bancroft a copy written by Lincoln for facsimile publication in *Autograph Leaves* along with a cover letter by Lincoln dated February 29. However, this Bancroft text was soon sent back to Lincoln because the page was too large for the proposed volume.

March 11: Lincoln sent to the editors of *Autograph Leaves* a new handwritten version, later called the Bliss text, written on paper with margins supplied by Alexander Bliss; the Bancroft was probably sent with it.[27]

It has already been established here that the Hay was not a prespeech draft; the DWills text, along with the written affirmation of David Wills, proves that the "authorized" version printed at Everett's behest by Little, Brown around January 30 has no connection to Lincoln. The chronology of the post-speech revisions above demonstrates that the Hay was not written after February 4, the date of Lincoln's cover letter for the Everett. The Hay cannot be made to fit into the sequence of the three clearly post-speech versions (the Everett, Bancroft, and Bliss) because they are virtually identical; this means that Lincoln used the previous text as the copy text in each instance. There are only two word differences among the three texts, and only a few, evidently deliberate, changes in punctuation, so within the sequence of the three texts, the many handwritten edits and additions found in the Hay text would have no purpose.[28] Lincoln knew that each of these last three versions would be made public; once he arrived at the words and punctuation of the Everett text in early February, he was careful about changes to the text, precluding a role for the Hay after February 4.

There is, then, only one role and one place chronologically, textually, and conceptually, for the Hay document: in order to write the Everett manuscript in response to Edward Everett's request of January 30, 1864. The maddening, confusing Hay document has been at the heart of the mystery of Lincoln's manuscripts for more than a century because its words display a puzzling combination of original text, edits, and additions, some of which are similar to the Nicolay document and some of which are similar to the reports of Lincoln's spoken words. Roy P. Basler, the lead editor of the long-standard *Collected Words of Abraham Lincoln*, even asserted that these variations meant that the relationship between the Nicolay and Hay texts "cannot now be established beyond question."[29] This has meant that, without a history, the Hay document could appear to be virtually anything, from a pre-Nicolay draft to a delivery text to a post-speech copy written as a souvenir.[30]

As it turns out, the seemingly inexplicable combinations in the Hay text were created by Lincoln consciously and deliberately because of the way he chose to respond to Everett's request for "the manuscript of your dedicatory remarks," a request that posed a clear and difficult problem. As James Speed noted, Lincoln recognized that his delivery text and his spoken words differed. More specifically, John Nicolay wrote in his 1894 *Century* article that "Lincoln saw" both that the delivery text "seemed incomplete" and that the newspaper reports of his spoken words were "imperfect."[31] This description of Lincoln's perception of the texts follows Nicolay's pattern of speaking not just about but for Lincoln, and as Lincoln's revisions reveal, it is probably an accurate portrayal of his mind as he undertook a post-speech revision to comply with Everett's request.

The deficiencies in the different versions of his speech led Lincoln, when responding to Everett's request, to create a new version that intentionally combined words and phrases from both his manuscript delivery text and from the printed reports of his spoken words (perhaps influenced by what he recalled saying) along with a few new phrases and words that he almost certainly did not say and that are not found in either his written delivery text or the reports of his speech; thus, the baffling combinations of edits, changes, and revisions in the manuscripts. According to Nicolay, at Lincoln's request, "his secretaries made copies of the Associated Press report as it was printed in several prominent newspapers." Lincoln then compared these newspaper reports to the delivery text and to his "fresh" recollection of what he had said, and he then prepared "a new autograph copy—a careful and deliberate revision." The Hay is a first sketch of that new revised version, and the Everett is the completed and finished version. John Nicolay, who was closely involved in the correspondence associated with the Everett and later texts, stated in a letter of 1885 that the Hay document was "the ms. notes of the revision" that Lincoln made after his speech, the word "notes" demonstrating that Nicolay knew the Hay was not the revised document itself. Nicolay's accurate perception of the Hay explains why in his 1894 *Century* article he did not refer to the document directly. As Robert Todd Lincoln later surmised, "it was not regarded as important by Nicolay, being merely a step in the revision process."[32]

Nicolay's precise description of the revision process also shows, however, that he incorrectly dated this post-speech revision, for in his article thirty years after the fact he associated it with David Wills's request in November for a copy of the manuscript.[33] Yet Lincoln did not send a manuscript to Wills, and we know, too, that Nicolay was not in Washington during the days following Wills's request.[34] The post-speech revision that Nicolay described as having occurred in November did take place, but in early February (when Lincoln's memory of his speech may or may not have been as "fresh" as Nicolay stated) and in response to Everett's request, as Lincoln's cover letter of February 4 stated.

It is even possible to identify the exact text that Lincoln used as his main copy text for the Hay document; the certainty of this evidence is the key to recognizing that, at last, the mysteries of the manuscripts, and of the Hay text in particular, no longer need to trouble the story of the Gettysburg Address. The current Hay document displays eight sites where a total of nine words were added, changed, or deleted. If all these changes and edits are ignored, then one arrives at an underlying text, called here the UrHay document. Lincoln may have made changes and edits as he was first putting words on the page, but it is also likely that some of the edits took place after all the words of the UrHay had been written. The UrHay, then, is conceived of not so much as an earlier form of the Hay, but more as the echo of the copy text that Lincoln worked from when writing the document that became the Hay on the way to the final written version, which is the copy he sent to Edward Everett.

Nicolay did not happen to mention the precise text that Lincoln both copied and actively edited as he was writing the UrHay. Yet we can know this copy text with great certainty: it was the "authorized" printed version in the official proceedings of the dedication ceremony published by Little, Brown and Company of Boston and sent to Lincoln by the great and wise Edward Everett within a day or so of January 30; Lincoln even mentioned receiving this publication in his cover letter to Everett of February 4. When combined with the chronological and circumstantial evidence, the textual evidence is virtually ironclad that Lincoln used what can be called the LittleBrown printed version as the copy text for his post-speech revision. To begin with, and to the extent that raw word counts are helpful, the UrHay is only twelve words different from the LittleBrown but is fifteen words different from the *New York Tribune* of November 20.[35] More important, there are three instances in which the LittleBrown and Lincoln's UrHay text and its descendants share an otherwise unique characteristic, not reflected in any other texts. Three may seem underwhelming, but because the LittleBrown is essentially a New York AP text, finding three unique traits shared by the UrHay and the LittleBrown and no other text is tantamount to a fingerprint.

The first textual evidence is the paragraph breaks. In all the dozens of AP versions and other texts consulted, and including the Nicolay text, only one has the same paragraphing as the UrHay and its descendants: the LittleBrown printed edition. The vast majority of newspaper texts had no paragraph divisions, but the processes of telegraphy also produced three or four main patterns of dividing Lincoln's speech into two or three paragraphs, some of which involved breaking sentences into different pieces; Charles Hale's version of spring 1864 has seven paragraphs. The paragraphing is perhaps the most powerful of the three traits in common because it is both unique and structural, affecting the way the entire speech looks on the page. In addition, it can be thought of as two decisions by Lincoln to conform to the LittleBrown copy text, or at least, two opportunities for Lincoln not to conform: after the first paragraph (which replicates the division in the Nicolay) and after the second (which differs). Given the existence of the DWills text in Everett's files (which was, of course, the copy text for the LittleBrown), and with so many ways that this textual trait could have been dissimilar, it is not a coincidence that the one text that is identical to the UrHay is the LittleBrown.

Another example is the unique combination of capitalization in the phrase, as rendered in the UrHay text, "a new nation, conceived in Liberty." This capitalization is found only in the DWills text and its descendant, the LittleBrown; almost every other text consulted has no capitalization; a few, like the *Tribune* version that David Wills used as his copy text, capitalize both "nation" and "liberty." The changes Wills made were deliberate because he also changed the capitalization of the other instances of "nation" that he found in the *Tribune* version. Lincoln adopted this pattern, which he found in the LittleBrown, and kept it through the Bliss text, even though this capitalization differed from his delivery text.

The third textual example confirming that Lincoln wrote the UrHay on the basis of the LittleBrown is "the" cause instead of "that" cause in the phrase "increased devotion to the cause for which they here gave the last full measure of devotion." This oddity is found only in the DWills, Little-Brown, and UrHay texts. Like "Liberty," this variation arose when David Wills copied the *Tribune* version to make the DWills text. Unlike the capital *L*, this may have been an inadvertent change. It is difficult to see why Wills would deliberately change only this one seemingly insignificant word and not take up the many other opportunities for similar word changes offered by the text. This unique word survived into the LittleBrown printed edition, and Lincoln then copied it into the UrHay when first setting about creating a manuscript in response to Everett's request. However, Lincoln then reverted to the wording of every other text (including the Nicolay delivery text) by striking out "the" and writing "that" above it, making this one of the nine word changes to the UrHay that created the current Hay text:

Nicolay:	to that	cause for which they here, gave
UrAP:	to that	cause for which they here gave
NYTrib20:	to that	cause for which they here gave
DWills:	to the	cause for which they here gave
LittleBrown:	to the	cause for which they here gave
UrHay:	to the	cause for which they here gave gave
Hay:	to that	cause for which they here gave
Everett:	to that	cause for which they here gave

| Bancroft: | to that | cause for which they here gave |
| Bliss: | to that | cause for which they gave |

There are several other examples of how the DWills and its original version, the UrDWills (for the current DWills document is based on an edited undertext), explain difficult editorial episodes that have long plagued the understanding of Lincoln's post-speech revisions—most importantly, as we shall see, the previously inexplicable "this/that government/s" phrase—but while they support the argument here, none are as decisive in proving the link between the LittleBrown and the UrHay as the three unique connections of paragraphing, "Liberty," and "the" cause. When such textual evidence so strongly supports the contextual and chronological evidence, the conclusion may be taken as proven. The mysteries of the manuscripts must finally give way before an inescapable syllogism: The LittleBrown text is unrelated to Lincoln and can be securely dated as having been first created after the speech; the Hay document was based on the LittleBrown; therefore, the Hay cannot be the delivery text or a prespeech draft.

The DWills/LittleBrown/UrHay sequence, which continued unbroken through the Everett version to the final Bliss copy, should also be recognized as final proof that hypothetical delivery texts are excluded by the contextual and textual evidence.[36] This alleged lost manuscript that Lincoln supposedly read to the crowd has been long sought but never found. In the 1990s, a well-known Lincolnist even produced what he claimed was a part of this document, weaving a tale that someone found it at a flea market and gave it to him for a few thousand dollars and a few photographs of Lincoln; had the document been authentic, it would have been worth many millions of dollars. So strong was the desire to find the lost delivery text that many were fooled—and yet the forger, seeking to provide a secure provenance, added an endorsement in what was supposed to pass as Lincoln's handwriting and signature, "For Hon Judge David Wills from A. Lincoln Nov 19, 1863." Wills did not become a judge until 1874, nor was he given that title at the time of the ceremony.[37] Thankfully, the forgery dropped from view after a few years. Since 1908, when the Hay text was discovered in John Hay's papers, confusion over its origins and the odd combinations of its edits allowed for doubts about the delivery text, but there seems little reason now to resort to hypothetical delivery texts.

One objection to viewing the Hay as a post-speech text has always been that the Hay, like the Nicolay delivery text, does not include the words "under God." It is sometimes asserted that, having said the words in his speech, Lincoln would never write a text that did not include them. This is undoubtedly true but only if referring to a document that Lincoln intended for public distribution. The Hay text, on the other hand, was a mere working draft that was created as part of a very deliberate revision process; Lincoln knew before he started to write it (or, more precisely, copy and revise it from the LittleBrown) that it would be superseded by a finished text—which is, of course, the Everett document, which was written within three or four days of the UrHay at most but which may well have been completed in the same writing session—and which, of course, does include the words "under God."

The UrHay/Hay/Everett compositional sequence, and consequently the final Bliss document, was based, then, not on either the delivery text or an AP text directly, but on an AP text as copied by David Wills with four word changes (one of which corrected "refinished," an error in the *New York Tribune*), which he then sent to Edward Everett for printing in the LittleBrown edition. Lincoln probably chose the LittleBrown as his copy text because it was a good approximation of his spoken words and because it was an "authorized" edition published by the respected Edward Everett, but probably not because he considered it the best version of his spoken words. For example, among the changes Lincoln made to the LittleBrown copy text, he ultimately rejected the three nontypographical word changes introduced by David Wills, which effectively returned the text to the *Tribune* version, and this has already been shown to be a telegraphically altered text.

Moreover, Lincoln's edits to the LittleBrown version during the post-speech revision support the original AP text defined here as probably the single best approximation of Lincoln's words. In three of the five words in which the UrAP and the LittleBrown differ, Lincoln actively edited the text of the LittleBrown in ways that recreated the UrAP wording, most importantly by restoring the word "poor," which is in the delivery text and in the UrAP but not in the *Tribune* text used by David Wills to make the LittleBrown. This suggests Lincoln used the LittleBrown in spite of its wording and because it was published by Everett, and it leaves the UrAP as the best approximation of Lincoln's spoken words.

Unfortunately, it is not possible to demonstrate that in making the UrHay or Hay texts, Lincoln sought only to replicate his spoken words, for his entire post-speech revision resulting in the Everett text ultimately added many words that he had almost certainly not spoken, and he also left out, at least momentarily, words that he almost certainly did say. Thus, it is not possible, except in a few instances (see below), to clearly distinguish between the different kinds of changes and the motives Lincoln may have had in making them when he wrote the UrHay or Hay texts. The result of Lincoln's post-speech revision, the Everett document, was a mixed text, based mainly on Lincoln's spoken words as printed in the LittleBrown but also incorporating changes that replicated the manuscript delivery text as well as new words that appear to be mainly stylistic rather than substantive.

And so, with the revised post-speech "Everett" manuscript, we have come full circle from the slightly altered *New York Tribune* text that David Wills sent to Edward Everett for printing, which itself was a version of the UrAP as telegraphed from Gettysburg the afternoon of November 19, taken down in shorthand, perhaps by John I. Davenport, while Lincoln stood on the platform and held in his hand the Battlefield Draft. The three key texts—the delivery document, the spoken words, and now, the post-speech revision—allow a kind of textual triangulation, illuminating previously difficult passages such as "under God" and allowing the path of Lincoln's words and thoughts to be read more fully and more coherently against the context provided by their history.

As Lincoln stepped forward to speak, he started with the Letterhead Page, very familiar to him by now, its opening words evoking his remarks to the serenade of July 7 welcoming the twin victories at Gettysburg and Vicksburg ("How long ago is it? Eighty-odd years") but now elevated by his desire to be able to say "some appropriate thing," as he told James Speed. The best contemporary evidence that Lincoln read his speech is the report in the *New York Times* from November 23 stating that Lincoln's speech was "delivered (or rather read from a sheet of paper the speaker held in his hand) in a very deliberate manner, with strong emphasis and a business like air." The self-correction in this statement demonstrates beyond argument that the reporter saw Lincoln holding paper and reading his speech. Still, John Nicolay and others recalled that Lincoln did not read the words closely, and some say he barely looked at the page; indeed, the similarities and the differences between the manuscript and the reports of his words suggest that Lincoln "read and spoke," just as the district attorney Robert Miller described.[38]

For the first sentences, presenting the Nicolay delivery text with line breaks at Lincoln's commas and other punctuation can help give a sense of how he might have read the lines, given that Lincoln tended to write and punctuate by ear. Lincoln followed nineteenth-century practice, taught in grammar books like Lindley Murray's *English Reader,* in which commas signaled a brief pause or beat, while periods represented a more definite rest.[39] Because Lincoln was reading so slowly, it is likely that the pauses would have been quite noticeable, which is probably one reason so many contemporary reports mention his deliberate, sincere, or earnest manner. These were the words Lincoln read as the sudden stillness settled on the crowd:

> Four score and seven years ago our fathers brought forth,
> upon this continent,
> a new nation,
> conceived in liberty,
> and dedicated to the proposition that "all men are created equal[.]"
>
> Now we are engaged in a great civil war,
> testing whether that nation,
> or any nation so conceived,
> and so dedicated,
> can long endure.

There is no significant difference among reliable contemporary reports of the first sentence, and very few in the first three sentences; perhaps Lincoln was reading particularly slowly and clearly at the beginning. Certainly the reporters were prepared and ready. Some might agree with John Defrees, the government printer who proofed and edited most of Lincoln's writings published while he was president, who thought Lincoln "used too many commas," but we can see in them Lincoln's emphatic style of presentation, a style that was very effective for some who heard him.[40] The quotation marks in the manuscript around the radical words of the Declaration of Independence seem to call for some kind of emphasis of tone or cadence and set off the words in a way unlike any others in the text, identifying the core of the issue.[41]

Most variations in the press reports of Lincoln's words are readily explained as telegraphic variations in the AP text, as in the second sentence above, where the Western Presses version and a few others read "testing the question" whether the nation would "remain." The Hale64 and UrAP agree that Lincoln did not say those words, nor are they found in any of the five manuscripts, setting the pattern by which the Western Presses version printed in papers beyond the Appalachians is revealed as an unreliable guide to Lincoln's spoken words; it is merely an AP version with peculiar variations. The next sentence in the delivery text, however, presents the first important differences when comparing it to the spoken words:

> NICOLAY: We are met on a great battle field of that war. We have come to dedicate a portion of it, as a final resting place for those who died here, that the nation might live. This we may, in all propriety do.
> UrAP: We are met on a great battle-field of that war; we are met to dedicate a portion of it as the final resting-place of those who here gave their lives that that nation might live. It is altogether fitting and proper that we should do this,

Because virtually all the spoken-word reports agree that Lincoln repeated "we are met" rather than saying "we are come," as written in the manuscript, this phrase helps clarify some of the difficulties in discovering the relationships among the texts, particularly when looking at the second part of the phrase:[42]

Nicolay:	We have come	to dedicate
UrAP:	we are met	to dedicate
NYTrib20:	We are met	to dedicate
Hale64:	We are met	to dedicate
DWills:	We are met	to dedicate
LittleBrown:	We are met	to dedicate
UrHay:	We are met	to dedicate
Hay:	We have come	to dedicate
Everett:	We have come	to dedicate
Bancroft:	We have come	to dedicate
Bliss:	We have come	to dedicate

In this sequence, changes from the Nicolay delivery text to the UrAP spoken words are explicable as the kind of unremarkable variation any speaker might introduce when working from a written text. In Lincoln's delivery manuscript, the prominently capitalized words in the phrases "We are met . . . We have come" are nearly above and below each other on the page, and in the case of the first one, the entire phrase "We are met" ends that line, so Lincoln's eye might naturally have been drawn to the phrase if he had looked up or was not reading closely. Then too, Lincoln's improvisation of "we are met" in this passage corresponds to other examples in which Lincoln added new repetitive words while speaking, words that reflected those already in the delivery text.

According to the order of texts presented here, when Lincoln afterward set about writing a version for Edward Everett, he first copied in the UrHay the words "We are met" that he found in the LittleBrown text that Everett had sent to him. Then, just as described by John Nicolay, Lincoln compared this published version with his delivery text, and in this case, Lincoln edited the UrHay and reverted to the wording of the delivery text and kept it through the last handwritten version. In most places where the delivery text and the LittleBrown version of his spoken words differed, however, Lincoln retained the wording of the LittleBrown.

For Lincoln, the spoken words constituted the essential text of his speech, and we can perhaps see one reason why in this passage:

Nicolay:	as a	final resting place	for	those who	died here,
UrAP:	as the	final resting-place	of	those who	here gave their lives
BosEveT20:	as a	final resting place	of	those who	have given their lives
PhilInq20:	as the	final resting place	of	those who	gave their lives
CinCm21:			to	those who	had died
Hale64:	as the	final resting-place	of	those who	have given their lives
LittleBrown:	as the	final resting-place	of	those who	here gave their lives
UrHay:	as the	final resting place	of	those who	here gave their lives
Hay:	as a	final resting place	for	those who	here gave their lives
Everett:	as a	final resting place	for	those who	here gave their lives,
Bancroft:	as a	final resting-place	for	those who	here gave their lives,
Bliss:	as a	final resting place	for	those who	here gave their lives

As he spoke, Lincoln elevated his tone from the rather stark factual statement "died here" to a formulation that was variously reported but that more expressively emphasized the reason why the soldiers voluntarily sacrificed themselves for the nation. Possibly, we are hearing in the new phrasing the same impulse that would bring him increasingly to make wholesale changes in his written manuscript as he spoke. Later, when revising the speech, Lincoln retained this new element of "here gave their lives" but returned to the original combination of "a" final resting place and "for" those who, as found in his delivery text for the first part of the phrase, a sign of how closely he was parsing the text as he revised.

Lincoln's improvisation while speaking evidently extended to a whole sentence when he said, "It is altogether fitting and proper that we should do this" instead of reading, "This we may, in all propriety do." Every text consulted gave very nearly the same wording as the UrAP, suggesting that Lincoln's statement here of the culturally current phrase "fitting and proper" was universally heard. This is a somewhat puzzling substitution; it is the only instance in the speech in which Lincoln when speaking replaced the words of a whole sentence, rather than augmenting or adding to a sentence or idea. The apparent ease of the substitution might suggest that Lincoln had thought about this change, or, perhaps more probably, he simply reverted to a stock phrase if, say, his eye failed to find the right place on the page or if he had spoken without referring to the manuscript. Possibly, the cadence of the new version is superior, as is avoiding the possible implication that something lacking in propriety might have been occurring, another sign of a more elevated and solemn tone and one more in keeping with the words of Reverend Stockton and Edward Everett.

> NICOLAY: But, in a larger sense, we can not dedicate—we can not consecrate—we can not hallow, this ground—The brave men, living and dead, who struggled here, have hallowed it, far above our poor power to add or detract. The world will little note, nor long remember what we say here; while it can never forget what they did here.
>
> UrAP: but in a larger sense we cannot dedicate, we cannot consecrate, we cannot hallow this ground. The brave men, living and dead, who struggled here have consecrated it far above our poor power to add or to detract. [Applause.] The world will little note, nor long remember, what we say here; but it can never forget what they did here. [Applause.]

These sentences form the pivot of the speech, with the appropriately underlined "did" here signaling the emotional high point. The spoken words are perhaps sharper than the manuscript's, the soft, somewhat abstract "hallowed it" becoming the harder edged, more concrete "consecrated it," which also avoids the possibly arch alliteration of "here have hallowed."

Yet such word play was a feature of Lincoln's style. The next sentence brings the rhyming "our poor power," for example. The word "poor" was long a point of contention because it is not found in the previously standard *Tribune* text, but the reconstruction here of the original AP report demonstrates that Lincoln did indeed say it, and perhaps did so wisely, for "our power" may well sound too facile on its own. The final sentence of this passage as spoken differs from the manuscript in only one word, the written "while" becoming "but," a change that sharpens the contrast Lincoln is making and, like other changes, hardens the sound and intensifies the impact.

The next line begins a new paragraph and is the last line on the page. This passage includes the familiar words "to stand here" that Lincoln struck out in pencil when he added new words in pencil to the Letterhead Page and then continued onto the Pencil Page (the words in pencil are indicated here in boldface). It is the most textually challenging section of the entire speech:

NICOLAY: It is rather for us, the living, ~~to stand here,~~ **we here be dedica** **// ted to the great task remaining before us—**
UrAP: It is for us, the living, rather to be dedicated here to the unfinished work that they have thus far so nobly carried on. [Applause.] It is rather for us here to be dedicated to the great task remaining before us;

Lincoln in this passage reportedly spoke more than twice as many words as written in the manuscript, his most extensive modification of the written text while speaking. Even more remarkable than the magnitude of the change is its placement, which becomes clearer when the written and spoken words are combined. In the following hypothetical construction of what the text would then look like, the new spoken words are underlined and the words of the delivery text that Lincoln did not say are struck through twice:

It is ~~rather~~ for us, the living, ~~to stand here,~~ <u>rather to be dedicated here</u> <u>to the unfinished work that they have thus far so nobly carried on. It is</u>

rather for us ~~we~~ here <u>to</u> be dedica // ted to the great task remaining before us;

This construction superimposes three compositional stages in the creation of Lincoln's speech: the underlying Washington Draft; the written pencil revisions in Gettysburg, and the spoken words. Nearly all the twenty-four words that Lincoln added while speaking could be inserted in a single block nested within the last line of the Letterhead Page after the word "living," precisely where Lincoln had edited the phrase "to stand here" that morning in pencil.

Whether Lincoln's changes to this passage were wholly deliberate or in some way a consequence of his earlier editing is an interesting question. One suggestive element is that, after the first few words of that line in the written text, Lincoln initiated the new block of spoken words before reading the similar words of the manuscript—these new words were not a repetition of something he had just said; rather, they were an anticipation. Having added this new phrase "dedicated here to the unfinished work," Lincoln then went on to read his delivery text essentially as written, which referred to being "dedica // ted to the great task." As Lincoln held the pages (each constituting the "half of a speech" he would later describe to James Speed) and slowly read and spoke, when he reached the last line of the Letterhead Page he would have seen "It is rather for us, the living, ~~to stand here,~~ we here be dedica" but would not have seen the continuing text that included the page he had first written that morning. This would have in a sense opened up the text, providing a moment or space that was not immediately filled with written text. This would present an opportunity for Lincoln to improvise more freely or to extend the basic idea of the words he had written in pencil that morning and that he might not have memorized as fully as those of the Letterhead Page, the legacy of the Washington Draft.

One reason for suggesting this possibility is that this passage is the only point at which Charles Hale of the *Boston Advertiser* heard Lincoln speak with increased emphasis or intensity:

> HALE64: It is for us, the living, rather, *to be dedicated*, here, to the unfinished work that they have thus far so nobly carried on. It is rather for us to be here dedicated to the great task remaining before us; that from these honored dead . . .

This emphasis falls upon the first of the repeated "dedicated" phrases, the one that was extemporaneously added while speaking. Lincoln's presentation must have been quite pronounced for Hale to have felt he needed to transcribe it. Probably this was an extension of the same emotional intensity that so many felt when they heard Lincoln evoke "what they <u>did</u> here" just seconds before, at the end of the previous sentence.

As with Lincoln's underlining of the word "<u>did</u>," the emphasis noted by Hale is probably a sign of the emotional and conceptual forces that had led Lincoln to revise his speech that morning. Upon his return from the battlefield Lincoln had added a fifth "dedicated" to his written text, yet now, while speaking, and before reaching that fifth written dedication, Lincoln felt compelled to add yet another iteration of the word, a sixth, spoken affirmation, a final repetition of a theme that had been building since, no doubt, Lincoln had closed the door behind William Saunders the night of November 17 and returned to his desk in the cabinet room to complete the final version of the Washington Draft.

Clearly, the same impulse or motivation was at work in both the written revision of the morning of the nineteenth and in the spoken addition of that afternoon. Together, the two phrases, "what they <u>did</u> here" and "*to be dedicated*" (as Hale reported it), move the focus from "the brave men," of the Letterhead Page to the actions that must be undertaken by "us, the living," as explained on the Pencil Page. Whether the added spoken words are strictly necessary for that transition is perhaps in the eye of the beholder; that is, it would be difficult to argue that the Nicolay text was in some sense incomplete, rendering the additional words necessary. Rather, it would seem that while speaking, Lincoln was led by his memory of the text as edited or by his anticipation of the ideas and words he knew were on the next page to expand and develop this crucial transition, which was perhaps not fully developed in his mind, having been written just that morning. Even after the speech, Lincoln continued to seek a way to perfect his expression of this passage. The version he wrote afterward for Edward Everett reads, "which they who fought here, have, thus far, so nobly advanced," making for six changed or added words in a passage that, as first created when Lincoln spoke, originally had only nine.

At this point in Lincoln's speech, one must imagine a wave of feeling or sympathetic emotion moving across at least some of those listening in order to account for the many news reports that emphasized exactly this moment. That feeling would continue naturally, though perhaps at a diminishing level of intensity, into the next sentences. Having completed the Letterhead Page with the second spoken "it is . . . rather," and evoked the "great task," Lincoln continued now to speak from the Pencil Page that he had written that morning, with its rolling, culminating series of resolutions and affirmations:

> NICOLAY: that, from these honored dead we take increased devotion to that cause for which they here, gave the last full measure of devotion—that we here highly resolve these dead shall not have died in vain;
> UrAP: that from these honored dead we take increased devotion to that cause for which they here gave the last full measure of devotion; that we here highly resolve that these dead shall not have died in vain. [Applause.]

Aside from the perpetually misleading Western Presses versions, there is no major disagreement among the published reports in this passage. But then we find the most notable innovation in the spoken words, a phrase that would have a long future but that at the time was not even remarked upon that:

Nicolay:	the nation,	shall have	a new birth of freedom,
UrAP:	the nation	shall, under God, have	a new birth of freedom,
NYTrib20:	the nation	shall, under God, have	a new birth of freedom;
PhilInq20:	the nation	shall, under God, have	a new birth of freedom,
PitGz21:	the nation	shall, under God, have	a new birth of freedom,
Hale:	the nation	shall, under God, have	a new birth of freedom,
LittleBrown:	the nation	shall, under God, have	a new birth of freedom,
UrHay:	this nation	shall have	a new birth of freedom;
Hay:	this nation	shall have	a new birth of freedom;
Everett:	this nation, under God,	shall have	a new birth of freedom—
Bancroft:	this nation, under God,	shall have	a new birth of freedom—
Bliss:	this nation, under God,	shall have	a new birth of freedom—

The significance of the words "under God" for Lincoln's personal beliefs will probably always inspire debate. Mary Todd Lincoln recalled in 1866 that it was after Willie's death that her husband "first thought" about religion and that he "felt religious More than Ever about the time he went to Gettysburg," but she was quick to add that "he was not a technical Christian."[43] Willie's death and Gettysburg were also linked in a story that appeared in a newspaper a year after the ceremony, which stated that not long before, Lincoln had told a clergyman, "When I left home to take this chair of State I requested my countrymen to pray for me, I was not then a Christian. When my son died, the severest trial of my life, I was not a Christian. But when I went to Gettysburg, and looked upon the graves of our dead heroes who had fallen in defence of their country, I then and there consecrated myself to Christ; I do love Jesus."[44] The language is clearly not Lincoln's, and the final assertion is so uncharacteristic as to be more than doubtful, but it may be that the anecdote accurately reflects some of the reverential and patriotic sensibility on the platform at Gettysburg that led Lincoln to add "under God" to his speech. Those words helped bring full cohesion and shared expression to a ceremony that had already seen Lincoln and many hundreds, perhaps even many thousands, bonded in prayer and tears under the influence of a most effective reverend and of a powerful orator. The fact that it was a spontaneous addition to that part of the speech, which had already been written and revised several times in Gettysburg (and undoubtedly in Washington before that), suggests that the contexts of time, place, and circumstance were particularly important in calling forth this expression at that moment.[45]

As spoken, "under God" was closely associated with "a new birth of freedom," which is the only wholly new and unprecedented element of Lincoln's speech. Building upon the foundation created by the Letterhead Page in Washington, Lincoln had with difficulty established a text and phrasing in Gettysburg that had suited the new reckoning that was beginning to shape his presidency, and yet here on the stand is a new element in addition to the changes he had made in the early evening the night before and incorporated in the Gettysburg Draft that he had undoubtedly completed before going to sleep. Even the Battlefield Draft created that morning was now, as Lincoln spoke, being strengthened and revisited. From the first moment Lincoln had been asked to participate in the ceremony he had sought the right tone—the occasion was indeed, as he was reported to have said on the train, "a novel and difficult one."[46] Over the days of writing and revision, he had found the words and come to a text that announced a hope for a new birth and the survival of the government of the fathers— and here on the platform, to safeguard and assure the highest ideals he held, he reached for the highest authority he could envision. This was the last significant change he made to his manuscript while speaking, the final creative impulse of that moment on the speakers' platform at Gettysburg, an act that combined thought and expression into a culturally powerful image with totemic words that both reaffirmed and radically redefined the work of the fathers.

The placement of "under God" in the reports of Lincoln's speech is uniform and consistent. Whether this was inaccurate or whether Lincoln on reflection thought it better placed differently, when he finally did insert the phrase into the Everett text he moved it before the verb "shall," giving the line a different cadence and rhythm, however one interprets its meaning.[47] Undoubtedly this move explains why he did not write the words "under God" in the UrHay/Hay, a suspicion that is supported by seeing that in the UrHay Lincoln had already begun to edit this passage by writing "this" nation instead of "the" nation as found in the LittleBrown and in his delivery text, an innovation he retained through to his final handwritten version. Evidently, at this point when writing the UrHay, he hesitated to place "under God" in his draft revision because in the LittleBrown copy text it was placed differently than he would like or than he remembered having spoken the words. Perhaps uncertain as yet of his solution, he appears to have reverted to the wording of the delivery text. Like so many elements of his speech, this hesitation can be read in several ways, but surely it is a sign of the evident care he took throughout the revision to ensure that he found the mix of his written delivery text, spoken words, and new rhetorical elements that suited his vision for the speech.

As the third of the four declarations associated with the dedication of the heroic dead, the "new birth of freedom" precedes the culmination of Lincoln's text, a phrase that has posed considerable difficulties:

NICOLAY: and that government of the people by the people for the
  people, shall not perish from the earth.
URAP: and that the government of the people, by the people and for the
  people, shall not perish from the earth. [Long applause.]

This central idea and probably at least some of the phrasing of this powerful conclusion had been part of Lincoln's speech since the Washington Draft, according to the evidence of Noah Brooks. Then, too, it may be that Seward provided some help with the last few words, but the difficulties this passage created for the history of the speech originated with the problems of telegraphy, compounded by the editing of David Wills. Remarkably, it is not the complex "of . . . by . . . and for" section that has caused trouble—virtually all the reports of his words include the word "and," for example—but the seemingly simpler phrase before it:

Nicolay:	and that	government
UrAP:	and that the	government
BaltoAm:	and that	Governments
HarrbDT20:	and that the	government
PhilNA20:	and that the	government
NYTrib20:	and that	Governments
PhilInq20:	and that the	Government
PitGz21:	and that the	Government
Hale:	and that	government
UrDWills:	and that	governments
DWills:	and that the	government
LittleBrown:	and that the	government
UrHay:	and that this	government
Hay:	and that this	government
Everett:	and that,	government
Bancroft:	and that	government
Bliss:	and that	government

The major press reports have several different combinations of definite articles and singular and plural formulations. When David Wills first wrote out the text for printing by Little, Brown and Company, he simply copied the words of the *New York Tribune,* but then, undoubtedly seeing that they made little sense, he edited the words he had written, probably with reference to another newspaper version, changing both the article and number. Lincoln evidently was dissatisfied with the words he found in the LittleBrown copy text, for it differed not only from what he reportedly said (and perhaps what he recalled saying) but also from what he had written in his manuscript. In his first revision of this passage Lincoln substituted "this" for the "the" added by Wills, perhaps so that "this government" would be parallel to "this nation" that Lincoln had also just written in the UrHay text. Lincoln's edit, then, created three different wordings in this passage (Nicolay, spoken words, Hay) with different claims to authority, a problem that cannot be resolved if the Hay text is regarded as a possible delivery text.

As with the great majority of the mysteries of the manuscripts, a more certain understanding of the sequence and history of the texts resolves this problem in a clear and conceptually compelling manner. As with "under God," when Lincoln set about writing a presentable manuscript to send to Everett, he changed the wording again, after already having changed it in the UrHay from his original copy text (the LittleBrown). With "under God," Lincoln eventually retained his spoken words as reported, but he moved the phrase to a place he preferred, a sign of deliberation and reflection. In the case of "government," Lincoln reverted to the language of the delivery text, which remained the definitive wording through to the Bliss text in mid-March, underscoring an essential continuity across the composition and revision of the speech, from Washington to Gettysburg and back again.

The brevity of Lincoln's remarks may have surprised many, but it is not surprising that the applause or response may have been muted, for the ceremony was not finished, and raucous demonstrations would have been out of place in any case. The AP report indicates "Long applause" at the end of the speech, which seems somewhat formulaic, but the six indications of applause it notes may be more than merely generic signs of approval by the crowd, for they seem to correspond to the rhythms of the speech. An "applause" marker ends the first sentence, but then follow just over 100 words with no applause; in contrast, there are five such marks in the last 130-odd words, which clearly form the emotional culmination of the speech.

As the speech progressed, it was not only the audience that found its voice. Lincoln began to depart much more frequently from the written words about a third of the way through his manuscript. When Lincoln spoke the first sixty-five words as written, he made no changes in words as measured by the UrAP; that is to say, the written and spoken words agree completely. Beginning with the repetition of "we are met" Lincoln appears to have begun to speak more freely, a trend that intensified when he reached the sentence that starts with the phrase "It is rather for us" on the last line of the Letterhead Page and then continues uninterrupted to the end of the speech on the Pencil Page. When Lincoln spoke the eighty-two written words of this passage, he reportedly made thirty word changes, almost all additions, a rate more than half again greater than for the middle section.

Just as with the image of Lincoln at Gettysburg, breaking the moment Lincoln spoke into fragments for analysis can prevent us from gaining a holistic sense of Lincoln's spoken words, an event that was creative as well as performative. Fortunately, we can gain a sense of the overall patterns in that moment through the testimony of an expert witness, a master of rhetoric, and a close and deeply interested observer of the scene who was listening from the best vantage point imaginable: Edward Everett. The ceremony at Gettysburg appears to have been the first time Everett heard Lincoln speak in public, and it made an impression upon him. The next morning, of course, Everett would write a letter to Lincoln praising the speech, but even three and a half months later Everett could still hear in his mind the cadence and emphasis that Lincoln gave his words that afternoon. In early March 1864, when Everett received Lincoln's handwritten copy in order to sell it at a charity fair, he inserted it into a bound volume that also contained the handwritten manuscript of his own "Oration at Gettysburg." The volume was arranged in such a way that when it was opened, every right-hand page showed a handwritten text. On the left, facing each of these pages, Everett then very carefully cut out and pasted into the volume the equivalent passage of the speeches as printed in the "authorized edition" by Little, Brown, which had been printed the month before.

A fastidious man was Mr. Edward Everett, and he noticed that the handwritten manuscript that Lincoln had just sent him differed from the printed LittleBrown version. Lincoln had, in fact, during the post-speech revision, made nineteen word changes in the handwritten text he sent Everett compared to the LittleBrown printed version that Everett had sent him. And so Everett quite carefully edited by hand, in pen, the printed words of the LittleBrown copy facing Lincoln's handwritten version to conform to most of the word changes Lincoln had made. But Everett also took the additional step of underlining in pen eleven different words in the printed copy facing Lincoln's handwritten version.

Everett's markings in the printed version of Lincoln's speech display a pattern similar to the applause markers and to the changes that Lincoln made while speaking, all of which can be thought of as proxies for intensity or cadence, for feeling or impact. Together, they express three different aspects of the same scene: the changes introduced by Lincoln, applause indications added by the AP report, and Everett's notes on what he heard. As expressed as a ratio of the words in each section of the speech, most marked is the gradual development, then a rise in the middle, reaching a peak around the third quarter of the speech, and finally a certain trailing off.

Section of Nicolay	Word changes, UrAP	Applause, UrAP	Everett's emphasis
First 65 words	0	1 (1:65)	1 (1:65)
Middle 92 words	21 (1:4.4)	2 (1:46)	6 (1:15)
Last 82 words	30 (1:2.7)	3 (1:27)	4 (1:20)

The arc of Lincoln's spoken words corresponds to these rhythms, which can be explained as translating a rise and development in Lincoln's presentation and the impact of his words. By adding the marks of emphasis to Lincoln's printed speech, Everett clearly intended to reveal to the best of his ability what he had heard Lincoln say, the intensity and feeling that, as a respected orator and a discerning critic, he had felt and heard while sitting on that little settee on the platform. Everett did not have to add the indications of Lincoln's spoken emphasis to the printed text, but he felt the emphasis needed to be conveyed, for he, too, had lived that moment. Transposing Everett's marks of emphasis (in **bold italics**) to the original AP report matches the spoken words more closely—to which can be added, too, Lincoln's underlined "did" and Hale's "*to be dedicated*"; the paragraphing here divides the speech according to the three-part pattern suggested by the word changes and applause markers. Here, then, is Abraham Lincoln's Gettysburg Address as it was heard by Edward Everett:[48]

Four score and seven years ago our fathers brought forth upon this continent a new nation, conceived in liberty and dedicated to the proposition that all men are created equal. [Applause.] Now we are engaged in a great civil war, testing whether that nation, or *any* nation so conceived and so dedicated, can long endure. We are met on a great battle-field of that war;

we are met to dedicate a portion of it as the final resting-place of those who here gave their lives that *that* nation might live. It is altogether fitting and proper that we should do this, but in a larger sense we cannot dedicate, we cannot consecrate, we cannot hallow this ground. The brave men, living and dead, who struggled here have consecrated it *far above our* poor power to add or to detract. [Applause.] The world will little note, nor long remember, what we *say* here; but it can *never* forget what they did here. [Applause.] It is for us, the *living*, rather *to be dedicated* here to the unfinished work that they have thus far so nobly carried on. [Applause.]

It is rather for *us* here to be dedicated to the great task remaining before us; that from these honored dead we take increased devotion to that cause for which *they here* gave the last full measure of devotion; that we here highly resolve that these dead shall not have died in vain. [Applause.] That the nation shall, under God, have a new birth of freedom, and that the government of the people, by the people and for the people, shall not perish from the earth. [Long applause.]

Lincoln seemingly emphasized while speaking some of the oppositions that are characteristic of his writings and speeches: "any" nation contrasted with "that" nation; "our" power contrasted with what "they here" gave; for "us" to be dedicated to the cause for which "they here" died; and, of course, the ephemeral nature of what we "say" here compared to the enduring memory of what they "did" here, which the world would "never" forget.

If the applause indications are more than formulaic, it may be that the increasing response of the crowd helped create the sympathy and exchange of emotion and outlook that is characteristic of great oratory and powerful communication. Many of the emotive and mythic depictions of Lincoln at Gettysburg center on this element of call and response, from Isaak Allen's emotion-laden depiction telegraphed the day after the ceremony, to William Makepeace Thayer's myth-building description of mid-1864, to Major Henry Lee's description from 1866. The evidence of the crowd's response over the course of the speech is perhaps too fragmentary or generic to confirm that this cycle of words and response was fully developed or sustained, but certainly something happened as Lincoln approached the "little note, nor long remember" phrase. It may well have been the emotional response of many who were listening, and of Lincoln himself, that accounted for the rhythm of Lincoln's words as the speech moved toward its conclusion.

One explanation for the new spoken words in the speech, then, is that Lincoln was in a sense carried along with the crowd by the inarguably powerful written text he had crafted over the previous days. Noah Brooks later recalled that Lincoln told him that he had made changes to the manuscript in Gettysburg and while "delivering it on the field," and there is also a secondhand account published by a journalist and former State Department official while Hay was secretary of state, stating, "Colonel Hay, his private secretary, says that he [Lincoln] wrote out a brief speech at the White House before leaving Washington, and, as usual on such occasions, committed it to memory; but the inspiration of the scene led him to make material changes."[49] Lincoln's speech, then, was in part an active process of creation, a performance, driven in part by the response of the crowd and the sense of the moment.

Together, a secure delivery manuscript, a clear choice as the best approximation of the spoken words, and a known sequence of texts eliminate the confusions and dead ends caused by the mysteries of the manuscripts, mysteries that have obstructed our ability to fully see the Gettysburg Address. Although there will always be a mystery about such creations, Lincoln's spoken words reveal that he was deeply inspired by the place and the moment when he completed the journey to Gettysburg that he had begun in Washington, when he had imagined what it would be like, "to stand here" with the graves of the heroic dead encircling him and the wooded hills all around.

Conclusion:
Who Wrote the Gettysburg
Address?

Away in Massachusetts the day after the Gettysburg ceremony, Henry Wadsworth Longfellow was catching up on some correspondence, thanking an old friend for having written a "very generous, and more than generous" article about him in the most recent edition of the *Atlantic*. Longfellow's reputation and popularity were at their peak, but the war years had been personally harrowing. His beloved wife had died in a fire in the early months of the war, and then in the summer of 1863 his son Charles, who had inspired Longfellow's touching poem "To a Child" and was just seventeen, had run off to join the army in spite of opposition from his father, who thought the lad too young. Just the week before, Longfellow had been shaken from sleep by a "thunderous knock on the front door," which he answered in fear of news from some far-off battlefield announcing his son's death. Many across the Union, and across the once and future nation, lived with the same fear in that fall of 1863, or had already received the telegram in the night. But this time it was a false alarm, so Longfellow could tell his friend, "We are all well here in this old house" and relate his happiness that their mutual friends, the scholar Charles Eliot Norton and the poet James Russell Lowell, had been named editors at the *North American Review*.

Another bit of news, about the cemetery dedication at Gettysburg, also caught Longfellow's attention that November morning. He had declined writing a poem for the occasion when David Wills was seeking a poet for the ceremony, and so he was perhaps particularly interested in reading about the event. It was not Everett's oration that caught his eye, however; Longfellow did not even mention it. Instead he noticed a relatively small item that was almost buried amid the extensive coverage devoted to the event by all the Boston newspapers and that, in some ways, must have spoken to his own fears of the sacrifices demanded by the war: "This morning's paper brings the report of Lincoln's brief speech at Gettysburg," wrote America's most esteemed poet, "which seems to me admirable."[1]

Longfellow's admiring friend, and the recipient of Longfellow's letter admiring "Lincoln's brief speech at Gettysburg," turns out to have been George W. Curtis. Critic and author, one-time denizen of the transcendentalist experiment at Brook Farm and the current political editor of *Harper's Weekly*, Curtis was one of the most influential figures in the interlinked and ingrown worlds of midcentury American literary, political, and cultural life. Whatever the role of Longfellow's recommendation, in his next *Harper's Weekly* column Curtis repeated the already standard comment that Everett's oration was "smooth and cold" but went on to glowingly praise Lincoln's speech—and there should be no doubt which passage he particularly commended: "The few words of the President were from the heart to the heart," he wrote. "They can not be read, even, without kindling emotion. 'The world will little note nor long remember what we say here, but it can never forget what they did here.' It was as simple and felicitous and earnest a word as was ever spoken." For good measure, the New Year's editorial in *Harper's Weekly* the next month again cited the same passage. In April 1864, the magazine went so far as to call Lincoln's speech "the most perfect piece of American eloquence" and, at a time when the classical era still represented the highest achievement of art and thought, to assert that it was "as noble and pathetic and appropriate as the oration of Pericles over the Peloponnesian dead."[2]

Opponents inadvertently underscored the high praise by asserting that Lincoln could not have possibly written the speech, leading the White House to officially announce in April 1864 that, with a few exceptions, the president personally wrote everything published over his name.[3] Not to be outdone in honoring the speech, Longfellow's and Curtis's friends Norton and Lowell at the *North American Review*, a periodical with a small circulation but wide influence, on the anniversary of the battle in July 1864 seconded the *Philadelphia Press* and anointed Lincoln's speech with the description that generations would take almost as part of its title: "immortal." The next year, after Lincoln's assassination, Lowell would write some of the most repeated lines of the emerging Lincoln myth:[4]

> Our children shall behold his fame,
> The kindly-earnest, brave, foreseeing man,
> Sagacious, patient, dreading praise, not blame,
> New birth of our new soil, the first American.

Lowell's "New birth of our new soil" evoking Lincoln's "new birth of freedom" after Lincoln's assassination links seamlessly with his journal's calling the speech "immortal" the year before, and harks further back to Curtis and *Harper's Weekly*, which set the tone during the war itself for what became a sustained campaign of praise in the nation's leading literary and political journals, and further back again, to the very morning of November 20, when the first printing of Lincoln's words reached America's first poet, who knew them to be admirable.

But the first compliment Lincoln received on his speech was, fittingly, that of Edward Everett. When Lincoln had finished speaking and sat down, a chorus sang a brief dirge in anticipation of college president Baugher's closing benediction, and then the ceremony was done. As artillery fired a salute and the Marine Band played, Lincoln, Everett, Stockton, and the others on the platform rose and congratulated and complimented each other, with Lincoln shaking hands all around as he made his way to his horse for the procession back to town. Wayne MacVeagh many years later recalled telling Lincoln on the platform that he thought it "an immortal address." Lincoln allegedly replied, "Oh, you must not say that. You must not be extravagant about it." John Russell Young recalled being surprised when Lincoln sat down so soon and asking somewhat impertinently if that was all. "Yes, for the present," Lincoln is supposed to have said.[5] Possibly the passing decades embroidered these memories, but it is certain that MacVeagh found the speech to be memorable, and that Everett congratulated Lincoln on the stand, probably just as Lincoln sat down after his speech, apparently saying something to the effect that Lincoln had said more in a few pages than all of his own oration, or perhaps that Lincoln's words would indeed be remembered.[6]

"We went home through crowded and cheering streets," John Hay wrote in his diary, striking a triumphalist note in an otherwise affectedly world-weary description of the day. Many of the press reports remarked on the enthusiastic cheering and greetings given Lincoln and the procession as it returned to the Diamond, perhaps a release of tension at the end of the funeral ceremony.[7] After a dinner at the Wills house, Lincoln and Governor Curtin formed a reception line, and while various bands played patriotic melodies, they shook hands with scores, if not hundreds, for an hour or so—a fitting image of the two Union war leaders working the crowd together, for Curtin had done so much to allow and encourage Lincoln's participation in an event that would give form to the words that are among the most enduring legacies of the war. Handsome Andrew reportedly kissed all the pretty girls who came down the line, but Lincoln forbore.[8]

At Lincoln's request, several of the marshals were sent to fetch the heroic John Burns, who had been on the speakers' platform but seemingly had not yet been introduced to the president; Burns was a longtime Democrat and something of an old coot, so David Wills may have deliberately tried to keep the local celebrity away from the president. Led by a band and the ever-present marshals, Burns and Lincoln then formed a little procession to a nearby church to hear a speech at an event organized by the Ohio delegation. "The poor president had to attend," wrote the sympathetic Everett in his diary; "I was too fatigued." Lucky for him, because it was "a long and verbose speech" according to the *New York World*. Lincoln, probably beginning to come down from the emotional heights of the day and probably feeling the effects of smallpox—and possibly, a late night writing his speech?—reportedly "bent his head on the back of the front seat and quietly slept." Lincoln's train left at about six that evening, and forty years later old-timers in Gettysburg could still recall it pulling out of the station, with Lincoln standing on the platform of the last car waving farewell until "lost to sight in the fast coming darkness."[9] They arrived in Washington at about one in the morning to find carriages waiting for them, much to Everett's relief; Stanton was nothing if not efficient. Lincoln's journey to Gettysburg and back again had lasted just over thirty-six hours.

The next day Everett, who had traveled to Washington on Lincoln's train, wrote his letter to Lincoln expressing "my great admiration of the thoughts expressed by you, with such eloquent simplicity & appropriateness," which could have simply been polite formality, except that the esteemed orator, who did not lack for vanity, also wrote, "I should be glad, if I could flatter myself that I came as near to the central idea of the occasion, in two hours, as you did in two minutes." Everett and Lincoln may have also exchanged compliments the Monday following, when Everett met Lincoln at the White House as part of his round of visits to cabinet officers and old friends in the capital. This and the other marks of appreciation earned by the speech seemingly got Lincoln to wondering about an address that had inspired a compliment he prized more than any other he had received. When his old friend James Speed accepted the post of attorney general, Lincoln was ready with the story. The composition process Lincoln described to Speed might easily have resulted in a jumbled mess, but it did not—and this seems to have been a large part of Lincoln's point in telling the story a year later. For Everett—Everett himself—had praised Lincoln's speech in words that went so deep that in telling the story a year later Lincoln actually "produced the letter," no doubt from the storied pigeonhole desk in his White House office, to show to his new attorney general and old friend, James Speed.

The central device of the dramatic narrative that Lincoln recounted to Speed that night in December 1864 or early 1865 was Lincoln's sense of the contrast between the high praise accorded the speech and its somewhat disjointed and unpromising origins. With the complicated and eventful story of the speech behind us, we can now perhaps more fully appreciate Lincoln's point. This was not a speech Lincoln set out to write. He "was anxious to go—and desired to be prepared to say some appropriate thing," as he told Speed, but mostly it was the "interesting ceremony," as he wrote to Stephen Logan on November 9, that brought Lincoln to undertake the journey, not the fact that he was asked, almost in passing, and with great hesitation, to say a few words as part of his role in the dedication ceremony.

Lincoln did not begin to work in earnest on his remarks until after he had made the final decision to attend, probably at the "urgent solicitation" of Andrew Curtin on Saturday, November 14. Then, out of concern to meet the expectations David Will clearly outlined in the invitation, he probably spoke with his friend Ward Lamon, the marshal of the day, and also asked William Saunders to come to him for a detailed examination of the cemetery plan. On the basis of the inspiration of his speech to the serenade of July 7, 1863, which connected the great victories at Gettysburg and Vicksburg to the Fourth of July, Lincoln then wrote a final version of the Washington Draft, probably on the night of November 17, that envisioned the war as part of the great project of freedom and equal rights begun by the founders. Judging from this first known version, Lincoln imagined what it would be like "to stand here," where the soldiers too had stood, with the battlefield surrounding him and the graves in the classical arcs elaborately described by Saunders. The cemetery became, then, a kind of meeting place of a revered past, a violent present, and an unformed future. The Washington Draft played upon dualities such as the fathers of the past and the struggle now in the present, and the sacrifices of the soldiers and the role now of the living—elements that Lincoln emphasized while speaking—and it probably reached a fairly well-developed conclusion relating the war to government by the people.

When he left Washington, Lincoln knew that he would want to review or work over some of the speech, but he did not do so on the train, instead talking politics with MacVeagh and kissing babies handed up to him on station platforms. After a long evening of introductions and speeches at the Wills house, he sent for his host to learn more about his "part" in the ceremonials and then, after about an hour, got his remarks into a shape that prompted consulting Seward. It seems likely that he completed or reworked the last part of his speech back at the Wills house, but there is little reason to think that up to that point the revisions or additions to the Washington Draft were extensive or structural, for it appears that in the Gettysburg Draft completed late on the night of November 18, he had left the Letterhead Page untouched.

The crisis came on the morning of the nineteenth, when events gave the twist to Lincoln's narrative to Speed and increased the sense of rush and confusion in an already compressed composition schedule. The visit to the battlefield is the most proximate event that may have sparked the new revision; it was certainly brought on by some new and more urgent, assertive, and emotionally powerful sense of the sacrifices of the soldiers and the obligations of the living that entailed three related changes: revision of the first page by adding a fifth "dedicated," emphasizing (probably) "what they did here," and rewriting, undoubtedly with some revisions, the last page wholly in pencil, including the only new and unprecedented phrase on the page, "a new birth of freedom." None of these changes center on the founders; the Washington Draft had taken up that theme from the July 7 victory celebration, but the Battlefield Draft was written under the influence of a new and altered understanding of the "devotion" of the soldiers—a word found in this speech only on the Pencil Page, twice. Influenced by the myth of the speech and its place in the national culture, which places Lincoln's words at the center of events that day in November, much of the scholarship and popular memory of the Gettysburg Address presents an incomplete view of the event and the causal relationships: not only did the speech help make Gettysburg a powerful image, but Lincoln's experience of Gettysburg also made the speech.

The paper Lincoln held as he spoke was the Nicolay document, called here the Battlefield Draft, which began with the Letterhead Page, the page Edward McPherson, following David Wills, described as "an official letter-sheet," with, as Dr. Daniel Slade ("Medicus") recalled, the "German text, 'Executive Mansion,' and blank space for date, being distinctly observed," the very same page that John Nicolay saw Lincoln editing that morning, the "half of a speech" that Lincoln himself told James Speed he wrote in Washington and then completed in Gettysburg. There is no direct historical or eyewitness evidence to support any other document as the delivery text to the exclusion of the Nicolay document. Virtually everything we know about Lincoln's delivery of his speech—from the contemporary reports confirming Lincoln's spoken emphasis upon evoking "what they did here" to the additional spoken words exactly at the ungrammatical juncture of the two pages—supports this conclusion.

The security of knowing the delivery text, as well as the sequence of other versions, creates new interpretive possibilities for gaining even greater understanding of this work, which has long been partially obscured by a haze of doubt. The two pages of the Battlefield Draft synthesize and express the double roots of the speech in Washington and Gettysburg, expressing the shifting emphasis of Lincoln's thought as he made his journey to the speakers' stand. The speech asserted the essential unity of the national project from the founders to the future across the broken divide of that fifth written "dedica // ted" that links Washington and Gettysburg, the ideals of the founders and the work and sacrifices and devotion of the new struggle for today and for the future. For the generation that carried on the war, Lincoln's speech reaffirmed their roots in the work of the "fathers" and inserted them into the world-historical founding myth of a unique experiment that promised a kind of political redemption for humankind. Although maintaining unity with the founders on the Letterhead Page, the speech on its Pencil Page of November 19 recognized the struggle of Lincoln's own day, with new aspirations suited to the splendor and power of a people in arms for a righteous cause. The Letterhead Page and the Pencil Page bring together in this way the two most powerful moments in American history, the founding era of the Revolution and Constitution, and the Civil War that brought massive upheaval and unprecedented mobilization.

This speech could not have been written only in Washington, sitting in quiet reflection at the cabinet table in the White House. Nor could it have been composed fully under the influence of the sacrifices of the dead upon the bloody field of Gettysburg. It was created in a final act of improvisational performance upon the very speakers' platform, when Lincoln joined his aspirations for the nation born from a lifetime of reflection on the meaning of the Declaration's recognition of human rights to his overwhelming sense of the human cost of the war and the importance of the ideals that gave such sacrifices meaning and significance.

Seeing the words of the emotional and conceptual pivot point of the speech as spoken, heard, and felt by Lincoln, Everett, and Charles Hale—and the vociferous crowd too—against the bright sky of that November day illuminates ever more clearly the reasons why Isaak Allen's stalwart officer broke down at this moment, and why many carried the memory to the end of their days:

> The world will little note, nor long remember, what we *say* here; but it can *never* forget what they <u>did</u> here. [Applause.] It is for us, the *living*, rather *to be dedicated* here to the unfinished work that they have thus far so nobly carried on. [Applause.]

It was that instant of speaking that most fully joined Lincoln's reflections at the White House to the sensibility of the Wills house, and that in the sixth "dedicated" helped create, in that moment in Gettysburg, a synthesis of words and pages and moments and ideas that fully joined the ideals of the founders and the blood of the soldiers in Lincoln's resolve for a "new birth of freedom."

As for the mysteries of the manuscripts, lining up the texts in sequential order helps reveal why the path taken by Lincoln's words has been so difficult to follow:

A. Lincoln writes and delivers his speech
   0. Hypothetical notes or drafts
   1. Washington Draft
   2. Gettysburg Draft

3. Battlefield Draft (the Nicolay document)
4. Lincoln's spoken words, the Gettysburg Address
B. Lincoln's words transcribed, telegraphed, and edited by others
    5. The original Associated Press report (UrAP)
    6. *New York Tribune*
    7. UrDWills/DWills
    8. LittleBrown printed version
C. Lincoln undertakes a post-speech revision
    9. UrHay/Hay (on the basis of the LittleBrown)
    10. Everett
    11. Bancroft
    12. Bliss

It was the middle stage that caused the trouble, when Lincoln's words took a detour down the telegraph lines to New York and then back to Gettysburg, where David Wills copied this transcribed, telegraphed text but also made deliberate changes before shipping the copy off to Edward Everett in Boston for printing. This meant that the UrHay/Hay document that Lincoln wrote on the basis of the version printed by Everett and Wills can look like a delivery text because it is so close in words to what Lincoln said—not because Lincoln read from the Hay text, but because Lincoln wrote the Hay text, the basis for his definitive revision, by copying and revising an edited and printed report of his spoken words.

The sequence of composition and order of texts presented here has never been previously suggested. Louis Warren had the right timing for the creation of the post-speech "revised version," associating it with Everett's request in late January 1864, but he also got lost in the thickets trying to show that the Hay was written before the Nicolay, a notion that had gained publicity during the confusion caused by the discovery of the Hay text among John Hay's personal papers in 1908.[10]

At that time, the Nicolay text, first published by John Nicolay in 1894, had been missing since 1901, when John Nicolay died, and it was presumed lost or stolen. Even after it was recovered in the files of John Hay in 1916, some suspected that somehow Nicolay had been the one who removed the two copies of the speech from the Lincoln papers. But possession is nine-tenths of the deed, and we must acknowledge that it was John Hay who had taken the two versions. He was a brilliant fellow, but he was also an avid Lincoln collector, and one does not become secretary of state and preside over a budding empire in the Philippines and the Caribbean without a streak of ruthlessness. Evidently, the heirs of Nicolay and Hay suspected what had happened, and so to cut off embarrassing questions they donated both the Nicolay and the Hay texts to the Library of Congress only a month after the surprising discovery of the Nicolay document bound in the late John Hay's signature red morocco leather among his other treasures.[11] No, it was not John Nicolay who stole the Gettysburg Address, but the suspicions surrounding the discovery of the Hay and then the Nicolay texts created such confusion that virtually any order of texts or origins of the Hay—delivery text, special-made souvenir, forgotten first draft—seemed more reasonable than the possibility that John Hay had succumbed to the frailties of our common humanity.

Another obstacle that prevented an accurate understanding of the composition and order of texts is that the overpowering legend of an "immortal" work of genius does not easily coexist with the concept of collaborators. Yet it was not Lincoln alone who wrote the Gettysburg Address, even aside from the phrases he took up from Daniel Webster, from the common wisdom of his day, or, in the first sentence, from the colonial governor of Connecticut, Samuel Huntington. We cannot be sure, but it may have been Edward Everett himself who provided the particular paragraph structure in the LittleBrown version that Lincoln incorporated in his revised version and kept through to his final copy. Everett's care for presenting Lincoln's words would suggest as much. Nor can we be sure exactly what the voluble secretary of state may have contributed, but he would not have been William H. Seward had he suddenly gone blank when Lincoln came calling the night before the ceremony to read or show him his speech.

Yet we do know the precise contribution of one of Lincoln's collaborators, and it is a beautiful and fitting legacy. David Wills labored tirelessly for months assuring that the wounded and dying were cared for, and that the dead were suitably honored, and that, finally, the ceremonial consecration of their burial place became an occasion unlike any in the history of the young Republic. Possibly he was among the cemetery agents who were not sure that Lincoln was up to the challenge of a "few appropriate remarks"—and, just maybe, he hoped for another nominee in 1864, because he certainly did not celebrate the incumbent's role in the affair, and his patron, Governor Curtin, hoped well into 1864 that Frémont would be the candidate. But Wills had his reward for his efforts on behalf of the Union.

Whenever we read Lincoln's words as he wrote them in their final form, we can see in a capital "L" a reminder and a legacy of the gift to his nation of David Wills: "Four score and seven years ago our fathers brought forth on this continent, a new nation, conceived in Liberty, and dedicated to the proposition that all men are created equal." David Wills eliminated all the nonstandard capitalization he found in the *New York Tribune* version that he copied for printing, but in this one case he seems to have deliberately retained the capital. Lincoln found it in the LittleBrown and kept it through the Hay, the Everett, the Bancroft, and finally to the Bliss. A small thing, perhaps, but who among us could expect such a portion of immortality?

And of course, Lincoln accepted a great deal of the work of the Associated Press reporter who gave printed form to the spoken words. It was probably John I. Davenport, just twenty years old and working the night shift when he was called upon to go to Gettysburg, but whoever it was, it seems unlikely that he was able to exactly replicate Lincoln's spoken words, even if we cannot know to what extent Lincoln's words may have differed from what was reported, or to what extent Lincoln's post-speech revision attempted to restore what he may have recalled saying two months earlier. Still, there are about fifty differences in words between the Nicolay delivery text and the Hay document that was based on the LittleBrown, so we can be reasonably sure that something of that reporter's work made it into the Civil War's most iconic statement of meaning and purpose. Certainly, there are many instances in which the punctuation of Lincoln's final versions do not reflect the Nicolay text but instead appear to have been taken from the AP report by way of the *New York Tribune* and David Wills and Little, Brown and Company of Boston. Furthermore, Lincoln even gave his last version a title suggested by John Pendleton Kennedy, a fading literary figure and one of the editors of *Autograph Leaves*: "Address delivered at the dedication of the Cemetery at Gettysburg."[12]

All these collaborators and contributions helped make the words, punctuation, and appearance of what has come down to us as "the Gettysburg Address," giving it the aspect not only of an individual creation by an artist-genius, but also of a socially created text, not just the work of one person's vision but also a collective cultural production. This impression is reinforced by the fact that for perhaps seventy-five years after the speech, many dozens, even hundreds, of different texts proliferated. Moreover, each passing decade brought new and changed understandings of and uses for Lincoln's words. Contemporaries emphasized the passage evoking "what they <u>did</u> here"; in contrast, "government by the people" was especially noted during World War I, and "under God" took on such resonance during the Cold War struggle against an atheist ideology that it was added to the Pledge of Allegiance.[13] True classics, despite their image of establishing an unchanging tradition, endure because they move with the times, and like the Gettysburg Address, they are created by continual reflection and take their meaning from the needs and aspirations of societies. The countless interpretations of Lincoln's meaning reflect the innumerable versions of the speech that have circulated, a collective national improvisation on a theme from Lincoln.

Lincoln himself appears to have witnessed the early esteem for his speech with pleasure and perplexity, a view that pervades his narrative to James Speed. According to the accounts by Noah Brooks, when talking about his speech at the time it was being written in Washington, he emphasized that it was "short, short, short" and not quite finished or wholly satisfactory, and on the train he seemingly noted the difficulty of his position in finding the right way to meet the "novel and difficult" occasion. This sense of concern or even anxiety during this time was also reflected in Lincoln's story to Speed, in Nicolay's descriptions of Lincoln's daunting task, and in Lamon's exaggerations. Once in Gettysburg, the reports founded in the recollections of David Wills depict Lincoln characterizing his speech as "a few thoughts," or "stray thoughts," or even "what I have been scribbling for a speech"; MacVeagh heard Lincoln call them "the few words he was expected to say."

These typically self-denigrating expressions found in later recollections of conversations are confirmed in Lincoln's own letter written to Everett the day after the speech, our most direct evidence for Lincoln's thoughts about his words at the time: "In our respective parts, yesterday, you could not have been excused to make a short address, nor I a long one. I am pleased to know that in your judgement, the little I did say was not entirely a failure." As with Lincoln's comparing the speakers' platform to a gallows before boarding the train to Gettysburg, it was not just modesty when writing to a noted rhetorician that led Lincoln to evoke the possibility of failure and to call his words "the little I did say." Almost all the comments about his speech ascribed to Lincoln at the time of the ceremony refer to its brevity in a way that suggests he dismissed its importance, most effectively in the speech itself when evoking how quickly "what we say here" would be forgotten.

And yet there is the Letterhead Page, essentially untouched through the revisions in Gettysburg, a sign that Lincoln recognized that there was something there that was worth saying. And after the speech, there was Everett's letter, which had prompted him to tell Speed that "he had never received a compliment he prized more highly." With the praise on the stand and after, and with his own reflection on a speech he took so much trouble to revise and rewrite, it seems that Lincoln began to gain a new appreciation for his words. As a first sign, when Lincoln on February 4, 1864, sent along the version he had written for Edward Everett, he called his speech "my remarks at Gettysburg," the first known reference by Lincoln to his words that did not also disparage or dismiss them. And too, in the spring of 1865 Lincoln copied the letter Charles Sumner had brought from the Duchess of Argyll mentioning Professor Goldwin Smith's praise for the speech and her own estimation that "the speech at the Gettysburg Cemetery must live." Then at last, there is Lincoln's own narrative to Speed, working out to his own satisfaction the problem of how a speech with such a story had inspired such notice.

But if the ideals of the speech have given it longevity, it is the politics at its core that give it life and strength. Crafted at a crucial time in the elaboration of Lincoln's Reconstruction policies, it is a full-blooded statement of ideology and was political in the best and most essential sense, as participating in the collective process of making decisions in a democracy. Perhaps the central argument in the speech is that it was vital to assure that the great project begun by the fathers and served by the soldiers was continued to ultimate victory. At a time when his governing coalition from Maryland to Missouri appeared ready to break apart over the perplexing compound of Union and slavery and when leading Democrats advocated an armistice and opposed the measures Lincoln thought necessary for victory—including emancipation, the revocation of habeas corpus, increased taxation, and the draft—Lincoln's argument for staying the course was not merely an abstract vision of national ideals; it was also the statement of an incumbent administration's governing philosophy.[14]

Too long relegated to the realm of misty abstractions, Lincoln's speech was, necessarily and rightfully, a statement of political purposes that cannot be distinguished from what opponents called partisanship, for the "new birth of freedom" stood for everything most Democrats (and all secessionists) stood against, including limited (at first) voting rights for freedmen, equal protection of all citizens, a renewed emphasis upon extending the emancipation policy even into Union slave states, and the first steps toward an antislavery amendment that Lincoln would insist upon as part of his reelection platform. This was the "great task" that inspired Lincoln to repeat six times his dedication and ours to assuring the survival of democratic government embracing freedom and equal rights for all: "the new birth of freedom."

"All honor to Jefferson," Lincoln once wrote in praise of the man who "had the coolness, forecast, and capacity to introduce into a merely revolutionary document, an abstract truth, applicable to all men and all times."[15] Yes, and all honor to Lincoln, who placed at the heart of our Civil War, the searing crisis of our maturation, a statement of ideals that renewed that promise and extended it to horizons not encompassed by the founders. And here is where we come most clearly to the importance of knowing which document Lincoln wrote in Washington, and which manuscript Lincoln took to the speakers' stand.

The literal meaning of the words in Lincoln's several handwritten texts differs very little, but only the Battlefield Draft encodes Lincoln's thought and experience in ways found in no other text. The Battlefield Draft alone reveals that in Lincoln's first known writing of the address, in Washington, he was building upon the founding and the cues provided by his first rough sketch of July 7, 1863, and only the Battlefield Draft provides in the penciled editing and the single, grand sentence on that second page in pencil the evidence that, at Gettysburg, Lincoln was moved in ways he did not initially envision, moved to bring a new sensibility and emphasis to his thought. And it was while speaking from the Battlefield Draft when standing before the living and the dead that Abraham Lincoln, in the inspiration of that Gettysburg moment, created the words and image of an enduring and authentic myth that across successive generations has been vital for elevating our vision and clarifying our purposes. Lincoln wrote his dedicatory remarks, but it took an entire nation to write "the Gettysburg Address." His journey to the "new birth of freedom" at Gettysburg is our nation's odyssey from the principles of the founding to the agony and grandeur of the Civil War. And in part because of Lincoln's journey and the larger passage toward an eternal ideal that he traced, we continue to make it a journey with the promise of hope.

■

Notes

Abbreviations

ACHS   Adams County Historical Society
Collected Works   *The Collected Works of Abraham Lincoln,* ed. Roy P.
                         Basler, 9 vols. (New Brunswick, N.J.: Rutgers University
                         Press, 1953–1955).
GNMP   Gettysburg National Military Park Archives
Lincoln Papers, LOC   Papers of Abraham Lincoln, Library of Congress
LOC   Library of Congress
MSHS   Massachusetts State Historical Society

Introduction: The Mysteries of the Manuscript

1. William Makepeace Thayer, *The Character and Public Services of Abraham Lincoln, President of the United States* (Boston: Dinsmoor, 1864), 17.

2. Barry Schwartz presents a tendentious definition of "post-heroic" politics; Schwartz, *Lincoln in the Post-heroic Era* (Chicago: University of Chicago Press, 2003), 7; see also Barry Schwartz, "The New Gettysburg Address: A Study in Illusion," in *The Lincoln Forum: Rediscovering Abraham Lincoln,* ed. John Y. Simon and Harold Holzer (New York: Fordham University Press, 2001).

3. Edwin Sparks, "The Long Story of a Short Oration," *Dial,* November 16, 1906, 320–321; James G. Randall, *Lincoln the President,* 4 vols. (New York: Dodd, Mead, 1945–1955), 2: 303. Benjamin P. Thomas notes that the only thing proven about the speech is "the existence of disagreement and uncertainty"; Thomas, *Portrait for Posterity: Abraham Lincoln and His Biographers* (New Brunswick, N.J.: Rutgers University Press, 1947), 241.

4. William E. Barton, *Lincoln at Gettysburg: What He Intended to Say; What He Said; What He Was Reported to Have Said; What He Wished He Had Said* (Indianapolis, Ind.: Bobbs-Merrill, 1930); Gabor Boritt, *The Gettysburg Gospel: The Lincoln Speech That Nobody Knows* (New York: Simon and Schuster, 2008); Michael Burlingame, *Abraham Lincoln: A Life*, 2 vols. (Baltimore: Johns Hopkins University Press, 2008); A. E. Elmore, *Lincoln's Gettysburg Address: Echoes of the Bible and Book of Common Prayer* (Carbondale: Southern Illinois University Press, 2009); Frank L. Klement, *The Gettysburg Soldier's Cemetery and Lincoln's Address: Aspects and Angles* (Shippensburg, Pa.: White Mane, 1993); Louis A. Warren, *Lincoln's Gettysburg Declaration: "A New Birth of Freedom"* (Fort Wayne, Ind.: Lincoln National Life Foundation, 1964); Carl F. Wieck, *Lincoln's Quest for Equality: The Road to Gettysburg* (DeKalb: Northern Illinois University Press, 2002); Garry Wills, *Lincoln at Gettysburg: The Words That Remade America* (New York: Simon and Schuster, 1992); Douglas Wilson, *Lincoln's Sword: The Presidency and the Power of Words* (New York, Knopf: 2006).

5. See Martin Johnson, "Who Stole the Gettysburg Address?" *Journal of the Abraham Lincoln Association* 24, no. 2 (Summer 2003): 2–19.

6. Lincoln to Edwin Stanton, December 23, 1863, in *The Collected Works of Abraham Lincoln*, ed. Roy P. Basler, 9 vols. (New Brunswick, N.J.: Rutgers University Press, 1953–1955), 7: 88 (hereafter *Collected Works*).

7. John R. Neff, *Honoring the Civil War Dead: Commemoration and the Problem of Reconciliation* (Lawrence: University Press of Kansas, 2005), 8, 222; see also James L. Huston, "The Lost Cause of the North: A Reflection on Lincoln's Gettysburg Address and the Second Inaugural," *Journal of the Abraham Lincoln Association* 33, no. 1 (Winter 2012): 14–37.

8. The reference is to the subtitle of Garry Wills, *Lincoln at Gettysburg: The Words That Remade America*; see also Merrill D. Peterson, *Lincoln in American Memory* (New York: Oxford University Press, 1994); Barry Schwartz, *Abraham Lincoln and the Forge of National Memory* (Chicago: University of Chicago Press, 2000).

9. "The Fourth of March," *Harper's Weekly*, March 11, 1865; Edward J. Blum, *Reforging the White Republic: Race, Religion, and American Nationalism, 1865–1898* (Baton Rouge: Louisiana State University Press, 2005); Andre M. Fleche, *The Revolution of 1861: The American Civil War in the Age of Nationalist Conflict* (Chapel Hill: University of North Carolina Press, 2012); Melinda Lawson, *Patriot Fires: Forging a New American Nationalism in the Civil War North* (Lawrence: University Press of Kansas, 2005).

10. On secession as one implication of popular sovereignty, see Christopher Childers, *The Failure of Popular Sovereignty: Slavery, Manifest Destiny, and the Radicalization of Southern Politics* (Lawrence: University Press of Kansas, 2012), 273.

11. The July 30, 1863, Order of Retaliation stated, "It is the duty of every government to give protection to its citizens, of whatever class, color, or condition"; *Collected Works*, 6: 357. General Order 329 enforced compulsory compensated

emancipation on all slave owners, loyal or rebel, if draft quotas were not met; *The War of the Rebellion: The Official Records of the Union and Confederate Armies*, series 3, 5 vols. (Washington, D.C.: GPO, 1899), 3: 860; William C. Harris notes that the policy was not always implemented as written; Harris, *Lincoln and the Border States: Preserving the Union* (Lawrence: University of Kansas Press, 2011), 274. James Oakes, *Freedom National: The Destruction of Slavery in the United States, 1861–1865* (New York: Norton, 2013), 464.

12. The 1863 Annual Message proposed equal pay; *Collected Works*, 7: 36. Lincoln supported but did not mandate voting rights for some blacks in Louisiana in December 1863, and in March 1864 he reaffirmed this position; LaWanda Cox, *Lincoln and Black Freedom: A Study in Presidential Leadership* (Columbia: University of South Carolina Press, 1981), 80. Phillip W. Magness and Sebastian N. Page argue that Lincoln continued to support colonization into 1865; Magness and Page, *Colonization after Emancipation: Lincoln and the Movement for Black Resettlement* (Columbia: University of Missouri Press, 2011). Lincoln publicly called for limited suffrage for freedmen on April 11, 1865; *Collected Works*, 8: 403.

13. The view here owes much to Herman Belz, *A New Birth of Freedom: The Republican Party and Freedman's Rights, 1861 to 1866* (New York: Fordham University Press, 2000; first ed., Westport, Conn.: Greenwood Press, 1976); Herman Belz, *Reconstructing the Union: Theory and Policy during the Civil War* (Ithaca, N.Y.: Cornell University Press, 1969); Daniel A. Farber, *Lincoln's Constitution* (Chicago: University of Chicago Press, 2003); George P. Fletcher, *Our Secret Constitution: How Lincoln Redefined American Democracy* (New York: Oxford University Press, 2001). For the classic treatment of these themes with a somewhat different emphasis, see James M. McPherson, *Abraham Lincoln and the Second American Revolution* (New York: Oxford University Press, 1991). For a recent survey of constitutional issues, see Brian R. Dirck, *Lincoln and the Constitution* (Carbondale: Southern Illinois University Press, 2012).

14. *Collected Works*, 7: 504.

15. Burlingame, *Abraham Lincoln: A Life*, 2: 591, quoting the *Springfield [Mass.] Republican* datelined November 24, 1863, and published November 28.

16. D. Wilson, *Lincoln's Sword*, 225.

Chapter 1. "It Will Be an Interesting Ceremony"

1. Lincoln on November 13 remarked that he started the message "today"; *New York World*, November 14. All dates refer to 1863 unless otherwise indicated. On November 25 Salmon Chase wrote Lincoln of his "great satisfaction" upon reading a draft of the message; Papers of Abraham Lincoln, Library of Congress (hereafter Lincoln Papers, LOC). Lincoln to Chase, November 17, in *The Collected Works of Abraham Lincoln*, ed. Roy P. Basler, 9 vols. (New Brunswick, N.J.: Rutgers University Press, 1953–1955), 7: 15; Stanton to Lincoln, November 17, endorsed by Lincoln; John Garret telegram to Stanton on November 17 accepting Stanton's proposed two-day schedule; *Collected Works*, 7: 16, and Lincoln Papers, LOC.

2. *Collected Works,* 7: 16.

3. *Collected Works,* 7: 16. Among others, the *Baltimore Daily Gazette,* the *Philadelphia Evening Bulletin,* the *Philadelphia Press,* and the *Cincinnati Daily Commercial* announced Lincoln's travel plans in articles datelined Washington, November 16, and printed in the November 17 editions. On the eighteenth, the *Boston Herald* and the *New York World* printed similar announcements, both datelined Washington, November 17.

4. Benjamin Brown French, *Witness to the Young Republic: A Yankee's Journal, 1828–1870,* ed. Donald B. Cole and John J. McDonough (Hanover, N.H.: University Press of New England, 1989), 437; Lincoln to Stephen Logan, November 9, in *Collected Works,* 7: 7.

5. Diary of Thomas H. Duval, quoted in James Marten, "'Dancing Attendance in the Ante-chambers of the Great': A Texas Unionist Goes to Washington, 1863," *Lincoln Herald* 90, no. 3 (Fall 1988): 84–86.

6. *Collected Works,* 7: 16; *Washington Evening Star,* November 17. Many newspapers reported this accurate schedule in their November 17 editions along with the fact that Nicolay would accompany the president, suggesting that it was Nicolay who announced the final schedule to the press sometime in the early afternoon; see, for example, the *New York Express,* November 17.

7. Speed's story is presented in the *Louisville Commercial,* November 12, 1879, in an "interview" with him, but Speed most probably gave a written account to the reporter for publication. All quotations from Speed are from this interview, unless otherwise noted. Speed reaffirmed its essential elements in the *New York Times,* April 20, 1887.

8. *Collected Works,* 7: 16.

9. Lincoln selected Speed as attorney general in early December 1864, and he was first introduced to the rest of the cabinet on December 16; Speed identified himself as a Democrat in a letter to Lincoln, November 15, 1859; Lincoln Papers LOC.

10. For example, the Gettysburg Address appeared in A. A. Griffith's *Lessons in Elocution . . . ,* 2nd ed. (New York: Barnes and Burr, 1865), 213. Perhaps the earliest known ceremonial use of the speech was on July 23, 1864, as noted in *Ceremonies at the Dedication of the Soldiers Monument* [Newton, MA] (Boston: Schism, Franklin Printing, 1864), 42. James Speed, *Address of the Hon. James Speed before the Society of the Loyal Legion, at Cincinnati, May 4, 1887 . . .* (Louisville, Ky.: John P. Morton, 1888).

11. *Philadelphia Press,* November 20; "The Color Guard," *North American Review* 99, no. 204 (July 1864): 172.

12. Thayer was a former pastor and Massachusetts state legislator who in 1864 had just become editor of the *Nation.* According to *Lincoln Lore* 917 (November 4, 1946) Lincoln may have owned Thayer's *The Pioneer Boy and How He Became President* (Boston: Walker and Wise, 1863) and *The Character and Public Services of Abraham Lincoln, President of the United States* (Boston: Dinsmoor, 1864). David C. Mearns concludes that Thayer conferred with Lincoln; Mearns, "Thayer's

The Pioneer Boy: A Second and Harder Look," *Library of Congress Quarterly Journal* 13, no. 3 (May 1956): 129–134. See also Allen C. Guelzo, "Holland's Informants: The Construction of Josiah Holland's *Life of Abraham Lincoln*," *Journal of the Abraham Lincoln Association* 23, no. 1 (Winter 2002): 1–27; Louis A. Warren, "Thayer's Pioneer Boy," *Lincoln Lore* 689 (June 22, 1942), 1–2.

13. *Harper's New Monthly Magazine* (January 1865), 264. Perhaps because of the article in *Macmillan's Magazine* (Goldwin Smith, "President Lincoln," *Macmillan's Magazine*, February 1865), Smith made the cover of the April 1865 issue of *Eclectic Magazine of Foreign Literature, Science, and Art*, which appeared before Lincoln's death. Lincoln, "Memorandum on Duchess of Argyll," March 22, 1865; Lincoln Papers, LOC. Charles Sumner, *The Promises of the Declaration of Independence: Eulogy on Abraham Lincoln, Delivered before the Municipal Authorities of the City of Boston, June 1, 1865* (Boston: Ticknor and Fields, 1865). In 1864 Smith recorded in his diary that he met Lincoln at the White House: "Tuesday, Nov. 16. With General Butler to Washington. Saw the President. His stories—The three pigeons. The manufacturing population. They would annex Hell as a market for their cottons. Mr Seward. Mr Fessenden. Manufactory of Notes in the Treasury. The White House"; quoted in Arnold Haultain, *Goldwin Smith, His Life and Opinions* (New York: Duffield, 1914), 260.

14. Smith, "President Lincoln," 302. The article was reprinted in *Littell's Living Age*, March 4, 1865, 426. Smith, however, took exception to the phrase "dedicated to the proposition" and said that Lincoln's delivery was "ungainly," though his source for this assessment is unknown.

15. Quoted in Haultain, *Goldwin Smith*, 262.

16. Everett began work on his oration immediately upon being asked by Frederick W. Lincoln, mayor of Boston, on September 23; diary, Edward Everett Papers, Massachusetts State Historical Society (hereafter, Everett Papers, MSHS).

17. Everett to Lincoln and Lincoln to Everett, November 20; Lincoln Papers, LOC.

18. Horatio King, *Turning On the Light: A Dispassionate Survey of President Buchanan's Administration* (Philadelphia: J. B. Lippincott, 1895), 238, reprinting an article King first published in the *Washington Critic* of February 17, 1888. On November 20 Lincoln did indeed deal with issues involving military justice, although Judge Holt is not named in the documents; *Collected Works*, 7: 25. Robert Todd Lincoln to Isaac Markens, November 5, 1913, in R. T. Lincoln, *A Portrait of Abraham Lincoln in Letters by His Oldest Son*, ed. Paul M. Angle (Chicago: Chicago Historical Society, 1968), 6.

19. Speed's word "flattering" possibly echoed the original's "flattered." Everett's letter was first published in John Nicolay and John Hay, "Abraham Lincoln: A History," *Century Magazine*, February 1890, 575. Isaac N. Arnold's *History of Abraham Lincoln and the Overthrow of American Slavery* (Chicago: Clarke, 1866), 424, appears to be the first mention in print of Everett's complimenting Lincoln while on the stand just after Lincoln's speech.

20. The invitation was first published in John Nicolay and John Hay, *Abraham Lincoln: A History*, 10 vols. (Philadelphia: Century, 1890), 8: 190.

21. The timing and circumstances of Lincoln's invitation have been important questions in the history of the speech; see Martin Johnson, "Lincoln's Contested Invitation to Gettysburg," *Journal of Illinois History* 13, no. 4 (Winter 2010): 238–264; Martin Johnson, "Lincoln's Response to His Invitation to Gettysburg," *Lincoln Lore: The Quarterly Bulletin of the Lincoln Museum* 1889 (Summer 2007): 18–23.

22. David Wills was quoted by the *Philadelphia Inquirer,* October 13, as saying that President Lincoln was expected to "perform the consecrational service," and the November 10, *Washington National Intelligencer* stated, "President Lincoln has determined to be present at the consecration." David Wills letter of November 7, *Adams County Sentinel [Gettysburg],* November 10; Joseph George Jr. argued that the *Inquirer* story of October 13 proved Lincoln had decided to attend at that early date; George, "The World Will Little Note? The Philadelphia Press and the Gettysburg Address," *Pennsylvania Magazine of History and Biography,* July 1990, 385–397.

23. David Wills to W. H. Seward, November 14; Gideon Welles Papers, microfilm reel 33, Library of Congress (LOC). This letter was mentioned by Frank L. Klement but not quoted; it undermines his contention that Lincoln had been asked to attend the dedication, and had firmly decided to go, long before receiving the formal invitation of November 2; Klement, *The Gettysburg Soldiers' Cemetery and Lincoln's Address: Aspects and Angles* (Shippensburg, Pa.: White Mane, 1993), 247n49.

24. The official representing Illinois at Gettysburg, Clark E. Carr, wrote in 1915 that the president gave no definite response to his invitation, "and it was not until about the time of his leaving Washington for Gettysburg that the [cemetery] Board was at all certain that he would speak"; *Galesburg Daily Republican-Register,* October 7, 1915. In 1890, Nicolay and Hay wrote, "President Lincoln expressed his willingness to perform the duty requested of him," but in 1894 John G. Nicolay more accurately noted, "There was even great uncertainty whether he could take enough time from his pressing official duties to go to Gettysburg at all" and said that "no definite arrangements for the journey" had been made until November 17; Nicolay and Hay, *Abraham Lincoln,* 8: 190; Nicolay, "Lincoln's Gettysburg Address," *Century Magazine,* February 1894, 597.

25. The *Gettysburg Compiler,* November 17, reported the expected attendance of several notable persons but did not mention Lincoln; similarly, the *Philadelphia Evening Bulletin* reported on November 14 that "many distinguished men from all parts of the country" would be present, again not naming Lincoln. An article in the *Cincinnati Daily Commercial*, November 17, datelined Washington, November 16, stated, "The President has changed his mind," and would go to Gettysburg. The *Boston Journal* reported on November 17 (dateline November 14), "[Although] it has been announced that the President will positively attend the inauguration of the

Gettysburg soldiers' cemetery, it can hardly be possible for him to leave at this time, when his public duties are so pressing."

26. The papers carrying such reports included the *Baltimore Daily Gazette,* the *Philadelphia Evening Bulletin,* the *Philadelphia Press,* and the *Cincinnati Daily Commercial,* all datelined Washington, November 16, and published November 17. On the eighteenth, the *Boston Herald* and the *New York World* printed similar announcements, both datelined Washington, November 17. Had Lincoln decided much before Saturday the fourteenth, his decision would doubtless have been published in the Saturday papers and in the few Sunday papers. The Sunday, November 15, edition of the *Washington Sunday Chronicle,* owned by John Forney, who was closely tied to the administration and was a major booster for the event, did not refer to Lincoln's plans. The *Philadelphia Public Ledger,* November 16, printed reports from Washington datelined Sunday but said nothing about Gettysburg.

27. Speed later confirmed, "He said he partially wrote it before he left Washington, and finished it up after arriving in Gettysburg"; *New York Times,* April 20, 1887.

28. As late as July 24, David Wills wrote, "Arms and legs and sometimes heads protrude [from shallow graves] and my attention has been directed to several places where the hogs were actually rooting out the bodies and devouring them"; David Wills to Governor Andrew Curtin, July 24, transcript in file 10-5a, Gettysburg National Military Park Archives (hereafter GNMP). Kathleen R. Georg, former Gettysburg Park historian, has produced the most detailed history of the founding of the cemetery to date: "This Grand National Enterprise: The Origins of Gettysburg's Soldiers' National Cemetery and Gettysburg Battlefield Memorial Association," May 1982, paper, GNMP and www.gdg.org/Research/BattlefieldHistories /kghgrand.html (accessed September 12, 2012). See also Gregory Coco, *A Strange and Blighted Land: Gettysburg, the Aftermath of a Battle* (Gettysburg, Pa.: Thomas Publications, 1995); George Sheldon, *When the Smoke Cleared at Gettysburg: The Tragic Aftermath of the Bloodiest Battle of the Civil War* (Nashville, Tenn.: Cumberland House, 2003); Jim Weeks, *Gettysburg: Memory, Market, and an American Shrine* (Princeton: Princeton University Press, 2003).

29. A. K. McClure, a longtime Curtin ally, in *Old Time Notes of Pennsylvania,* 2 vols. (Philadelphia: John C. Winston, 1905), 2: 55.

30. *Report of the Select Committee Relative to the Soldiers' National Cemetery* (Harrisburg, Pa.: Singerly and Myers, State Printers, 1864), 62, written by David Wills.

31. William A. Frassanito, *Early Photography at Gettysburg* (Gettysburg, Pa.: Thomas Publications, 1995), 400; *History of Cumberland and Adams Counties* (Chicago: Warner, Beers, 1886), 375, biographical entry for David Wills.

32. Wills to Curtin, August 26, *Adams County Sentinel [Gettysburg],* September 15.

33. *Philadelphia Inquirer,* October 13. As early as September 18, David Tod, governor of Ohio, wrote David Wills that he would attend; Earl W. Wiley, "Buckeye Criticism of the Gettysburg Address," *Speech Monographs* 23, no. 1 (March

1956), 2; Clark E. Carr, *Lincoln at Gettysburg: An Address,* 4th ed. (Chicago: McClurg, 1909), 18.

34. On Carr, see Johnson, "Lincoln's Contested Invitation." Louis A. Warren mentioned Carr only to undermine his credibility; Warren, *Lincoln's Gettysburg Declaration: "A New Birth of Freedom"* (Fort Wayne, Ind.: Lincoln National Life Foundation, 1964), 44. Even so judicious an authority as David H. Donald felt compelled to take sides, flatly declaring that "the invitation to the President was not an afterthought"; Donald, *Lincoln* (New York: Simon and Schuster, 1995), 460. Among recent authors, only Douglas L. Wilson devotes a paragraph to Carr's story, although William E. Barton cited Carr approvingly; Wilson, *Lincoln's Sword: The Presidency and the Power of Words* (New York: Knopf, 2006), 210; Barton, *Lincoln at Gettysburg: What He Intended to Say; What He Said; What He Was Reported to Have Said; What He Wished He Had Said* (Indianapolis, Ind.: Bobbs-Merrill, 1930), 48. Recent works that do not discuss Carr's account include A. E. Elmore, *Lincoln's Gettysburg Address: Echoes of the Bible and Book of Common Prayer* (Carbondale: Southern Illinois University Press, 2009); Gabor Boritt, *The Gettysburg Gospel: The Lincoln Speech That Nobody Knows* (New York: Simon and Schuster, 2008); Klement, *The Gettysburg Soldier's Cemetery.*

35. Wills to Curtin, October 23, cited in Klement, *The Gettysburg Soldiers' Cemetery,* 9. A public letter by Wills on November 7 and published in the *Adams County Sentinel [Gettysburg],* on November 10, addressed to Curtin, supports the conclusion that their discussion involved Lincoln's invitation, stating that Lincoln had been invited "at your suggestion" and "upon consultation with representatives from the other States." Note that Wills did not state that Lincoln had responded or would attend, or even that the others had agreed to the invitation. Lamon's invitation was dated October 30; all the others to Washington were dated November 2; Lamon Papers, Huntington Library, San Marino, California; *Report of the Select Committee,* 15. See also David Wills to William Seward, November 2; Seward Papers, University of Rochester Library.

36. Simon Cameron warned Lincoln, "[Curtin] aspires to have your place, in the White House"; October 10, Lincoln Papers, LOC. The *Harrisburg Daily Telegraph* several times floated a trial balloon for Curtin, as on November 4. Thomas G. Mitchell details the ways Curtin and the radical John Andrew, governor of Massachusetts, worked closely in promoting Frémont; Mitchell, *Anti-slavery Politics in Antebellum and Civil War America* (New York: Praeger, 2007), 289.

37. *Report of the Select Committee,* second part, 5.

38. Wills to Lincoln, November 2; Lincoln Papers, LOC; *Report of the Select Committee,* 47.

39. Carr, *Lincoln at Gettysburg,* 76.

40. Johnson, "Lincoln's Response," 19. Presumably the discussion with Lincoln took place before Lamon accepted the position in a letter dated November 4; *Washington National Intelligencer,* November 10; Lincoln to Lamon, in *Collected Works,* 7: 7.

41. Stanton to Lincoln, in *Collected Works*, 7: 16. See below for a description of Lincoln's visit to the battlefield.

42. *Boston Herald*, November 18; *New York World*, November 18. Governor Curtin brought his wife and son to the ceremony and may have mentioned his plans to Lincoln in their meeting on November 14.

43. Like so many inaccurate or half-accurate stories about Gettysburg, this one seems to originate with William Barton's *Lincoln at Gettysburg*, 49. Carl Sandburg's influential *Abraham Lincoln: The War Years*, 4 vols. (New York: Harcourt Brace, 1939), 2: 462, repeated the story, as did Catherine Clinton's *Mrs. Lincoln: A Life* (New York: Harper, 2009), 208. Tad had smallpox, which he gave to his father, according to Armond S. Goldman and Frank C. Schmalstieg Jr., in "Abraham Lincoln's Gettysburg Illness," *Journal of Medical Biography* 15 (2007): 104–110.

44. *Philadelphia Press*, November 17. The journalist John Russell Young, who was "for a time" the "private secretary" to Forney, called the *Chronicle* "the Administration newspaper"; Young, *Men and Memories: Personal Reminiscences*, ed. May D. Russell Young, 2 vols. (New York: F. Tennyson Neely, 1891–1901), 1: 48.

45. In January 1863 Lincoln corrected an article by "Occasional," and in May 1863, he complimented an article in the *Chronicle*; *Collected Works*, 6: 62, 6: 214. Harry J. Carman and Reinhard H. Luthin give examples of the patronage requests Lincoln accorded Forney and cite contemporary reports that the government purchased 10,000 copies of the *Chronicle* for distribution to the Army of the Potomac; Carman and Luthin, *Lincoln and the Patronage* (New York: Columbia University Press, 1943), 119. John Nicolay described Forney as "an astute politician" who was particularly sensitive to the "Curtin-Cameron contention"; unpublished note, box 9, folder 80, Nicolay Papers, LOC.

46. Phillip Shaw Paludan notes Forney's role in the "Union League" and at its national convention in Cleveland in mid-May 1863; Paludan, *The Presidency of Abraham Lincoln* (Lawrence: University Press of Kansas, 1994), 225.

47. Forney to Lincoln, November 12, Lincoln Papers, LOC. Peter Connor Shannon was a judge and state legislator from Pittsburgh; the other visitor was fleet surgeon Jonathan N. Foltz.

48. John Forney to Edward Everett, November 11, Everett Papers, MSHS.

49. Lincoln to Logan, in *Collected Works*, 7: 7.

50. Sandburg, *Abraham Lincoln*, 2: 440; Barton, *Lincoln at Gettysburg*, 52; Garry Wills, *Lincoln at Gettysburg: The Words That Remade America* (New York: Simon and Schuster, 1992), 25.

51. Gideon Welles, *Diary of Gideon Welles: Secretary of the Navy under Lincoln and Johnson*, ed. Howard K. Beale, 3 vols. (New York: Norton, 1960), 1: 480, undated entry, probably early December 1863; Edward Bates, *The Diary of Edward Bates, 1859–1866*, vol. 4 of *Annual Report of the American Historical Association, 1930*, ed. Howard K. Beale (Washington, D.C.: GPO, 1933), 316; *The Salmon P. Chase Papers*, ed. John Niven et al., 5 vols. (Kent, Ohio: Kent State University Press, 1993–1998), 4: 192. At one point Stanton, too, was expected to go;

Wayne MacVeagh, "Lincoln at Gettysburg," *Century Magazine,* November 1909, 21. The *New York Evening Express,* November 16 reported that William Seward, Montgomery Blair, Edward Bates, and Gideon Welles would accompany Lincoln.

52. Aside from his cabinet, Lincoln personally invited or encouraged at least six other people to the ceremony: E. W. Andrews, Ward Lamon, Stephen Logan, Wayne MacVeagh, William McDougall, and William Saunders.

53. *Boston Herald,* November 18; *Boston Journal,* November 20.

54. Curtin to Lincoln, October 27, Lincoln Papers, LOC. Over the next few weeks Curtin would be particularly insistent about a post for his wife's brother. Curtin wrote to Morton McMichael that Lincoln's plans were "not definitely settled" when he left Washington, but he added, "I have no doubt the President will go [to Gettysburg] direct by Baltimore"; November 16, Curtin Papers, Pennsylvania State Archives, quoted in Boritt, *The Gettysburg Gospel,* 38.

55. John Hay diary, November 28, 1863, and January 9, 1864, *Inside Lincoln's White House: The Complete Civil War Diary of John Hay,* ed. Michael Burlingame and John R. Turner Ettlinger (Carbondale: Southern Illinois University Press, 1997), 120, 141. Wayne MacVeagh, the party chair in Pennsylvania and a Curtin man, also spoke with Hay that day, but Hay did not connect these incidents, so possibly Curtin was not involved. On January 28, 1864, Lincoln agreed to meet with Forney, Cameron, and the leader of the Pennsylvania House, but for what purpose is not certain; *Collected Works,* 7: 157.

56. For example, the *New York Tribune,* November 18.

Chapter 2. The Washington Draft

1. Louis A. Warren, misinterpreting a statement by John Hay, argued that the Nicolay text was written in Washington, D.C., using the Hay text as a copy text, but this problematic scenario has not found favor with others across the ensuing sixty years; Warren, *Lincoln's Gettysburg Declaration: "A New Birth of Freedom"* (Fort Wayne, Ind.: Lincoln National Life Foundation, 1964), 155.

2. Many discuss Lincoln's "delivery text," but none focuses extensively on the text written in Washington, although Douglas L. Wilson devotes several pages to Lincoln's prespeech drafts; Wilson, *Lincoln's Sword: The Presidency and the Power of Words* (New York: Knopf, 2006), 210.

3. Waldo W. Braden briefly mentioned all four in the context of composing the speech in Washington, the only account to do so; Braden, *Abraham Lincoln, Public Speaker* (Baton Rouge: Louisiana State University Press, 1988), 62. Unsourced newspaper clippings cited by Warren provide two other accounts; both are secondhand recollections of decades-old conversations with informants (Simon Cameron and John Defrees) who had died long before the account was published; Warren *Lincoln's Gettysburg Declaration,* 53. Even if both were accepted at face value, they would add little to the evidence provided by the direct eyewitnesses.

4. *Louisville Commercial,* November 12, 1879; *New York Times,* April 20, 1887.

5. John G. Nicolay, "Lincoln's Gettysburg Address," *Century Magazine,* Feb-

ruary 1894, 599. William Lambert was the first to name both the Nicolay and Hay documents; Lambert, *The Gettysburg Address: When Written, How Received, Its True Form* (Philadelphia: J. B. Lippincott, 1909; reprinted from the *Pennsylvania Magazine of History and Biography* 33 [October 1909]; page references are to the Lippincott edition.

6. Nicolay, "Lincoln's Gettysburg Address," 599, 601. Nicolay stated that "we may infer" there was a second page.

7. Nicolay to R. W. Gilder, September 19, 1885, and Nicolay to David Wills, January 20, 1894, in "Some Correspondence Regarding a Missing Copy of the Gettysburg Address," *Lincoln Lore* 1437 (November 1957), 2.

8. Noah Brooks, *Lincoln Observed: Civil War Dispatches of Noah Brooks,* ed. Michael Burlingame (Baltimore: Johns Hopkins University Press, 1998), 4. Possibly because he was scheduled to replace Nicolay, Brooks ever after conducted a smoldering feud with Hay and Nicolay; on July 14, 1888, Hay wrote that Brooks's recollections were "rubbish"; Hay, *At Lincoln's Side: John Hay's Civil War Correspondence and Selected Writings,* ed. Michael Burlingame (Carbondale: Southern Illinois University Press, 2000), xiv.

9. Lamon Papers, Huntington Library, San Marino, California. Brooks seems not to have attended the event. Brooks's newspaper articles during this time demonstrate his special access to the president; Brooks, *Lincoln Observed,* 76.

10. Noah Brooks, "Personal Reminiscences of Lincoln," *Scribner's Magazine,* February 1878, 565. Brooks later quoted Lincoln as saying, "It was very kind in Mr. Everett to send me this, in order that I might not go over the same ground as he has. There is no danger that I shall. My speech is all blocked out. It is very short"; Brooks, *Abraham Lincoln: The Nation's Leader in the Great Struggle through Which Was Maintained the Existence of the United States* (Washington, D.C.: National Tribune, 1888), 377–379. Brooks in 1894 noted, "When he came back from Gettysburg, Lincoln told me that he made several changes in the manuscript of his own address after he got to Gettysburg, and others 'as he went along' while delivering it on the field"; Brooks to R. W. Gilder, February 3, 1894, in Brooks, *Lincoln Observed,* 89. Yet another account with slightly different details appears in Brooks's article "Glimpses of Lincoln in Wartime," *Century Magazine,* January 1895, 457–467, which was reprinted that same year in his *Washington in Lincoln's Time* (Philadelphia: Century, 1895).

11. Gabor Boritt rejected Brooks's account because of apparent contradictions; Boritt, *The Gettysburg Gospel: The Lincoln Speech That Nobody Knows* (New York: Simon and Schuster, 2008), 82. Douglas L. Wilson accepted Brooks's evidence; Wilson, *Lincoln's Sword,* 210.

12. Knowing the inaccuracies of telegraphy, Everett on November 14 had the *Boston Advertiser* print an advance copy of his oration for distribution to the press by mail; diary, Everett Papers, MSHS. The *Philadelphia Press* of November 20 mentioned that Everett's speech "was furnished in proofsheets from the office of the *Boston Advertiser* yesterday afternoon."

13. Another questionable source places Everett's speech in Lincoln's hands before the ceremony: in 1954 Edward Ringwood Hewitt wrote that his father-in-law, Ohio representative James M. Ashley, who had died in 1896, had said that he and his wife sat behind Lincoln on the train to Gettysburg and that they both recalled that Lincoln had a copy of Everett's oration; David C. Mearns and Lloyd A. Dunlap, "Notes and Comments on the Preparation of the Address," in *Long Remembered: Facsimilies of the Five Versions of the Gettysburg Address,* ed. David C. Mearns and Lloyd A. Dunlap (Washington, D.C.: Library of Congress, 1963), n.p. [4]. Ashley himself said nothing of this in his many postwar speeches—for example, *Reminiscences of the Great Rebellion: Calhoun, Seward and Lincoln : Address of Hon. J. M. Ashley at Memorial Hall, Toledo, Ohio, June 2, 1890* (New York: Evening Post, 1890)—nor was this story known to Ashley's biographer, Robert F. Horowitz; Horowitz, *The Great Impeacher: A Political Biography of James M. Ashley* (New York: Brooklyn College Press, 1979). Hewitt also told a similar story but without mentioning Everett's oration; Hewitt, *Those Were the Days: Tales of a Long Life* (New York: World Book, 1943), 180.

14. The line "Solid men of Boston, make no long orations" arose in a somewhat off-color British political ditty from the eighteenth century; much reprinted, even quoted by Edmund Burke on the floor of the House of Commons, the song eventually crossed the Atlantic, where articles in popular history journals explained its long lineage; "Billy Pitt and the Farmer by Captain [Thomas] Morris," in John Almon, ed., *An Asylum for Fugitive Pieces,* 2 vols. (London: J. Debrett, 1786), 2: 246. One immortal line gives a sense of its flavor: "Straitaways she snatch'd up the vessel that she p——ss'd in, to dash at the head of this daring Philistine." For Burke, see *The Parliamentary Register; or, History of the Proceedings and Debates of the House of Commons . . . during the Fourth Session of the Seventeenth Parliament . . .* (London: J. Debrett, 1794), 38: 10; *Memoirs of the Right Honourable Edmund Burke,* ed. Charles McCormick (London: Lee and Hurst, 1798), 371. See also "Solid Men of Boston," *Historical Magazine and Notes and Queries Concerning the Antiquities, History and Biography of America,* February 1857, 39.

15. Melvin R. Sylvester, *Black Experience in America: Negro Periodicals in the United States, 1840–1960. An Annotated Bibliography* (Westport, Conn.: Negro Universities Press, 1960), 396, citing *Frederick Douglass' Monthly* of January 1861. Seward used the phrase in 1860; Seward, *The Works of William H. Seward,* ed. George E. Baker, 5 vols. (Boston: Houghton Mifflin, 1884), 4: 83. Both "John Cotton and His Memorial Tablet," *American Church Monthly* 2, no. 3 (September 1857), 200, and *An Account of the Pilgrim Celebration at Plymouth, August 1, 1853* (Boston: Crosby, Nichols, 1853), 167, name Everett as one of the "solid men of Boston." Webster quoted the line in an 1852 speech at Faneuil Hall in Boston; quoted in George Ticknor Curtis, *Life of Daniel Webster,* 2 vols. (Philadelphia: Appleton, 1870), 2: 619. Webster also applied the phrase to himself in a letter of 1849; Webster, *The Private Correspondence of Daniel Webster,* ed. Fletcher Webster, 2 vols. (Boston: Little, Brown, 1857), 2: 304.

16. Others find a similar phrase by Theodore Parker more likely; see Gary Wills, *Lincoln at Gettysburg: The Words That Remade America* (New York: Simon and Schuster, 1992), 90; Carl F. Wieck, *Lincoln's Quest for Equality: The Road to Gettysburg* (DeKalb: Northern Illinois University Press, 2002), 4.

17. Diary, November 14, Everett Papers, MSHS; John Hay, *Inside Lincoln's White House: The Complete Civil War Diary of John Hay*, ed. Michael Burlingame and John R. Turner Ettlinger (Carbondale: Southern Illinois University Press, 1997), 109; D. Mark Katz, *Witness to an Era: The Life and Photographs of Alexander Gardner* (New York: Viking, 1991), 112.

18. See, for example, Gillian Cohen and Martin Conway, *Memory in the Real World*, 3rd ed. (New York: Psychology Press, 2008); Katz, *Witness to an Era*, 114.

19. Among those who agree that Lincoln had Everett's oration are William E. Barton and Louis A. Warren; Barton, *Lincoln at Gettysburg: What He Intended to Say; What He Said; What He Was Reported to Have Said; What He Wished He Had Said* (Indianapolis, Ind.: Bobbs-Merrill, 1930), 54; Warren, *Lincoln's Gettysburg Declaration*, 53. Douglas Wilson supports Brooks in general but discounts the notion that Lincoln had the oration in Washington; Wilson, *Lincoln's Sword*, 211. Isaac Markens found five instances in which Everett's oration influenced Lincoln's speech; Markens, *Lincoln's Masterpiece: A Review of the Gettysburg Address New in Treatment and Matter* (New York: Isaac Markens, 1913), 10. Garry Wills suggests Lincoln saw Everett's speech in Gettysburg, as does Gabor Boritt; Wills, *Lincoln at Gettysburg*, 30; Boritt, *The Gettysburg Gospel*, 93.

20. Brooks to Gilder, February 8, 1894, in Brooks, *Lincoln Observed*, 89.

21. Lamon may have been embittered by his failure after the war to secure the governorships of the Idaho or Colorado territories; Benjamin P. Thomas, *Portrait for Posterity: Abraham Lincoln and His Biographers* (New Brunswick, N.J.: Rutgers University Press, 1947), 33. For an even-handed assessment, see Rodney O. Davis's "Lincoln's 'Particular Friend' and Lincoln Biography," *Journal of the Abraham Lincoln Association* 19, no. 1 (Winter 1998): 21–38.

22. Lamon's unpublished notes, Lamon Papers, as quoted by D. Wilson in *Lincoln's Sword*, 211; *Philadelphia Times*, October 4, 1887, reprinted in Horatio King, *Turning On the Light: A Dispassionate Survey of President Buchanan's Administration* (Philadelphia: J. B. Lippincott, 1895), 239; Benjamin Brown French, *Witness to the Young Republic: A Yankee's Journal, 1828–1870*, ed. Donald B. Cole and John J. McDonough (Hanover, N.H.: University Press of New England, 1989), 430.

23. Quoted in D. Wilson, *Lincoln's Sword*, 212. Lamon had published yet another quite similar version in the *Philadelphia Times*, October 4, 1887. Lamon's posthumous *Recollections of Abraham Lincoln, 1847–1865* (Chicago: McClurg, 1895), 171–173, edited by his daughter Dorothy Lamon Teillard, translated the Latin *haec verba* as meaning "in substance, if not in exact words." See also William Smith and Theophilus D. Hall, *A Copious and Critical English-Latin Dictionary* (New York: American Book Company, 1871), 509; Bryan A. Garner, *A Dictionary of Modern Legal Usage*, 2nd ed. (New York: Oxford University Press, 2001), 446.

24. It was not unusual for Lincoln to worry beforehand about his speeches; he was also reportedly concerned about his speech at the Cooper Union. According to his friend and law partner William Herndon, "We had many misgivings—and he not a few himself—of his success in the great metropolis"; quoted in Harold Holzer, *Lincoln at Cooper Union: The Speech That Made Abraham Lincoln President* (New York: Simon and Schuster, 2006), 54.

25. Because of the insurmountable problems posed by Warren's argument that the Nicolay text was based on the Hay text as a copy text (see note 1 above), (and as confirmed by evidence to be presented farther along), no one today argues that the Hay text was written in Washington, meaning that this foolscap version was not the Hay document.

26. Unsourced newspaper clipping quoting the *Chicago Tribune* with the handwritten notations "1886" and "Probably in February"; I would like to thank Patty Mosher of the Galesburg [Illinois] Public Library for sending me this clipping. Louis Warren apparently cited the same article as 1886 or 1889; Warren, *Lincoln's Gettysburg Declaration*, xvii, 125. In later accounts, Lamon attributed to Lincoln words that he had in earlier accounts expressed as his own opinion.

27. John G. Nicolay and John Hay, *Abraham Lincoln: A History,* 10 vols. (New York: Century, 1890), 8: 199. John Nicolay wrote the section on the Gettysburg Address; "Schedule of Chapters," box 9, Nicolay Papers, LOC. For Nicolay, see Helen D. Bullock, "The Papers of John G. Nicolay, Lincoln's Secretary," *Library of Congress Quarterly of Current Acquisitions* 7, no. 3 (May 1950): 3–8; Michael Burlingame, "Nicolay and Hay: Court Historians," *Journal of the Abraham Lincoln Association* 19, no. 1 (Winter 1998): 1–20; John G. Nicolay, *With Lincoln in the White House: Letters, Memoranda, and Other Writings of John G. Nicolay, 1860–1865,* ed. Michael Burlingame (Carbondale: Southern Illinois University Press, 2000); David Herbert Donald, *"We Are Lincoln Men": Abraham Lincoln and His Friends* (New York: Simon and Schuster, 2003); Helen Nicolay, *Lincoln's Secretary: A Biography of John G. Nicolay* (New York: Longmans, Green, 1949); John R. Sellers, "Serving President Lincoln: The Public Career of John G. Nicolay," in *Lincoln Reshapes the Presidency*, ed. Charles M. Hubbard (Macon, Ga.: Mercer University Press, 2003), 52–64.

28. For example, John Hay letter to R. W. Gilder, January 26, 1891: "Lincoln's Gettysburg speech cannot be considered in any sense 'an extemporaneous effort.' It was not only carefully considered, but was reduced to writing before it was delivered,—and very little changed in the subsequent copy"; Hay, *Letters of John Hay and Extracts from His Diary*, ed. Clara Hay and Henry Adams, 3 vols. (Privately printed, 1908), 2: 214.

29. Nicolay to R. W. Gilder, September 19, 1885, in "Some Correspondence," 2; Nicolay and Hay, *Abraham Lincoln*, 8: 199.

30. Nicolay and Hay, *Abraham Lincoln*, 8: 199; letter dated April 29, 1865, by Richard C. McCormick, a New York journalist and Republican politician, *New York Evening Post,* May 3, 1865.

31. Nicolay and Hay, *Abraham Lincoln*, 8: 199.

32. Clark E. Carr to John Nicolay, March 14, 1864, Lincoln Papers, LOC, in which Carr mentions speaking with Nicolay in Washington.

33. Nicolay, "Lincoln's Gettysburg Address."

34. For examples of a whole full sheet of letterhead paper, see Lincoln to Montgomery Blair, November 2; to Governor Bradford, November 2; to Nathaniel Banks, November 5; to Zachary Chandler, November 20; all in Lincoln Papers, LOC. Compared to these and other documents, the Letterhead Page is narrower overall, and its left margin is noticeably narrow, meaning that after the full sheet was cut, creating what Nicolay accurately described as a "half sheet of letter paper," the left side of the first page was trimmed.

35. Brooks, *Lincoln Observed*, 89.

36. According to Nicolay, who is not contradicted by direct evidence, those earlier notes were not the Hay text, which is sometimes identified (incorrectly) as Lincoln's speaking text, or his "second draft." Nicolay in 1885 described the Hay as a draft written after the speech; "Some Correspondence," 2. On the confusion surrounding the discovery of the Hay document, see Martin Johnson, "Who Stole the Gettysburg Address?" *Journal of the Abraham Lincoln Association* 24, no. 2 (Summer 2003): 2–19.

37. David C. Mearns characterized the idea of the Hay text as the "reading copy" as "absurd"; Mearns, "The Mysteries of the Manuscripts," unpublished typescript, Mearns Papers, LOC, 87.

38. John G. Nicolay, *An Oral History of Abraham Lincoln: John G. Nicolay's Interviews and Essays*, ed. Michael Burlingame (Carbondale: Southern Illinois University Press, 1996), 107.

39. William Saunders, "Memoir of Gettysburg," in *Congressional Record* 70, no. 3 (February 12, 1929): H3321–3323.

40. Boritt suggests this was when Lincoln first began to write his speech; *The Gettysburg Gospel*, 81.

41. None of Saunders's early drawings for the cemetery survive, but the plan Lincoln saw that night was probably similar to the one published by Saunders in February 1864 in the "authorized" version of the speeches published by Edward Everett, *Address of Honorable Edward Everett at the Consecration of the National Cemetery at Gettysburg 19th November, 1863, with the Dedication Speech of President Lincoln and the Other Exercises of the Occasion* (Boston: Little, Brown: 1864). Several newspapers also published maps; see the *New York Herald,* the *New York World,* and the *Philadelphia Inquirer* for November 20, and also the more elaborate plan published in late December 1863 as part of the City of Boston's official report on the cemetery, *City Document No. 106: Report of the Joint Special Committee on the Burial of the Massachusetts Dead at Gettysburg* (Boston: J. E. Farwell, 1863).

42. In *Report of the Select Committee Relative to the Soldiers' National Cemetery* (Harrisburg: Singerly and Myers, 1864), 38. Saunders also described the cemetery in Forney's *Washington Daily Morning Chronicle,* November 5.

43. Saunders, "Memoir of Gettysburg," H 3321–3323.

44. For example, Lincoln reworked the draft of his speech later given at Cooper Union when the venue changed; Holzer, *Lincoln at Cooper Union*, 74. Everett met with Boston mayor Frederick Lincoln and John B. Bachelder; diary, November 9, Everett Papers, MSHS.

45. Saunders, "Memoir of Gettysburg," H 3321–3323.

46. William Saunders, "Landscape Gardening," *Report of the Commissioner of Agriculture for the Year 1869* (Washington, D.C.: GPO, 1870), 161; Saunders, "Memoir of Gettysburg," H3321–3323. Garry Wills placed the Gettysburg cemetery in the "rural" category suited to the romantic temperament, but its creator probably deemed its form classical; G. Wills, *Lincoln at Gettysburg*, 69.

47. Saunders, "Journal," December 20, 1898, Saunders Papers, LOC. Saunders rendered the phrase "admirable and benefiting," and Garry Wills gave it as "advisable and benefitting"; Saunders, "Memoir of Gettysburg," H3322; G. Wills, *Lincoln at Gettysburg*, 29.

48. Saunders, "Memoir of Gettysburg," H3322. Saunders remarked that he did not think he traveled on Lincoln's train, a sign that the Scotsman was not seeking to elevate his role or associate himself with the great speech and the iconic train journey. In fact, Saunders traveled on a different train and, just as he said, brought the famous plan with him; *Washington Daily Morning Chronicle*, November 21.

49. *Washington Daily Morning Chronicle*, July 8, reporting Lincoln's speech of the night before. For more on the July 7 speech, see Martin Johnson, "Abraham Lincoln Greets the Turning Point of the Civil War: July 7, 1863," *Lincoln Herald* 106, no. 3 (Fall 2004): 102–115.

50. William Barton opined that Lincoln on July 7 did not have time to do the math; *Lincoln at Gettysburg*, 28. David H. Donald has suggested that Lincoln simply did not get his math right; Donald, *Lincoln* (New York: Simon and Schuster, 1995), 462.

51. Carl Sandburg noted that Lincoln at Gettysburg used the phrase for the first time during his presidency "on a dramatic occasion," but this is too ungenerous to the July 7 speech, which was also delivered at a dramatic moment; Sandburg, *Abraham Lincoln: The War Years*, 4 vols. (New York: Harcourt, Brace, 1939), 2: 476.

52. Lincoln, "Speech in Independence Hall, Philadelphia," February 22, 1861, in *The Collected Works of Abraham Lincoln*, ed. Roy P. Basler, 9 vols. (New Brunswick, N.J.: Rutgers University Press, 1953–1955), 4: 240.

53. *Collected Works*, 4: 438. The term "southern strategy" is taken from Michael Vorenberg, *Final Freedom: The Civil War, the Abolition of Slavery, and the Thirteenth Amendment* (New York: Cambridge University Press, 2001), 26.

54. Samuel Huntington, quoted in Jonathan Elliot, *The Debates in the Several State Conventions on the Adoption of the Federal Constitution, as Recommended by the General Convention at Philadelphia, in 1787 . . .* , 2nd ed., 2 vols. (Washington, D.C.: Jonathan Elliot, 1836), 2: 201. According to Harold Holzer, both Lincoln and Douglas consulted Jonathan Elliot's *Debates* when they were sparring,

and Lincoln did so again to prepare the Cooper Union speech; Holzer, *Lincoln at Cooper Union*, 35.

55. Grow had even used the word "Fourscore"; cited in Don E. Fehrenbacher, *Lincoln in Text and Context: Collected Essays* (Palo Alto, Calif.: Stanford University Press, 1987), 285; *Washington National Intelligencer,* July 7, 1863.

56. *Collected Works,* 4: 439.

57. Lincoln to James N. Brown, October 18, 1858, in *Collected Works,* 3: 327.

58. Speech at Cooper Institute, in *Collected Works,* 3: 522; speech of August, 31, 1864, to the 148th Ohio Regiment, in *Collected Works,* 7: 528.

59. Response to a Serenade, November 8, 1864, in *Collected Works,* 8: 96.

60. Annual Message, December 8, in *Collected Works,* 8: 53.

61. *Pittsburgh Daily Commercial,* November 23, as quoted in Michael Burlingame, *Abraham Lincoln: A Life,* 2 vols. (Baltimore: Johns Hopkins University Press, 2008), 2: 572; also quoted in Boritt, *The Gettysburg Gospel,* 94.

62. See also G. Wills, *Lincoln at Gettysburg,* 29.

63. Roy P. Basler, "Did President Lincoln Give the Smallpox to William H. Johnson?" *Huntington Library Quarterly* 35, no. 3 (May 1972): 279–284; Lincoln to Samuel Atlee, November 18, in *Collected Works,* 8: 526.

64. James Marten, "'Dancing Attendance in the Ante-chambers of the Great': A Texas Unionist Goes to Washington, 1863," *Lincoln Herald* 90, no. 3 (Fall 1988): 84–86.

65. Wayne MacVeagh, "Lincoln at Gettysburg," *Century Magazine,* November 1909, 20.

66. Lincoln's story to the escorting officer in James B. Fry, "General James B. Fry," in *Reminiscences of Abraham Lincoln, by Distinguished Men of His Time,* ed. Allen Thorndike Rice (New York: North American Pub. Co., 1886), 403; Clark E. Carr, *Lincoln at Gettysburg: An Address,* 4th ed. (Chicago: McClurg, 1909), 21; Lincoln to Everett, November 20, Lincoln Papers, LOC.

Chapter 3. A Celebrated Railway Journey

1. *Philadelphia Press,* November 21. The day before, the ever-vigilant Stanton had asked Lincoln, "Please furnish me the names of those whom you may invite that they may be furnished with tickets and unauthorized intrusion prevented"; *The Collected Works of Abraham Lincoln,* ed. Roy P. Basler, 9 vols. (New Brunswick, N.J.: Rutgers University Press, 1953–1955), 7: 16; box 1, Nicolay Papers, LOC.

2. *National Anti-slavery Standard,* November 28. On Blair and Stevens, see Michael Green, *Freedom, Union, and Power: Lincoln and His Party during the Civil War* (New York: Fordham University Press, 2004), 117. Blair feared "the enslavement of whites" if Radicals rewrote the constitutions of the reconstructed states; Blair to Charles Sumner, October 24, microfilm reel 22, Blair Papers, LOC.

3. Edward Bates, diary entry for October 17, in *The Diary of Edward Bates, 1859–1866,* vol. 4 of *Annual Report of the American Historical Association,* 1930,

ed. Howard K. Beale (Washington, D.C.: GPO, 1933); Chase to William Sprague, November 26, quoted in William Frank Zornow, *Lincoln and the Party Divided* (Norman: University of Oklahoma Press, 1954), 25; Chase letter of regrets to David Wills, November 16, in *Address of Honorable Edward Everett at the Consecration of the National Cemetery at Gettysburg 19th November, 1863, with the Dedication Speech of President Lincoln and the Other Exercises of the Occasion* (Boston: Little, Brown: 1864), 20. Chase wrote to his daughter Kate, on November 18, "I should like to go; but cannot leave my work. The Report is hardly begun, and I must finish, if possible, before Congress comes together"; *The Salmon P. Chase Papers,* ed. John Niven et al., 5 vols. (Kent, Ohio: Kent State University Press, 1993–1998), 4: 192.

4. *Cincinnati Daily Gazette,* November 24, datelined November 18; Francis B. Carpenter states that Chase said Lincoln had repeated the story to the Cabinet; Carpenter, *Six Months at the White House with Lincoln: The Story of a Picture* (New York: Hurd and Hudson, 1867), 38.

5. Quoted in Henry Blumenthal, *A Reappraisal of Franco-American Relations, 1830–1871* (Chapel Hill: University of North Carolina Press, 1959), 140.

6. The quotation is from *Macbeth,* act 5, scene 8, perhaps Lincoln's favorite play. Seward to Lincoln, November 15, Lincoln Papers, LOC. Washington mayor Richard Wallach introduced some visitors from "Montreal" to Lincoln on the sixteenth; *Washington National Republican,* November 16, cited at www.TheLincoln Log.org (accessed September 14, 2012). Both sources for McDougall's invitation stated that McDougall was invited very late and on the spur of the moment and that Alexander Galt, who would also later be considered one of the Fathers of Confederation, was unable to make the journey. McDougall's nephew, F. C. L. Jones, a barrister in Toronto, Canada, said that McDougall told him of the journey in the 1890s. The other informant was William Houston, a journalist and later librarian of the Ontario Provincial Library. See George Maclean Rose, *A Cyclopedia of Canadian Biography: Being Chiefly Men of the Time* (Montreal: Rose Publishing, 1886), 556. Both accounts are quoted in "More about Canadian Link with Lincoln" by Canadian senator Norman Lambert, reprinted in the *Ottawa Journal,* July 19, 1947, citing different accounts by the two men written many years before. I would like to thank Suzanne Zeller, author of the McDougall article in the *Dictionary of Canadian Biography Online,* http://www.biographi.ca/index-e.html (accessed September 15, 2012), for help with this material.

7. *Philadelphia Inquirer,* November 21. Gabor Boritt provides a description and illustration of the car that Lincoln may have used; Boritt, *The Gettysburg Gospel: The Lincoln Speech That Nobody Knows* (New York: Simon and Schuster, 2008), 58. James B. Fry stated that Lincoln did not write while on the train; Fry, "General James B. Fry," in *Reminiscences of Abraham Lincoln, by Distinguished Men of His Time,* ed. Allen Thorndike Rice (New York: North American Pub. Co., 1886), 40. John Hay, *Inside Lincoln's White House: The Complete Civil War Diary of John Hay,* ed. Michael Burlingame and John R. Turner Ettlinger (Carbondale:

Southern Illinois University Press, 1997), 111; John G. Nicolay, "Lincoln's Gettysburg Address," *Century Magazine,* February 1894, 601.

8. *Philadelphia Inquirer,* November 21; Henry Clay Cochrane, "With Lincoln to Gettysburg, 1863," in *Abraham Lincoln: Military Order of the Loyal Legion of the United States, Commandery of the State of Pennsylvania. Memorial Meeting, February 13, 1907* ([Philadelphia,] 1907), 9. Cochrane thought it possible that Lincoln wrote on the train, but this is an inference, not an eyewitness recollection. Lincoln had indeed passed over these tracks going to Congress in 1847; John W. Starr, *Lincoln and the Railroads: A Biographical Study* (New York: Dodd, Mead, 1927), 48.

9. *Baltimore Daily Gazette, Baltimore American,* and *Baltimore Clipper,* November 19; Cochrane, "With Lincoln to Gettysburg," 10.

10. Cochrane, "With Lincoln to Gettysburg," 9.

11. Jackson, quoted in J. W. Jones, *The Story of American Heroism: Thrilling Narratives of Personal Adventures during the Great Civil War as Told by the Medal Winners and Roll of Honor Men* (Springfield, Ohio: Werner, 1895), 106. Cochrane recalled that all was quiet as they passed through the streets; Cochrane, "With Lincoln to Gettysburg," 10.

12. Donn Piatt, Schenck's chief of staff, recalled that Lincoln severely chastised Schenck for the heavy-handed nature of the recruitment of slaves in Maryland, which had provoked the shooting of a black federal draft agent; Piatt, *Memories of the Men Who Saved the Union* (New York: Belford, Clarke, 1887), 4; Hay diary, October 22, *Inside Lincoln's White House,* 97. Lincoln's letter to Charles Drake, October 5, in *Collected Works,* 6: 499, mentions the "perplexing compound."

13. *The War of the Rebellion: The Official Records of the Union and Confederate Armies,* series 3, 5 vols. (Washington, D.C.: GPO, 1899), 3: 860. See also William C. Harris, *Lincoln and the Border States: Preserving the Union* (Lawrence: University Press of Kansas, 2011), 274.

14. Cochrane, "With Lincoln to Gettysburg," 10; E. W. Andrews, "Lincoln's Kindness of Heart," in Rice, *Reminiscences of Abraham Lincoln,* 295.

15. I. Wayne MacVeagh, "Lincoln at Gettysburg," *Century Magazine,* November 1909, 21. Ward Lamon twenty years earlier had published a similar story in a different circumstance, but MacVeagh evidently did not know of it, for he stated that he thought the story had not been repeated anywhere since Lincoln had told it on the train; Ward Hill Lamon, *Recollections of Abraham Lincoln, 1847–1865,* ed. Dorothy Lamon Teillard (Chicago: McClurg, 1895), 196.

16. E. W. Andrews, "Lincoln's Kindness," 511.

17. McCormick letter dated April 29 published in the *New York Post,* May 3, 1865, also reprinted in *Littell's Living Age,* June 1865, 328. McCormick had helped host Lincoln during his 1860 visit to New York to speak at Cooper Union; many of his recollections in the article can be verified from other sources and appear to be reliable.

18. J. G. Holland, *The Life of Abraham Lincoln* (Springfield, Mass.: Gurdon

Bill, 1866), 423, preface dated November 1865. See also Allen C. Guelzo, "Holland's Informants: The Construction of Josiah Holland's *Life of Abraham Lincoln*," *Journal of the Abraham Lincoln Association* 23, no. 1 (Winter 2002): 1–27.

19. Isaac N. Arnold, *The History of Abraham Lincoln and the Overthrow of American Slavery* (Chicago: Clarke, 1866), 422–423.

20. Harriet Beecher Stowe, *Men of Our Times; or, Leading Patriots of the Day* (Hartford, Conn.: Hartford Publishing, 1868), 80. Stowe's *Men of Our Times* is clearly a summary of Arnold's *History of Abraham Lincoln*.

21. John P. Usher lecture at Lawrence, Kansas, reported in the *Chicago Daily Tribune*, May 2, 1882. This train scene is not mentioned in Usher's book *President Lincoln's Cabinet, by Honorable John P. Usher, Secretary of the Interior January 7, 1863–May 15, 1865, with a Foreword and a Sketch of the Life of the Author by Nelson H. Loomis* . . . (Omaha, Neb., 1925), in the book by Elmo R. Richardson and Alan W. Farley, *John Palmer Usher: Lincoln's Secretary of the Interior* (Lawrence: University Press of Kansas, 1960), or in Usher's essay "Lincoln and Slavery," in Rice, *Reminiscences of Abraham Lincoln*, 203–226.

22. Noah Brooks, "Personal Recollections of Abraham Lincoln," *Harper's New Monthly Magazine*, July 1865, 222–230. Brooks again mentioned Lincoln writing on pasteboard in "Personal Reminiscences of Lincoln," *Scribner's Magazine*, February 1878, 561–569.

23. Isaac N. Arnold, *The Life of Abraham Lincoln* (Chicago: Jansen, McClurg, 1885), 328. Arnold mentioned in this edition that he was "indebted to Governor Dennison, the Postmaster General and an eye-witness, for some of the incidents detailed in the text." William Dennison was not on Lincoln's train and he died in 1882, so he could not be an eyewitness for either the 1866 or the 1885 material relating to the train journey. Arnold provided no source for the reference to a pencil, which was not mentioned by Usher, but it is almost certainly an inference based on the fact that the dip pens of 1863 (and 1885) rendered it essentially impossible to write in ink under the conditions described by Usher.

24. Robert Todd Lincoln to Belle F. Keyes, co-owner of what would later be called the Everett copy of the Gettysburg Address, December 18, 1885, quoted in William E. Barton, *Lincoln at Gettysburg: What He Intended to Say; What He Said; What He Was Reported to Have Said; What He Wished He Had Said* (Indianapolis, Ind.: Bobbs-Merrill, 1930), 108–109. Robert later adopted Nicolay's view that no part of the speech was written on the train; Robert Todd Lincoln, *A Portrait of Abraham Lincoln in Letters by His Oldest Son*, ed. Paul Angle (Chicago: Chicago Historical Society, 1968), 22.

25. William Augustus Mowry and Arthur May Mowry, *A History of the United States for Schools* . . . (Boston: Burdett, 1896), 407.

26. Nicolay, "Lincoln's Gettysburg Address," 601. James Daniel Richardson states, "[The] consensus of valid opinion is against the 'legend' that it was written on an envelope on the train"; Richardson, ed., *A Compilation of the Messages and Papers of the Presidents*, vol. 8 (New York: Joint Committee on Printing: Bureau of

National Literature, 1897), 3373. Emma Miller Bolenius noted, "The story goes that on the train he sat buried in thought and then jotted down some few sentences on an old envelope"; Bolenius, ed., *The Boys' and Girls' Readers: Fourth–Sixth Reader*, vol. 3 (Boston: Houghton Mifflin, 1919), 162.

27. The spurious story was reprinted many times, including by the *Lancaster [Pa.] Inquirer*, April 23, 1887; the *Springfield [Mass.] Republican*, July 20, 1888; the *New York Times*, August 7, 1893; all clippings found in the "Political, A. Lincoln" file of the Edward McPherson Papers, LOC.

28. See Boritt, *The Gettysburg Gospel*, 188; Jay Monaghan, *Lincoln Bibliography, 1839–1939*, 2 vols. (Springfield: Illinois State Historical Library, 1943), 1: 390. The publisher claimed there were fifty-seven printings of Andrews's story and 500,000 copies in print by 1937.

29. Modern observers tend to doubt that Lincoln wrote while on the train but often leave the question open. Douglas L. Wilson notes that Lincoln may have worked on his speech, but he appears doubtful, as do David C. Mearns and Lloyd A. Dunlap; Wilson, *Lincoln's Sword: The Presidency and the Power of Words* (New York: Knopf, 2006), 217; Mearns and Dunlap, "Notes and Comments on the Preparation of the Address," in *Long Remembered: Facsimiles of the Five Versions of the Gettysburg Address*, ed. David C. Mearns and Lloyd A. Dunlap (Washington, D.C.: Library of Congress, 1963). Neither Gabor Boritt nor Garry Wills addresses the question of Lincoln writing on the train; Boritt, *The Gettysburg Gospel;* Wills, *Lincoln at Gettysburg: The Words That Remade America* (New York: Simon and Schuster, 1992). Louis A. Warren argues against the depiction in "The Perfect Tribute" but does not arrive at a clear conclusion about Lincoln writing; in Warren, *Lincoln's Gettysburg Declaration: "A New Birth of Freedom"* (Fort Wayne, Ind.: Lincoln National Life Foundation, 1964), 63. Frank L. Klement and Michael Burlingame dismiss the possibility that Lincoln wrote on the train; Klement, *The Gettysburg Soldiers' Cemetery and Lincoln's Address: Aspects and Angles* (Shippensburg, Pa.: White Mane, 1993), 87; Burlingame, *Abraham Lincoln: A Life*, 2 vols. (Baltimore: Johns Hopkins University Press, 2008), 2: 570.

30. On the same page Carpenter mentions Wayne MacVeagh as a source for another train story, but no source is mentioned in this case, suggesting it was not MacVeagh; Carpenter, *Six Months*, 242.

31. John Defrees, superintendent of government printing and former chair of the Indiana Republican Party, wrote on August 8, 1865, to J. G. Holland that Lincoln "thought Mr. Seward's style too verbose—too much like 'machine writing'"; quoted in Guelzo, "Holland's Informants," 46.

32. Frederick Weiser, "Lincoln's Trip to Gettysburg," *Lincoln Herald* 55, no. 1 (Summer 1953): 2; *Encounter at Hanover: Prelude to Gettysburg* (Shippensburg, Pa.: White Mane, 1988; reprinted from Hanover, Pa.: Hanover Chamber of Commerce, 1962; page references are to the 1988 edition), 192.

33. In 1952, York County inhabitant Russell Bowman discovered that photographs long said to be of Hanover Junction, Virginia, were actually of Hanover

Junction, Pennsylvania, and a figure on the rail station platform was identified as Lincoln, prompting Helen Nicolay's visit; *Baltimore Sun,* June 1, 1953. The identification as Lincoln was quickly refuted; the photographs undoubtedly depict Ward Hill Lamon and his parade marshals on November 17, when they were stranded overnight at the station; Benjamin Brown French, *Witness to the Young Republic: A Yankee's Journal, 1828–1870,* ed. Donald B. Cole and John J. McDonough (Hanover, N.H.: University Press of New England, 1989), 432; *Encounter at Hanover,* 192–193, citing "a statement" by "Captain" Eichelberger, who headed up a local militia unit in the 1840s; John Gibson, ed., *A Biographical History of York County, Pennsylvania* (Chicago: Genealogical Publishing, 1886), 63; Weiser, "Lincoln's Trip to Gettysburg," 3.

34. *Encounter at Hanover,* 192–193; Hay, *Inside Lincoln's White House,* 111; MacVeagh, "Lincoln at Gettysburg," 20. McPherson was a "lame duck," having been defeated in the recent elections, but Lincoln would help him be appointed clerk of the House early in the new Congress, a position he held until 1875.

35. Abraham Lincoln to I. Wayne MacVeagh, October 13, in *Collected Works,* 6: 512; A. K. McClure, *Old Time Notes of Pennsylvania,* 2 vols. (Philadelphia: John C. Winston, 1905), 2: 55. McClure, a long-time Pennsylvania insider, described the 1855 Cameron-Curtin struggle as "the most disgraceful free-for-all fight for the senatorship that has ever been witnessed at Harrisburg." John Russell Young, *Men and Memories: Personal Reminiscences,* ed. May D. Russell Young, 2 vols. (New York: F. Tennyson Neely, 1891–1901), 1: 61; "I. Wayne MacVeagh," *Encyclopaedia of Contemporary Biography, of Pennsylvania . . .* (New York: Atlantic Publishing, 1899), 3: 227–228.

36. MacVeagh later wrote that only the support of the soldiers had reelected Curtin in 1863; quoted in William H. Egle, *The Life and Times of Andrew G. Curtin* (Philadelphia: Thompson, 1895), 159. McClure described amending the state constitution; *Old Time Notes of Pennsylvania,* 2: 56.

37. Hay diary, September 17, *Inside Lincoln's White House,* 85. Cameron warned Lincoln of Curtin's presidential ambitions; October 10, Lincoln Papers, LOC.

38. Carpenter, *Six Months,* 242; Dennis K. Boman, *Lincoln's Resolute Unionist: Hamilton Gamble, Dred Scott Dissenter and Missouri's Civil War Governor* (Baton Rouge: Louisiana State University Press, 2006), 215, 225; Hay diary, November 19, *Inside Lincoln's White House,* 111.

39. Burlingame, *Abraham Lincoln,* 2: 554; Hay diary, November 19, *Inside Lincoln's White House,* 111.

40. *Cincinnati Daily Gazette,* November 23; Burlingame, *Abraham Lincoln: A Life,* 2: 543, 553; Hay diary, December 9 and 10, *Inside Lincoln's White House,* 123; Harris, *Lincoln and the Border States,* 334; see also Dennis K. Boman, *Lincoln and Citizens' Rights in Civil War Missouri: Balancing Freedom and Security* (Baton Rouge: Louisiana State University Press, 2011).

41. Mary Shaw Leader, in the *Hanover Spectator.* A plaque inaugurated in

Hanover on Veteran's Day 1942 and transcribed in *Encounter at Hanover*, 182, includes many details based on oral traditions and local sources. Weiser, "Lincoln's Trip to Gettysburg," 5; *Philadelphia Inquirer*, November 21. It appears that the *Spectator* and the *Citizen* based their stories on that of the *Inquirer*, adding details of their own.

42. The Republican *Hanover Spectator* prudently avoided mentioning Lincoln's question, perhaps because it did not reflect well on either Lincoln or his audience; *Encounter at Hanover*, 184, 248, 114. *Hanover Citizen*, reprinted in Weiser, "Lincoln's Trip to Gettysburg," 5; *Philadelphia Inquirer*, November 21. The *Daily Richmond [Va.] Examiner*, November 25, ridiculed Lincoln's question and the response.

43. E. W. Andrews, "Lincoln's Kindness," 300. Lincoln's words and little Jackie Melsheimer are mentioned in the plaque at Hanover; *Encounter at Hanover*, 182. The *Philadelphia Inquirer*, November 21, described the departure.

Chapter 4. Revisions in Gettysburg

1. Diary, November 18, Everett Papers, MSHS; John Russell Young, *Men and Memories: Personal Reminiscences*, ed. May D. Russell Young, 2 vols. (New York: F. Tennyson Neely, 1891–1901), 1: 59.

2. The *Philadelphia Inquirer*, November 21, noted the carriage and the visit to Lincoln's car. Hay diary, November 19, *Inside Lincoln's White House: The Complete Civil War Diary of John Hay*, ed. Michael Burlingame and John R. Turner Ettlinger (Carbondale: Southern Illinois University Press, 1997), 111; diary, November 18, Everett Papers, MSHS; Benjamin Brown French, *Witness to the Young Republic: A Yankee's Journal, 1828–1870*, ed. Donald B. Cole and John J. McDonough (Hanover, N.H.: University Press of New England, 1989), 434. Montgomery Blair was serenaded at the home of lawyer D. A. Buehler; whether he was also lodging there is unclear; *Gettysburg Star and Banner*, November 26. William A. Frassanito, *Early Photography at Gettysburg* (Gettysburg, Pa.: Thomas Publications, 1995), 80.

3. "The Diary of Josephine Forney Roedel," ed. Elsie Singmaster, *Pennsylvania Magazine of History and Biography*, October 1943, 397. The *Washington Daily Morning Chronicle*, November 21, noted souvenirs for sale. Henry Sweeney to Andrew Sweeney, November 29, file 190, Adams County Historical Society, Gettysburg, Pennsylvania (hereafter ACHS).

4. Since Jennie Wills Quimby was born in December, she must have heard the dinner spoken of in her family; *Philadelphia Public Ledger*, undated clipping stamped February 11, 1931 or 1921, formerly at the Lincoln Museum, Fort Wayne, now the Lincoln Financial Foundation Collection held by the Indiana State Museum, Indianapolis, and the Allen County [Indiana] Public Library. David Wills's father, James, also lived with the family in 1860 according to the U.S. census record, accessed through Ancestry.com, September 4, 2012. Linda Giberson Black states that there were twenty at dinner, citing Frank L. Klement and Philip B. Kunhardt Jr.; Black, *Gettysburg Remembers President Lincoln: Eyewitness Accounts of*

November 1863 (Gettysburg, Pa.: Thomas Publications, 2005), 20; Klement, *The Gettysburg Soldiers' Cemetery and Lincoln's Address: Aspects and Angles* (Shippensburg, Pa.: White Mane, 1993); Kunhardt, *A New Birth of Freedom: Lincoln at Gettysburg* (Boston: Little, Brown, 1983). Both Klement and Kunhardt are unreliable on events in the Wills house that evening, giving no sources for many details not found elsewhere.

5. Edward Everett, *Orations and Speeches on Various Occasions,* vol. 4 (Boston: Little Brown, 1868) 744, speaking on November 24, 1864. The meal Everett referred to might have taken place the next afternoon after the speech, when his diary mentioned "Dinner at M. Wills' for a very large company," whereas in the entry for the eighteenth Everett states only that he went to tea; however, it seems likely that the tea was earlier and Everett simply omitted mention of dinner on the eighteenth; diary, Everett Papers, MSHS. Everett's remarks in Boston, for example, mentioned no governors present, and he was fairly careful about such matters, suggesting it was a dinner for the party that had just arrived on the train, for the next day many governors were probably at the table. In addition, several newspapers mention a supper on the eighteenth as if it were a notable event; for example, the *New York World,* November 20, stated that a band played "after the President and the members of the cabinet who accompanied him had taken supper."

6. William A. McIlhenny, quoted in L. Black, *Gettysburg Remembers,* 24. McIlhenny had been wounded in mid-October 1863, according to the service record summarized at www.emmitsburg.net/archive_list/articles/history/civil_war/coles_cavalrymen/mchiihenny.htm (accessed September 6, 2012); diary, November 18, Everett Papers, MSHS.

7. Hay diary, November 19, *Inside Lincoln's White House,* 112; *Washington Daily Morning Chronicle,* November 20. The Fahnestocks were prominent merchants in the town. Benjamin French noted in his diary that at the courthouse "we made all the necessary arrangements for the following day"; *Witness to the Young Republic,* 434.

8. Albertus McCreary, quoted in John Alexander and Jim Slade, *Firestorm at Gettysburg: Civilian Voices June–November 1863* (Atglen, Pa.: Schiffer, 2004), 171; *Philadelphia Inquirer,* November 21; E. W. Andrews, "Lincoln's Kindness of Heart," in *Reminiscences of Abraham Lincoln, by Distinguished Men of His Time,* ed. Allen Thorndike Rice (New York: North American Pub. Co., 1886), 301.

9. *Philadelphia Inquirer,* November 21; Clark E. Carr, *Lincoln at Gettysburg: An Address,* 4th ed. (Chicago: McClurg, 1909), 140.

10. *New York Tribune,* November 20, which is also the text reprinted in *The Collected Works of Abraham Lincoln,* ed. Roy P. Basler, 9 vols. (New Brunswick, N.J.: Rutgers University Press, 1953–1955), 7: 17. This version was part of an Associated Press report that was widely reprinted, but many papers also included their own summaries. Aside from the case noted below, there are only a few substantive differences among the versions. The November 21 *New York Times,* how-

ever, reported, "The President said he was tired, and did not feel like speaking, and a man who did not feel like talking was apt to say foolish things," while the November 20 *Philadelphia Press* stated, "The President said he was happy to see so many of his friends present to participate in the ceremonies." *Boston Evening Transcript*, November 20.

11. The *New York Tribune* version included in *Collected Works,* 7: 17, has someone shout out the words "if he can help it" attributed here to Lincoln. This interruption appears to be a mistake in the telegraphic message as it was printed in New York. It is found only in the November 20 *New York Tribune, New York Herald,* and *New York World.* The *Times* included its own, very brief, summary with no interruption, as did a second article in the *World.* The interruption is not found in the same Associated Press report as published in cities telegraphically closer to Gettysburg, such as Philadelphia, Baltimore, or Washington, nor is it in the Associated Press report or summaries and special reports published by many papers across the Union, from Boston to Columbus and from Pittsburg to Chicago. For this reason, the analogous sentence from the *Baltimore American,* November 20, is given in the speech instead of the *Tribune* text that has the New York interruption. *Philadelphia Inquirer*, November 21.

12. Junius B. Remensnyder, "Personal Memories of Lincoln: President Lincoln's Address at Gettysburg." *Outlook,* February 13, 1918, 243, reprinting an article that had first appeared in 1914. On Remensnyder, see William S. Pelletreau, *Historic Homes and Institutions and Genealogical and Family History of New York*, 4 vols. (New York: Lewis Publishing, 1907), 4: 36–37.

13. Hay diary, November 19, *Inside Lincoln's White House,* 112. Nicolay seems to have remembered nothing of his night in Gettysburg, or at least nothing he cared to reveal; Nicolay, "Lincoln's Gettysburg Address," *Century Magazine,* February 1894, 596–608.

14. The *Pittsburgh Post,* November 22, attacked Lincoln's serenade response for not praising the soldiers, adding for good measure, "The few formal remarks addressed by him the next day would not have been given to the assemblage had they not been written out for him by another."

15. Francis Carpenter noted that Lincoln once mocked a diplomatic statement that Seward had written for him, reading it aloud in "a waggish manner" and concluding "with sly humor," "There, I like it. It has the merit of originality"; Carpenter, *Six Months at the White House with Lincoln: The Story of a Picture* (New York: Hurd and Hudson, 1867), 129.

16. *New York Tribune*, November 20; Nicolay, "Lincoln's Gettysburg Address," 601.

17. Two similar versions of Seward's speech appeared in the press on November 20; the one used here appeared in the *New York Tribune* and was reprinted in the official *Report of the Select Committee Relative to the Soldiers' National Cemetery* (Harrisburg, Pa.: Singerly and Myers, State Printers, 1864), 72, and in William H.

Seward, *The Works of William H. Seward,* ed. George E. Baker, 5 vols. (Boston: Houghton Mifflin, 1884), 5: 489. Gabor Boritt, *The Gettysburg Gospel: The Lincoln Speech That Nobody Knows* (New York: Simon and Schuster, 2008), 77. Henry Sweetser Burrage states that David Wills believed that Seward thought Gettysburg was below the Mason-Dixon line; Burrage, *Gettysburg and Lincoln: The Battle, the Cemetery, and the National Park* (New York: G. P. Putnam's Sons, 1906), 97. *Cincinnati Daily Commercial,* November 21.

18. Seward's speech was closely parsed in the press, including the *Pittsburgh Post,* November 22; the *Liberator,* January 15, 1864; and the *National Anti-Slavery Standard,* December 5.

19. I. Wayne MacVeagh, "Lincoln at Gettysburg," *Century Magazine,* November 1909, 21; diary, November 18, Everett Papers, MSHS; Young, *Men and Memories,* 1: 61; Hay diary, November 19, *Inside Lincoln's White House,* 112.

20. Hay diary, November 19, *Inside Lincoln's White House,* 112; MacVeagh, "Lincoln at Gettysburg," 21.

21. *Philadelphia Press,* November 20. Young, whom Hay mentioned as among the journalists covering the speech, was even more generous to Forney's remarks in his later memoir, saying that the "proud, gallant Forney" felt "the banner of the dead Douglas was in his keeping, and it was ever unfurled"; Young, *Men and Memories,* 1: 61; Hay diary, November 19, *Inside Lincoln's White House,* 112.

22. *Gettysburg Compiler,* November 23; Hay diary, November 19, *Inside Lincoln's White House,* 112; *Milwaukee Sentinel,* November 28; *Cincinnati Daily Gazette,* November 21.

23. I. Wayne MacVeagh, "Lincoln at Gettysburg," *Century Magazine,* November 1909, 22. Like his summary of Forney's remarks, MacVeagh's description of Seward's speech shows no sign of contamination by later reading.

24. Michael Burlingame, *Lincoln: A Life,* 2 vols. (Baltimore: Johns Hopkins University Press, 2008), 2: 672, details Lincoln's views on his reelection.

25. MacVeagh, "Lincoln at Gettysburg," 21; Hay diary, *Inside Lincoln's White House,* 113; Young, *Men and Memories,* 1: 61.

26. MacVeagh, "Lincoln at Gettysburg," 22.

27. A. K. McClure, *Old Time Notes of Pennsylvania,* 2 vols. (Philadelphia: John C. Winston, 1905), 1: 338; Edward McPherson, letter to the editor, *Nation,* September 9, 1875, 164. McPherson's publications included *The Political History of the United States during the Great Rebellion* (1864; 2nd ed., 1865; 3rd ed., 1876), *The Political History of the United States of America during the Period of Reconstruction* (1871; 2nd ed., 1875), *A Political Manual* (published annually from 1866 to 1869), and *A Handbook of Politics* (published biennially from 1868 to 1894).

28. David Wills, "Statement Given by Judge Wills to Charles M. McCurdy, about 1890," quoted in Henry E. Luhrs, *Lincoln at the Wills Home and the Gettysburg Address* (Shippensburg, Pa.: Lincoln Publishers, 1938), 17. All citations here of Wills's 1890 statement refer to this photograph of the document, which is the only published version that is not a transcription. This document has the same

wording as the Wills letter that is quoted in full in "Some Correspondence Regarding a Missing Copy of the Gettysburg Address," *Lincoln Lore* 1437 (November, 1957): 1, with no source citation given. This *Lincoln Lore* article, probably written by editor R. Gerald McMurtry or perhaps Louis Warren, states that the copy of the Wills letter it quotes was included in a letter from David Wills to John G. Nicolay of January 19, 1894, in which Wills explained, "Years ago I wrote out the facts I knew about it [Lincoln's speech] and they were published in some of the newspapers." No such newspaper account has been found, but there is no reason to doubt Wills's statement on this point. The 1894 version is probably the same as the letter referred to by Garry Wills in *Lincoln at Gettysburg: The Words That Remade America* (New York: Simon and Schuster, 1992), 268n17, which states that it is preserved in the Manuscript Room of the Library of Congress; a transcript identical in words to the McCurdy letter is among the David Wills papers there. The Wills statement appears to have reached its final form after September 10, 1885, because in the letter on that date to R. W. Gilder, Wills offered to have a photo taken of a facsimile of the Bliss text that he owned, and in the 1890 statement Wills states he actually has such a photograph; "Some Correspondence," 1. The first publication of the statement by Wills appears to have been in *Encyclopaedia of Contemporary Biography, of Pennsylvania . . .* , 4 vols. (New York: Atlantic Publishing, 1899), 3: 44–47.

29. On the Gilder Age, see Herbert F. Smith, *Richard Watson Gilder* (New York: Twayne Publishers, [1970]), 13. Wills to Gilder, September 10, 1885, and Nicolay to Gilder, September 19, 1885; both in *Lincoln Lore* 1437.

30. "In this temple, as in the hearts of the people for whom he saved the Union, the memory of Abraham Lincoln is enshrined forever"; inscription behind Lincoln's statue in the Lincoln Memorial. I would like to thank Marcus R. Pratt of the Gettysburg National Military Park for providing floor plans of the Wills house as it stood in 1863. The David Wills House Museum in Gettysburg, now operated by the Military Park, has restored the room to its appearance in 1863 to the extent possible. It cannot be asserted as a certainty that Wills was not already on the second floor, or for that matter, was not on the third level, when Johnson found him. Nor is it certain that Bigham was there at that moment, or that the table was not, for example, borrowed or new—but the table was there, as Bigham was there and the washstand and the towels, which really were embroidered, but perhaps they were on the bureau, for example.

31. "I went and found him writing,"; Isaac Markens, *Lincoln's Masterpiece: A Review of the Gettysburg Address New in Treatment and Matter* (New York: Isaac Markens, 1913), 12, quoting a newspaper report that included a letter from Wills read at a 1909 commemorative event in Philadelphia.

32. Sixty years later a lawyer claimed that when he was a young law student, David Wills told him that he had given Lincoln the paper, a story that created yet another element in the growing legend; Edward Newton Haag in the *Philadelphia Public Ledger*, February 21, 1921. Unfortunately, the story of Wills providing the

paper was repeated by Frank Klement in *Blue and Gray Magazine,* December 1990, 36, reprinted in Klement, *The Gettysburg Soldiers' Cemetery,* 74. This inaccurate story is repeated in the insightful reflection by Kent Gramm, *November: Lincoln's Elegy at Gettysburg* (Bloomington: Indiana University Press, 2001), 131, and in Doris Kearns Goodwin's *Team of Rivals: The Political Genius of Abraham Lincoln* (New York: Simon and Schuster, 2005), 584.

33. McPherson in the *Philadelphia Press,* cited in the *[Springfield] Illinois State Journal,* November 17, 1879. Gabor Boritt recognized that McPherson based his story on what Wills told him; Boritt, *The Gettysburg Gospel,* 318.

34. John Bartlett, *Familiar Quotations: Being an Attempt to Trace to Their Source Passages and Phrases in Common Use,* 7th ed. (Boston: Little, Brown, 1875). The preface notes the selection criteria is that "the general reader would readily recognize them as old friends" (vii). The seventh edition was the first expanded edition since the fifth edition of 1868; by this measure, then, Lincoln's words had become "old friends" sometime between 1868 and 1875.

35. Medicus also stated that the words were written on alternate lines of perhaps four pages; *New York Tribune,* May 28, 1882. Medicus was writing to refute Usher's lecture stating that Lincoln on the train had written on pasteboard balanced on his knee, and knowing that it was not possible to write in ink under those conditions, Medicus specifically disputed the notion that Lincoln wrote in pencil, which, as he stated, was the "inference" of Usher's account. While the description of alternate lines and lack of penciled text is troubling, the mention of letterhead paper would seem to be conclusive that Medicus saw Lincoln reading the Letterhead Page. Daniel Denison Slade was born in Boston in 1823, graduated from Harvard in 1844, and was a professor of applied zoology at Harvard from 1870 to 1882. He wrote under the pen name "Medicus" and served in the U.S. Sanitary Commission at Baltimore in 1863. For a full biography, see Edward Wheelwright, *Memoir of Daniel Denison Slade, M.D.* (Cambridge, Mass.: University Press, 1900), 23.

36. Accounts based upon the recollections of Edwin Newton Haag (for example, in the *Philadelphia Public Ledger,* February 6, 1921) cannot be relied upon, as they directly contradict David Wills. Henry Sweetser Burrage quotes a letter from the husband of Jennie Wills that adds nothing to David Wills's 1890 statement; Burrage, *Gettysburg and Lincoln,* 99.

37. R. S. Chilton of Clifton, Ontario (Canada), *New York Times,* July 23, 1881, reprinting an undated article from the *Toronto Daily Mail.* In 1868 Chilton was an official at the State Department, according to Gregory A. Waselkov and Kathryn E. Holland Braund, eds., in *William Bartram on the Southeastern Indians* (Lincoln: University of Nebraska Press, 2002), 268. In 1877 he was listed as the U.S. consul in Clifton, Ontario (near Niagara, New York); *Canadian Almanac and Directory* (Toronto: Scobie and Balfour, 1877), 64; R. S. Chilton Jr. Papers, Georgetown University Library, Washington, D.C., http://www.library.georgetown.edu/dept /speccoll/chilton/index.htm (accessed September 13, 2012).

38. All three begin by mentioning that Lincoln stayed at the Wills home and that Wills went to Lincoln's room; Lincoln was writing or about to write (the 1875 and 1881 versions describe the paper, as well); Lincoln was writing a "few thoughts" or "stray thoughts," or he was "scribbling"; what Lincoln was writing was the same as the speech given at the ceremony; and Lincoln wrote a definitive copy for the Baltimore Fair in 1864.

Chapter 5. The Gettysburg Draft

1. *Philadelphia Press*, November 21.

2. *Philadelphia Press*, November 21.

3. Everett's diary and many newspaper reports agree that Curtin arrived in Gettysburg and at the Wills house at about eleven; for example, *Baltimore Daily Gazette*, November 21; *Philadelphia Press*, November 21.

4. Wills to Gilder, September 10, 1885, in *Lincoln Lore* 1437; Curtin, as quoted in Horatio King, *Turning On the Light: A Dispassionate Survey of President Buchanan's Administration* (Philadelphia: J. B. Lippincott, 1895), 237, reprinting an article from the *Washington Critic*, February 18, 1888. Curtin had first told King and others this story at the 1885 reunion and the 1888 article was published after King had again consulted with Curtin. King had briefly served as postmaster general during the last days of the Buchanan administration.

5. Edwin M. Stanton to Abraham Lincoln, Wednesday, November 18, Lincoln Papers, LOC; Robert Fortenbaugh, *Lincoln and Gettysburg* (Gettysburg, Pa.: Bookmart, 1949), 46.

6. William McSherry, *History of the Bank of Gettysburg, 1814–1864, the Gettysburg National Bank, 1864–1914, of Gettysburg* (Gettysburg, Pa.: Gettysburg National Bank, 1914), 63; U.S. census records accessed through Ancestry.com; recollections collected in the early 1920s by Sara McCullough, a granddaughter of one of the soldiers, file 190, ACHS; Hugh Bigham letter of January 14, 1922, quoted in Charles McCurdy, *Gettysburg: A Memoir* (Pittsburgh: Reed and Witting, 1929), 32. Secondhand versions of Bigham's statement sometimes state that he saw Lincoln writing that night, but the sources written directly by Bigham make no such claim.

7. Undated letter by Hugh Bigham transcribed in an unidentified auction catalog preserved in file 10-18, GNMP. This letter is very similar but not identical to the 1922 letter quoted in McCurdy, *Gettysburg*, 32. Mary Lincoln telegram quoted in Fortenbaugh, *Lincoln and Gettysburg*, 12, and Gabor Boritt, *The Gettysburg Gospel: The Lincoln Speech That Nobody Knows* (New York: Simon and Schuster, 2008), 90. None of the telegrams Lincoln received in Gettysburg is known to have been published before the 1940s, so Bigham's detailed knowledge of one of them provides strong support for his reliability.

8. Curtin to Nicolay, April 7, 1892, box 118, Nicolay Papers, LOC. The wording of this letter is given slightly differently by David C. Mearns and Lloyd A. Dunlap in "Notes and Comments on the Preparation of the Address," in *Long*

Remembered: Facsimilies of the Five Versions of the Gettysburg Address, ed. David C. Mearns and Lloyd A. Dunlap (Washington, D.C.: Library of Congress, 1963), n.p. The 1892 letter and the version in King's *Turning On the Light,* 237, also differ slightly, as noted below.

9. Accounts of the Curtin story traceable to King's son, General Horatio King Jr., stated that Curtin had copied out Lincoln's speech or that Lincoln had read his speech to a group at a Gettysburg hotel; William Augustus Mowry and Arthur May Mowry, *A History of the United States for Schools . . .* (Boston: Burdett, 1896), 407; Emma Miller Bolenius, ed., *The Boys' and Girls' Readers: Fourth–Sixth Reader,* vol. 3 (Boston: Houghton Mifflin, 1919), 162; Noah Brooks, *Washington in Lincoln's Time* (Philadelphia: Century, 1895).

10. Edward Ringwood Hewitt, *Those Were the Days: Tales of a Long Life* (New York: World Book, 1943), 180. The story shows strong signs of being influenced by other accounts, especially that of Curtin; Ashley died in 1896, so the conversation was about fifty years old in 1943.

11. Boritt provides an excellent account of Johnson and his relationship to Lincoln; *The Gettysburg Gospel,* 54, 83.

12. Bigham letter of January 12, 1922, reprinted in McCurdy, *Gettysburg,* 32.

13. The note adds, "Presumption—finishing his speech"; Philip Bikle, interviewed on February 20, 1925, by Sara McCullough, file 190, ACHS.

14. *Washington Daily Morning Chronicle,* November 21. A later section of this report is signed "J. H." and appears to have been written mainly by John Hay on the presidential train during the trip back to Washington after the ceremony. The first section also bears signs of Hay's style and discusses some of the same public events as his diary but also includes many details about events Hay could not have participated in, including a journey to Gettysburg that does not correspond to the trip on Lincoln's train.

15. Cross to Seward, November 23, microfilm edition, reel 81, Seward Papers, University of Rochester Library.

16. Like many of the men of the town, Robert Harper, the editor of the *Sentinel,* a Republican paper, had found it prudent to be elsewhere during the invasion.

17. Benjamin Brown French, *Witness to the Young Republic: A Yankee's Journal, 1828–1870,* ed. Donald B. Cole and John J. McDonough (Hanover, N.H.: University Press of New England, 1989), 433. Seward's taste for the finer things like cigars and conversation is evident from a gift he received from Ward Lamon two weeks after the ceremony: two cases of Martell brandy, which Seward found "very fine"; Lamon to Seward, December 7, and Seward to Lamon, December 9, microfilm edition, reel 81, Seward Papers.

18. Seward's role in these stories confirms that the episode took place at Harper's, for Seward was not known to have been at the Wills house that evening; *Ottawa Journal,* July 19, 1947, citing accounts by the two men written many years before. As noted in chapter 3 above, one of the informants was McDougall's nephew, F. C. L. Jones, a barrister in Toronto, Canada, who said that McDougall

told him the story in the 1890s. The second was William Houston, a journalist and later librarian of the Ontario Provincial Library.

19. Douglas L. Wilson, *Lincoln's Sword: The Presidency and the Power of Words* (New York: Knopf, 2006), 218. Wilson discusses examples of Seward's editorial influence on the First Inaugural (59), the July 4, 1861, message to Congress (94), and the Emancipation Proclamation (117). Francis Carpenter also gives examples of Lincoln editing his writings in response to comments from Seward and others; Carpenter, *Six Months at the White House with Lincoln: The Story of a Picture* (New York: Hurd and Hudson, 1867), 23, 123, 129. John Russell Young expressed relief that he would not have to transcribe Seward's remarks; Young, *Men and Memories: Personal Reminiscences*, ed. May D. Russell Young, 2 vols. (New York: F. Tennyson Neely, 1891–1901), 2: 60.

20. The word "perish" appears on at least thirty-two different pages, sometimes multiple times per page, in *The Works of William H. Seward*, ed. George E. Baker, 5 vols. (Boston: Houghton Mifflin, 1884), in volumes 4 and 5, devoted to the 1850s and the war. A speech titled "On the True Greatness of the American People" that Seward gave several times in the 1840s stated, "If, now, after imparting these sublime and beneficent instructions, this people could at once perish from the earth . . . " (3: 18). One of Lincoln's uses of the word had occurred only the month before: "You and Burnside now have him [the enemy] by the throat, and he must break your hold, or perish"; Lincoln to General Rosecrans, October 12, in *The Collected Works of Abraham Lincoln*, ed. Roy P. Basler, 9 vols. (New Brunswick, N.J.: Rutgers University Press, 1953–1955), 6: 510. Garry Wills has suggested that "perish" reflects the influence of Everett's oration; Wills, *Lincoln at Gettysburg: The Words That Remade America* (New York: Simon and Schuster, 1992), 268n19.

21. The story evidently arose in a letter by "W. Farquhar," May 26, 1921, quoted in John M. Taylor, *William Henry Seward: Lincoln's Right Hand* (New York: HarperCollins, 1991), 224. Farquhar gave many details he could not have witnessed, and this story appears to be one of them. This would appear to be Arthur Biggs Farquhar, who was also quoted as telling this story by James Edward Kelly and William B. Styple in their *Tell Me of Lincoln: Memories of Abraham Lincoln, the Civil War, and Life in Old New York* (Belle Grove, Pa.: Belle Grove Publishing, 2009), 267. However, Farquhar did not mention it in his autobiography, *The First Million the Hardest* (New York: Doubleday, 1922).

22. Wills statement of 1890, quoted in Henry E. Luhrs, *Lincoln at the Wills Home and the Gettysburg Address* (Shippensburg, Pa.: Lincoln Publishers, 1938), 17; Bigham letter in file 10-18, GNMP; French, *Witness to the Young Republic*.

23. There was a good deal of confusion in the press as to the exact name of the choir, but the *Baltimore American,* November 21, noted that the formal name of the Union Glee Club was the National Union Musical Association of Baltimore; see also the chapter on music at Gettysburg in Frank L. Klement's *The Gettysburg Soldiers' Cemetery and Lincoln's Address: Aspects and Angles* (Shippensburg, Pa.: White Mane, 1993), 192–211.

24. Bigham letter in file 10-18, GNMP; Bigham letter quoted in McCurdy, *Gettysburg,* 32; *Baltimore American,* November 20.

25. Wills's daughter Jennie, who was just about to be born, many years later told a newspaper reporter a story that seems to have been much influenced by Curtin's account: after Lincoln went to the Harpers', he "returned shortly with the explanation that he must complete his address for the next day. He retired to the guest bedroom and there rewrote from a rough draft the words which have become a classic"; newspaper clipping, probably the *Philadelphia Evening Ledger,* February 11, 1921 (or 1931?), preserved at the former Lincoln Museum, Fort Wayne, now the Lincoln Financial Foundation Collection held by the Indiana State Museum, Indianapolis, and the Allen County [Indiana] Public Library.

26. Curtin to Nicolay, April 7, 1892, box 118, Nicolay Papers, LOC. The 1888 interview states more briefly, "He said, 'I will go and show it to Seward,' who stopped at another house, which he did, and then returned and copied his speech on a foolscap sheet"; Curtin, quoted in King, *Turning On the Light,* 237.

27. *Washington Daily Morning Chronicle,* November 21; diary, Everett Papers, MSHS; French, *Witness to the Young Republic,* 435.

28. William Saunders, "Memoir of Gettysburg," in *Congressional Record 70,* no. 3 (February 12, 1929): H3322.

Chapter 6. The Battlefield Draft

1. Mrs. Jacob A. Clutz [Liberty Hollinger Clutz], *Some Personal Recollections of the Battle of Gettysburg* (privately printed, n.d.), 19, quoted in Linda Giberson Black, *Gettysburg Remembers President Lincoln: Eyewitness Accounts of November 1863* (Gettysburg, Pa.: Thomas Publications, 2005), 28.

2. Clutz, *Some Personal Recollections,* 28. See also David Cleutz, *Rebels in the Front Yard: Liberty at Gettysburg* (Gettysburg, Pa.: Gettysburg Publishing, 2012). David Cleutz is one of Liberty's descendants.

3. Note to Edwin Stanton, December 23, in *The Collected Works of Abraham Lincoln,* ed. Roy P. Basler, 9 vols. (New Brunswick, N.J.: Rutgers University Press, 1953–1955), 7: 88.

4. *Harper's Weekly,* August 22, publishing engravings based upon photographs by Matthew Brady's studio. Gardner issued a photo that claimed to be of the spot, but probably was not; William A. Frassanito, *Gettysburg: A Journey in Time* (New York: Scribner, 1975), 222. A few weeks after the Gettysburg ceremony, Lincoln met with Reynolds's sister and supported her plea for promotion for the aide who had carried Reynolds from the battlefield; note to Edwin Stanton, December 23, in *Collected Works,* 7: 88.

5. Edward J. Nichols, *Toward Gettysburg: A Biography of General John F. Reynolds* (New York: Pennsylvania State University Press, 1958), 220; Stephen W. Sears, *Gettysburg* (New York: Houghton Mifflin, 2004), 40.

6. Donn Piatt to Abraham Lincoln, July 2, Lincoln Papers, LOC; *Washington Daily Morning Chronicle,* November 21.

7. *New York Herald*, August 6 and November 20; Emily Bliss Thacher Souder, *Leaves from the Battlefield of Gettysburg* (Philadelphia: Caxton, 1864), 137; *Ohio State Journal*, November 23; *Cleveland Plain Dealer*, November 23.

8. Schenck's sighting of Lincoln is mentioned in an undated newspaper clipping in Louis A. Warren, *Lincoln's Gettysburg Declaration: "A New Birth of Freedom"* (Fort Wayne, Ind.: Lincoln National Life Foundation, 1964), 72; William Houston on McDougall in the *Ottawa Journal*, July 19, 1947; Tisdale in James Edward Kelly and William B. Styple, *Tell Me of Lincoln: Memories of Abraham Lincoln, the Civil War, and Life in Old New York* (Belle Grove, Pa.: Belle Grove Publishing, 2009), 233.

9. *Philadelphia Press*, November 21. Alfred R. Waud's illustration of the death of Reynolds may be seen at the Library of Congress, http://www.loc.gov/pictures /resource/cph.3a09687/. Reynolds's portrait and biography were published in the July 18 issue of *Harper's Weekly*. Ellie Reynolds, letter, July 5, preserved at Franklin and Marshall College Library archives, http://library.fandm.edu/archives/Reynolds /JFR/transcriptions/s127.htm (accessed September 12, 2012).

10. *Washington Daily Morning Chronicle*, November 21. Gabor Boritt was probably the first to point out the importance of Lincoln's remark; Boritt, *The Gettysburg Gospel: The Lincoln Speech That Nobody Knows* (New York: Simon and Schuster, 2008), 92. The woodlot was actually owned by McPherson's neighbor; today it is called Reynolds Woods; William A. Frassanito, *Early Photography at Gettysburg* (Gettysburg, Pa.: Thomas Publications, 1995), 59.

11. William Saunders, "Memoir of Gettysburg," in *Congressional Record 70*, no. 3 (February 12, 1929): H3321–3323.

12. *Cincinnati Daily Commercial*, November 23.

13. *Philadelphia Press*, November 21; *Milwaukee Sentinel*, November 21.

14. John G. Nicolay, "Lincoln's Gettysburg Address," *Century Magazine*, February 1894, 602.

15. Orton H. Carmichael, *Lincoln's Gettysburg Address* (New York: Abingdon Press, 1917), 87–88; *History of Cumberland and Adams Counties, Pennsylvania* (Chicago: Warner, Beers, 1886), 87; U.S. census records accessed through Ancestry.com.

16. Carmichael, *Lincoln's Gettysburg Address*, 87–88.

17. David C. Mearns and Lloyd A. Dunlap were unwilling to use Rebert's evidence because he never directly said it was Lincoln's speech he saw; Mearns and Dunlap, "Notes and Comments on the Preparation of the Address," in *Long Remembered: Facsimiles of the Five Versions of the Gettysburg Address*, ed. David C. Mearns and Lloyd A. Dunlap (Washington, D.C.: Library of Congress, 1963), n.p. Douglas L. Wilson suggests that Lincoln was working on "other presidential business"; Wilson, *Lincoln's Sword: The Presidency and the Power of Words* (New York: Knopf, 2006), 219.

18. Nicolay to Gilder, September 19, 1885, and Nicolay to Wills, January 20, 1894, in "Some Correspondence Regarding a Missing Copy of the Gettysburg Address," *Lincoln Lore* 1437 (November, 1957): 2.

19. David C. Mearns described Nicolay's article as "so filled with palpable error as to arouse speculation as to whether, in any particular, it may be correct"; Mearns, "The Mysteries of the Manuscripts," unpublished typescript, Mearns Papers, LOC, 3. More balanced but still critical are John R. Sellers, "Serving President Lincoln: The Public Career of John G. Nicolay," in *Lincoln Reshapes the Presidency*, ed. Charles M. Hubbard (Macon, Ga.: Mercer University Press, 2003); and Michael Burlingame, "Nicolay and Hay: Court Historians," *Journal of the Abraham Lincoln Association* 19, no. 1 (Winter 1998): 1–20.

20. Nicolay to Wills, January 20, 1894, in "Some Correspondence," 2.

21. Michael Burlingame, *Abraham Lincoln: The Observations of John G. Nicolay and John Hay* (Carbondale: Southern Illinois University Press, 2007), 35.

22. The respected scholar Gabor Boritt, former director of the Civil War Institute at Gettysburg College, is the most recent authority to advance this claim; Boritt, *The Gettysburg Gospel*, appendix C. The textual analysis he presents there with H. Van Dyke Parunak and Anita Gene Parunak assumes, among other things, that "the reading draft," whatever it might have been, is "an accurate record of what Lincoln said" (282). If this were a valid assumption, there would not have been 100 years of doubt about the Hay text, for it has always been recognized as the Lincoln document closest in words to the reports of his spoken words.

23. Wilson, *Lincoln's Sword*, 216; Garry Wills, *Lincoln at Gettysburg: The Words That Remade America* (New York: Simon and Schuster, 1992), 193. Wilson suggests that the words of a lost delivery text were similar to the Associated Press report and the Hale version; Wills suggests that they were instead those of the version printed later by David Wills and Edward Everett.

24. The existence of a hypothetical page written in pencil that may have preceded the existing Pencil Page is very much open to question, for this hypothesis contradicts Nicolay and involves positing several steps and reversals that are not required by a more conservative reading of the evidence.

25. Lincoln to Cuthbert Bullitt, July 28, 1862, in *Collected Works*, 5: 344; Lincoln to Erastus Corning, June 12, in *Collected Works*, 6: 265.

26. Speech at Cooper Institute, in *Collected Works*, 3: 522; speech of August 31, 1864, to the 148th Ohio Regiment, in *Collected Works*, 7: 528; response to a serenade, November 8, 1864, in *Collected Works*, 8: 96.

27. *Pittsburgh Daily Commercial*, November 23, as quoted in Michael Burlingame, *Abraham Lincoln: A Life*, 2 vols. (Baltimore: Johns Hopkins University Press, 2008), 2: 572, and also in Boritt, *The Gettysburg Gospel*, 94.

28. While it is possible to parse the structure of the speech in a variety of ways, the dashes in Lincoln's final handwritten version, the Bliss copy, clearly reveal that, at least at that point, he saw a four-part fulfillment of the great task: "—that from . . . —that we here . . . —that this nation . . . —and that government . . . ."

29. Lincoln to Stephen Logan, November 9, in *Collected Works*, 7: 7. In 1856 Lincoln had also used the phrase "to establish a dedication" to mean a public right of way or public use of a street; *Collected Works*, 2: 336.

30. Garry Wills argued that the underlined word meant this was not the delivery text; G. Wills, *Lincoln at Gettysburg*, 194.

31. *New York World,* November 14, dateline Washington, November 13, reported that Lincoln said he began his message to Congress "today"; *Chicago Times,* November 24, reported that Lincoln had finished the message; *Baltimore American,* November 25, reported that the section of the message dealing with slavery was finished; Chase wrote Lincoln on November 25 that the message gave him "great satisfaction"; Lincoln Papers, LOC.

32. The actual beginning of the message has all the marks of having been written by Seward, although Roy P. Basler, the editor of Lincoln's *Collected Works,* suggests the author was Lincoln; *Collected Works,* 7: 48.

33. *Collected Works,* 7: 49.

34. Lincoln later changed "new review" to "another review," perhaps to avoid the facile rhyme.

35. The July 30, 1863, Order of Retaliation stated, "It is the duty of every government to give protection to its citizens, of whatever class, color, or condition"; *Collected Works,* 6: 357. General Order 329 of October 3, 1863, imposed compulsory, compensated emancipation on all slave owners, loyal or rebel, in the Union slave states if draft quotas were not met; *The War of the Rebellion: The Official Records of the Union and Confederate Armies* (Washington, D.C.: GPO, 1899), ser. 3, vol. 3, p. 860. The 1863 Annual Message proposed equal pay; *Collected Works,* 7: 36. Lincoln supported voting rights for some blacks in Louisiana in December 1863; LaWanda Cox, *Lincoln and Black Freedom: A Study in Presidential Leadership* (Columbia: University of South Carolina Press, 1981), 80. Phillip W. Magness and Sebastian N. Page argue that Lincoln continued to support colonization into 1865; Magness and Page, *Colonization after Emancipation: Lincoln and the Movement for Black Resettlement* (Columbia: University of Missouri Press, 2011). Lincoln has been criticized for not publicly advocating black suffrage in 1863, but even the radical Wade-Davis bill of mid-1864 did not do so.

36. Burlingame, *Abraham Lincoln: A Life,* 2: 591, quoting the *Springfield Republican,* November 28. David W. Blight has argued that Lincoln's increasing radicalism was in part due to the influence of his acquaintance with Frederick Douglass, whom Blight calls "the intellectual godfather of the Gettysburg Address"; Blight, *Race and Reunion: The Civil War in American Memory* (Cambridge, Mass.: Harvard University Press, 2001), 15.

Chapter 7. *"What They Did Here"*
1. *Philadelphia Press,* November 21; John Russell Young, *Men and Memories: Personal Reminiscences,* ed. May D. Russell Young, 2 vols. (New York: F. Tennyson Neely, 1891–1901), 1: 63; *Boston Advertiser,* November 23; Storrick in the *Gettysburg Star and Sentinel,* November 23, 1940.

2. "The Diary of Josephine Forney Roedel," ed. Elsie Singmaster, *Pennsylvania*

Magazine of History and Biography, October 1943, 398; *New York World,* November 21.

3. *[Columbus] Ohio State Journal,* November 23; *Washington Daily Morning Chronicle,* November 20; Orton H. Carmichael, *Lincoln's Gettysburg Address* (New York: Abingdon Press, 1917), 52.

4. *Washington Daily Morning Chronicle,* November 20, and the report on November 21 by "J. H.," which in this second section of the article appears to reflect very closely the experience and outlook of John Hay. Linda Giberson Black, *Gettysburg Remembers President Lincoln: Eyewitness Accounts of November 1863* (Gettysburg, Pa.: Thomas Publications, 2005), 30; *Boston Advertiser*, November 2; *Boston Journal,* November 23.

5. Harvey Sweeney, file 190, ACHS; *Cincinnati Daily Gazette,* November 23; *Philadelphia Inquirer,* November 21; *Indianapolis Daily Journal,* November 23.

6. Named in various news reports were governors Andrew Curtin (Pennsylvania); David Tod, William Dennison, John Brough (Ohio); Augustus Bradford (Maryland); Oliver Morton, Joseph Wright (Indiana); Horatio Seymour (New York); Joel Parker (New Jersey); Arthur Boreman, Francis Pierpont (West Virginia); and Abner Coburn (Maine); *Baltimore American,* November 23.

7. William A. Frassanito, *Early Photography at Gettysburg* (Gettysburg, Pa.: Thomas Publications, 1995), 128; Henry Eyster Jacobs, *Lincoln's Gettysburg World-Message* (Philadelphia: United Lutheran Publication House, 1919), 63.

8. Clark E. Carr, *Lincoln at Gettysburg: An Address,* 4th ed. (Chicago: McClurg, 1909), 37; John Hay, *Inside Lincoln's White House: The Complete Civil War Diary of John Hay,* ed. Michael Burlingame and John R. Turner Ettlinger (Carbondale: Southern Illinois University Press, 1997), 113; Young, *Men and Memories,* 1: 63; *Boston Advertiser,* November 23.

9. A map in the *New York Herald,* November 20, indicated the route. Just over a thousand reburials had taken place at the time of the ceremony. The *New York World,* November 21, *Cincinnati Daily Commercial,* and *Indianapolis Daily Journal,* November 23, described the graves. "J. H." in the *Washington Daily Morning Chronicle,* November 21.

10. Emily Bliss Thacher Souder, *Leaves from the Battlefield of Gettysburg* (Philadelphia: Caxton, 1864), 139.

11. The *Washington Daily Morning Chronicle,* November 20, noted that journalists were seated "at desks" on the platform. *Ohio State Journal,* November 23. William Frassanito used photographic and other evidence to demonstrate the location of the stand, which had long been a point of contention; Frassanito, *Early Photography,* 163. *Washington Daily Morning Chronicle,* November 21, mentioned "tickets" to enter the stand. The platform was too small and was raised only 3 feet, according to Hale in the *Boston Advertiser,* November 23. *New York World,* November 21. Cochrane recalled that some in the crowd inadvertently trampled the graves in the crush; Henry Clay Cochrane, "With Lincoln to Gettysburg, 1863," in *Abraham Lincoln: Military Order of the Loyal Legion of the United States, Com-*

mandery of the State of Pennsylvania. Memorial Meeting, February 13, 1907 ([Philadelphia,] 1907), 11. *Philadelphia Daily Evening Bulletin,* November 20.

12. The *Cincinnati Daily Commercial,* November 23; *Chicago Tribune,* November 21; and *Washington Daily Morning Chronicle,* November 20, describe Lincoln's arrival. From left to right facing the stand the seating arrangement of the middle of the first row appears to have been Saunders, French, Thomas Stockton, Henry Baugher, Everett, Lincoln, Seward, Curtin, Seymour, and Tod, according to Frank L. Klement, *The Gettysburg Soldiers' Cemetery and Lincoln's Address: Aspects and Angles* (Shippensburg, Pa.: White Mane, 1993), 95, and Louis A. Warren, *Lincoln's Gettysburg Declaration: "A New Birth of Freedom"* (Fort Wayne, Ind.: Lincoln National Life Foundation, 1964), 95. *Cincinnati Daily Gazette,* November 23.

13. *Boston Journal,* November 23. The Associated Press (AP) report datelined Gettysburg, November 19, that began with the words "The ceremonies attending" included the standard AP version of Lincoln's speech; *New York Tribune,* November 20.

14. *New York Herald,* November 20; "J. H." in the *Washington Daily Morning Chronicle,* November 21.

15. Diary, November 19, Everett Papers, MSHS; Young, *Men and Memories,* 1: 64.

16. *Philadelphia Daily Evening Bulletin,* November 20; Edmund Wilson, *Patriotic Gore* (New York: Norton, 1962).

17. *Chicago Tribune,* November 2; *Cincinnati Daily Commercial,* November 21; Young, *Men and Memories,* 1: 66.

18. *Report of the Select Committee Relative to the Soldiers' National Cemetery* (Harrisburg, Pa.: Singerly and Myers, State Printers, 1864), 77. Everett, who listened closely to all the speeches that day, thought it "highly rhetorical, but otherwise extremely well written"; diary, November 19, Everett Papers, MSHS. Hay diary, November 19, *Inside Lincoln's White House,* 113; I. Wayne MacVeagh, "Lincoln at Gettysburg," *Century Magazine,* November 1909, 21. *Baltimore Daily Gazette,* November 21, wrote archly that the prayer was "remarkable for its length."

19. *[Chambersburg, Pa.] Franklin Repository,* December 9; *Ohio State Journal,* November 23. The *Cincinnati Daily Commercial,* November 23, agreed that the prayer brought tears to the eyes of thousands. *Cincinnati Daily Gazette,* November 23. *Baltimore American,* November 20.

20. "J. H." in the *Washington Daily Morning Chronicle,* November 21.

21. The editorial in the Democratic *New York World,* November 20, opined, "This imitation of a passage in a Greek orator is rather a substitute for true feeling than an evidence of it."

22. Everett to Frank P. Blair, October 18, 1862, boasting of his correspondence with presidents, quoted in Paul Revere Frothingham, *Edward Everett: Orator and Statesman* (Port Washington, N.Y.: Kennikat Press, 1971; reprint of Boston: Houghton Mifflin, 1925; page references are to the 1971 edition), 449. See also

Paul A. Varg, *Edward Everett: The Intellectual in the Turmoil of Politics* (Selinsgrove, Pa.: Susquehanna University Press, 1992); Ronald F. Reid, *Edward Everett: Unionist Orator* (New York: Greenwood, 1990); *Cincinnati Daily Gazette*, November 23.

23. Edward Everett, *Orations and Speeches on Various Occasions*, vol. 4 (Boston: Little, Brown, 1868), 622–659. I have silently modernized some spelling. News reports confirm Everett's diary entry of November 19, that he spoke from memory; Everett Papers, MSHS.

24. *Cincinnati Daily Commercial*, November 23; *Chicago Tribune*, November 21; *Cincinnati Daily Gazette*, November 23. Everett's student Ralph Waldo Emerson wrote of his "radiant beauty"; "Edward Everett," in *Dictionary of American Biography* (New York: Charles Scribner's Sons, 1936), as it appears at *Biography in Context*, http://ic.galegroup.com.proxy.lib.muohio.edu/ic/bic1/ReferenceDetails Page/ReferenceDetailsWindow?failOverType=&query=&prodId=BIC1&window state=normal&contentModules=&mode=view&displayGroupName=Reference& limiter=&currPage=&disableHighlighting=false&displayGroups=&sortBy=&source =&search_within_results=&action=e&catId=&activityType=&scanId=&docu mentId=GALE%7CBT2310013896&userGroupName=muohio_main&jsid=e667f dd94ba897dc323f6f45foed510a (accessed September 14, 2012).

25. *Boston Daily Journal*, November 23. Charles Hale also wrote of Lincoln crying during Everett's speech; *Boston Advertiser*, November 23. Benjamin Brown French noted his own tears and emotion in his diary; French, *Witness to the Young Republic: A Yankee's Journal, 1828–1870*, ed. Donald B. Cole and John J. McDonough (Hanover, N.H.: University Press of New England, 1989), 435.

26. Lincoln to Everett, November 20, Lincoln Papers, LOC; *The Collected Works of Abraham Lincoln*, ed. Roy P. Basler, 9 vols. (New Brunswick, N.J.: Rutgers University Press, 1953–1955), 8: 236, quoting the *Washington Daily Morning Chronicle*, January 25, 1865.

27. *Philadelphia Public Ledger*, November 23.

28. *Boston Advertiser*, November 23; Charles Hale to Edward Everett Hale, November 24, Hale Family Papers, Smith Library Archives.

29. Lincoln to Everett, November 20, Lincoln Papers, LOC. In contrast, the *New York World*, November 21, derided Everett's argument. *Cincinnati Daily Commercial*, November 23.

30. Diary, November 19, Everett Papers, MSHS; Young, *Men and Memories*, 1: 72. Clark E. Carr also recalled that Lincoln "rose to grasp his [Everett's] hand and say something I could not hear"; *Chicago Tribune*, February 12, 1900.

31. Charles Hale to Edward Everett Hale, November 24, Hale Family Papers, Smith Library Archives.

32. *Memoirs of Henry Eyster Jacobs: Notes on the Life of a Churchman*, ed. Henry E. Horn (Huntington, Pa.: Church Management Service, 1974), 148; "Reminiscences of Isaak Jackson Allen," ed. John Simon, *Ohio History* 73 (Autumn 1964), 231; *Cincinnati Commercial*, November 23.

33. French, diary for December 2, in *Witness to the Young Republic*, 439; *Cleveland Plain Dealer*, November 25; MacVeagh, "Lincoln at Gettysburg," 22. Isaak Allen wrote that Lincoln on the train had a headache from being in the sun; Allen, typescript "Reminiscences" [1904], Allen Papers, LOC, 24. Armond S. Goldman and Frank C. Schmalstieg Jr. argue that Lincoln's illness was indeed smallpox and was quite serious, and that he contracted it from Tad and passed it to William Johnson; Goldman and Schmalstieg, "Abraham Lincoln's Gettysburg Illness," *Journal of Medical Biography* 15 (2007): 104–110. See also Roy P. Basler, "Did President Lincoln Give the Smallpox to William H. Johnson?" *Huntington Library Quarterly* 35, no. 3 (May 1972): 279–284. Calvin Hamilton thought Lincoln "listless"; quoted in Carmichael, *Lincoln's Gettysburg Address*, 74. See also Donald R. Hopkins, *The Greatest Killer: Smallpox in History*, rev. ed. (Chicago: University of Chicago Press, 2002), 277.

34. *Cincinnati Daily Commercial*, November 23; Carr, *Lincoln at Gettysburg*, 57; *New York Times*, November 4. The famous photograph of Lincoln on the stand at Gettysburg at the National Archives was probably taken just as he arrived on the platform; http://blogs.archives.gov/prologue/?p=2564 (accessed September 14, 2010). Philip B. Kunhardt Jr. discusses the possible identities of those in the photograph, including the conclusions of Josephine Cobb, who in 1952 first recognized that this previously unidentified photograph actually showed Lincoln at Gettysburg; Kunhardt, *A New Birth of Freedom: Lincoln at Gettysburg* (Boston: Little, Brown, 1983), 190.

35. Jacobs, *Lincoln's Gettysburg World-Message*, 63; the family had kept detailed records of the weather for decades. *Washington Daily Morning Chronicle*, November 21.

36. *Greenfield [Mass.] Daily Recorder*, December 1, 1921, reporting the death of Benjamin Tuttle; clipping in File 10-8a, GNMP; *Bellingham [Pa.] Herald*, January 20, 2009.

37. *Washington Daily Morning Chronicle*, November 20; *Philadelphia Inquirer*, November 20; *Boston Journal*, November 23.

38. *Cincinnati Daily Gazette*, November 23. Hay had originally written "words of consecration" and then changed it to "lines"; Hay, *Inside Lincoln's White House*, 113. Curtin, quoted in Horatio King, *Turning On the Light: A Dispassionate Survey of President Buchanan's Administration* (Philadelphia: J. B. Lippincott, 1895), 237; *Philadelphia Evening Bulletin*, November 20; Elias Price letter dated November 23, file 10-18, GNMP; *Indianapolis Daily Journal*, November 23.

39. John G. Nicolay and John Hay, *Abraham Lincoln: A History*, 10 vols. (New York: Century, 1890), 8: 199; Carr, *Lincoln at Gettysburg*, 52; *Boston Advertiser*, November 23; *Philadelphia Evening Bulletin*, November 20.

40. Lincoln to James Conkling, August 37, in *Collected Works*, 6: 414; Hale quoted in John A. Andrew, *Address of His Excellency John A. Andrew, to the Two Branches of the Legislature of Massachusetts, January 8, 1864* (Boston: Wright and Potter, 1864), lxxii. On Lincoln as an orator, see Wayne C. Temple, "Lincoln the

Lecturer," *Lincoln Herald* 101, no. 3 (Fall 1999): 94–110, and 101, no. 4 (Winter 1999): 146–163; Waldo W. Braden, *Abraham Lincoln, Public Speaker* (Baton Rouge: Louisiana State University Press, 1988); Lois J. Einhorn, *Abraham Lincoln the Orator: Penetrating the Lincoln Legend* (Westport, Conn.: Greenwood, 1992).

41. *Boston Advertiser,* November 23; *Cincinnati Daily Gazette,* November 23; *Hanover Spectator,* November 25, quoted in *Encounter at Hanover: Prelude to Gettysburg* (Shippensburg, Pa.: White Mane, 1988; reprinted from Hanover, Pa.: Hanover Chamber of Commerce, 1962; page references are to the 1988 edition), 197; City of Boston, *City Document No. 106: Report of the Joint Special Committee on the Burial of the Massachusetts Dead at Gettysburg* (Boston: J. E. Farwell, 1863), 20; *Philadelphia Age,* November 21; *New York World,* November 20. Every history of the speech discusses the press response, but see also Robert S. Harper, *Lincoln and the Press* (New York: McGraw-Hill, 1951); Louis M. Starr, *Bohemian Brigade: Civil War Newsmen in Action* (New York: Knopf, 1954); Joseph George Jr., "The World Will Little Note? The Philadelphia Press and the Gettysburg Address," *Pennsylvania Magazine of History and Biography,* July 1990, 385–397; Earl W. Wiley, "Buckeye Criticism of the Gettysburg Address," *Speech Monographs* 23, no. 1 (March 1956): 1–8; Jared Peatman, "'Lincoln Acted the Clown': Virginia's Newspapers and the Gettysburg Address," in *Virginia at War, 1863,* ed. William C. Davis and James Robertson Jr. (Lexington: University of Kentucky Press, 2009); Ronald F. Reid, "Newspaper Response to the Gettysburg Addresses," *Quarterly Journal of Speech* 53, no. 1 (February 1967): 50–60.

42. Sarah's young hero, William Earnest Goodman, received a Congressional Medal of Honor for service at Chancellorsville; www.cmohs.org (accessed September 20, 2012). Young, *Men and Memories,* 1: 67. The *Washington Daily Morning Chronicle,* November 21, mentioned a photographer, "prominently placed at the outskirts of the main crowd." Frassanito suggests the photographer was David Bacharach; *Early Photography,* 163.

43. Robert Miller, at the time of the ceremonies in Gettysburg, was thirty-six years old and married with two children, though his wife was soon to deliver a third. A younger son, he was the prosperous owner of $2,400 in real property in 1860, according to U.S. census records accessed through Ancestry.com and a family genealogy Web site, http://www.gmccuistion.com/mcquiston15909/b15403.htm (both accessed on September 14, 2012). He was also a member of the Ohio state legislature, according to William H. Lambert, *The Gettysburg Address: When Written, How Received, Its True Form* (Philadelphia: J. B. Lippincott, 1909; reprinted from *Pennsylvania Magazine of History and Biography* 33 [October 1909]; page references are to the Lippincott edition), 9. George W. Hawes, abstract from *Ohio State Gazetteer and Business Directory for 1860–1861,* 2nd ed. (Indianapolis, Ind., 1860), http://ohpreble.ohgenweb.net/eaton.htm (accessed September 14, 2012).

44. Allen's manuscript autobiography written about 1906 similarly stated, "He spoke but seven minutes. But, before he had spoken five minutes that whole assembled multitude were sobbing, and sympathetic tears were dimming all eyes"; Allen

Papers, LOC, also available online at www.jacksonfamilygenealogy.com (accessed September 14, 2012); and "Reminiscences of Isaak Jackson Allen," ed. Simon, 207–238. Before 1863 Allen had briefly met Lincoln on several occasions in Cincinnati. Harper suggests that Allen was angling for a job; *Lincoln and the Press*, 288.

45. "Reminiscences of Isaak Jackson Allen," ed. Simon, 207–238.

46. David Wills, quoted in *Report of the Select Committee,* 50; *Philadelphia Press,* November 21 and 25.

47. Carr, quoted in *Galesburg Evening Mail,* February 13, 1901, and in *Galesburg Daily Republican,* October 7, 1915; *Washington Daily Morning Chronicle,* November 21; *Philadelphia Public Ledger,* November 23.

48. Azor Howitt Nickerson, "Personal Recollections of Two Visits to Gettysburg," *Scribner's Magazine,* July 1893, 27.

49. "Proceedings of the Pennsylvania State Teachers' Association—Thirteenth Annual Session," *Pennsylvania School Journal* 15, no. 171 (September 1866): 51–74. See also Samuel P. Bates, *The Battle of Gettysburg* (Gaithersburg, Md.: Ron R. Sickle Military Books, 1987; reprint of Philadelphia: Davis, 1875; page references are to the 1987 edition), 214; Michael A. Dreese and Timothy H. Smith, *The 151st Pennsylvania Volunteers at Gettysburg: Like Ripe Apples in a Storm* (Jefferson, N.C.: McFarland, 2009), 36; Henry T. Lee, *Address Commemorative of the Services of the Alumni and Former Students of Lafayette College in the War for the Union* (Lafayette, Pa.: Lafayette College, 1867).

50. MacVeagh, "Lincoln at Gettysburg," 22.

51. *New York Times,* May 1, 1864; MacVeagh Family Papers, Pennsylvania Historical Society, http://www2.hsp.org/collections/manuscripts/m/macveagh1616 .htm (accessed September 16, 2012).

Chapter 8. "My Remarks at Gettysburg"

1. Lincoln to Everett, February 4, 1864, Lincoln Papers, LOC.

2. Long-distance messages were "repeated" by automated rekeying, which was notorious for introducing errors; the *Cincinnati Daily Gazette,* November 23, noted that reports to the city had to be "repeated" five times. On the fractured versions of Lincoln's address published in Ohio, see Earl W. Wiley, "Buckeye Criticism of the Gettysburg Address," *Speech Monographs* 23, no. 1 (March 1956): 1–8. See also George B. Prescott, *History, Theory, and Practice of the Electric Telegraph* (Boston: Ticknor and Fields, 1860); Menahem Blondheim, *News over the Wires: The Telegraph and the Flow of Public Information in America, 1844–1897* (Cambridge, Mass.: Harvard University Press, 1994); Richard J. John, *Network Nation: Inventing American Telecommunications* (Cambridge: Cambridge University Press, 2010); Richard Allen Schwarzlose, *The Nation's Newsbrokers,* 2 vols. (Evanston, Ill.: Northeastern University Press, 1989).

3. The reporter who transmitted the Western Presses version wrote in the *Cincinnati Daily Gazette,* November 23, that the version published on the twenty-first had been "murdered" by the telegraph operators and then presented what was

claimed to be the accurate version, which was essentially the AP version as published in New York. This means the Western Presses reporter did not consider his version independent or authentic in comparison to the AP version. Leaving aside two obvious typographical misprints, the text of the *Cincinnati Daily Gazette*'s corrected version of the twenty-third (CincyGZ23) differs in three words from the version published in the *New York Tribune* on November 21; in those three words, the *Tribune* version is the same as the Nicolay delivery text and virtually all other reports of Lincoln's spoken words, suggesting the Western version is not to be preferred.

4. Prescott, *History, Theory, and Practice of the Electric Telegraph,* 385. Boston's five major dailies, for example, all use the words "have given" their lives that the nation might live, while the New York texts consulted read "here gave." Several Baltimore papers read any "other" nation so conceived and so dedicated, a variation repeated further down the line in many of the Washington papers.

5. Other newspapers in the three cities published the speech but they include wider variations. The *Harrisburg Daily Telegraph, Philadelphia North American,* and *Baltimore American,* because of their similarities, bring us closest to the text as telegraphed, rather than to the text as printed in various places. York, Pennsylvania, did not have a daily paper, and its weekly, the *York Gazette,* November 24, took its account from the *Philadelphia Age,* an opposition paper that did not print the speech.

6. Others have sought to create the best version of Lincoln's words or of the AP text of his speech. The most sophisticated version is that in Douglas L. Wilson's *Lincoln's Sword: The Presidency and the Power of Words* (New York: Knopf, 2006), 222, which offers a *New York Tribune* text edited to include three changes based on other AP texts. Similarly, John Carbonell created an "eastern AP" text from New York, Boston, and other papers; Carbonell, *The Early Printings of Abraham Lincoln's Gettysburg Address and What They Reveal about His Spoken Words* (New Castle, Del.: Oak Knoll Press, 2008), 16.

7. Obvious telegraphic variations in the *Harrisburg Daily Telegraph, Philadelphia North American,* and *Baltimore American* versions, the three base texts for reconstructing the original AP text, UrAP, include "general" instead of "great" battle-field, for example; there is no instance in which the three texts give three different wordings for the same passage, nor do the *Harrisburg Daily Telegraph* and *Baltimore American* ever agree with each other against the *Philadelphia North American.* William Lambert similarly identified the *Philadelphia North American* as "freer from obvious errors" than any other AP text; Lambert, *The Gettysburg Address: When Written, How Received, Its True Form* (Philadelphia: J. B. Lippincott, 1909; reprinted from *Pennsylvania Magazine of History and Biography* 33 [October 1909]; page references are to the Lippincott edition), 15.

8. William E. Barton, *Lincoln at Gettysburg: What He Intended to Say; What He Said; What He Was Reported to Have Said; What He Wished He Had Said* (Indianapolis, Ind.: Bobbs-Merrill, 1930), 86, 95, 189. A question about the AP report was raised in the *New York Times,* July 7 and 10, 1887. Gilbert's daughter's story is in the *Philadelphia Evening Bulletin,* November 12, 1940, B-14.

9. Joseph L. Gilbert, "Lincoln in 1861," in *Nineteenth Annual Convention, National Shorthand Reporter's Association: Proceedings of the Annual Meeting Held in the City of Cleveland, Ohio, August 13–16, [1917], at the Hotel Statler* (LaPorte, Ind.: Chase and Shepard, 1917): 131–140. A. E. Elmore also consulted Gilbert's article directly but still accepts Barton's interpretation; Elmore, *Lincoln's Gettysburg Address: Echoes of the Bible and Book of Common Prayer* (Carbondale: Southern Illinois University Press, 2009), 130.

10. John Russell Young, *Men and Memories: Personal Reminiscences,* ed. May D. Russell Young, 2 vols. (New York: F. Tennyson Neely, 1891–1901), 1: 70. An earlier version of Young's memoir was given in the *Philadelphia Evening Star,* July 25, 1891. The circumstances surrounding Gilbert's recollection are given by his daughter in the *Philadelphia Evening Bulletin,* November 12, 1940, B-14.

11. Garry Wills built much of his interpretation of the texts, including his argument for a hypothetical text he called the "Wills Text" as the delivery text, on the inaccurate Barton version of the Gilbert story; Wills, *Lincoln at Gettysburg: The Words That Remade America* (New York: Simon and Schuster, 1992), 191, 195. Gabor Boritt does not mention Barton or Gilbert; Boritt, *The Gettysburg Gospel: The Lincoln Speech That Nobody Knows* (New York: Simon and Schuster, 2008). Douglas Wilson saw that Barton had misinterpreted Gilbert; *Lincoln's Sword,* 216, 220, 221.

12. Gilbert gave a personal memory of seeing Lincoln leading the parade back to town after the ceremony, but he said nothing about talking with Lincoln or receiving the manuscript from anyone. Gilbert even criticized reports that indicated applause during the speech, stating, "I heard none," yet the AP report he has long been credited with writing included six indications of "applause" during Lincoln's speech. As Gilbert had carefully said, "I was relied on" to take shorthand notes, but he did not say he had done so; Gilbert, "Lincoln in 1861," 135, 134. Even this statement essentially repeats John Russell Young's statement that "it was my duty" to take down the speech and Young's admission that he did not do so; Young, *Men and Memories,* 1: 59.

13. "A. S." in the *New York Times,* July 7 and 10, 1887. "A. S." was probably Abram S. Mitchell, one of the principal *New York Times* reporters in Washington during the war, although at that time he signed his dispatches "York"; J. Cutler Andrews, *The North Reports the Civil War* (Pittsburgh, Pa.: University of Pittsburgh Press, 1955), 40; Louis M. Starr, *Bohemian Brigade: Civil War Newsmen in Action* (New York: Knopf, 1954), 311.

14. The highly detailed memoir, written from contemporary notes and diary entries, by the AP agent in Washington gives no indication that he was at Gettysburg; Louis A. Gobright, *Recollection of Men and Things at Washington, during the Third of a Century,* 2nd ed. (Philadelphia: Claxton, Remsen, and Haffelfinger, 1869), 339. *Cincinnati Daily Gazette,* November 23.

15. Davenport was working the night shift at the paper while studying law. Not long after the ceremony, he was appointed an assistant provost marshal and served

in the Bureau of Military Information. After the war he became a lawyer and was a prominent elections reformer; Amzi B. Davenport, *Supplement to the History and Genealogy of the Davenport Family* (Stamford, Conn.: Printed by the author, 1876), 324; Richard Gleason Greene, *The International Cyclopedia: A Compendium of Human Knowledge* (New York: Dodd, Mead, 1890), 4: 901. L. Starr consulted the *Tribune* archive but did not connect Davenport to the AP report; Starr, *Bohemian Brigade,* 226.

16. David Wills in his 1890 statement mentioned "stenographers" taking down Lincoln's speech; David Wills, "Statement Given by Judge Wills to Charles M. McCurdy, about 1890," in *Lincoln at the Wills Home and the Gettysburg Address,* by Henry E. Luhrs (Shippensburg, Pa.: Lincoln Publishers, 1938), 17. When Charles Hale published his own version of the speech in 1864, he stated that the newspaper reports were incorrect; he would not have made this claim had the manuscript been given to the reporters; John A. Andrew, *Address of His Excellency John A. Andrew, to the Two Branches of the Legislature of Massachusetts, January 8, 1864* (Boston: Wright and Potter, 1864), xxxv. Similarly, "J. H." of the *Chronicle* mentioned reporters comparing their "phonographic" reports afterward on the train returning to Washington. Because Stockton's prayer and Everett's oration were already printed, this comment would seem to refer to Lincoln's remarks, but such comparisons would not be needed had the manuscript been made available; *Washington Daily Morning Chronicle,* November 21. *Cincinnati Commercial,* November 21.

17. James Speed, in the *Louisville Commercial,* November 12, 1879; the wording seems to imply that this comparison took place directly after the speech and so could be construed as supporting John Russell Young's assertion that the speech was given to the reporter for the AP, but Lincoln's story rules this out. It is more likely that Speed had compressed events, and that what he described was Lincoln having told him about his revisions of the speech back in Washington after the ceremony. Brooks also mentioned that afterward Lincoln revised his speech, but his statements are ambiguous about the nature and purpose of the revision; Noah Brooks, *Abraham Lincoln: The Nation's Leader in the Great Struggle through Which Was Maintained the Existence of the United States* (Washington, D.C.: National Tribune, 1888), 377; Brooks to Richard Gilder, February 3, 1894, in *Lincoln Observed: Civil War Dispatches of Noah Brooks,* ed. Michael Burlingame (Baltimore: Johns Hopkins University Press, 1998), 89. John G. Nicolay, "Lincoln's Gettysburg Address," *Century Magazine,* February 1894, 602. See also Michael Burlingame, "Lincoln Spins the Press," in *Lincoln Reshapes the Presidency,* ed. Charles M. Hubbard (Macon, Ga.: Mercer University Press, 2003), 65–78.

18. Reports that may have been independently prepared include those in the *Philadelphia Inquirer,* November 20 (PhilInq20); *Washington Daily Morning Chronicle,* November 20; *Cincinnati Commercial,* November 21; City of Boston, *City Document No. 106: Report of the Joint Special Committee on the Burial of the Massachusetts Dead at Gettysburg* (Boston: J. E. Farwell, 1863), 20, first published in December 1863. All combine different traits across the usual geographic

lines, suggesting consultations across texts; all are also incomplete, suggesting a technical explanation for at least some of their unusual traits. Their collective impact when comparing texts is nearly zero, however, for their idiosyncrasies cancel each other out, and they never agree against the major texts. Carbonell's close study of these and other reports similarly concludes that "a published text could just be the result of plausible wording from partial notes, vague memories, specific information from others, or general hearsay, all somehow cobbled together"; Carbonell, *The Early Printings*, 30.

19. Hale, quoted in Andrew, *Address of His Excellency*, xxxv. Twelve years later the *Boston Advertiser*, September 3, 1875, added that Hale had taken his notes "in longhand." James G. Randall wrongly thought that the text published in the *Boston Advertiser* in November 1863 was the Hale text (the Hale text was actually published in spring 1864), an error followed by L. Starr, invalidating his comparison of texts, and, more seriously, followed also by Garry Wills; Randall, *Lincoln the President*, 4 vols. (New York: Dodd, Mead, 1945–1955), 2: 314; Starr, *Bohemian Brigade*, 230; Wills, *Lincoln at Gettysburg*, 294n15.

20. Most notably, the Hale64 has "have given" but not "poor" power, a combination that is found only in Boston papers, such as the *Boston Evening Transcript*, November 20 (BosEveT20). The one exception is the *Cincinnati Daily Gazette* of November 21, which is clearly a western text; all the western texts consulted have "poor" except the *Gazette*; the lack of "poor" in the *Gazette* appears to be an accident. The lack of "poor" in the Hale64 undermines its claims to independence, as this conforms to the pattern of the disappearance of "poor" from AP texts published in New York and to the north. Perhaps Hale was correct and the Boston texts also just happen to have arrived at the same words by accident, but the fact that the Nicolay delivery text and the UrAP are unlike the Hale64 in both cases argues against Lincoln having said this precise combination.

21. Perhaps the most significant difference between these two is that the UrAP refers to "our poor power to add or to detract," whereas the Hale64, like the New York versions of the AP that were long taken as definitive (and, as noted, like the Boston texts), does not have "poor" or the "to" in "to detract." Nor is "poor" in the *Cincinnati Commercial* summary, although it is in most of the Western Presses texts. "Poor" has been retained in the UrAP version because it is found in all three of the base UrAP texts; in addition, it is in the Nicolay delivery text and in all of Lincoln's later handwritten versions.

22. Louis A. Warren, *Lincoln's Gettysburg Declaration: "A New Birth of Freedom"* (Fort Wayne, Ind.: Lincoln National Life Foundation, 1964), 155.

23. Microfilm reel 46, Everett Papers, MSHS. Carbonell's *Early Printings*, 19–20, is the only other source to discuss this document, but Carbonell argues on the basis of the placement of two dashes that it was not the one printed by Everett in the Little, Brown edition; rather, Carbonell argues that Everett was working from a text now lost, possibly sent him by John Hay.

24. Everett to David Wills, January 9, 1864, Everett Papers, MSHS, in which

Everett does not mention a text of Lincoln's speech in a short list of items he was waiting to receive. David Wills wrote William Lambert about using a newspaper version; in Lambert, *The Gettysburg Address*, 17. Had David Wills ever received a Lincoln text, he would have been very interested in pointing this out in his correspondence and statements, a fact underscored by Edward McPherson, who wrote Nicolay on November 28, 1893, that he was "quite confident that Mr. Lincoln did not comply with the request" to send Wills a manuscript; box 5, Nicolay Papers, LOC.

25. What is called here the DWills document, which exists, is not the hypothetical Wills Text that Garry Wills asserts was Lincoln's manuscript delivery text that he sent to David Wills for printing; G. Wills, *Lincoln at Gettysburg*, 195; see note 11 above. Variations among the versions of the speech as printed in various cities easily identify the DWills text as a New York version, and the punctuation of the DWills text as first written most closely matches the *Tribune*'s text; for example, the *New York Times* differs from both in reading "Fourscore." David Wills changed four words in the NYTrib20 text in the DWills document as last written: (1) "refinished" in the *Tribune* became "unfinished," an obvious correction; (2) "that" cause became "the" cause, probably a copying error; (3 and 4) "Governments" became "the government," but in this phrase the DWills text as first written (the UrDWills) followed the NYTrib20 text perfectly, meaning that David Wills deliberately edited this phrase, probably on the basis of another newspaper version.

26. Wills to Lincoln requesting the manuscript, November 23, 1863; Everett to Lincoln, January 30, 1864, promising to send soon the official publication of the cemetery dedication proceedings and asking for the manuscript in order to sell it and Lincoln's letter to him of November 20; Lincoln to Everett, February 4, 1864, noting, "Yours of Jan. 30th was received four days ago; and since then the address mentioned has arrived"; Everett to Lincoln, March 3, 1864, thanking Lincoln for his letter of February 4 (Everett accidentally wrote "January") and for the manuscript, both of which arrived "this day"; all in Lincoln Papers, LOC. On Nicolay's absence, see John Hay, *Inside Lincoln's White House: The Complete Civil War Diary of John Hay*, ed. Michael Burlingame and John R. Turner Ettlinger (Carbondale: Southern Illinois University Press, 1997), 117, 122. In his diary between November 23 and December 9, Hay does not mention speaking with Nicolay. There are no writings by Nicolay in his papers from this time until December 7; John G. Nicolay, *With Lincoln in the White House: Letters, Memoranda, and Other Writings of John G. Nicolay, 1860–1865*, ed. Michael Burlingame (Carbondale: Southern Illinois University Press, 2000), 121. Given that Wills's request was dated November 23, a note of December 1 from John Hay to John Dix supports the argument that Lincoln's illness would have prevented him from responding immediately: "I have not been permitted until today to present to the President your communication of the 23rd November," and Hay added that Lincoln remained quite ill; Lincoln Papers, LOC. Everett to Nicolay, March 3, 1864, thanking him for his letter of February 29 sending the manuscript; Everett Papers, MSHS. The

"Everett" document had probably not been sent upon its completion in early February because Nicolay was too busy: John Hay was away from Washington from January 14 to March 24, and Nicolay at this time complained bitterly about the amount of work he faced every day; see Nicolay, *With Lincoln in the White House*, 127, 131, 142, 183.

27. Lincoln to George Bancroft, February 29, 1864, transmitting what would be called the Bancroft manuscript intended for use in *Autograph Leaves*; John P. Kennedy to Lincoln and John P. Kennedy to Seward, March 4, 1864, requesting a new copy; Alexander Bliss to Nicolay, Monday, March 7, 1864, sending a sheet with the proper margins and promising to return the Bancroft text in case Lincoln needed it for copying (Bliss added, "I shall send the previous copy with great regret as being a certainty in hand and also because I had promised my father [his step-father, George Bancroft] to return it to him after the lithographing. I therefore beg that you will return it with the new copy"); all in Lincoln Papers, LOC. The cover letter of March 11, 1864, by Lincoln or Nicolay transmitting the Bliss (and probably the Bancroft) appears to be missing, but the date is given in Nicolay, "Lincoln's Gettysburg Address," 605.

28. The hypothesis that Lincoln could have copied all three from a now lost text is rendered implausible by the fact that the one-word change between the Everett and the Bancroft ("upon" in "upon this continent" being replaced by "on") was also continued into the Bliss. From the Bancroft to the Bliss, Lincoln also deleted "here" in the phrase that first read, "that cause for which they here gave the last full measure of devotion." Lincoln deleted eight commas from the Everett to the Bliss; he also added one hyphen to the Bancroft but then removed it in the Bliss, for no net change, another sign of care. Given the complex punctuation of certain passages of the Everett text (which, for example, has seven dashes), this consistency is strong evidence that the few changes between the Everett and Bliss texts were the result of intentional thought. Nicolay came to the same conclusion, seemingly based on his participation in the correspondence involving the three final texts; Nicolay, "Lincoln's Gettysburg Address," 605.

29. *The Collected Works of Abraham Lincoln*, ed. Roy P. Basler, 9 vols. (New Brunswick, N.J.: Rutgers University Press, 1953–1955), 7: 18. David C. Mearns and Lloyd A. Dunlap stated that uncertainty about the "Hay" text is the reason why we cannot know "when and where the Gettysburg Address was written"; Mearns and Dunlap, "Notes and Comments on the Preparation of the Address," in *Long Remembered: Facsimilies of the Five Versions of the Gettysburg Address*, ed. David C. Mearns and Lloyd A. Dunlap (Washington, D.C.: Library of Congress, 1963), n.p.

30. The discovery in 1908 of the Hay text among the papers of John Hay raised delicate questions of ownership, which prompted a variety of explanations about the origins of the Hay, including that Lincoln gave or made it for John Hay as a souvenir; see James Grant Wilson in the *New York Times*, June 29, 1913, and his "Recollections of Lincoln," *Putnam's Magazine*, February 1909, 515–529. Two

important studies have argued that the Hay was made as a souvenir for John Hay: Mearns and Dunlap's "Notes and Comments," n.p., and Garry Wills's *Lincoln at Gettysburg,* 200; compare Martin Johnson's "Who Stole the Gettysburg Address?" *Journal of the Abraham Lincoln Association* 24, no. 2 (Summer 2003): 2–19. Among those who have argued that the Hay was the delivery text are William E. Barton in *Lincoln at Gettysburg,* 69; Roy P. Basler in *Collected Works,* 7: 18; Gabor Boritt in *The Gettysburg Gospel,* 119; Robert Fortenbaugh in *Lincoln and Gettysburg* (Gettysburg, Pa.: Bookmart, 1949), 12; and Carl Sandburg in *Abraham Lincoln: The War Years,* 4 vols. (New York: Harcourt, Brace: 1939), 2: 445.

31. Nicolay, "Lincoln's Gettysburg Address," 604.

32. Nicolay to Richard W. Gilder, September 19, 1885, in "Some Correspondence Regarding a Missing Copy of the Gettysburg Address," *Lincoln Lore* 1437 (November 1957), 2. Nicolay's decision to ignore the Hay caused tremendous confusion in the scholarship of the speech and even contributed to the suspicion that John Nicolay had stolen or inappropriately seized Lincoln's delivery text and had shaped his 1894 article to cover his crime; for a different view, see Johnson, "Who Stole?" 18. Robert Todd Lincoln to Isaac Markens, December 8, 1915, in R. T. Lincoln, *A Portrait of Abraham Lincoln in Letters by His Oldest Son,* ed. Paul M. Angle (Chicago: Chicago Historical Society, 1968), 21.

33. Nicolay, "Lincoln's Gettysburg Address," 604. Nicolay incorrectly thought Wills had a text written by Lincoln. This probably led him to more readily associate Lincoln's post-speech revision with Wills's request for a manuscript, which Nicolay knew was the only way Wills could have a copy written by Lincoln; Nicolay to Richard W. Gilder, September 19, 1885, in "Some Correspondence," 2. Another mistake by Nicolay has also caused confusion: without access to earlier post-speech versions, Nicolay simply published the words of the Bliss text as those of Lincoln's post-speech revision, based on his conviction that Lincoln had made no changes in the wording; this was an error of interpretation, but it is not evidence that Nicolay was trying to mislead future researchers.

34. Louis Warren also argued that the post-speech revision took place in response to Everett's request, but he did not associate this revision with the Hay document; Warren, *Lincoln's Gettysburg Declaration,* 162.

35. Most of the changes Wills made to the NYTrib20 replicate other published versions (notably, that in the *Baltimore American*), so they cannot prove that the LittleBrown was Lincoln's copy text. Three of the twelve word changes Lincoln made when copying and writing the UrHay are evidently copying errors by Lincoln and so have no apparent conceptual basis: a doubled word is deleted, and two words, without which the phrases in question make no sense, were omitted and later reinserted.

36. Garry Wills argued that the LittleBrown was actually a copy of a "Lincoln text" and contains the words of Lincoln's now lost delivery text; G. Wills, *Lincoln at Gettysburg,* 195. Others who also have advocated for a now lost delivery text include A. E. Elmore in *Lincoln's Gettysburg Address,* 232; Frank L. Klement in *The*

Gettysburg Soldiers' Cemetery and Lincoln's Address: Aspects and Angles (Shippensburg, Pa.: White Mane, 1993), 145; and Douglas L. Wilson in *Lincoln's Sword*, 288.

37. Lloyd Ostendorf brought the document forward formally in "Turning the Pages of History: A New Draft of the Gettysburg Address Located," *Gettysburg Magazine*, January 1, 1992, 107–112. Frank L. Klement revised his history of the speech to incorporate this "sixth copy"; Klement, *The Gettysburg Soldiers' Cemetery*, 145. Correspondence and a noncommittal laboratory report on the paper may be found in the "Lost Copy" file, drawer 6, of the former Lincoln Museum, Fort Wayne, now the Lincoln Financial Foundation Collection held by the Indiana State Museum, Indianapolis, and the Allen County [Indiana] Public Library. The Library of Congress transcription of Wills's November 2 letter inviting Lincoln to Gettysburg also incorrectly described Wills as a judge; "David Wills to Abraham Lincoln, Monday, November 02, 1863," *The Abraham Lincoln Papers at the Library of Congress*, http://memory.loc.gov/cgi-bin/query/r?ammem/mal:@field(DOCID+@lit(d2778300)) (accessed September 14, 2012).

38. Nicolay, "Lincoln's Gettysburg Address," 602; *Eaton [Ohio] Register*, November 30.

39. Rudolph R. Reeder, *The Historical Development of School Readers and of Method in Teaching Reading* (New York: Macmillan, 1900), 39.

40. John Defrees, quoted in Allen C. Guelzo, "Holland's Informants: The Construction of Josiah Holland's *Life of Abraham Lincoln*," *Journal of the Abraham Lincoln Association* 23, no. 1 (Winter 2002): 46.

41. The fact that Lincoln's manuscript is unique in these and similar markers, including capitalization, provides additional evidence that Lincoln's manuscript was not copied for any of the newspaper reports. The version published in the city of Boston's *City Document No. 106*, 20, first published in December 1863, which is very different from the delivery text and spoken words, also placed the phrase in quotes. This is probably a coincidence, but it is not impossible that the authors, who were part of the official delegation of the city of Boston, saw the first page while Lincoln was speaking, just as "Medicus" saw the letterhead; *New York Times*, May 22, 1882.

42. Even the variation in the *Pittsburgh Gazette* of November 21 states that Lincoln used the word "met"; only the summary in *Cincinnati Commercial*, November 21, reads "come," probably a coincidental similarity. This passage provides strong evidence that, at least in this passage, Lincoln when creating the Hay was not attempting to recreate his spoken words.

43. Douglas L. Wilson and Rodney O. Davis, *Herndon's Informants: Letters, Interviews, and Statements about Abraham Lincoln* (Urbana: University of Illinois Press, 1998), 360.

44. This anecdote has long been known but was believed to have first appeared only after Lincoln's assassination, lessening its value and authority. One "KHirsch" writing on WikiQuote.org, however, discovered that it appeared first in the *New*

York Evangelist 35, no. 46 (November 17, 1864): 4; http://en.wikiquote.org/wiki /Talk:Abraham_Lincoln#I_do_love_Jesus (accessed September 14, 2012).

45. John Nicolay included "under God" among the changes he suggests that Lincoln had decided upon during the ceremonies; Nicolay, "Lincoln's Gettysburg Address," 604. Carl Sandburg asserted that Lincoln had decided upon "under God" the night before but did not change his delivery text (which Sandburg believes to have been the Hay); Sandburg, *Abraham Lincoln,* 2: 445. Garry Wills noted that Everett mentioned "under Providence"; G. Wills, *Lincoln at Gettysburg,* 268n19. For an alternative to the view taken here, see Elmore, *Lincoln's Gettysburg Address,* 129. The literature on Lincoln's belief is ably surveyed in Samuel W. Calhoun and Lucas E. Morel, "Abraham Lincoln's Religion: The Case for His Ultimate Belief in a Personal, Sovereign God," *Journal of the Abraham Lincoln Association* 33, no. 1 (Winter 2012): 38–74.

46. R. C. McCormick, *New York Evening Post,* May 3, 1865.

47. The only printed version with the placement Lincoln adopted is *City Document No. 106* (CD106), printed in December 1863, which Lincoln may have consulted during the post-speech revision because CD106 is also the only printed text with the words "who fought here," which Lincoln also included in the Everett, but it may be that these are coincidences; City of Boston, *City Document No. 106,* 20.

48. Barton, *Lincoln at Gettysburg,* 106, mentioned Everett's underlining, which is also recreated in a note in box 83 of the Mearns Papers, LOC, but not on the basis of the UrAP.

49. William Eleroy Curtis, *The True Abraham Lincoln* (Philadelphia: J. B. Lippincott, 1902), 88; Brooks, *Lincoln Observed,* 89.

Conclusion: Who Wrote the Gettysburg Address?

1. Longfellow to G. W. Curtis, November 19, in *The Letters of Henry Wadsworth Longfellow,* ed. Andrew Hilen, vol. 4 (Cambridge, Mass.: Harvard University Press, 1972), 366, 368.

2. "The Lounger," *Harper's Weekly,* December 5; *Harper's Weekly,* January 9, 1864, and April 23, 1864.

3. *Frank Leslie's Illustrated Newspaper,* April 16, 1864; "Lincoln never in his life thought in the style of the address at Gettysburg," according to *Wilkes' Spirit of the Times,* November 28.

4. "The Color Guard," *North American Review* 99, no. 204 (July 1864), 172; James Russell Lowell, "Ode Recited at the Harvard Commemoration, July 21, 1865," in *The Poetical Works of James Russell Lowell* (London: Ward, Lock, 1880), 293.

5. *Philadelphia Evening Bulletin,* November 20; *New York World,* November 21. MacVeagh claims to have repeated his praise on the train returning to Washington, when Lincoln again modestly said, "You are more extravagant than ever, and you are the only person who has such a misconception of what I said"; I. Wayne MacVeagh, "Lincoln at Gettysburg," *Century Magazine,* November 1909, 22.

John Russell Young, *Men and Memories: Personal Reminiscences,* ed. May D. Russell Young, 2 vols. (New York: F. Tennyson Neely, 1891–1901), 1: 69.

6. The first published version of Everett's compliment on the stand appears to be, "Ah, Mr. Lincoln, how gladly I would exchange all my hundred pages, to have been the author of your twenty lines," but other versions circulated; Isaac N. Arnold, *The History of Abraham Lincoln and the Overthrow of American Slavery* (Chicago: Clarke, 1866), 424. Ward Lamon's later story of Everett and Seward expressing disappointment appears to translate Lamon's own response to the speech; see Rodney O. Davis, "Lincoln's 'Particular Friend' and Lincoln Biography," *Journal of the Abraham Lincoln Association* 19, no. 1 (Winter 1998), 25.

7. John Hay, *Inside Lincoln's White House: The Complete Civil War Diary of John Hay,* ed. Michael Burlingame and John R. Turner Ettlinger (Carbondale: Southern Illinois University Press, 1997), 113; *Washington Daily Morning Chronicle,* November 21; *Baltimore American,* November 20; *Boston Daily Journal,* November 23; *Indianapolis Daily Journal,* November 23; *Milwaukee Sentinel,* November 25.

8. An anonymous newspaper clipping dated 1923 records the recollection of Mrs. Clara McCrea, who claimed to have seen Curtin's gallantry in person; Lincoln Museum, Fort Wayne, now the Lincoln Financial Foundation Collection held by the Indiana State Museum, Indianapolis, and the Allen County [Indiana] Public Library. Seventy years later Mrs. Malcomb Orlando Smith stated that Lincoln kissed her at Gettysburg—she must have been a child at the time; *Baltimore American,* May 27, 1934.

9. Diary, November 19, Everett Papers, MSHS; *Milwaukee Sentinel,* November 25; *Philadelphia Press,* November 21; *New York World,* November 21. On the Ohio ceremony, see Earl W. Wiley, "Colonel Charles Anderson's Gettysburg Address" *Lincoln Herald* 54, no. 1 (Spring 1952): 14–21. Curtin took the opportunity to thank Everett, though he was not present; *Cincinnati Daily Commercial,* November 23. Orton H. Carmichael, *Lincoln's Gettysburg Address* (New York: Abingdon Press, 1917), 78, citing the recollections of old Gettysburgers.

10. Louis A. Warren, *Lincoln's Gettysburg Declaration: "A New Birth of Freedom"* (Fort Wayne, Ind.: Lincoln National Life Foundation, 1964), 152.

11. Martin Johnson, "Who Stole the Gettysburg Address?" *Journal of the Abraham Lincoln Association* 24, no. 2 (Summer 2003): 2–19.

12. Wills referred to the speech as "remarks" in his letters to Lincoln of November 2 and November 23; Lincoln Papers, LOC. Everett followed this vocabulary in his letters to Lincoln of November 20, 1863, and January 30, 1864. News reports at the time of the speech generally called it "dedicatory remarks" or "dedicatory speech"; in the program for the ceremony it was titled "Dedicatory Remarks by the President of the United States"; microfilm reel 46, Everett Papers, MSHS. Wills may have been the first to formally call the speech an "address," writing "President Lincoln's Address" at the top of the copy he made for printing, but before sending it to Everett he changed it to "Dedicatory Address of President Lincoln," which is

the title as published in the Little, Brown "authorized" edition. Kennedy suggested the eventual title in a letter to Lincoln, March 4, 1864; Lincoln Papers, LOC.

13. Richard J. Ellis, *To the Flag: The Unlikely History of the Pledge of Allegiance* (Lawrence: University Press of Kansas, 2007), 125.

14. See, for example, Lincoln's speeches of August 18 and 22, 1864; Lincoln Papers, LOC. This was the context behind Lincoln's dramatic Blind Memorandum of August 23, 1864, which committed the cabinet to exceptional measures to win the war before the inauguration of a new president, because afterward military victory would be impossible. This was also when Lincoln met with Frederick Douglass to initiate a federally supported underground railroad system to remove enslaved people from a possibly independent Confederacy. The Democratic Party platform of 1864 called for an armistice and negotiations with the Confederacy.

15. Lincoln in a letter intended for publication and addressed to Henry L. Pierce, April 6, 1859, in *The Collected Works of Abraham Lincoln,* ed. Roy P. Basler, 9 vols. (New Brunswick, N.J.: Rutgers University Press, 1953–1955), 3: 174.

Bibliography

Archives

Adams County Historical Society, Gettysburg, Pa.

Carr, Clark E., file. Galesburg Public Library, Galesburg, Ill.

Chilton, R. S., Jr., Papers. Georgetown University Library, Washington, D.C. http://www.library.georgetown.edu/dept/speccoll/chilton/index.htm.

Everett, Edward, Papers. Massachusetts State Historical Society, Boston.

Franklin and Marshall College Library Archives. http://library.fandm.edu/archives/.

Gettysburg National Military Park Archives. Gettysburg, Pa.

Hale Family Papers. Smith College Library, Northhampton, Mass.

Lamon, Ward, Papers. Huntington Library, San Marino, Calif.

Library of Congress, Washington D.C. Papers of Isaak Jackson Allen; Montgomery Blair; Abraham Lincoln; Edward McPherson; David C. Mearns; John G. Nicolay; William Saunders, Gideon Welles.

Lincoln Museum, Fort Wayne, now the Lincoln Financial Foundation Collection held by the Indiana State Museum, Indianapolis, and the Allen County [Indiana] Public Library.

MacVeagh Family Papers. Pennsylvania Historical Society, Philadelphia. http://www2.hsp.org/collections/manuscripts/m/macveagh1616.htm.

National Archives. www.archives.gov/.

Seward, William H., Papers. University of Rochester Library, Rochester, N.Y.

Published Works

An Account of the Pilgrim Celebration at Plymouth, August 1, 1853. Boston: Crosby, Nichols, 1853.

Address of Honorable Edward Everett at the Consecration of the National Cemetery at Gettysburg 19th November, 1863, with the Dedication Speech of President Lincoln and the Other Exercises of the Occasion. Boston: Little, Brown, 1864.

Alexander, John, and Jim Slade. *Firestorm at Gettysburg: Civilian Voices June– November 1863*. Atglen, Pa.: Schiffer, 2004.

Allen, Isaak Jackson. "Reminiscences of Isaak Jackson Allen." Edited by John Simon. *Ohio History* 73 (Autumn 1964): 207–238.

Almon, John, ed. *An Asylum for Fugitive Pieces*. 2 vols. London: J. Debrett, 1786.

Andrew, John A. *Address of His Excellency John A. Andrew, to the Two Branches of the Legislature of Massachusetts, January 8, 1864*. Boston: Wright and Potter, 1864.

Andrews, E. W. "Lincoln's Kindness of Heart." In *Reminiscences of Abraham Lincoln, by Distinguished Men of His Time*, edited by Allen Thorndike Rice, 287–304. New York: North American Pub. Co., 1886.

Andrews, J. Cutler. *The North Reports the Civil War*. Pittsburgh, Pa.: University of Pittsburgh Press, 1955.

Arnold, Isaac N. *The History of Abraham Lincoln and the Overthrow of American Slavery*. Chicago: Clarke, 1866.

———. *The Life of Abraham Lincoln*. Chicago: Jansen, McClurg, 1885.

Ashley, James M. *Reminiscences of the Great Rebellion: Calhoun, Seward and Lincoln. Address of Hon. J. M. Ashley at Memorial Hall, Toledo, Ohio, June 2, 1890*. New York: Evening Post, 1890.

Bartlett, John. *Familiar Quotations: Being an Attempt to Trace to Their Source Passages and Phrases in Common Use*. 7th ed. Boston: Little, Brown, 1875.

Barton, William E. *Lincoln at Gettysburg: What He Intended to Say; What He Said; What He Was Reported to Have Said; What He Wished He Had Said*. Indianapolis, Ind.: Bobbs-Merrill, 1930.

Basler, Roy P. "Did President Lincoln Give the Smallpox to William H. Johnson?" *Huntington Library Quarterly* 35, no. 3 (May 1972): 279–284.

Bates, Edward. *The Diary of Edward Bates, 1859–1866*. Vol. 4 of *Annual Report of the American Historical Association, 1930*. Edited by Howard K. Beale. Washington, D.C.: GPO, 1933.

Bates, Samuel P. *The Battle of Gettysburg*. Gaithersburg, Md.: Ron R. Sickle Military Books, 1987. Reprint of Philadelphia: Davis, 1875. Page references are to the 1987 edition.

Belz, Herman. *A New Birth of Freedom: The Republican Party and Freedman's Rights, 1861 to 1866*. New York: Fordham University Press, 2000. First ed., Westwood, Conn.: Greenwood Press, 1976.

————. *Reconstructing the Union: Theory and Policy during the Civil War.* Ithaca, N.Y.: Cornell University Press, 1969.

Black, Edwin. "Gettysburg and Silence." *Quarterly Journal of Speech* 80, no. 1 (February 1994): 21–36.

Black, Linda Giberson. *Gettysburg Remembers President Lincoln: Eyewitness Accounts of November 1863.* Gettysburg, Pa.: Thomas Publications, 2005.

Blight, David W. *Race and Reunion: The Civil War in American Memory.* Cambridge, Mass.: Harvard University Press, 2001.

Blondheim, Menahem. *News over the Wires: The Telegraph and the Flow of Public Information in America, 1844–1897.* Cambridge, Mass.: Harvard University Press, 1994.

Blum, Edward J. *Reforging the White Republic: Race, Religion, and American Nationalism, 1865–1898.* Baton Rouge: Louisiana State University Press, 2005.

Blumenthal, Henry. *A Reappraisal of Franco-American Relations, 1830–1871.* Chapel Hill: University of North Carolina Press, 1959.

Bolenius, Emma Miller, ed. *The Boys' and Girls' Readers: Fourth–Sixth Reader.* Vol. 3. Boston: Houghton Mifflin, 1919.

Boman, Dennis K. *Lincoln and Citizens' Rights in Civil War Missouri: Balancing Freedom and Security.* Baton Rouge: Louisiana State University Press, 2011.

————. *Lincoln's Resolute Unionist: Hamilton Gamble, Dred Scott Dissenter and Missouri's Civil War Governor.* Baton Rouge: Louisiana State University Press, 2006.

Boritt, Gabor. *The Gettysburg Gospel: The Lincoln Speech That Nobody Knows.* New York: Simon and Schuster, 2008.

Braden, Waldo W. *Abraham Lincoln, Public Speaker.* Baton Rouge: Louisiana State University Press, 1988.

————. *Building the Myth: Selected Speeches Memorializing Abraham Lincoln.* Urbana: University of Illinois Press, 1990.

Brooks, Noah. *Abraham Lincoln: The Nation's Leader in the Great Struggle through Which Was Maintained the Existence of the United States.* Washington, D.C.: National Tribune, 1888.

————. "Glimpses of Lincoln in Wartime." *Century Magazine,* January 1895, 457–467.

————. *Lincoln Observed: Civil War Dispatches of Noah Brooks.* Edited by Michael Burlingame. Baltimore: Johns Hopkins University Press, 1998.

————. "Personal Recollections of Abraham Lincoln." *Harper's New Monthly Magazine,* July 1865, 222–230.

————. "Personal Reminiscences of Lincoln." *Scribner's Magazine,* February 1878, 561–569.

————. *Washington in Lincoln's Time.* Philadelphia: Century, 1895.

Bullock, Helen D. "The Papers of John G. Nicolay, Lincoln's Secretary." *Library of Congress Quarterly of Current Acquisitions* 7, no. 3 (May 1950): 3–8.

Burke, Edmund. *Memoirs of the Right Honourable Edmund Burke.* Edited by Charles McCormick. London: Lee and Hurst, 1798.

Burlingame, Michael. *Abraham Lincoln: A Life.* 2 vols. Baltimore: Johns Hopkins University Press, 2008.

———. *Abraham Lincoln: The Observations of John G. Nicolay and John Hay.* Carbondale: Southern Illinois University Press, 2007.

———. "Lincoln Spins the Press." In *Lincoln Reshapes the Presidency.* Edited by Charles M. Hubbard, 65–78. Macon, Ga.: Mercer University Press, 2003.

———. "Nicolay and Hay: Court Historians." *Journal of the Abraham Lincoln Association* 19, no. 1 (Winter 1998): 1–20.

Burrage, Henry Sweetser. *Gettysburg and Lincoln: The Battle, the Cemetery, and the National Park.* New York: G. P. Putnam's Sons, 1906.

Calhoun, Samuel W., and Lucas E. Morel. "Abraham Lincoln's Religion: The Case for His Ultimate Belief in a Personal, Sovereign God." *Journal of the Abraham Lincoln Association* 33, no. 1 (Winter 2012): 38–74.

Canadian Almanac and Directory. Toronto: Scobie and Balfour, 1877.

Carbonell, John. *The Early Printings of Abraham Lincoln's Gettysburg Address and What They Reveal about His Spoken Words.* New Castle, Del.: Oak Knoll Press, 2008.

Carman, Harry J., and Reinhard H. Luthin. *Lincoln and the Patronage.* New York: Columbia University Press, 1943.

Carmichael, Orton H. *Lincoln's Gettysburg Address.* New York: Abingdon Press, 1917.

Carpenter, Francis B. *Six Months at the White House with Lincoln: The Story of a Picture.* New York: Hurd and Hudson, 1867.

Carr, Clark E. *Lincoln at Gettysburg: An Address.* 4th ed. Chicago: McClurg, 1909.

Ceremonies at the Dedication of the Soldiers Monument [Newton, Mass.]. Boston: Schism, Franklin Printing, 1864.

Chase, Salmon P. *The Salmon P. Chase Papers.* Edited by John Niven et al. 5 vols. Kent, Ohio: Kent State University Press, 1993–1998.

Childers, Christopher. *The Failure of Popular Sovereignty: Slavery, Manifest Destiny, and the Radicalization of Southern Politics.* Lawrence: University Press of Kansas, 2012.

City of Boston. *City Document No. 106: Report of the Joint Special Committee on the Burial of the Massachusetts Dead at Gettysburg.* Boston: J. E. Farwell, 1863.

Cleutz, David. *Rebels in the Front Yard: Liberty at Gettysburg.* Gettysburg, Pa.: Gettysburg Publishing, 2012.

Clinton, Catherine. *Mrs. Lincoln: A Life.* New York: Harper, 2009.

Clutz, Mrs. Jacob A. [Liberty Hollinger Clutz]. *Some Personal Recollections of the Battle of Gettysburg.* Privately printed, n.d.

Cochrane, Henry Clay. "With Lincoln to Gettysburg, 1863." In *Abraham Lincoln:*

Military Order of the Loyal Legion of the United States, Commandery of the State of Pennsylvania. Memorial Meeting, February 13, 1907, 9–12. [Philadelphia,] 1907.

Coco, Gregory. *A Strange and Blighted Land: Gettysburg, the Aftermath of a Battle.* Gettysburg, Pa.: Thomas Publications, 1995.

Cohen, Gillian, and Martin Conway. *Memory in the Real World.* 3rd ed. New York: Psychology Press, 2008.

"The Color Guard." *North American Review* 99, no. 204 (July 1864): 172.

Cox, LaWanda. *Lincoln and Black Freedom: A Study in Presidential Leadership.* Columbia: University of South Carolina Press, 1981.

Curtis, George Ticknor. *Life of Daniel Webster.* 2 vols. Philadelphia: Appleton, 1870.

Curtis, William Eleroy. *The True Abraham Lincoln.* Philadelphia: J. B. Lippincott, 1902.

Davenport, Amzi B. *Supplement to the History and Genealogy of the Davenport Family.* Stamford, Conn.: Printed by the author, 1876.

Davis, Rodney O. "Lincoln's 'Particular Friend' and Lincoln Biography." *Journal of the Abraham Lincoln Association* 19, no. 1 (Winter 1998): 21–38.

Dirck, Brian R. *Lincoln and the Constitution.* Carbondale: Southern Illinois University Press, 2012.

Donald, David Herbert. *Lincoln.* New York: Simon and Schuster, 1995.

———. *"We Are Lincoln Men": Abraham Lincoln and His Friends.* New York: Simon and Schuster, 2003.

Dreese, Michael A., and Timothy H. Smith. *The 151st Pennsylvania Volunteers at Gettysburg: Like Ripe Apples in a Storm.* Jefferson, N.C.: McFarland, 2009.

"Edward Everett," in *Dictionary of American Biography* (New York: Charles Scribner's Sons, 1936), as it appears at *Biography in Context,* http://ic.galegroup .com.proxy.lib.muohio.edu/ic/bic1/ReferenceDetailsPage/ReferenceDetailsWin dow?failOverType=&query=&prodId=BIC1&windowstate=normal&content Modules=&mode=view&displayGroupName=Reference&limiter=&currPage =&disableHighlighting=false&displayGroups=&sortBy=&source=&search_ within results=&action=e&catId=&activityType=&scanId=&documentId= GALE%7CBT2310013896&userGroupName=muohio_main&jsid=e667fdd94 ba897dc323f6f45foed510a (accessed September 14, 2012).

Egle, William H. *The Life and Times of Andrew G. Curtin.* Philadelphia: Thompson, 1895.

Einhorn, Lois J. *Abraham Lincoln the Orator: Penetrating the Lincoln Legend.* Westport, Conn.: Greenwood, 1992.

Ellis, Richard J. *To the Flag: The Unlikely History of the Pledge of Allegiance.* Lawrence: University Press of Kansas, 2007.

Elliot, Jonathan. *The Debates in the Several State Conventions on the Adoption of the Federal Constitution, as Recommended by the General Convention at Philadelphia, in 1787* .... 2nd ed. 2 vols. Washington, D.C.: Jonathan Elliot, 1836.

Elmore, A. E. *Lincoln's Gettysburg Address: Echoes of the Bible and Book of Common Prayer.* Carbondale: Southern Illinois University Press, 2009.

Encounter at Hanover: Prelude to Gettysburg. Shippensburg, Pa.: White Mane, 1988. Reprinted from Hanover, Pa.: Hanover Chamber of Commerce, 1962. Page references are to the 1988 edition.

Encyclopaedia of Contemporary Biography, of Pennsylvania .... 3 vols. New York: Atlantic Publishing, 1899.

Everett, Edward. *Address of Honorable Edward Everett at the Consecration of the National Cemetery at Gettysburg 19th November, 1863, with the Dedication Speech of President Lincoln and the Other Exercises of the Occasion.* Boston: Little, Brown: 1864.

———. *Orations and Speeches on Various Occasions.* Vol. 4. Boston: Little, Brown, 1868.

Farber, Daniel A. *Lincoln's Constitution.* Chicago: University of Chicago Press, 2003.

Farquhar, Arthur Biggs. *The First Million the Hardest.* New York: Doubleday, 1922.

Fehrenbacher, Don E. *Lincoln in Text and Context: Collected Essays.* Palo Alto, Calif.: Stanford University Press, 1987.

Fleche, Andre M. *The Revolution of 1861: The American Civil War in the Age of Nationalist Conflict.* Chapel Hill: University of North Carolina Press, 2012.

Fletcher, George P. *Our Secret Constitution: How Lincoln Redefined American Democracy.* New York: Oxford University Press, 2001.

Fortenbaugh, Robert. *Lincoln and Gettysburg.* Gettysburg, Pa.: Bookmart, 1949.

Frassanito, William A. *Early Photography at Gettysburg.* Gettysburg, Pa.: Thomas Publications, 1995.

———. *Gettysburg: A Journey in Time.* New York: Scribner, 1975.

French, Benjamin Brown. *Witness to the Young Republic: A Yankee's Journal, 1828–1870.* Edited by Donald B. Cole and John J. McDonough. Hanover, N.H.: University Press of New England, 1989.

Frothingham, Paul Revere. *Edward Everett: Orator and Statesman.* Port Washington, N.Y.: Kennikat Press, 1971. Reprint of Boston: Houghton Mifflin, 1925. Page references are to the 1971 edition.

Fry, James B. "General James B. Fry." In *Reminiscences of Abraham Lincoln, by Distinguished Men of His Time,* ed. Allen Thorndike Rice, 387–404. New York: North American Pub. Co., 1886.

Garner, Bryan A. *A Dictionary of Modern Legal Usage.* 2nd ed. New York: Oxford University Press, 2001.

Georg, Kathleen R. "This Grand National Enterprise: The Origins of Gettysburg's Soldiers' National Cemetery and Gettysburg Battlefield Memorial Association." Paper, May 1982. Accessed September 12, 2012. http://www.gdg.org/Research /BattlefieldHistories/kghgrand.html.

George, Joseph, Jr. "The World Will Little Note? The Philadelphia Press and the

Gettysburg Address." *Pennsylvania Magazine of History and Biography*, July 1990, 385–397.

Gibson, John, ed. *A Biographical History of York County, Pennsylvania*. Chicago: Genealogical Publishing, 1886.

Gilbert, Joseph L. "Lincoln in 1861." In *Nineteenth Annual Convention, National Shorthand Reporter's Association: Proceedings of the Annual Meeting Held in the City of Cleveland, Ohio, August 13–16, [1917] at the Hotel Statler*, 131–140. LaPorte, Ind.: Chase and Shepard, 1917.

Gobright, Louis A. *Recollection of Men and Things at Washington, during the Third of a Century*. 2nd ed. Philadelphia: Claxton, Remsen, and Haffelfinger, 1869.

Goldman, Armond S., and Frank C. Schmalstieg Jr. "Abraham Lincoln's Gettysburg Illness." *Journal of Medical Biography* 15 (2007): 104–110.

Goodwin, Doris Kearns. *Team of Rivals: The Political Genius of Abraham Lincoln*. New York: Simon and Schuster, 2005.

Gramm, Kent. *November: Lincoln's Elegy at Gettysburg*. Bloomington: Indiana University Press, 2001.

Green, Michael S. *Freedom, Union, and Power: Lincoln and His Party during the Civil War*. New York: Fordham University Press: 2004.

Greene, Richard Gleason. *The International Cyclopedia: A Compendium of Human Knowledge*. New York: Dodd, Mead, 1890.

Griffith, A. A. *Lessons in Elocution . . . .* 2nd ed. New York: Barnes and Burr, 1865.

Guelzo, Allen C. "Holland's Informants: The Construction of Josiah Holland's *Life of Abraham Lincoln*." *Journal of the Abraham Lincoln Association* 23, no. 1 (Winter 2002): 1–27.

Harper, Robert S. *Lincoln and the Press*. New York: McGraw-Hill, 1951.

Harris, William C. *Lincoln and the Border States: Preserving the Union*. Lawrence: University Press of Kansas, 2011.

Haultain, Arnold. *Goldwin Smith, His Life and Opinions*. New York: Duffield, 1914.

Hawes, George W. Abstract from *Ohio State Gazetteer and Business Directory for 1860–1861*. 2nd ed. (Indianapolis, Ind. 1860). Accessed September 14, 2012. http://ohpreble.ohgenweb.net/eaton.htm.

Hay, John. *At Lincoln's Side: John Hay's Civil War Correspondence and Selected Writings*. Edited by Michael Burlingame. Carbondale: Southern Illinois University Press, 2000.

———. *Inside Lincoln's White House: The Complete Civil War Diary of John Hay*. Edited by Michael Burlingame and John R. Turner Ettlinger. Carbondale: Southern Illinois University Press, 1997.

———. *Letters of John Hay and Extracts from His Diary*. Edited by Clara Hay and Henry Adams. 3 vols. Privately printed, 1908.

Hewitt, Edward Ringwood. *Those Were the Days: Tales of a Long Life*. New York: World Book, 1943.

History of Cumberland and Adams Counties. Chicago: Warner, Beers, 1886.

Holland, J. G. *The Life of Abraham Lincoln.* Springfield, Mass.: Gurdon Bill, 1866.

Holzer, Harold. *Lincoln at Cooper Union: The Speech That Made Abraham Lincoln President.* New York: Simon and Schuster, 2006.

———, ed. *The Lincoln Mailbag: America Writes to the President, 1861–1865.* Carbondale: Southern Illinois University Press, 1998.

Hopkins, Donald R. *The Greatest Killer: Smallpox in History.* Rev. ed. Chicago: University of Chicago Press, 2002.

Horowitz, Robert F. *The Great Impeacher: A Political Biography of James M. Ashley.* New York: Brooklyn College Press, 1979.

Huston, James L. "The Lost Cause of the North: A Reflection on Lincoln's Gettysburg Address and the Second Inaugural." *Journal of the Abraham Lincoln Association* 33, no. 1 (Winter 2012): 14–37.

"I. Wayne MacVeagh." *Encyclopaedia of Contemporary Biography, of Pennsylvania . . . .* New York: Atlantic Publishing, 1899.

Jacobs, Henry Eyster. *Lincoln's Gettysburg World-Message.* Philadelphia: United Lutheran Publication House, 1919.

———. *Memoirs of Henry Eyster Jacobs: Notes on the Life of a Churchman.* Edited by Henry E. Horn. Huntington, Pa.: Church Management Service, 1974.

John, Richard J. *Network Nation: Inventing American Telecommunications.* Cambridge: Cambridge University Press, 2010.

"John Cotton and His Memorial Tablet." *American Church Monthly* 2, no. 3 (September 1857): 200.

Johnson, Martin. "Abraham Lincoln Greets the Turning Point of the Civil War: July 7, 1863." *Lincoln Herald* 106, no. 3 (Fall 2004): 102–115.

———. "Lincoln's Contested Invitation to Gettysburg." *Journal of Illinois History* 13, no. 4 (Winter 2010): 238–264.

———. "Lincoln's Response to His Invitation to Gettysburg." *Lincoln Lore: The Quarterly Bulletin of the Lincoln Museum* 1889 (Summer 2007): 18–23.

———. "Who Stole the Gettysburg Address?" *Journal of the Abraham Lincoln Association* 24, no. 2 (Summer 2003): 2–19.

Jones, J. W. *The Story of American Heroism: Thrilling Narratives of Personal Adventures during the Great Civil War as Told by the Medal Winners and Roll of Honor Men.* Springfield, Ohio: Werner, 1895.

Katz, D. Mark. *Witness to an Era: The Life and Photographs of Alexander Gardner.* New York: Viking, 1991.

Kelly, James Edward, and William B. Styple. *Tell Me of Lincoln: Memories of Abraham Lincoln, the Civil War, and Life in Old New York.* Belle Grove, Pa.: Belle Grove, 2009.

King, Horatio. *Turning On the Light: A Dispassionate Survey of President Buchanan's Administration.* Philadelphia: J. B. Lippincott, 1895.

Klement, Frank L. *The Gettysburg Soldiers' Cemetery and Lincoln's Address: Aspects and Angles*. Shippensburg, Pa.: White Mane, 1993.

Kunhardt, Philip B., Jr. *A New Birth of Freedom: Lincoln at Gettysburg*. Boston: Little, Brown, 1983.

Lambert, William H. *The Gettysburg Address: When Written, How Received, Its True Form*. Philadelphia: J. B. Lippincott, 1909. Reprinted from *Pennsylvania Magazine of History and Biography* 33 (October 1909). Page references are to the Lippincott edition.

Lamon, Ward Hill. *Recollections of Lincoln, 1847–1865*. Edited by Dorothy Lamon Teillard. Chicago: McClurg, 1895.

Lawson, Melinda. *Patriot Fires: Forging a New American Nationalism in the Civil War North*. Lawrence: University Press of Kansas, 2005.

Lee, Henry T. *Address Commemorative of the Services of the Alumni and Former Students of Lafayette College in the War for the Union*. Lafayette, Pa.: Lafayette College, 1867.

Lincoln, Abraham. *The Collected Works of Abraham Lincoln*. Edited by Roy P. Basler. 9 vols. New Brunswick, N.J.: Rutgers University Press, 1953–1955.

Lincoln, Robert Todd. *A Portrait of Abraham Lincoln in Letters by His Oldest Son*. Edited by Paul M. Angle. Chicago: Chicago Historical Society, 1968.

Lincoln Lore [newsletter] 917 (November 4, 1946).

Longfellow, Henry Wadsworth. *The Letters of Henry Wadsworth Longfellow*. Edited by Andrew Hilen. Vol. 4. Cambridge, Mass.: Harvard University Press, 1972.

Lowell, James Russell. "Ode Recited at the Harvard Commemoration, July 21, 1865." In *The Poetical Works of James Russell Lowell*. London: Ward, Lock, 1880.

Luhrs, Henry E. *Lincoln at the Wills Home and the Gettysburg Address*. Shippensburg, Pa.: Lincoln Publishers, 1938.

MacVeagh, I. Wayne. "Lincoln at Gettysburg." *Century Magazine*, November 1909, 20–23.

Magness, Phillip W., and Sebastian N. Page. *Colonization after Emancipation: Lincoln and the Movement for Black Resettlement*. Columbia: University of Missouri Press, 2011.

Markens, Isaac. *Lincoln's Masterpiece: A Review of the Gettysburg Address New in Treatment and Matter*. New York: Isaac Markens, 1913.

Marten, James. "'Dancing Attendance in the Ante-chambers of the Great': A Texas Unionist Goes to Washington, 1863." *Lincoln Herald* 90, no. 3 (Fall 1988): 84–86.

McClure, A. K. *Old Time Notes of Pennsylvania*. 2 vols. Philadelphia: John C. Winston, 1905.

McCurdy, Charles. *Gettysburg: A Memoir*. Pittsburgh: Reed and Witting, 1929.

McPherson, James M. *Abraham Lincoln and the Second American Revolution*. New York: Oxford University Press, 1991.

McSherry, William. *History of the Bank of Gettysburg, 1814–1864, the Gettysburg National Bank, 1864–1914, of Gettysburg.* Gettysburg, Pa.: Gettysburg National Bank, 1914.

Mearns, David C. "The Mysteries of the Manuscripts." Unpublished typescript. Mearns Papers, Library of Congress.

———. "Thayer's *The Pioneer Boy*: A Second and Harder Look," *Library of Congress Quarterly Journal* 13, no. 3 (May 1956): 129–134.

Mearns, David C., and Lloyd A. Dunlap. "Notes and Comments on the Preparation of the Address." In *Long Remembered: Facsimilies of the Five Versions of the Gettysburg Address,* edited by David C. Mearns and Lloyd A. Dunlap. Washington, D.C.: Library of Congress, 1963.

Mitchell, Thomas G. *Anti-slavery Politics in Antebellum and Civil War America.* New York: Praeger, 2007.

Monaghan, Jay. *Lincoln Bibliography, 1839–1939.* 2 vols. Springfield: Illinois State Historical Library, 1943.

Mowry, William Augustus, and Arthur May Mowry. *A History of the United States for Schools . . . .* Boston: Burdett, 1896.

Neff, John R. *Honoring the Civil War Dead: Commemoration and the Problem of Reconciliation.* Lawrence: University Press of Kansas, 2005.

Nichols, Edward J. *Toward Gettysburg: A Biography of General John F. Reynolds.* New York: Pennsylvania State University Press, 1958.

Nickerson, Azor Howitt. "Personal Recollections of Two Visits to Gettysburg." *Scribner's Magazine,* July 1893, 19–28.

Nicolay, Helen. *Lincoln's Secretary: A Biography of John G. Nicolay.* New York: Longmans, Green, 1949.

Nicolay, John G. "Lincoln's Gettysburg Address." *Century Magazine,* February 1894, 596–608.

———. *An Oral History of Abraham Lincoln: John G. Nicolay's Interviews and Essays.* Edited by Michael Burlingame. Carbondale: Southern Illinois University Press, 1996.

———. *With Lincoln in the White House: Letters, Memoranda, and Other Writings of John G. Nicolay, 1860–1865.* Edited by Michael Burlingame. Carbondale: Southern Illinois University Press, 2000.

Nicolay, John G., and John Hay. "Abraham Lincoln: A History." *Century Magazine,* February 1890, 561–576.

———. *Abraham Lincoln: A History.* 10 vols. New York: Century, 1890.

Oakes, James. *Freedom National: The Destruction of Slavery in the United States, 1861–1865.* New York: Norton, 2013.

Ostendorf, Lloyd. "Turning the Pages of History: A New Draft of the Gettysburg Address Located." *Gettysburg Magazine,* January 1, 1992, 107–112.

Paludan, Phillip Shaw. *The Presidency of Abraham Lincoln.* Lawrence: University Press of Kansas, 1994.

The Parliamentary Register; or, History of the Proceedings and Debates of the

House of Commons . . . during the Fourth Session of the Seventeenth Parliament . . . . London: J. Debrett, 1794.

Peatman, Jared. "'Lincoln Acted the Clown': Virginia's Newspapers and the Gettysburg Address." In *Virginia at War, 1863,* ed. William C. Davis and James Robertson Jr., 115–132. Lexington: University of Kentucky Press, 2009.

Pelletreau, William S. *Historic Homes and Institutions and Genealogical and Family History of New York.* 4 vols. New York: Lewis Publishing, 1907.

Peterson, Merrill D. *Lincoln in American Memory.* New York: Oxford University Press, 1994.

Piatt, Donn. *Memories of the Men Who Saved the Union.* New York: Belford, Clarke, 1887.

Prescott, George B. *History, Theory, and Practice of the Electric Telegraph.* Boston: Ticknor and Fields, 1860.

"Proceedings of the Pennsylvania State Teachers' Association—Thirteenth Annual Session." *Pennsylvania School Journal* 15, no. 171 (September 1866): 51–74.

Randall, James G. *Lincoln the President.* 4 vols. New York: Dodd, Mead, 1945–1955.

Reeder, Rudolph R. *The Historical Development of School Readers and of Method in Teaching Reading.* New York: Macmillan, 1900.

Reid, Ronald F. *Edward Everett: Unionist Orator.* New York: Greenwood, 1990.

———. "Newspaper Response to the Gettysburg Addresses." *Quarterly Journal of Speech* 53, no. 1 (February 1967): 50–60.

Remensnyder, Junius B. "Personal Memories of Lincoln: President Lincoln's Address at Gettysburg." *Outlook,* February 13, 1918, 243.

Report of the Select Committee Relative to the Soldiers' National Cemetery. Harrisburg, Pa.: Singerly and Myers, State Printers, 1864.

Richardson, Elmo R., and Alan W. Farley. *John Palmer Usher: Lincoln's Secretary of the Interior.* Lawrence: University Press of Kansas, 1960.

Richardson, James Daniel, ed. *A Compilation of the Messages and Papers of the Presidents.* Vol. 8. New York: Joint Committee on Printing: Bureau of National Literature, 1897.

Roedel, Josephine Forney. "The Diary of Josephine Forney Roedel." Edited by Elsie Singmaster. *Pennsylvania Magazine of History and Biography,* October 1943, 390–411.

Rose, George Maclean. *A Cyclopedia of Canadian Biography: Being Chiefly Men of the Time.* Montreal: Rose Publishing, 1886.

Sandburg, Carl. *Abraham Lincoln: The War Years.* 4 vols. New York: Harcourt, Brace, 1939.

Saunders, William. "Landscape Gardening." *Report of the Commissioner of Agriculture for the Year 1869.* Washington, D.C.: GPO, 1870.

———. "Memoir of Gettysburg." In *Congressional Record* 70, no. 3 (February 12, 1929): H3321–3323.

Schwartz, Barry. *Abraham Lincoln and the Forge of National Memory.* Chicago: University of Chicago Press, 2000.

————. *Lincoln in the Post-heroic Era.* Chicago: University of Chicago Press, 2003.

————. "The New Gettysburg Address: A Study in Illusion." In *The Lincoln Forum: Rediscovering Abraham Lincoln,* ed. John Y. Simon and Harold Holzer, 160–186. New York: Fordham University Press, 2001.

Schwarzlose, Richard Allen. *The American Wire Services: A Study of Their Development as a Social Institution.* New York: Arno, 1979.

————. *The Nation's Newsbrokers.* 2 vols. Evanston, Ill.: Northeastern University Press, 1989.

Sears, Stephen W. *Gettysburg.* New York: Houghton Mifflin, 2004.

Sellers, John R. "Serving President Lincoln: The Public Career of John G. Nicolay." In *Lincoln Reshapes the Presidency,* ed. Charles M. Hubbard, 52–64. Macon, Ga.: Mercer University Press, 2003.

Seward, William H. *The Works of William H. Seward.* Edited by George E. Baker. 5 vols. Boston: Houghton Mifflin, 1884.

Sheldon, George. *When the Smoke Cleared at Gettysburg: The Tragic Aftermath of the Bloodiest Battle of the Civil War.* Nashville, Tenn.: Cumberland House, 2003.

Smith, Goldwin. "President Lincoln." *Macmillan's Magazine,* February 1865, 300–305.

Smith, Herbert F. *Richard Watson Gilder.* New York: Twayne Publishers, [1970].

Smith, William, and Theophilus D. Hall. *A Copious and Critical English-Latin Dictionary.* New York: American Book Company, 1871.

"Solid Men of Boston." *Historical Magazine and Notes and Queries Concerning the Antiquities, History and Biography of America,* February 1857, 39.

"Some Correspondence Regarding a Missing Copy of the Gettysburg Address." *Lincoln Lore* 1437 (November 1957): 1–5.

Souder, Emily Bliss Thacher. *Leaves from the Battlefield of Gettysburg.* Philadelphia: Caxton, 1864.

Sparks, Edwin. "The Long Story of a Short Oration." *Dial,* November 16, 1906, 320–321.

Speed, James. *Address of the Hon. James Speed before the Society of the Loyal Legion, at Cincinnati, May 4, 1887* .... Louisville, Ky.: John P. Morton, 1888.

Starr, John W. *Lincoln and the Railroads: A Biographical Study.* New York: Dodd, Mead, 1927.

Starr, Louis M. *Bohemian Brigade: Civil War Newsmen in Action.* New York: Knopf, 1954.

Stowe, Harriet Beecher. *Men of Our Times; or, Leading Patriots of the Day.* Hartford, Conn.: Hartford Publishing, 1868.

Sumner, Charles. *The Promises of the Declaration of Independence: Eulogy on Abraham Lincoln, Delivered before the Municipal Authorities of the City of Boston, June 1, 1865.* Boston: Ticknor and Fields, 1865.

Sylvester, Melvin R. *Black Experience in America: Negro Periodicals in the United States, 1840–1960. An Annotated Bibliography.* Westport, Conn.: Negro Universities Press, 1960.

Taylor, John M. *William Henry Seward: Lincoln's Right Hand*. New York: Harper-Collins, 1991.

Temple, Wayne C. "Lincoln the Lecturer." *Lincoln Herald* 101, no. 3 (Fall 1999): 94–110; 101, no. 4 (Winter 1999): 146–163.

Thayer, William Makepeace. *The Character and Public Services of Abraham Lincoln, President of the United States*. Boston: Dinsmoor, 1864.

———. *The Pioneer Boy and How He Became President*. Boston: Walker and Wise, 1863.

Thomas, Benjamin P. *Portrait for Posterity: Abraham Lincoln and His Biographers*. New Brunswick, N.J.: Rutgers University Press, 1947.

Usher, John P. "Lincoln and Slavery." In *Reminiscences of Abraham Lincoln, by Distinguished Men of His Time*, ed. Allen Thorndike Rice, 203–226. New York: North American Pub. Co., 1886.

———. *President Lincoln's Cabinet, by Honorable John P. Usher, Secretary of the Interior January 7, 1863–May 15, 1865, with a Foreword and a Sketch of the Life of the Author by Nelson H. Loomis. . . .* Omaha, Neb., 1925.

Varg, Paul A. *Edward Everett: The Intellectual in the Turmoil of Politics*. Selinsgrove, Pa.: Susquehanna University Press, 1992.

Vorenberg, Michael. *Final Freedom: The Civil War, the Abolition of Slavery, and the Thirteenth Amendment*. New York: Cambridge University Press, 2001.

The War of the Rebellion: The Official Records of the Union and Confederate Armies. Series 3. 5 vols. Washington, D.C.: GPO, 1899.

Warren, Louis A. *Lincoln's Gettysburg Declaration: "A New Birth of Freedom."* Fort Wayne, Ind.: Lincoln National Life Foundation, 1964.

———. "Thayer's Pioneer Boy." *Lincoln Lore* 689 (June 22, 1942): 1–2.

Waselkov, Gregory A., and Kathryn E. Holland Braund, eds. *William Bartram on the Southeastern Indians*. Lincoln: University of Nebraska Press, 2002.

Webster, Daniel. *The Private Correspondence of Daniel Webster*. Edited by Fletcher Webster. 2 vols. (Boston: Little, Brown, 1857).

Weeks, Jim. *Gettysburg: Memory, Market, and an American Shrine*. Princeton: Princeton University Press, 2003.

Weiser, Frederick. "Lincoln's Trip to Gettysburg." *Lincoln Herald* 55, no. 1 (Summer 1953): 1–4, 5, 8.

Welles, Gideon. *Diary of Gideon Welles: Secretary of the Navy under Lincoln and Johnson*. Edited by Howard K. Beale. 3 vols. New York: Norton, 1960.

Wheelwright, Edward. *Memoir of Daniel Denison Slade, M.D*. Cambridge, Mass.: University Press, 1900.

Wieck, Carl F. *Lincoln's Quest for Equality: The Road to Gettysburg*. DeKalb: Northern Illinois University Press, 2002.

Wiley, Earl W. "Buckeye Criticism of the Gettysburg Address." *Speech Monographs* 23, no. 1 (March 1956): 1–8.

———. "Colonel Charles Anderson's Gettysburg Address." *Lincoln Herald* 54, no. 1 (Spring 1952): 14–21.

Wills, David. "Statement Given by Judge Wills to Charles M. McCurdy, about 1890." In *Lincoln at the Wills Home and the Gettysburg Address,* by Henry E. Luhrs, 17. Shippensburg, Pa.: Lincoln Publishers, 1938.

Wills, Garry. *Lincoln at Gettysburg: The Words That Remade America.* New York: Simon and Schuster, 1992.

Wilson, Douglas L. *Lincoln's Sword: The Presidency and the Power of Words.* New York: Knopf, 2006.

Wilson, Douglas L., and Rodney O. Davis. *Herndon's Informants: Letters, Interviews, and Statements about Abraham Lincoln.* Urbana: University of Illinois Press, 1998.

Wilson, Edmund. *Patriotic Gore.* New York: Norton, 1962.

Wilson, James Grant. "Recollections of Lincoln." *Putnam's Magazine,* February 1909, 515–529.

Young, John Russell. *Men and Memories: Personal Reminiscences.* Edited by May D. Russell Young. 2 vols. New York: F. Tennyson Neely, 1891–1901.

Zornow, William Frank. *Lincoln and the Party Divided.* Norman: University of Oklahoma Press, 1954.

Index